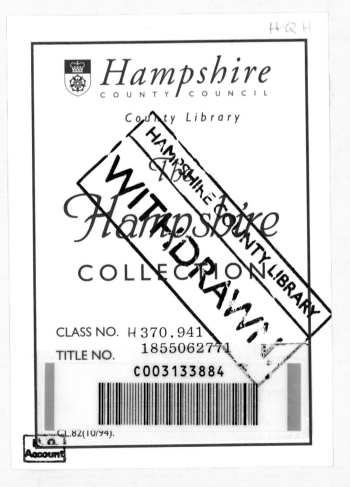

CLASSICS IN
EDUCATION

Printed and Bound by
Antony Rowe Ltd., Chippenham, Wiltshire

NINE PAMPHLETS

Volume I

Richard Dawes

Introduced by Jeffrey Stern

UNIFACMANU

THOEMMES PRESS

© Thoemmes Press 1994

Co-published in 1994 by

Thoemmes Press
11 Great George Street, Bristol BS1 5RR
England

———————— & ————————

Unifacmanu Trading Company Ltd.
4F, 91 Ho-Ping East Road
Sec 1, Taipei 10609, Taiwan

ISBN 1 85506 277 1

This is a reprint, in two volumes, of the 1847–57 Editions

Publisher's Note

These reprints are taken from original copies of each book.
In many cases the condition of those originals is not perfect,
the paper, often handmade, having suffered over time and
the copy from such things as inconsistent printing pressures
resulting in faint text, show-through from one side of a leaf
to the other, the filling in of some characters, and the break
up of type. The publisher has gone to great lengths to ensure
the quality of these reprints but points out that certain
characteristics of the original copies will, of necessity, be
apparent in reprints thereof.

INTRODUCTION

Richard Dawes (1793–1867) was born in Yorkshire and entered Trinity College, Cambridge, in 1813. He was ordained in 1818 and by 1836 was rector of King's Somborne, Hampshire. It was through observing the progress of the children in his parish that he began to notice the shortcomings of their education and in 1842 he founded his own school. King's Somborne School became one of the most truly innovatory schools in the country and it was visited by all who were interested in popular education. The nine pamphlets reprinted in this volume constitute all Dawes's important educational writings.

King's Somborne School received a great deal of attention from the Inspectors, no doubt because it was educationally so far in advance of other schools of its type. The most detailed report was made by the Rev. Henry Moseley, one of the most perceptive of the early Inspectors. He pointed out that in school hygiene, reading, spelling, width of curriculum, attendance, and length of time spent at school, King's Somborne excelled all other schools of its type. The average attendance was 89 per cent, compared with the 66 per cent of other schools; 32 per cent of the pupils remained at school after the age of eleven years, compared with 23 per cent at other schools. As in the case of all successful and happy schools, the appearance and demeanour of the children spoke for itself. Every girl had a hairbrush and comb, and regular washing and brushing of the teeth was the rule. Inspectors noticed that the children looked intelligent, modest and purposeful. Significantly, the children created their own voluntary circles. A dozen of the older boys organized a voluntary chemistry class which met on Saturday mornings, and many of the pupils kept journals in which observations on natural history at different seasons of the year were kept. Moseley also discovered that the width of the curriculum had a very beneficial effect on the children's powers of reading, for at one of his examinations 40 per cent of the children read with 'tolerable ease and correctness', whereas at other schools the percentage was under 17, despite the fact that at these schools scarcely anything but reading was taught.

The demonstration of this proposition alone would have ensured Dawes's place as an innovator, for it gave implicit support to the contention that the policy hitherto pursued by religious and charitable bodies was educationally unsuccessful. Dawes himself was convinced of this, and condemned the narrow aims and religious bias of the National Society, becoming one of the leaders of the progressive wing of the Society in opposition to the policies of the conservative Archdeacon Denison, whom he described as 'struggling in a direction so contrary to the feelings of the age...'. Dawes was a strong supporter of Kay-Shuttleworth and his efforts for state education, the policy of the Committee of Council, and the work of the Inspectors. He condemned the labours of the National Society as 'a national deception, retarding the cause of education rather than advancing it', and described the instruction given in many of their schools as 'absolutely valueless'.

If the National Schools suffered in comparison with Dawes's standards of education, neither could they match his social attitudes. Though in making King's Somborne a comprehensive school for the rural lower and middle classes he admittedly aimed at connecting 'these lower adjoining and important links in the social chain'. Moseley considered that one of the secrets of the success of King's Somborne lay in the abandonment of the idea that the poor were the natural objects of charity and the unquestioning recipients of 'a fragment of our own education', and the acceptance of Dawes's 'abundant faith in the affection of a labouring man for his children' and his adoption of education suitable to their wants.

Stewart and McCann, *Educational Innovators*, I, pp. 132–3.

Jeffrey Stern
York, 1994

CONTENTS

HINTS

ON AN

IMPROVED AND SELF-PAYING SYSTEM

OF

NATIONAL EDUCATION,

SUGGESTED FROM THE

WORKING OF A VILLAGE SCHOOL IN HAMPSHIRE.

WITH

OBSERVATIONS, FROM PERSONAL INSPECTION,

ON THE

IRISH NATIONAL SCHOOLS.

BY THE
REV. RICHARD DAWES, A.M.

SECOND EDITION.

·LONDON:
GROOMBRIDGE AND SONS,
PATERNOSTER ROW.
1847.

PRINTED BY C. AND J. ADLARD,
BARTHOLOMEW CLOSE.

KING'S SOMBORNE

NATIONAL SCHOOL.

THE success of the National School of this village, and the mode of instruction adopted in it, having been such as to attract considerable attention, I am induced, in compliance with a wish repeatedly expressed by the Rev. Mr. Allen, her Majesty's Inspector of Schools, to submit an account of it to the public, under a hope that, in so doing, I am giving some assistance to those who have the same object in view as myself,—the establishing an efficient system of education in their own parishes.

There is no way of promoting an object of a practical kind, better than by explaining plans of working it out, which have been found by experience to be successful, as it must be admitted that what has been done in one case, may, under similar circumstances, be done in another.

Dr. Hook says, we live in an age when the question is, *not whether*, but *how*, the people are to be educated.

To the question, *how* the people are to be educated,

I conceive the plan adopted here, and now entering on its fifth year, to be a successful and practical answer, so far as regards my own parish, and that at no great expense to the State; how far this answer may be a general one, and apply to other districts, those who read will judge for themselves, but I can see no difficulty, wherever the trial is fairly made.

It has always appeared to me, that a system of National Education embracing the wants of the labouring classes, and those immediately connected with them, uniting both, might be established on something like a self-paying principle, and in this way a system, so far as education is concerned, better in its kind, and having a much stronger hold on the affections of the people of all classes, might be brought about, and with a greater probability of permanent success, than on any other plan of a less pretending kind, which confines itself merely to the education of the poor; but in order to effect this, it is necessary that the educational acquirements to be had at our schools, should be sufficient for all the wants of industrial life, and bearing upon their every-day occupations; for instance, in the rural districts, equal to all that is wanted by the occupying class of farmers, and such trades as are connected with the occupation of land, and although, in order to accomplish this, there are prejudices to be overcome, yet, from my own experience here, I know it can be effected.

In this way, and keeping in view the principle of uniting the education of the children of the labourer with those of his employer, I have endeavoured to supply the educational wants of my own parish, and, with the hope of inducing others to attempt the same, I venture to publish the result of the experiment.

That there is something of unwillingness, even amongst many of the educated classes, to extend secular education among the poor, there can be no doubt; but by raising the standard of secular acquirements, we should at the same time, by proper attention, promote the blessing of a sound scriptural education, in a much higher degree than on any system which aims at so small an amount of knowledge as that which is to be acquired in the great majority of our National Schools.

Of this unwillingness I had an instance, about the time of my commencing this school. Being present in a party where the education of the labouring classes was the subject of conversation, and a particular school being mentioned, in which the clergyman of the parish took great interest, one of the party very significantly observed, "Poor man, he is teaching the children geography!" and this, in a way as if the man was much to be pitied who could think of such a thing, and as I saw that the feeling of those present went with the speaker, it required an effort of courage on my part, to avow that I intended doing the same, *and more.*

Such feelings are by no means uncommon, we hear less of them now than a few years ago, because the tide of education is against them.

Improved education for the labourer is not generally popular with the farmer. One wants to know if it will make a boy plough a straighter furrow ; another quaintly asks, if it will make his turnips grow (he knows hard work will) : and I actually know a case, where the farmers of a parish turned against the clergyman's plan, because he proposed teaching geography ; saying, " they would not have the labourers' toes treading on their heels :" such prejudices are fast giving way, and will in a little time give no trouble.

A common complaint among the middle classes of agricultural life, is the expense of education ; but, as soon as it is found that a better one is to be had at our National Schools, than they are in the habit of giving their own children, and at a much less cost, they will readily embrace the opportunity of sending them, and, in this way, not only benefit themselves, but indirectly assist in educating the children of those around them, and have the satisfaction of seeing that moral improvement among the labouring classes which in any other way it would be vain to expect. The classes above the labourer would always have the advantage of being able to send their children to school to a greater age, and thus they would come out into the world, in point of education, in advance of those who in the social chain stand below them. In the school here, there is no difference whatever, either in the instruction or in the treatment of the children, arising from one class paying more than another; everything works and harmonizes well, on the principle, of those who are able to do so, sending their children for a longer period.

With respect to the standard of acquirements to be had at most of our National Schools, all seem to agree that it is far below what it ought to be, and that this is the case, no one of any experience can doubt.

I have myself been in some (and there are many of a like kind), where the more advanced children did not know whether the months of July and August were summer or winter months, and could not answer many other questions equally simple.

There are at present in the school here, three brothers lately come, who walk every day a distance of four miles, the eldest of them fourteen years of age, fine healthy lads, so far as the building up of the animal is concerned, and children of parents well able to pay for their education ; these children have been sent to a village school more than three years, and actually cannot read fluently words of one syllable, and are in every other respect equally ignorant ; and this in no way owing to deficiency on the part of the children themselves. How can parents be expected to take any interest in schools where such are the results?

This is owing, in a great measure, to the total unfitness of the schoolmaster; and, in one instance of a school which I visited, and on the building of which a great deal of money had been spent, making some observations to the master about a stove which was in it, he replied, " I likes he very well:" and his mode of expressing himself, on all other subjects, was equally incorrect.

From the daily working of this school, and from every observation which I can make, as to the interest which parents take in it, from the tendency which is shown on the part of those immediately above the labouring class, and who have hitherto never dreamt of schools of this kind, as places of education for their own children, but who now show a most lively interest in doing so, I should say, rather than aim at a system of state education of the labouring classes, apart from that of the class immediately above them, aim at a system of good practical and industrial education, bearing upon the wants of both, for, up to a certain point, the wants both of the labouring class and the immediate employer of labour are the same; let the labourer feel that by his own industry a good education for his children is within his power, and he will not only take the greater interest in it, but much greater respectability attaches to himself by his being made the instrument

through which it is to be had; let the upper class experience the benefits to their own children from such
schools, a benefit which they will not be slow to understand, and one which their children's increasing intelligence will very soon prove to them, that *they* are the
party most deeply interested in the success of schools
of this kind : do this, and there will be no difficulty in
the maintenance of them.

One great objection to a plan of educating the poor,
as a class entirely apart from their fellow-men, is, that
it assumes them to be paupers as to one of the most
important wants of life ; for certainly, next to food,
clothing, and shelter, education is the most important.
Why should all the world preach, and talk, and declaim
against pauperism, and then show, by the plans which
they adopt, that in respect to education it must be assumed as a principle that the whole of the labouring
classes are paupers? why disconnect these adjoining
and important links in the social chain—the very main-
stay and support of the whole fabric—when they might
be united by a much stronger tie than any which holds
them together at present; that of an education in
common? their wants are alike in this respect, and
the system of education in the class of life immediately
above the labourer is quite as defective, and a better
system quite as much wanted as for the labouring class:
and the present would appear to be a favorable time,

when a system uniting the two might be attempted with success.

No doubt many jarring elements between these two classes would give way, and the feelings between them be much softened and subdued, by an united education which is sound and practically good; "producing a sympathy between the employer and the employed, a sense of their mutual dependence and mutual duties, a pleasure in the recognition of each other's joys, and reciprocal condolence in those sorrows which fall to the lot of every rank."

The following passage, from the 'Records of Creation,' by Dr. Sumner, the present Bishop of Chester, is so much to the purpose, and carries so much greater weight with it than anything which I could say, both as to the benefits arising from educating the poor, and making them as far as possible the instruments through which it is to be done, that I cannot but quote it :—
"Of all obstacles to improvement ignorance is the most formidable, because the only true secret of assisting the poor is by making them agents in bettering their own condition, and to supply them, not with a temporary stimulus, but with a permanent energy. As fast as the standard of intelligence is raised, the poor become more and more able to co-operate in any plan proposed for their advantage, and more likely to listen to any reasonable suggestion, and more able to understand,

and therefore more willing to pursue it. Hence it follows, that when gross ignorance is once removed, and
right principles are introduced, a great advantage has
been already gained against squalid poverty. Many
avenues to an improved condition are opened to one
whose faculties are enlarged and exercised; he sees his
own interest more clearly, he pursues it more steadily,
and he does not study immediate gratification at the
expense of bitter and late repentance, or mortgage the
labour of his future life without an adequate return.
Indigence, therefore, will rarely be found in company
with good education."

My own experience here strongly confirms the truth
of these sentiments, and I invariably find that those
parents (of whom there are many) who do not avail
themselves of the school, are not those who have the
lowest wages, or earn the least money, but they are the
most ignorant, and their habits of life are of so low and
degraded a nature, that they are not only indifferent to
the welfare and moral conduct of their own children,
but are perfectly regardless of the good opinion of those
around them: many of them, such as are living in
crowded cottages, and, from the force of habit and bad
management, can make no effort to keep their children
decently clean; and, in fact, their standard of moral
feeling is so low, whether arising out of their physical
condition, I do not know, as to make them appear to
have little beyond the animal instinct of feeding their

young, so as to keep the body alive, and have not the slightest notion of anything which is not of a gross and sensual nature.

I would have it inculcated by every father in his family, by every schoolmaster in his school, by every clergyman in his parish, that the man who *needlessly* throws himself for support on the industry of others, lowers himself in the scale of human beings, and in some respects partakes of the character of a dishonest man; that he does not act up to the precepts of Christianity which he professes; and that the strong feeling of the labouring class, which prevails more particularly in the south of England, of " Why spare the parish?" and which is encouraged by the strangely mistaken principles on which the farmers act, not only has a tendency in every possible way to lower their condition, by interfering with the price of labour, and thus lowering their standard of social comforts, by totally destroying every feeling of self-respect and of manly independence; but also that in past times it had almost destroyed the whole social system to which they belong, and may do so again if not guarded against, by a system of education of the lower classes, which shall teach them more of forethought in what concerns their own domestic affairs, and give them a greater insight as to how all this bears upon the well-being, not only of their own class, but of the country to which they belong.

In saying this of the labouring class I do not throw the blame upon them, as regards the past, far from it; I think much greater blame attaches itself to the classes above them, who, without having the excuse of want of education, have not paid that attention to their condition, physical and moral, which it was their duty to do.

Nor would I less press upon the attention of the rising generation, those of them likely to be the future employers of labour, that "the labourer is worthy of his hire;" that the wages of the industrious labourer, in a healthy state of society, ought to be equal to all the decent wants and respectabilities of his station in life; and although political economy may say the state of the labour market is not regulated by considerations of this kind, yet, youth trained up in these ideas, and, with kindly feelings arising out of them, impressed in early life, will not afterwards be able to shake them off at the suggestions of avarice; but will be content to think, that such a portion of the value of a commodity as is equal to all his proper wants belongs to the producer, who has the first claim, and that the merchant, the landlord, or the farmer, ought to be content with what remains after the producer is provided for.

Should any of these classes thus trained up at school transgress these wholesome maxims instilled into them in youth, conscience will be continually telling them they are wrong, and they will have that sort of uncomfortable feeling about them, which every man has, when he knows he is doing an act which he dare not talk of to his neighbours, and which both his early education, and his own conscience, unite in telling him is morally wrong.

These remarks are multiplying to a so much greater length than I had intended, that I fear I may be looked upon as "building great gates to a very small city," I will, therefore, at once give such statistics of this educational experiment as are necessary to form an opinion of its worth.

The parish contains an area of 7500 acres, with a population, according to the last census, of 1125; of this population about 800 live in the village, the rest are very much scattered, and at various distances of from two to three miles; the farms are large, many of them uniting what formerly used to be two, three, and even four farms, making the case less favorable to the kind of plan which I am advocating, than if the parish had been divided into smaller ones.

The school and master's house * were built from the Council of Education Plans for 110 children, previous to which there was nothing but a Sunday-school, with two Dame-schools, of the usual class in villages like this.

On the opening of the school in October, 1842, I examined into the books published by the different Educational Boards, and it ended by my adopting,

---

* They are built on the site of a palace of John of Gaunt, and the window-sills, of Caen stone, are out of the old foundation : the ground belonged to Lady Mildmay, and was given in the same kind and liberal way in which she does everything connected with the welfare of the poor principally the secular books published by the Irish National Board, and by Mr. Sullivan, in connexion with it, together with others by our own Societies.

The payments for the labourer's children are twopence per week for one, and a penny for every additional child in the same family. For the children of all those above the mere labourer, and whose parents are living in the parish, six shillings, and for those of a similar class out of the parish, ten shillings per quarter.

The school opened in October, 1842, with 38 children, which in October, 1843, had increased to 106.

At the end of the second year, to 110.

At the end of the third year, to 144.

At the end of the fourth year, to 158.

On the opening of the school, the number of children paying by the quarter was 11, increased at the end of the year to 25, of which number one was from an adjoining parish.

At the end of the second year the number was 27, of which three were out of other parishes.

At the end of the third year 34, of which there were 10, and at the end of the fourth year 36, of which 14 were from other parishes; and at this present time the number is 45, of which 22 are from neighbouring parishes.

The amount of school payments for the successive years are as follow, the first column being the total amount, including books, &c.; the second being for books alone, and showing the amount to which they have been purchased by themselves.

	£	s.	d.	£	s.	d.
Payments of 1st year to Michaelmas 1843	56	17	3	7	5	5
2d year to ditto 1844	68	11	7	8	0	6
3d year to ditto 1845	84	6	1	11	5	3
4th year to ditto 1846	93	5	5	15	8	0

The payments of the children alone for the *present quarter*, taking the numbers as they stand in the books, will amount to £26 10s. 4d. :* the yearly expenses from £110 to £120.

The Salaries of Teachers.

Master and Mistress, man and wife, £70, a house and garden.

A Second Master £25, a boy of 17, educated at the school.

Four paid Monitors, two in each school.

A very respectable Dame-school in the village is, as a preparatory school to this, more flourishing than it ever was before.

The increase in the number of children who pay by the quarter in each successive year, shows very distinctly, that the prejudice in the classes above the labourer, against sending their children to our National Schools, are gradually giving way, and at this moment there are *fourteen*, the children of farmers and respectable tradesmen, lodging in the village from Monday to Friday night, when they go home, and return the

* The actual amount at the end of the quarter was £32 14s. 9d. ; of which £5 6s. 11d. was for books, and £27 7s. 9d. payments for schooling.

following Monday morning. Of these, six are the children of three families, relations who have joined and taken a small house, and placed a relation in it to take care of them, and four are from a parish where there is an endowment of upwards of £90 a year for educational purposes, and one from a parish, which jointly with two others, has an endowment of a very much larger amount.

Soon after the opening of the school I recommended the children to buy the books, in order that they might have an opportunity of reading their lessons at home in the evening, and before the end of the first quarter I made it a positive rule they should do so, and in this there has not been the slightest difficulty. The extent to which they buy them, as shown by the preceding figures, is a very convincing proof of the. way in which the parents estimate the education their children are getting; their being thus enabled to interest those around them at home in an evening, has been one of the causes which has contributed very much to the success of the school.

Of one small book, called the 'Sequel,' as coming between No. 2 and No. 3 of the 'Dublin Reading Books,' price 7d., no fewer than five dozen copies were bought by the children in less than so many months after its introduction, and within the year upwards of a hundred. Of a set of small Maps, 6d. each, published by Betts in the Strand, 63 were bought in a very few weeks, and a very considerable number since.

The parents themselves take great interest in getting their children to point out places on the map which interest them, and in one instance, when a child said its father wished it to have a map of Australia, I was curious to know why; it was, that some of their relations had gone out there as emigrants.

As a model school, I conceive this to have been of very great service in this part of the country: it has not only been the means of introducing a better class of books into many of the schools of the neighbourhood, but improved modes of teaching, arising from the teachers, as well as those taking an interest in village education, having visited it.

There are at present four children from it employed as teachers in other schools; and the boy whom I have placed in the position of a second master, has, through the school and his own industry, qualified himself for any situation of the kind, and is perfectly competent to teach anything which is taught here.

Schools of an effective kind in different parts of the country, would be of great assistance in providing masters for the smaller parishes in their neighbourhood. In many instances it would be found that boys, in other respects disqualified for occupations requiring great bodily activity, would, by being taken as paid monitors, or assistants, not only help in the success of the parent school, but would in the end be qualified to conduct others; and there are at present here several boys, who, if they could be continued two years longer, or even one, by a small allowance to their parents, would be qualified for the smaller schools; or if taken into our training schools for a year, would be well fitted in everything, excepting age, for masters where greater attainments are required.

These pecuniary results are more striking, from the fact that we have no resident gentry in the parish to assist or take any interest whatever in education; neither does it differ in any way from the ordinary run of agricultural parishes and from its neighbours, excepting in a sort of bad notoriety* in the annals of pauperism, previous to the passing of the New Poor Law Amendment Act.

I mention this to show, that the prospect of realizing much in the way of school-payments was not very great in the commencement, and as a ground of encouragement, that where the education in our schools is made to bear on practical life, the parents themselves will make a much greater effort to pay for it than they have hitherto had credit for.

* The poor-rate and road-rate for this parish (the latter being equally a poor-rate with the first, and no separate account kept) actually amounted on an average of the seven years preceding Christmas, 1835, to £1600 a year, the population being 1040, according to the census of 1830, or upwards of thirty shillings a head on the whole population. This implies a degree of immorality and a state of things which it is frightful to contemplate.

2

Many of the poor tell me that the expenses of the schooling and books are more than saved to them from the more orderly and cleanly habits the children have acquired.

Formerly you could scarcely ride through this village without being in danger of riding over half-a-dozen children, now during school hours there are few to be seen.

After the school had been opened about two years, finding the usefulness of it of a much more extensive kind than I had anticipated, I saw the importance of adding a class room, not only for separate instruction for the more advanced boys, but as a room for several things in the way of school apparatus, which it was highly desirable to have; for instance, a small collection of the ores of metals most in use—of the raw material, and also in the worked-up state of our textile manufacture—specimens of the different woods, or any other particular vegetable products of the parish or of the country—models of any simple kind of machinery—a small philosophic apparatus, such as an air-pump, and a few common hydrostatic things—in fact, anything of that kind which might interest or help in the purposes for which education is intended.

This has, after some delay, been effected, and is at present in use.

In any attempt to educate the children of the poor there is a great difference between their case and that of

the educated classes ; all the home-influences are against
you, their habits of life, manner of expressing themselves, &c. ; in fact, out of school they are, from their
habits, unlearning what they have learnt when there; and
this tells in many ways, but more particularly does it
make difficult the teaching them to read tolerably well.

The bad reading, I observe is a general complaint
in the Inspectors' Reports, but unless children are continued at school until all the mechanical difficulties of
reading are got over, education would not afford them
in after-life that kind of enjoyment in their hours of
leisure which otherwise might be expected from it ; but
these are difficulties which will gradually become less
and less as education spreads.

But uneducated as the parents of the present generation are, and short as the time is which this school
has been at work, I could enumerate very many instances in which they have told me how much the happiness of their firesides, and their social and domestic
comfort is increased by hearing their children read to
them in an evening, and telling them of what they read
at school; by the interest which they take in seeing
them learning their tasks, and doing the little exercises
they have to do at home : generally such account as
they can give in writing, of some Scripture character,
or what they may know of some substance or thing used
in common life.

No one, without experience, can believe how much

of conversation and of interest among themselves, in their cottages, instruction of this kind gives rise to.

I may mention such questions as the following, which they do in writing as well as they can :

Point out the various uses of soap, how it adds to our comforts and cleanliness; and the different purposes for which iron is used ; the advantages of being able to convert it into steel; how many kinds of tools they can enumerate which are made of it. Write down what they know of sugar, tea, coffee, and where we get them from : trace a little sketch, and put down the names of all the counties which a ship will coast along in bringing coals from Newcastle to Southampton; and, in fact, an infinity of little questions of this kind.

Then again, in arithmetic, they are occasionally set questions to take home, such as the following :

If each person consume   lbs. of sugar in a year, how much will the whole family consume, and what will it cost at   per lb. ?

Give the number of acres of the parish, and population ; how many to an acre, number of houses, how many in a house ?

The population of the parish in 1831 was 1040, at the census of 1841 it had increased 7 per cent., what is it at present ?

Twenty per cent. of the population ought to be at school, but there are only 15 per cent., how many are there, and how many absent who ought to be there ?

It would be useless to multiply these questions here, but I have known some of them to afford amusement to a whole family for an evening; and they lead to considerable discussion among themselves, as to whether they do use more or less of such and such articles.

Hitherto they have thought little in this way, and these suggestions are of great use to them.

The more advanced boys have also a very competent knowledge of the mensuration of regular figures, whether solid or superficial; of finding out the weight of a body, from knowing its specific gravity; how a knowledge of the properties of a few simple geometrical figures simplifies, and can be applied, to all the measurements of the things with which they have to do, and this not in a parrot-like way, but are led to understand them as a matter of reasoning, and whatever they do, it is shown to them how it bears upon practical life; in fact, the three-foot rule is to the village school what Liebig says the "balance is to the laboratory." The axiom of Euclid, that "things which are equal to the same are equal to one another," does a great deal of work if properly applied.

To show what an interest this mode of teaching excites in them, I will mention an occurrence which happened a few days ago; writing in my study, I heard a noise of joyous voices, which I found proceeded from half a dozen boys who, after school-hours, had come to measure my garden-roller; the master of the school had been teaching them how to find the solid contents of a roller, such as the farmers use in the fields (a hollow iron cylinder), and from knowing the specific gravity of iron to find its weight; my garden-roller occurring to them, they had come to practise upon it.

I have often been much struck by the degree of intelligence marked in the answers of the boys to questions of this kind, showing that their minds had been occupied by what they had been taught, and that they thoroughly understood many of the principles as applied to common life.

Questioning a class of boys who knew a little more than is ordinarily taught of geography, I asked whether the same body would weigh more at the equator or at the pole? I observed the eyes of one of them glistening with delight, thinking he had it, who answered, " At the pole, sir—at the pole;" twice repeated. " Why?"—" Because, sir, at the equator one sweats so much." Now this, although not exactly the answer I expected, was that of a reasoning mind. This boy would not have sent out a cargo of patent skates to Buenos Ayres, as Swainson, in his ' Discourse on Natural History,' states that a Sheffield cutler did, in 1806.

They have also made considerable progress in singing on the Hullah system, which is kindly taught them by one of my parishioners, and enables them to sing with correctness in church, and is a great improvement upon the old system of village psalmody; and the little moral songs which they learn are a source of amusement to many of them, both at school and at home.

On the subject of religion, great pains are taken to ground them well in scriptural knowledge, but the Bible is not used as a text-book, as it is in some of our National Schools. On a Friday, the lessons for the following Sunday, together with the Psalms of the day, are read and explained to them, and their exercise given them to write on a Friday night, for the Monday morning is generally a scriptural one : this interests the parents as well as the children. As I have not time to attend the Sunday-school during the day, the first class of boys and girls come to me an hour on alternate Sunday evenings for scriptural reading and instruction, and I have no hesitation in saying that their knowledge of Scripture, and the interest they take in it, are much increased by the knowledge they have of their own language, and of other subjects, through the medium of secular books.

Since the 1st of January last, up to the present time, November 1st, a period of ten months, upwards of sixty prayer-books have been bought by the children themselves.

From the opening of the school I have never had one single question asked, either as to what was taught or what was not taught.

After the school had been opened rather more than two years I began giving to the teachers, and the more advanced of the school children, short explanations of a philosophic kind, and in a common-sense sort of way, of the things almost daily passing before their eyes, but of the nature of which they had not the slightest conception; such as some of the peculiar properties of metals, glass, and other substances in common use; that the air had weight, and how this pressure of the atmosphere helped them to pump up water; enabled them to amuse themselves with squirts and pop-guns; to suck up water, as they called it, through a straw; why the kettle top jumped up when the water was boiling on the fire; why, when they wanted to know whether it boiled or not, they seized the poker, and placing one end on the lid and the other to their ear, in order to know whether it actually boiled; why a glass sometimes breaks when hot water is poured into it, explaining the reason of the unequal expansion of the two surfaces; these, and similar things, I found so excessively amusing to them, and at the same time so instructive, that I have scarcely missed a week explaining some principle of this nature, and in questioning them on what had been done before.

In subjects of this kind, and to children, mere verbal explanations, as every one will perceive, are of no use whatever; but when practically illustrated before their eyes by experiment, they become not only one of the most pleasing sources of instruction, but absolutely one of the most useful.

For instance, a teacher may talk to them about a thermometer, and find in the end they just know as much about it as they did when he began, but if he shows them one, and then grasps it in his hand, telling them to look at the fluid as it rises, or plunge it into hot or cold water, and let them see the effect, they then begin to open their eyes in a wonderful manner, light breaks in upon them, and information thus given leaves an impression which in after life they turn to a source of instruction, by the reasoning powers of their own minds.

The teachers here, who at first knew but little of these matters, are now well qualified to give instruction in them; to teach the mechanical principles of the tools they use, the spade, the axe, the plough; and to explain such things as the common pump, barometer, pair of bellows; metals varying in volume, according to the quantity of heat which is in them, or, as it is termed, expanding by heat and contracting by cold;

why one substance feels colder to the hand than another; the way in which metals are separated from their ores; how water is converted into steam, and again condensed; how their clothes are dried, and why they feel cold in sitting in wet clothes; why one body floats in water and another sinks; how much in volume, and how much in weight, a floating body displaces of the fluid in which it floats; why, on going into the school on a cold morning, they sometimes see a quantity of water on the glass, and why it is on the inside and not on the outside; why, when their ink is dried up, does it leave a substance behind, which does not go away; the substances water holds in solution; water of the springs taking up some of the soil through which it has fallen; chalk, &c.; equal volumes of water varying in weight according to what is taken up.

All this is mentioned to suggest to the teachers in our schools to qualify themselves for this sort of instruction.

Speaking from experience, I am quite sure there is no kind of knowledge when intelligently given, more likely to raise the character of the village school than this; but previously to attempting it, all the mechanical difficulties of reading are supposed to have been got over, and that the principles of common arithmetic, and all its applications to the ordinary purposes of life, are well understood.

One thing intended by this pamphlet is, to point out the kind and extent of secular knowledge given in what has been thought a successful attempt (so far as a trial of four years is concerned) to raise the standard of acquirement to be had at a National School, and in that way bring together the children of the labouring classes, and their employers, for the purposes of education; a thing of such importance in its consequences to both classes after leaving school, and if effected, likely to have such an influence for good on the social relations of both, that any attempt to carry it out, however imperfect, must, I think, meet with a favorable reception.

Hitherto it has been too much assumed as a principle in educating the poor, to confine the instruction to a mere reading of Scripture, and to getting over the mechanical difficulties of doing so, and that it was in no way necessary to give them any knowledge of the material world around them; the consequence of which has been, that the merely being able to read is very often but imperfectly accomplished, and many of the parents have been in the habit of sending their children from motives entirely apart from the instruction to be had at our schools.

But it may be asked, do the children remain to an age to profit from instruction of this kind?

The labourers generally do not send their children, particularly the boys, beyond the age, however young, at which they can find employment for them, but there are some who do, and many more who are anxious to do it, and in this respect every year will bring about an improvement.

The parents of this class are too apt to think them educated when they can write a little : a little writing being, in the idea of most of them, the perfection of education : with the rising generation a better standard will be adopted, and it will even now be found that there are many cases of labourers, who from being more successful, or perhaps more prudent than their neighbours, from having, in some instances, had a little property left them, some, from placing a higher value upon education than others, are most anxious to send their children beyond the very early age at which they have been in the habit of sending them out to work. I have known a father say, " Sir, it gives me such pleasure to see what my boy is doing, that I would even live on bread and water to send him longer to school." This is no uncommon feeling, but they are so circumstanced as not to be able to act upon it ; surely feelings of this kind tend to humanize and improve !

At this present time there is a class of fifteen boys to whom this kind of instruction is given, and who are well capable of understanding it ; six of them are the children of labourers, the rest those of tradesmen and farmers.

In agricultural districts, the employer does not

encourage the labourer to educate his child, on the contrary, his mode of thinking and of acting is in every way against it. He has no feeling that the respectability of the labouring classes would be advanced by education; or if he has, he immediately becomes jealous of their being brought nearer to himself, not seeing that the class to which he belongs will in the end be equally advanced.

In fact, he has no notion of worth in the labourer, as a man, or as a fellow-creature, but only values him as a machine, or instrument, by which a certain quantity of work is to be performed; and does not think that although he professes to be a Christian, it is any part of his duty, as such, to endeavour to improve the moral condition of the labourers about him, by making them more intelligent, more sober, and better conducted in every relation of life, or that, by doing so, he adds to his own respectability.

In the eyes of too many of the employers, the labourer who spends his money at the beer-house, neglects his family, and is perfectly regardless as to how they are brought up, is considered quite as useful as the one who would struggle hard to get his children an education, and try to raise them above those low and degraded habits to which they have hitherto been accustomed. Let those who act thus, if higher motives will not influence them, weigh well the observation of a modern writer, that, " independent of moral grounds,

the kindness, sympathy, and attention of an employer
to his workmen is the safest and most profitable
money speculation in which he can engage."

I have never known a single instance of a farmer
encouraging the labourer to send his children for a
longer period to school, however trifling the work for
which he wanted them. I have known instances of a
parent wishing to continue a child, but his employer
preventing him by requiring his services when so
young, that it would have been far more creditable to
have employed an older boy. Conscience never steps
in and says (or if it does they do not listen), "now I
should be doing a very kind act, and only what is my
Christian duty to this poor boy, if I were to delay
employing him for six months and send him to school,
or enable his father to do so by giving him an additional shilling a week, or even to allow his parents to
continue him as long as they are able."

True, the education within their reach has hitherto
never been such as to make either class set much value
upon it; there is therefore nothing strange in their
not reasoning about it in this way.

I have also introduced instruction of an elementary
kind connected with chemical agriculture, adopting as
a school book the Catechism on this subject published
by Professor Johnston, and illustrating it by a small
apparatus which I had on my own premises, but now
placed in the class room of the school : placing before

them, as clearly as possible, what was meant by
organic and inorganic matter; calling their attention
to the ashes remaining after any substance of a vegetable kind was burnt; how small a portion remained;
that the quantity of ashes was different in different
parts of the same plant; the difference in weight
between the ashes remaining when burning a given
weight of the straw and of the grain; what the ashes
consisted of; that in burning vegetable matter the
ash remained which might be turned to a useful purpose, as they all were aware, in manuring the ground
and again feeding other plants; and how the volatile
parts were subservient to the same purpose; how
plants were nourished, and that they cannot take up
their food in a solid state, &c.; telling them to observe
when they are burning different kinds of wood in
their own cottages, how much the quantity of ash
varies, particularly to notice the difference between
elm and willow, &c.

The different tables in the book of the quantity of
ashes remaining after burning given weights of certain
vegetable substances, and the nature of the products
which are left, and of the composition of soils, may
be made most instructive, by showing them what the
plant is made up of, and reasoning from this what
ought to be found in the ground in addition to what
is supplied through the atmosphere, in order that it
may be a healthy and productive plant; calling their

attention to the much greater quantity of some particular substances taken out of the ground by some crops than by others, and that therefore a succession of crops of the same kind would exhaust the ground of that particular substance, and would be bad farming; that knowing the particular substances taken out of the ground by a crop of wheat, oats, barley, rye, grass, &c., as shown them by these tables, they should endeavour to find · out such manures as would give it back to the ground.

Then again with respect to animals—the food which they eat must contain all the elements necessary to form the flesh, bones, muscles, &c., as it was clear they could be formed in no other way; but we had also direct proof, as the chemist could take them to pieces, as it were, and show what bone, muscle, &c. was made of; and on examination it was found that they were made up of the very same elementary things as the food which the animals fed upon; that perhaps one particular vegetable did not contain all the materials necessary, but some contained one and some another, and that a variety of food within certain limits was good; that if a young animal ate a food which contains what would make fat and flesh, but had nothing in it of which bone was made, it could not make bone, and would most likely die; that milk of animals was found to be a perfect nutriment, and containing everything necessary for making bone, muscle, flesh, &c., and was therefore good for young people; that the farmer very often makes the observation from experience, that such a field or pasture is good for young stock,—another field for fattening; which means, that in the first pasture, there are certain plants, or grasses, which contain all the elements of bone, flesh, muscle, sinews, and which are necessary for building up a strong and healthy animal; in the second, that the plants and grasses are more favorable for producing fatty matter, and as grown up animals do not want to make bone, this is the kind of pasture for them.

This is a subject clearly within their comprehension, and not only that, but one in which, if intelligently taught, they will take great delight. The interest which many of the children here, even in the little which has been attempted, seem to take is of the most lively kind, and has often brought across my mind an account which I read many years ago, in Ellis's ' Polynesian Researches,' of the great curiosity and astonishment shown by the South Sea Islanders, on seeing the first printed sheets issue from the press. The very mention of things, such as that grass contains bone, or the elements of it, is quite as strange to this class of children, as printing was to the natives of the South Sea Islands.

The bearing of this subject being so completely on what is to be the future occupation in life of the great majority here, whether as labourers or as the employers of labour in agriculture, gives it a value, both in the eyes of the parents and children, which no other subject can have, independent of its being so attractive in itself to every inquiring mind.

If introduced into our National Schools, where the standard of acquirement is such as to admit of it (and this ought to be the case in all), it would not only have a tendency to bring the children of the farmer to the village school, but would be the means of introducing among the agricultural class a kind of knowledge which, at the same time that it is intimately connected with their occupations, has a great tendency to cultivate the mind, and is one of which the present race of farmers are entirely ignorant; they are, however, no readers, and I fear that such works as those on Chemical Agriculture by Prof. Johnston, admirable as they are, will find but few to read them among the occupying class of farmers in the south of England.

Some time ago, wanting a copy of the 'Western Agriculturist,' the first three numbers containing Lectures on Chemical Agriculture by Mr. Conybeare, I wrote to the publisher at Axminster, who told me in reply, that the attempt to continue this little work, notwithstanding the cheapness of it, and the great attraction of Mr. Conybeare's name, had entirely failed; and that so illiterate and prejudiced were the farmers there, that only ONE in the parish (one of the

largest in the county), had condescended to read
Mr. Conybeare's Lectures ; such would be the case in
any part of the south of England, until a generation
rises up instructed in this kind of knowledge at our
parish schools.

The personal cleanliness of the children, more particularly of the girls, has been a matter of general
remark, so much so, that strangers have said—" they
cannot be the children of the labouring class—your
labourers must have higher wages than are usually
given ;" now, the fact is, these children have become
more orderly, and are beginning to feel that cleanliness and well-mended clothes are necessary to their
comfort ; their parents find it attended with no greater
expense than rags and dirt, only requiring better
regulated habits. Habits of this kind in the girls,
who are taught to be good workers, having one half
of the day for sewing, will have the greatest influence
on the next generation.

A little girl, of five or six years old, not giving a
very wise answer to a question asked her by a lady,
on the latter asking her what she thought her little
head was given for, curtsied, and said, " to comb
ma'am ;" so that it was quite clear that in this case,
at all events, lessons of cleanliness had made an
impression.

No one can have had much intercourse with our
peasantry, without having to regret the great want of

truth which prevails among them in matters of daily life : this want of openness in their dealings has been, in a great measure, brought about by the way in which they are treated by their employers ; many of whom take advantage of any improvement in their circumstances which may render them a little less dependent upon daily labour for their living. I hope the rising generation will be trained up in better principles.

Observing to a father, whose boy had been guilty of telling a falsehood, how important it was to bring up his children with a greater regard to truth, he answered, " I always tells my children nothing *bates* the truth ;" but in a tone of indifference, which showed he did not care whether they did so or not. I have always instructed the teachers to be extremely careful never to frighten and ferret a child into a lie; and have strictly enjoined them, always, and at once, with great and small, to believe them, unless they have strong reasons for the contrary ; to express great satisfaction with any openness of character and candour which they may see in any of them ; and I have myself, on all occasions, treated them as if they would scorn a lie. From this I conceive great good has arisen ; and the bold way in which they avow their faults, or confess, for instance, they have not complied with certain school rules in matters of cleanliness, and in which they might easily deceive, is most pleasing to see. On such occasions the clean ones are placed at the top of the class for the morning, giving the others great credit for telling the truth, which is a Christian virtue which stands before cleanliness, but that those who have acted up to both must be preferred.

I find, almost daily, circumstances occurring, which, trifling in themselves, throw great light upon the way in which education works; and, although I could relate many, I will confine myself to two, which occurred within the last few days.

Calling at the cottage of a school-girl, who was sick, and who was living with her grandmother—on saying, I hoped she would be well enough to be in school again in a few days, the grandmother said, " You may be sure of that, sir, if she is well, for there is no keeping her away from it;" and the girl gently replied, " I am sure, grandmother, you would not wish me to stay away;" when the old woman very affectionately answered, " No, indeed, my dear child, I would not." Such an instance of the humanizing effects of education is very pleasing

At another cottage, the mother said, " You cannot think how pleasantly we spend our evenings now, compared with what we used to do; the girls reading and getting their lessons while I am sewing, and their father working with them; and he is so disappointed, sir, if *the evening task is above him*, so that he cannot help in it."

In two or three instances, it has been told me, " Well, sir, for the first three or four months my child was at the National School, I thought it could not read a chapter in the Testament a bit better than it did when at the dame's school, and I was dissatisfied; but I now find out I was under a sad mistake, it is now quite astonishing what he is doing, and all that time he was learning something, which helped him on wonderfully." In one case, the mother actually sent a message to the school, " That she hoped they would not teach her child all that nonsense, as she would rather it learned nothing than that"—a little piece of poetry with a good moral to learn by heart:—such is the absurdity of some of the parents!

During the four years which the school has been at work, I do not think there have been half a dozen cases where the children have not provided themselves with the necessary books, and every child may be seen going home with what Mr. Moseley, in his Report, calls, " the accustomed satchel," either over his shoulder or in his hand, having the means to instruct himself at home, and to add cheerfulness to his father's fireside. Nothing connected with this school has given me more pleasure (in fact, it has amply repaid me for all I have done) than the satisfaction which I have heard expressed by many of the parents, of the increase of their own domestic happiness, arising from the interest they take in their children's learning, and the way in which they are now able to spend their evenings at home, in listening to their reading.

At first, the parents were too apt to attempt to interfere in the discipline; this very soon ceased, but in the first year, not fewer than thirty were taken away, because they would not conform to the rules of the school; in one instance, where a boy had been kept in at noon, the father went and took him away to a cricket match; the boy actually begged his father, who was afterwards very sorry for what he had done, to let him return in order to undergo his punishment, and not run the risk of losing the benefit of the school.

The good effects, as shown in the children, are that they are more respectful and obedient to their parents, and to all around them—more alive to the decencies and respectabilities of life—more truthful—more honest—have stronger feelings of self-respect, and their conduct in every way is very striking, when contrasted with that of those who have not availed themselves of the advantages which the school offers. There is a modesty and pleasingness of demeanour in the girls, which must be evident to every one who sees them; and there are several instances of those who are out at service having already realized all that one expected from them, and are, I hope, becoming what every well-wisher of society would have the working population to be—" cheerful and contented with their lot in this life, and looking confidently forward, through the atoning merits of their Redeemer, to the life of the world to come."

Of all classes in society, there is none so powerful for good in this matter of education as the clergy; and, in the rural districts at least, it almost wholly depends upon them whether an efficient system can be established or not; in small parishes it is impossible to have a thoroughly good school on anything like a self-paying principle, but they might still maintain the kind of school they do at present for the younger children; for their wants beyond this, they would naturally connect themselves with the larger schools in the neighbourhood, and if those who have the power would set about it in earnest, it would not be too much to expect that, within a very few years, schools of an efficient kind for the joint education of the labouring classes, and those immediately above them, might be very extensively established in every county in England.

Theoretical writers and speakers may stir up a temporary feeling in favour of education in the public mind, and this will help to a first establishment of the necessary machinery for working it out; but, after all, the more vital part rests with those who are to be the instruments of doing it, and both from his position, his acquirements, his constant residence, no one can be so effective as the clergyman of the parish.

Some, perhaps, will say this is becoming village

schoolmaster, but it is no such thing; it only requires a small amount of time, systematically given, and I think almost every one will agree, that in no other way could an hour a day for three or four days in the week be productive of anything like the same amount of good as when spent in the village school. With many of those who are grown up, and whose habits are formed, humanly speaking, little good can be effected; their ignorance is so great, that religion in them can scarcely be regarded as anything more than a superstition acting upon their fears, and with no influence whatever upon their conduct as men in any of the relations of life; it is only through the children, and that by educating them, that any extensive good can be effected.

Since the school here was established, I have given almost constantly an hour, and sometimes an hour and a half a day to it; looking at the exercises, hearing them read, giving a cheering word to one, and an encouraging look to another, pointing out their faults: in this way much is done in a little time, and the best possible effects arise from it.

The clergyman's support, or that of some influential and educated person, is not only wanted in the school, but he may do much by endeavouring to raise the social position of the schoolmaster, and by supporting his authority in matters where the parents, from ignorance, are sometimes too apt to interfere; but where the education is good, it only requires firmness to get the better of all this.

The real difficulty of the question is not with the people, or the classes to be educated, but in getting it out of the hands of the talking men, and into those of the practical and working ones; and in persuading those who are to direct and do the work of it, to do it in a common-sense way, and with common-sense views; instead of starting difficulties to begin with, many of which are of an imaginary kind—and would in practice never arise—to begin on a plan, good in itself, so far as the knowledge to be had at the school is concerned; and if this is done, I feel persuaded the classes to be educated will throw no difficulties whatever in the way.

I should be satisfied in having made public this account of the working of a village school, if it in any way affords encouragement to those of the clergy, or of any other class who contemplate improvements in the matter of education in their own parishes, or in their own neighbourhoods. They cannot have greater obstacles to contend with than here, nor do I pretend to say they will meet with less. From the first I formed no extravagant notions as to its success; I never imagined that every parent would send his children, but, as a matter of common sense, that the more respectable ones would do so in the first instance, and the rest would follow; that the parents, from ignoance, and from not knowing and properly estimating the difficulties of the schoolmaster, would, in some instances, act very absurdly, but in the end that they would have their eyes opened and see their mistake; neither did I expect every child to turn out well, who had been educated at the school (I certainly expected to have those pointed out to me who turned out ill); neither do I deny, that an educated man may be more powerful for evil than if he had not been educated, but this, I think, only applies when those about him have been brought up in ignorance, and that if one in any way turns out ill, the rest are made much more capable of resisting the bad example. These opinions I feel strengthened every day by the experience which this school affords.

It has often been remarked to me, " all this seems to be very good which you are doing, and to go on very successfully, but wait and see how they turn out," and various sorts of dampers, such as—" a succeeding incumbent may not take the interest in it that you do, and then all this will fall to the ground." Now, the successor to a person who takes up a plan which has been successful, would have a much easier task than the person who originates it; our growing institutions for the training of masters would make it a much more easy thing to find qualified teachers. An effective school, when it has once taken root, stands a much better chance of being made lasting than one of a less pretending kind; instead of having only one person, the clergyman, feeling an interest in it; all classes, the parents of every class, would feel an interest in the well-working of what they had found so beneficial to themselves, and would take a lively interest in securing the same advantages to their children; besides this, an efficient system of inspection, and taking place more frequently than at present, would, in a great measure, be a guarantee against future relapse.

Inspection is not only good, as to seeing what is taught, and how a school is conducted, but, if attended with examination into the acquirements of the school, it gives rise to a sort of emulation on the part of the more advanced children, to stand well in the opinion of the inspector, as well as increased exertion on the part of the teachers, that they may do so.

It also attaches an idea of importance to education in their eyes, which it is right to encourage, as well as a feeling that there are others in the world beside those immediately about them, who feel an interest in their welfare.

On the occasion of Mr. Allen's last visit here, this was very forcibly shown, from the way in which they worked for a few weeks previous to his coming. At his examination, he gave the first class, of both boys and girls, a few written questions, to be answered also in writing; with their answers he expressed great satisfaction, and seeing the effect of this, I desired

them to provide copybooks for the purpose of occasionally entering their school exercises with the
dates; these books to be shown to the Inspector on
his next visit, as a test of what they were doing, and
as a·means of judging of the progress made between
his periods of inspection. A few questions asked on
these exercises, would at once show the examiner, how
far they understood what they had been.doing.

Such books have been kept, and having told them
a few weeks ago that Mr. Allen was likely to be down
in December, there is clearly more pains taken by
many of them, both in the writing and in the matter,
with a view to his good opinion when looking over
the book, as well as greater attention in their school
lessons, from a wish to do well in the examination.

It is a good plan, to point out more particularly
certain subjects for them to attend to, previous to
an inspector's visit, which teaches them to fix their
attention.

The difficulties of establishing a school on anything
like a self-paying system, has always appeared to me
to be much greater in an agricultural parish, than in
a town where the population is not extended over so
large a surface, and where the number of tradesmen,
&c., and of those who are able to pay such sums as 6s.
and 10s. per quarter; and even larger sums, is much·
greater. I have no doubt, whatever in my own mind,
that in every town of 1000 people, there are all the

necessary elements of a self-paying system ; and I would also extend the observation to all agricultural parishes, of the same amount of population.

I have no wish to hold this up as an example for more than it is worth, or to wish, that those who read it, may draw larger conclusions than the data justify them in doing ; whether the number of facts explained, are sufficient to entitle it to the attention of those interested in the promotion of education, those who read must judge; I am not aware of leaving out anything, which might help them to a right conclusion, or of inserting anything, which might lead them to a wrong one.

It has been a matter of complaint, that the better educated masters and mistresses brought up in our training schools, leave their profession for other employments in which they are better paid : this is natural, and cannot be blamed ; but, might not some system of superannuation after a certain number of years' service, (I mean of good and effective service), and after having arrived at a certain age, be adopted, as an inducement to remain ?

Surely in a profession so useful to the public, it is worthy the consideration of government, to see whether any such plan could be adopted. The system of inspection, if properly carried out, would guard the public against abuse.

Perhaps also, a plan of a mutual benefit society for

schoolmasters of a county or large district, might be worth consideration.

Some may think it is going too far, to say that a general theory or system can be attempted, founded on a single experiment, but still there are cases in which a single experiment may amount almost to a demonstration of the general proposition, and this I conceive to be the nature of the case here.

" The evidence of a theory becomes stronger, by the number of facts which it explains, and the accuracy with which it explains them, and diminishes by the number which it does not explain."

Now what are the conditions under which the experiment is made?

What are the facts which it will explain? and what are those it will not explain?

The experiment is tried in an agricultural parish, having a certain amount of population scattered over a given area,—their occupations chiefly agriculture and the trades it gives rise to,—their educational wants and present state of education,—their feelings in favour or against it,—their means of paying for it,— their condition, moral and physical;—all these may be taken as of an average kind, and belonging to the same number of people in any of the rural districts in England,—the schoolmaster fairly qualified and anxious to improve,—the clergyman taking up education in earnest, and desirous to advance it,—the kind of education such as is described before—these are the data.

The facts proved are,—

That the poor, as a class, have shown themselves willing and more ready to pay for their education, books, &c., than they have hitherto had credit for.

That the classes immediately above the labourer, their employers, are glad to avail themselves of a good education, in conjunction with the labouring class, and their former prejudices against our National Schools and schools of that kind, as places of education for their own children, entirely vanish.

That schools established on this principle of united education of a really effective kind, when the first expenses of building, of school apparatus, fittings, &c., are provided for, would in many districts be absolutely self-paying ; and in others so nearly so, that the expenses falling upon those who made themselves responsible, would not be great; much less than in schools where the standard of education is of a lower kind.

That the moral effects both on children and parents, so far as can be judged from an experience of four years, are of the most encouraging kind.

That such schools might be very extensively established in the larger parishes throughout England, by the assistance of the clergy and others interested in the education of the poor.

The difficulty no doubt is (and this the experiment cannot explain) in getting the clergyman, or others who are competent to the task, in the locality where a school is to be established, to take such an interest in it as will ensure success; hence arises the necessity of looking out for such places as, all things considered, model schools would be likely to succeed in; this of course is more particularly the business of boards of education, and of those who, from their situation in life, may have influence beyond the locality in which they live; the material to work upon is the same or nearly the same in every district in England, and, through our training schools, the difficulty of finding qualified teachers is becoming every day less, and the feeling in favour of education greater: these considerations afford ground for hope that all difficulties of whatever kind may shortly be overcome.

These observations, whether from my not having sufficiently compressed what I wanted to say, or from what other cause I do not know, are certainly of greater length than I had intended them to be; the opinions expressed have arisen from watching with an observing eye the daily working of the school here for the last four years, its effects both upon children and upon parents, and are in no way the result of mere theory, or of opinions formed before I took this in hand; looking at them in this light as the result of experience, I have thought them worth offering to the public. I am no enthusiast in the matter; I know and see that great practical good is attainable, and that the difficulties, so far as the people to be educated are concerned, (and I think I know them well,) are by no means so great as they have hitherto been looked upon. Should the cause of education be in any way advanced by publishing these observations, my wishes will be attained.*

---

* There is a lending library in connexion with the school; the number of books taken out, from 1st of Jan. 1845, to 29th Dec., was 540, calling each little separate thing a book. Of the usefulness of this, there can be no doubt, and although the actual reading is confined, or nearly so, to those who are, or have been at school—in fact very few of the others can read—yet through the children, it is a source of instruction both to young and old.

There are three instances of girls, who had had a little education such as the dames give, but who were too old to come to school when it opened, who have, through these books, and the help of their younger brothers and sisters, managed to educate themselves,—one now gone out into respectable service, and in two of the cases, with the exception of writing, they are nearly as well educated, as those at school.

IRISH NATIONAL SCHOOL.

HAVING spent about two months, at the end of last
summer, in Ireland, I took the opportunity of visiting
a very considerable number of National and other
schools, and, in a great many cases, of personally examining into the kind of education given, the numbers
that attended, the acquirements of the children, the
feelings of the people on the subject, and into any
other points which might enable a stranger to form a
correct opinion, as to how far the National system of
education was a successful one, and whether it gave
promise of realizing those practical good effects on the
country at large, which its friends and supporters say
are likely to result from it.

I certainly entertain an opinion, as far as my own
experience goes justly so, that there is a want of
information in England on the Irish National system,
and that the public have been labouring under great
mistakes, as to the view and intentions of the Board
appointed to work it out, and have little or no knowledge either of the books published by the Board, or

the kind of education to be had at the schools under their control. Many, I think, have entertained opinions against the books, and against the system, without in any way having examined into either, and others, again, have entertained feelings in favour of them with quite as little foundation for their opinion.

There is also a good deal of misunderstanding as to the origin of the system : some labouring under the idea that it was a hastily got up plan in 1831, by the then government, and that it had none of that consideration, given to it, which is due to a plan calling itself National ; others, that it, as well as the books adopted in the schools, originated entirely with the present Board of Education, who had, in fact, nothing whatever to do with framing it, but are a body appointed for working out the system adopted by the State.

The plan itself is mainly founded on a Report, made in 1812, of a Commission issuing from the Crown in 1806, at the head of which was the then primate, and the Report is signed by him, by the then Archbishop of Cashel, the Bishop of Killala, and Dr. Elrington then Provost of Trinity College—a recommendation coming with greater church authority one can scarcely conceive.

It was adopted by a commission from the Crown in 1825, by a committee of the House of Commons in 1828, and again in 1830, so that the plan, so far from being a hastily got up one, seems to have been under the contemplation of the different governments from 1812 to the time when it was adopted in 1831.

This Report of 1812, after stating that the various plans hitherto adopted had failed, goes on to say—" No plan, however wisely and unexceptionally contrived in other respects, can be carried into effectual execution in this country, unless it be explicitly avowed, and clearly understood as its leading principle, that no attempt shall be made to influence or disturb the peculiar religious tenets of any sect or description of Christians ;" it then recommends a Board constituted like the present, its selection of proper books, and, amongst these, extracts from Scripture of the kind published by it; and although not being acted upon for so long a period, may imply that it was attended with difficulty, yet this, if it were so, also proves that no government, or commission, or committee could devise any better system, than the one which has been adopted : such was the origin of the plan.

On the subject of the books published by the Board, the Scriptural Extracts, and the mode of using them in the National Schools, there is, also, a good deal of misconception among us.

Many of the clergy, as well as others who take an interest in education, imagine that the Bible is excluded from the National Schools in Ireland, and that the Extracts alone are permitted to be read.

This, on inquiry they will find is an error. So far as the secular books are concerned, I have put them into the hands of many of my neighbours and others, who have uniformly acknowledged the excellence of them, and I should have no hesitation whatever, in putting the Extracts into the hands of any child in whose education I took an interest, with the same views with which they are introduced into the National Schools.

The following extract from the preface to the Scripture Lessons will show the views of the Commissioners in introducing them.

" These selections are offered, not as a substitute for the Sacred Volume itself, but as an introduction to it, and they have been compiled in the hope of their leading to a more general and more profitable perusal of the Word of God.

" The Board of Commissioners of Education earnestly and unanimously recommend these lessons to be used in all the schools receiving aid from them.

" And to the religious instructors of the children they cheerfully leave, in communicating instruction, the use of the Sacred Volume itself, as containing those doctrines and precepts, a knowledge of which must be at the foundation of all true religion."

The Extracts being a part of the regular school books, may be read at the school hours for secular instruction, the Bible or the catechism of any particular church, only at the time appointed for religious instruction, at which time the teacher attends, and assists the clergyman of his own persuasion in giving religious instruction to the pupils.

The following observations arise out of my own personal knowledge, and from having examined with somewhat the eye of an inspector into a very great number of schools, not less than fifty or sixty, many of them in rural districts taken as chance threw them in my way, in a ramble in part over all the four provinces. In many of these I entered into that kind of examination, which a person conversant in matters of this kind, and taking an interest in them, is likely to do, and in doing which, in Ireland a stranger will always find the greatest encouragement, both on the part of the school-masters and of the Boards of management connected with them; in others I was a mere looker-on.

One of the first things which occurs to an English-man on entering an Irish school, in the rural districts more particularly, is the ragged condition of the children, want of shoes, &c., when compared with the same class in his own country; but when he looks on the surrounding cabins and reflects on the social condition of the peasantry, he sees at once that it would be unreasonable to expect to see them otherwise.

My first visit commenced in the south of Ireland, with the schools which happened to be on or near the roadside, and in almost every case I found the attendance much greater than from the nature of the district I should have expected; many of the children coming a distance of four or five Irish miles; another thing very observable was the greater ages of the children of both sexes than in our schools, but this no doubt is in part explained by the great want of employment, which applies to all ages; but, independent of this, there is a more lively and active feeling among the labouring classes in favour of education, than exists at present in this country, and there is a great aptness and quickness in the children which give them an interest in what they are doing.

In this class of schools, I found in most of them, I may say in all where the master had been trained to the work, a knowledge of their reading books—(I am speaking of the secular books of the Board, parts of which are relating to Scripture history)—of geography, grammar, and of arithmetic, which it was most pleasing to find, and which, I cannot hesitate to say, was much greater than is to be found, or even aimed at, in our own National Schools in the rural districts.

The previous knowledge which I had of the books, and of their contents, gave me great facility in examining; and I was much amused with the master in one which I visited in company with an Irish gentleman, who from my not having explained that I was an English stranger, on our leaving the school, took an opportunity of asking if I was a commissioner, and if so, he hoped I would represent his school to the Board in Dublin as I had found it. The children did very well, and although there were only a few scattered cabins in the immediate neighbourhood, upwards of

a hundred were present, many of them coming a
distance of four Irish miles. The school hours, from
ten to four. The master here had one great difficulty
to contend with, and which is the case with many
others, teaching the children a language which many
of the parents do not speak.

This district was one in which there were very few
Protestants, and on my asking the question whether
there were any Protestant children in the school, the
answer was " No." " Why?" " Because they are
too proud." This answer must not be mistaken; its
real meaning was, that there were very few Protestants
in the parish, and those of a class above sending their
children to the National Schools.

This would apply to the greater part of the south of
Ireland.

In one school, of a larger kind than the previous
ones, the master was a young man of whose qualifications, from conversation, I thought more favorably
than of any I had yet met with. He had just been
advanced to the first class of trained masters, that is,
the class receiving £20 a year from the Board; and,
although I had not an opportunity of seeing his
scholars, it being vacation, yet I was much pleased by
his intelligence and manner, his clean and neat appearance, and by the lively interest he took in his
profession. In this school, of 120 boys, there were
as many as eighteen or twenty reading the fifth book

of Lessons, and he had been advanced to the first class of masters, from the Inspector, on his last visit, having been so much pleased with the *class in science* which he had formed; this was the first time I had heard the expression made use of in speaking of education in a National School, and it forcibly attracted my attention; although I had not an opportunity of testing its meaning and its worth, as applied to his own school, it was not lost upon me in those I visited afterwards.

From observation I was led to think that the system of classification of the teachers by the Board, and of increasing the salaries of those who may be considered deserving, worked well; it is only for three years at a time, thus holding out an inducement for continued exertion, in order to retain the increase when it has once been granted.

The whole country is divided into 32 school districts, each having a superintendent who inspects, and reports each school in his district, at least three times in each year; and examinations are held from time to time by the superintendents, with the view of raising meritorious teachers to a higher class, or of depressing others who may have conducted themselves improperly, or in whose schools the attendance has considerably decreased.

The next I examined was in a small town: there were present 105 in the boys' school; the principal class of more than twenty, were many of them of a much more advanced age than any I had yet seen ; some of them qualifying themselves for being surveyors, and occupations of a similar description, and belonging to a class of life, who were able to pay for their instruction ; some paying as high as 7s. 6d. per quarter.

The master asked me if I should wish to hear them examined in any particular subject, and, on my answering in anything he liked, he called out "Geometers, come forward." This I thought was rather grand, but, to my astonishment, a class of not fewer than eighteen, whose ages were from fifteen to twenty, came forward. He set them two propositions in the first book of Euclid, which they demonstrated with accuracy, and I then asked them various questions connected with the properties of simple geometrical figures, and as to how far they were able to apply what they knew to those purposes of practical mensuration, which, in them, constituted the real value of this kind of knowledge ;—to all this they answered well.

Bearing in mind what the master at a previous school had said about having formed a class in science, I then asked a variety of questions on ordinary subjects of this nature, and I am not aware of having asked one to which I did not receive an intelligent answer.

To the questions on the fourth and fifth reading-books of the Board, their answers were equally satisfactory.

The clergyman here, I understood, was a supporter of the National system, and had broken up his own school, and sent all the children to this.

In the larger towns I found, in many of the National Schools, three or four hundred boys, and, in nearly all, a large class reading the fourth and fifth books; in some of them, as in the one I have just mentioned, books of a mathematical kind are introduced, of a more extensive nature than those published by the Board. There seems to be a greater desire for this kind of knowledge in the south of Ireland, particularly, and a more general acquaintance with it, than in this country.

In nearly all these schools I found the more advanced pupils well acquainted with the subjects of the books of the National Board, and having a very fair knowledge of things connected with them,—geography, grammar, arithmetic, all very good. The great attention paid to grammar arises, I suppose, from the English being taught, in some measure, as a foreign language.

To the questions which I asked on the lessons connected with Scripture history, in the different books published by the Board, very satisfactory answers were given; and I have no reason to suppose that less attention is given to this department of their reading-books, belonging to the ordinary school-hours, than to any other.

I did not ask any questions which might be supposed to infringe upon the school rules, and therefore cannot speak on my own authority beyond this. The Board sees that one day a week, at least, is set apart for religious instruction, and to say that the children are neglected in this respect, would be to accuse, of a neglect of duty, those to whom it particularly belongs, to see that this important part of their instruction is not neglected.

At Limerick the National system does not seem to prevail, as I could find no schools in connexion with it. There is a very large school for about 400 under the Christian Brothers, but it being vacation, I had no opportunity of forming an opinion of the instruction given, beyond what was implied in the books and educational apparatus, which seemed to be very good.

I observed also that the National School books were not introduced into the schools of the poor-house, so that, I suppose, there may be some opposition to the system here, with which I am not acquainted.

During my stay in Dublin I made frequent visits to the Model Schools in Marlborough street. The buildings are spacious and well adapted to the purposes for which they are intended ; school-rooms well supplied with every kind of educational apparatus, and the whole bearing an appearance of doing its work well. This I found, on examination, to be the case.

Both schools of boys and girls, having from 400 to 500 in each, will, in point of cleanliness, bear a comparison with any large schools I have ever seen ; although I fear, in the girls' school, to an English eye, there appears to be a little propensity to finery.

The regularity and order with which everything was conducted—the business-like manner and energy displayed in the teaching department—the amount and kind of instruction which I listened to, as being given to the more advanced pupils, and the interest which they appeared to take in it,—all this denoted a superior organization, and made an impression upon my mind of the most pleasing kind. I found, on examination, the acquirements in both schools quite equal to what the appearance led me to expect.

One morning I was present when the head master was teaching the senior part of the boys' school in a separate class-room, when, to oblige me, he went into an examination of them, in which I also joined ; in this they gave proof of a knowledge of the subjects of their books, and of things connected with them,— of the application of their knowledge of arithmetic, and of similar subjects, which convinced me that these boys had received a good education, and one fitting them for all the purposes of ordinary life. The knowledge of geography in both schools was remarkable, but in a large class of the senior part of the girls' school, fitting themselves for teachers, I had never seen in females anything like the knowledge which they had on this subject.

The training department for teachers is under very able management, and is effecting a great deal every year towards improving the class of school teachers all over the country; the number trained last year was 260.

In Ireland more particularly, it is highly important to give the teaching as much of an industrial character as possible, and of this the Board seems to be aware, having established a model farm at Glasnevin, a short distance from Dublin, in order to give the teachers a practical knowledge in agriculture; and there are also three or four other smaller agricultural schools established. They have, however, not yet been able to carry out their plans of this kind to anything like the extent which is desirable, but this I believe is owing to want of funds, and not from any doubt as to the necessity of it, having resolved upon establishing 32 model schools, one in each school district, and many of them of an industrial kind.

In the schools of the north of Ireland I found, where the teachers had been trained, the instruction and acquirements much of the same character and equally satisfactory with those I have mentioned before: to go into details would lengthen these observations far beyond what I wish; but there is a small agricultural school at Larne, in the county of Antrim, deserving of particular mention. The school-room good and well appointed in every respect, the cleanliness and outward appearance of the children, the extent and kind of knowledge in which they are instructed, fitting them, both in practice and in theory, as young pioneers for introducing a new and improved system of farming in the neighbourhood, gives this school in such a country as Ireland a very peculiar interest.

After having walked with the master over the six acres of ground connected with the school, and seen the improved way in which it is managed, I spent some time in examining the pupils, both in their ordinary school acquirements and in their knowledge of chemical agriculture. In all this they acquitted themselves extremely well, and some of them interested me very much by the good sense way in which they came to their conclusions, showing they were well instructed, and did credit to the master.

Schools like this ought, if possible, to be established very extensively in Ireland, and, if encouraged by the landed proprietors, would no doubt lead to the most beneficial results.

This is a proof of how much individuals may do in their own neighbourhood, as I believe a great deal of the getting up of this school, and the energy in working it, is owing to Dr. Kirkpatrick, of Larne, whom I regret not having had the pleasure of seeing on the occasion of my visit.

On the subject of mixed education in this part of

Ireland, I will quote a letter by the Rev. J. Smith, A.M., Rector of Island-magee, and addressed to the Bishop of Cashel, he says, " I have visited and personally examined into the circumstances of several National Schools, in the county of Antrim,—I think not less than twenty, possibly more, all of which are found within a circle of ten or fifteen miles around the neighbourhood (Larne). In *no one* of these schools, as far as I can recollect, have I found a class of children exclusively of one religion, excepting one (his own) parish, in which the whole number of Roman Catholic children is under twenty. In Larne, where I reside, in the principal male and female National Schools, the proportion of Roman Catholic children in each school is nearly one fourth, the remaining three fourths being chiefly Presbyterian children, with some of the Established Church, and some of other denominations : I have also visited other National Schools in this county, more distant than those before mentioned, and a few in some of the adjoining counties : and in no one school can I recollect an instance of a perfectly unmixed class of scholars, in regard of their religious faith ; and I may add, from observation and correct information, that it will very generally be found in the counties of Antrim and Down, and also in other northern counties, that united education prevails under the National Board, and that, while in the two former counties, the greater proportion of children, in attendance at the National Schools in most places, may be Presbyterians ; yet that, in these schools, and generally in the rural districts of the North of Ireland, the classification of children, as regards their religious faith, will be found in a very fair ratio with that of the surrounding population."

The town of Armagh he speaks of as an exception to this rule. Here there is a very good school of a model kind, under the Church Education Society, which I visited. In this town in particular, the children of the Church schools appear cleaner in their persons, better clothed than those of the National Schools, and this, in point of appearance and of clothing, might apply to other places; but the peculiar circumstances connected with Armagh are sufficient to account for this ; but even here, my impression was, that the acquirements of a school of this kind were not equal to those of the best National Schools. One of the National Schools was closed at that time, not having a master : another, a large one full of children, all Roman Catholics, was ill-ventilated, although in other respects doing well.

The school at Sligo appeared to me a very interesting one, but I had no opportunity of examining it. I had some conversation with the master in the school on the subjects taught, and the manner of teaching them. He was clearly well trained, and took great interest in his work. He had various specimens of the rocks and minerals in the county and neighbourhood, and knew how to take advantage of local circumstances in order to interest his school. This it is in a teacher which ensures success, and it cannot be too much impressed upon our schoolmasters to talk to the children of the nature of the things about them—the animals, vegetables, minerals, and, in fact, to interest them in that part of the creation which is rubbing against them at every step : if a teacher knows well how to do this, the children will smooth all difficulties with the parents, and it gives a life and action to the whole, which nothing else will do.

As a school of an industrial kind, the design of the one just now built at the fishing village of Cladagh, close to the town of Galway, is very interesting—the Piscatory National School. The building is a particularly neat one, and its intention is, by a good education bearing upon their own occupations, to open out more extensive fields of industry in nautical life to the rising generation in and about Cladagh, which, from prejudice and from ignorance of more improved methods used in other fisheries, has hitherto been confined to their own sea-coast.

The day I spent in Galway was one of their annual fairs, and truly the Irish collect in great numbers on such occasions, but I am not aware of having seen one single instance of drunkenness during the day.

The opinion which I formed of the National Schools

which came under my observation, and which were sufficiently numerous to give a tolerably correct idea of the working of the whole, was, that in all those schools where the masters had been trained, there was a degree of school-acquirement displayed by the children in the knowledge of the subjects of their reading books, grammar, geography, Scripture history, arithmetic—and, in the larger schools, of the higher parts of arithmetic and mensuration, as applied to the business of life, far greater in amount than I had expected to find, and which showed that they were getting an efficient education, and one sufficient for all the wants of their class, and which had a strong hold on the feelings both of parents and of children, as was shown from the numbers which are to be found in every school.

The girls' schools did not appear to me in so satisfactory a state as the boys', chiefly from the want of needlework, giving an idea of a deficiency in this respect, but to which it will be difficult to find a remedy in the rural districts.

This success is no doubt owing to the steadiness of purpose with which the Board have pursued their plans from the beginning, and the business-like way in which they have worked them out; and in no small degree has it contributed to their success, their having in the commencement of their proceedings, put forth a set of educational books, embodying a system of instruction of a definite kind; and it has always been to me a matter of great surprise, that something of the same kind should not have been done by our own National Society long ago : the progress of education in England has been very much retarded by its not having done so.

The great numbers also, which, from their plans, the training department have been able to send out, has worked great and rapid improvement in the staple of the teachers.

The head of this department, being acquainted with the Inspector's reports, with the merits of the school-masters under the Board, and whether trained or not, knows the age, habits, state of school, of each school-master, and whether (all things considered), there is sufficient of promise in him to make him worth train-ing; and if so, he is brought up to Dublin for the pur-pose, his school in the meantime being conducted by some one approved of by the inspector of his district. In this way the best or most promising ones are selected; the Board having about 100 masters at the same time, to attend lectures, and undergo a system of training for six months, to which time it is limited for the teachers brought up from the country, in order to extend the advantages to the whole as rapidly as pos-sible; and it is found, that short as this time is, it effects a very great improvement on those who receive it ; and the reports of them afterwards are in general highly satisfactory.

The numbers so sent out last year were 260 for National Schools, of whom 173 were males and 87 females; and also 30 teachers, who support themselves, for schools not National, of whom six were males and 24 females : there is also a special class in the Training Schools, consisting of about 30, fifteen of each sex, who remain for two years ; and a few training for agricultural schools.

The observations about training apply also to the female teachers.

To the question, has the system answered as one of mixed education ? it will, I believe, generally be found that where the clergy of the Established Church are decidedly opposed to the National system, that the children of their own persuasion do not attend the National Schools in any great numbers, and that in those cases, owing to this opposition, it has not answered as a system of mixed education to the extent which is desirable, but that with all other Protestant denominations it has; and I scarcely found one person, among those with whom I ordinarily conversed, both in the lower and middle classes, who did not look upon the National system as one of the greatest blessings ever conferred upon Ireland.

That the system has a strong hold on the feelings and opinions of the great mass of the Irish population, both Roman Catholic and Protestant, there can I think be no doubt ; and this is very strongly shown by the fact, that the number of schools in Ulster (the province in which Protestants of that class in life for which the National Schools are intended, are principally to be found) is greater than in any other part of Ireland. .

There is I believe a party among the Roman Catholics who are opposed to it ; but when it is seen that at the end of 1845 there were 3426 schools in connexion with the Board, and attended by 432,844 children, being an average of upwards of 120 in each, and, in addition to this, the Board had at that time undertaken to make grants towards the building of 276 school-houses, which were then to be completed, and at which they expected an attendance of about 27,172 additional children, and there were then also five agricultural model schools in operation, and grants promised to five more : this bespeaks a great and general interest in the system.

The average annual increase of schools, from 1840 to the end of 1845, is 293, and of the yearly increase of children for the same time, 40,056.

The Board some years ago made a calculation, as appears by their returns, that, taking the children between the ages of seven and thirteen, they would require school room for 570,000. Considering the time it has been established ; the numbers at the end of 1845, as given above, are a very satisfactory and encouraging result.

In speaking of the numbers of schools and of
children, the foregoing numbers include the workhouse
schools, which the guardians have placed in connexion
with the Board : the number of these at the end of
1845 was 90 out of 123, the whole number of unions
in Ireland.

So great a number placing their schools under the
superintendence of a Board of Education is a very
strong fact; and in reference to it the Commissioners
make the following observations in their Report :—
"That the Boards of Guardians of the different unions
comprise Protestants and Roman Catholics, and have
amongst them men of the highest rank and station :
that the schools are attended by Protestants and
Roman Catholics indiscriminately : and that the duty
of giving religious instruction to those of each creed
belongs to a chaplain of their own communion : that
here, therefore, we see the National system carried into
complete effect : that here we see how peculiarly
adapted it is to the circumstances of Ireland : and that
here, too, we see how decidedly it carries the opinion
of the country with it."

The number of children is so great in many of the
Irish poor-houses, that the school department becomes
one of the greatest importance. In many of those
which I visited, such as Killarney, Listowel, &c. I
found as many as 200 children, and in some, a much
greater number.

In all, so far as the arrangements of the buildings are concerned, the school is well cared for—large and separate school-rooms, and extensive playgrounds for the boys and girls—children clean, and in this respect a great improvement upon their home habits ;—all getting some education, and in many places good, and there is a wish to make that which is defective better—most of their schools furnished with maps, &c. The sites of the poor-houses seemed well chosen, generally in some elevated situation out of the town, and the organization and internal arrangement appeared better than in England ; so far as a traveller can form an opinion from having visited a considerable number, seen over the internal arrangements, examined their schools, seen the people at their meals, and made all the inquiry which it was in his power to do, I should say, that the system worked extremely well, and did credit to those concerned in the administration of it ; and I believe it is found, that the workhouses are doing their part well under the present circumstances and difficulties in which Ireland is placed.

Of the schools under the Church Education Society, I visited a good many, and it appeared to me with a very few exceptions, judging from the books, from the kind of instruction given, and the numbers present, that they did not aim at that amount of secular instruction which is to be found in the National Schools ;

and that, in this respect, as places of education, they were far inferior to them; that continued opposition on the part of the clergy, must in all places, with the exception of a very few, such as Armagh and Dublin, have the effect of placing the children of the Established Church in a much worse position, in point of education, than those of any other denomination.

If the education at the Church schools is not equal to the wants of the present time, the parents will, no doubt, and I believe are now doing so on these very grounds, send their children to the National Schools, which offer greater educational advantages. In the last Report of the Church Education Society, the numbers at the end of December, 1844, were 104,968, and at the end of 1845, were 100,755, showing a decrease of 4213. To maintain anything like an efficient system, even for children belonging to the Church, on a voluntary principle, must be difficult under any circumstances, and in opposition to a Board like the National one, a thing impossible; and under these circumstances, it is deeply to be regretted, that so many of the clergy should feel themselves obliged to oppose the National system.

Education in Ireland has, as respects the practical good which is to arise from it, greater difficulties to contend with than in England: not greater as to giving the people a certain amount of intellectual education, or of knowledge bearing upon the arts of industrial life—for the Irish are in all these respects a most teachable people—but the greater difficulty is, in finding a field for productive labour when they leave school.

That education, which teaches them greater skill in what are likely to be their after employments—greater steadiness and fixity of purpose in what they undertake, producing also a disposition to habits of industry and good order, will have the effect of bringing about increased confidence in those who have it in their power to give employment there can be no doubt; and will thus, in the end, it is to be hoped, open out new fields of home employment of a productive kind in a system of improved agriculture—of a more extended commerce — increased employment in their fisheries, their mines, and other resources belonging to Ireland, which hitherto have, comparatively speaking, been but little thought of.

As a proof of what may be done in this way, even by an individual, a most striking instance is given in ' Facts from Gueedore,' just now published, by Lord George Hill : let any one read the petition of Patrick McKye, the master of the National School, to the Lord Lieutenant of Ireland, in 1837, and then read the list of things sold at Lord George Hill's store, and that in articles there mentioned, *the very same people* to whom the petition applies, laid out £550 in the *quarter*, ending the 19th of December, 1844; and that they delivered at the store, and sold that *same year* oats to the amount of £1100 ;* and it must convince him, that the people of Ireland may yet do much for themselves, if they would only set about it in the right way; an experiment so full of instruction at this present time, is most cheering, and must be gratifying to every one to see. Patrick McKye's petition is worth reading for its graphic description of things about him.

The most useful lesson which can be taught the Irish labourer, and one which ought to be instilled into him in youth, is, that a system of working for wages would place him in a state of much greater comfort than the occupation of a small patch of land is ever likely to do, and create in him feelings of a different kind from those he has at present, giving a taste for a better dwelling, better clothes, and better food ; and make him feel that there is a kind of happiness and comfort within his reach, far above that in which he is at present dragging on his threescore years and ten, vegetating upon what has been termed the lazy root of Ireland, and in a state of existence, such as is scarcely to be found in any other civilized part of the world.

I know of nothing that gives a stranger a clearer insight into the state of the small holders of land in

---

* Previous to this, they were never in the habit of selling their grain, but made it, and all they could procure besides, into poteen. 'Facts from Gweedore' also mention, that in 1845, upwards of three hundred pounds' worth of exciseable articles were sold at the store ; a proof, that improvements in Ireland, are not *necessarily* unproductive to the Exchequer.

Ireland, occupiers of from two, up to ten or perhaps twenty acres, than in looking on at one of their markets, particularly if immediately after harvest. I happened to be at Gort, a small town in the county of Clare, on their weekly market-day at the end of August; the number of people, some having one pig —two perhaps—another, one, two, three sheep; some with a small quantity of grain, oats, barley, or wheat; but in no case more than about a sack, and in many instances beat out by whipping the sheaf over a stone, leaving the straw to get a sort of threshing at a more convenient time; this small quantity in most cases being their whole produce of that kind; then the women with a few fowls, perhaps a turkey or two, a few eggs, showing clearly, that no part whatever of the produce beyond the potatoes and buttermilk, went for their own support.

It is rather curious to contemplate how little the discoveries and inventions of modern times, and the progress of things supposed to have an influence on the comforts and happiness of mankind, have done for the Irish peasant.

Beginning with his cabin, to what period of time must we go back to contemplate a state of things more rude, or requiring less of art to construct than it does, or having fewer of those things which man in the progress of civilization has adopted in his dwelling, than we find here.

Then, again, in England we speak of the produce of

our colonies, sugar and coffee from the West, tea from the East, reaching our cottages; but how few of these ever reach the Irish cabin; with the exception of tobacco, that bane of Irish peasant life, few or none of these things find their way there; and hope, that sweetener of life, has hitherto never opened a prospect to him of a more cheering kind, than that of vegetating upon the produce of his potato land, and bringing up his children to tread in the same steps.

Still with all this I have never travelled among a peasantry who were more cheerful, more obliging, or more alive to kindness than they are.

To my mind no feature in Ireland offers so cheering a prospect for the future as her National Schools. May all classes unite in promoting a system of education already so well commenced, and so likely to be productive of lasting good. May they all endeavour to realize the words of their countryman, Professor Kane, that " with temperate habits, and with the education which the National system will give to every individual of the growing race, there is no danger but that industry may be accompanied by intelligence, intelligence by morality, and all by the steadiness of purpose and tranquillity of habits, on which the happiness of the family, and the peace of the community depend." This is the result which it should be the object of all to promote.

C. AND J. ADLARD, PRINTERS, BARTHOLOMEW CLOSE.

AN ACCOUNT

OF THE

KING'S SOMBORNE SCHOOL.

EXTRACTED FROM THE

"MINUTES OF THE COMMITTEE OF COUNCIL ON EDUCATION, 1847-8."

LONDON:

R. GROOMBRIDGE AND SONS,

5, PATERNOSTER ROW.

Printed by C. and J. Adlard, Bartholomew Close.

Committee of Council on Education,
Privy Council Office, Downing Street,
March 14, 1849.

GENTLEMEN,

I have to acknowledge the receipt of your letter of the 12th instant, in which, as the publishers of the works of the Rev. R. Dawes, you request permission "to reprint that portion of the 'Minutes of the Committee of Council on Education, for 1847-8,' which relates to the King's Somborne School."

In reply, I am to state that my Lords have no objection whatever to the proposed reprint of a portion of their 'Minutes.'

Their Lordships are of opinion that it is very desirable that the attention of persons interested in the improvement and extension of elementary education, should be drawn effectually to the real character of the causes which have combined to render the National School of King's Somborne a model worthy of imitation.

I am,

Gentlemen,

Your obedient servant,

HARRY CHESTER.

MESSRS. GROOMBRIDGE and SONS,
5, *Paternoster Row.*

KING'S SOMBORNE SCHOOL.

KING'S SOMBORNE is a parish of 7500 acres. Its population is 1125, of whom 160 belong to the hamlet of Up-Somborne, about two miles and a half from the school; another 160 live scattered in various parts more or less remote from it, and the remaining 800 live in the village in which the school is situated, distant three miles from Stockbridge. The occupation of the people is wholly agricultural, the growing of corn and feeding of sheep. The farms are large, many of them uniting what used to be two, three, or even four farms; and five or six farmers occupying the whole parish.* The wages of a labourer vary from 6s. to 9s. a week, and the rent for a cottage from £2 10s. to £5 a year. There are no means of employing women and children otherwise than on the farms. There is no squire or other person resident in the place above the condition of the farmer, except the rector.

Neither is there any indirect influence of non-resident landlords or neighbouring gentry favorable to the schools, to account for their success. The exercise of any such influence by the rector himself would be opposed to his view of the principle on which that success depends.

The National schools consist of—

A Boys' school of 92 children, taught by a master and assistant master.

Girls'	,,	93	,,	,,	mistress.
Infants'	,,	34	,,	,,	mistress.

Making a total of 219 children.

* A parish in which there were many small farms would offer a much more favorable field for a self-paying system of education.

a §

There are, besides, two dame schools in the parish, containing, together, 49 children.

Of the children who attend the National school, there are 53 belonging to other parishes, leaving a total of 215 of the children of the parish, or more than one sixth of its population under education—one seventh being in its National schools,* and one forty-second part in other schools. As somewhat less than one fourth of the population are probably of an age to go to school (from 4 to 14), this leaves about one twelfth as the proportion who ought to be at school and are not. Of the 53 children who come from other parishes, 26 are the sons of labourers, and 27 of the class above the labourer. Of the latter, 17 reside in lodgings in the village, that they may attend the school, bringing with them from home on the Monday morning a portion of their provisions for the week.† The rest walk a distance of from two to four miles daily to the school.

The school is wholly self-supporting. The children buy their own books, and their fees pay the salaries of the teachers. No child is admitted to the school free of charge. No arrears of the school fee are allowed. The following is the scale of payments. For the labourers' children, 2d. per week for one, and 1d. for every additional child in the same family. For the children of all those above the mere labourer, and whose parents are living in the parish, 6s. ; and for those of a similar class out of the parish, 10s. per quarter.

The school opened in October, 1842, with 38 children, of

* The fact that so large a proportion as one seventh of the actual population is in the National schools, proves, in opposition to an assertion which has sometimes been made, that the King's Somborne school, whilst it educates the farmers' and tradesmen's children, is, to a much greater extent than National schools generally are, the school also of the labouring poor of the parish. It is in this union, to which the interest of neither class appear to be sacrificed, but which identifies them, that consists its chief excellence.

† Of these, six are the children of three families, relations, who have joined and taken a small house, and placed a relation in it to take care of them ; and four are from a parish where there is an endowment of upwards of £90 a year for educational purposes, and one from a parish which, jointly with two others, has an endowment of a much larger amount.

whom 11 paid by the quarter. The following table exhibits its subsequent progress.

Years from the Commencement of the School.			Whole Number of Children.	Number of Children paying by the Quarter.		Sum received for Fees.	Sum received for Books.
				From Somborne.	From other Parishes.		
						£ s. d.	£ s. d.
1st	year to	1843	106	24	1	56 17 3	7 5 5
2d		1844	110	24	3	68 11 7	8 0 6
3d		1845	144	24	10	84 6 1	11 5 3
4th	Michaelmas	1846	158	22	14	93 5 5	15 8 0
5th		1847	219	23	26	145 6 6	24 18 1

The following is a statement of the ages of the children.

KING'S SOMBORNE SCHOOL.

Ages in Years.	No. of Children.		Ages in Years.	No. of Children.	
	Boys.	Girls.		Boys.	Girls.
Under 6	—	2	From 13 to 14 . .	2	6
„ 7	14	9	„ 14 to 15 . .	4	6
From 7 to 8 .	13	12	„ 15 to 16 . .	1	2
„ 8 to 9 .	12	7	„ 16 to 17 . .	2	2
„ 9 to 10 .	13	13			
„ 10 to 11 .	10	11	Total	90	82
„ 11 to 12 .	9	6			
„ 12 to 13 .	10	6	Average age . .	10½ years.	

King's Somborne is a secluded place, not situated upon any high road, or near any great town. Its schools stand in view of the open downs near the church, and are built for 110 children, according to the simplest and the most economical of the plans of the Committee of Council; the site being a plot of ground of an acre, the gift of the lady of the manor.*

* They are built on the site of a palace of John of Gaunt, and the window-sills, of Caen stone, are out of the old foundation: the ground belonged to Lady Mildmay, and was given in the same kind and liberal way in which she does everything connected with the welfare of the poor. (*Hints*, &c., p. 8.) Her ladyship has during the present year added half an acre to the site.

The teachers, at my first visit to the school, in May, 1847, were a. master, a second master, a mistress, and four paid monitors, two in each school. At my second visit the monitors had been replaced by six apprenticed pupil teachers.

The master and mistress have jointly a salary of £75, with a house and garden. The second master, a youth of 18, educated in the school, has £30 a-year. To these salaries are now added the Government allowances for teaching the apprentices.

In the year which intervened between my first and second visits, a village school, heretofore taught by a dame, had been incorporated with the National schools as an infant school, and one of the apprenticed teachers was constantly employed in it.

On entering the school a stranger, attracted there by the reputation it has gained, would, I think, be struck by the absence of those things intended to catch the eye, which have sometimes awakened his suspicions in other schools of local celebrity. There is a reality in the scene which will impress him favorably in respect of it. It is a village school that he sees before him ; the better learning of the children, obvious in the intelligence of their looks, has not taken away their rusticity ; a school crowded with sturdy, healthy, shy-looking cottagers' children, clad somewhat better, perhaps, than the children of other schools,* but in garments of the same rude fashion and coarse texture. In regard to cleanliness, a marked difference is, however, on closer observation, apparent. It is particularly to be seen in the hair of the girls ; down to the

* "The personal cleanliness of the children, more particularly of the girls, in this school has been a matter of general remark, so much so, that strangers have said,—' They cannot be the children of the labouring class ; your labourers must have higher wages than are usually given.' Now, the fact is, these children have become more orderly, and are beginning to feel that cleanliness and well-mended clothes are necessary to their comfort ; their parents find it attended with no greater expense than rags and dirt, only requiring better regulated habits. Habits of this kind in the girls, who are taught to be good workers, having one-half of the day for sewing, will have the greatest influence on the next generation.

" A little girl, of five or six years old, not giving a very wise answer to a question asked her by a lady, on the latter asking her what she thought her little head was given for, curtsied, and said, ' To comb, ma'am ;' so that it was quite clear that in this case, at all events, lessons of cleanliness had made an impression."—*Hints on a Self-paying System*, &c., p. 23.

least child in the school, the head of each is as cleanly, and the hair as glossy, as though a nursery-maid had bestowed daily care upon it.* All this cleanliness is the result of the attention which the governess has been directed to give to the subject, and to a public opinion favorable to it, which has, by judicious management, been created among the children themselves. Every girl is provided with a hair-brush and comb, purchased by herself, and wears her hair separated in front, and long enough to be placed behind the ears.

The injustice is not committed of robbing her of her hair, to keep her humble and cleanly. A girl's hair is an ornament Nature has given to her; her pride in it is an instinct to which violence cannot be done with impunity. Her character, thwarted of its natural development in that direction, will grow deformed in some other.

Personal cleanliness is not, however, encouraged among these children in the matter of their hair only, but in other things not less likely to make it habitual.

Twice, for instance, in every week every child is asked whether it has washed its feet, and there is reason to believe that ablutions of this kind are general in the school.†

Every child has, moreover, a tooth-brush, and washes its teeth daily, a practice which Mr. Dawes was led to introduce in the school, thinking it would more firmly fix habits of cleanliness in regard to other things, and because he was informed on the authority of an eminent dentist that it was a precaution tending greatly to the preservation of the teeth, and, therefore, of the health.

---

* There is a penny clothing club in the school, which is now in its fourth year. It consists at present of 129 children, who pay 1d. per week for 48 weeks in the year, and the rector adds 1s. to the whole sum thus paid in by each. A week or two before Christmas orders are given by the schoolmaster for useful articles of clothing, to the amount of their deposits, on three shops, two in the village, and one in a neighbouring town, to give them the choice of a market.

† There was at first considerable opposition on the part of the parents to the washing of their children's feet in cold water, lest it should injure their health. It will be admitted that the attention which is given to this habit of cleanliness is not without reason, when I state that, from inquiries made to ascertain how far it is observed among the poor, there is, I am told, reason to believe that the feet of labouring men are rarely or ever washed from the time of their childhood.

It is a characteristic distinction of this from other village schools, that it includes with the children of labourers those of shopkeepers and farmers. It was made up of these classes in the following proportions at my two visits.

Station.	Payments.		May, 1847.	May, 1848.
	£ s. d.			
	1 0 0 per quarter.		1	..
	0 10 0 ,,		28	30
Farmers and tradesmen .	0 6 0 ,,		19	26
	0 3 0 ,,		3	5
	0 0 3 per week		..	9
Labourers	0 0 2 and 1d. per week		112	136
Sent by Trustees of a small fund for education . . .	. . . .		..	7
	Gratis		..	9
Total	. . . .		163	222*

To this statement, with which Mr. Dawes has obligingly favoured me, he has appended the following note:

"There are none paying £1 per quarter; some time ago I thought of making a class pay £1, and one boy did so, but doubting the policy of it, I gave it up, and now I think I was right in doing so.

"Of those paying 10s., two are sons of a professional man, who hires a couple of rooms in a farm-house, and sends a person to take care of them. The rest are the children of farmers and tradesmen; but I doubt whether more than 10 or 12 of them would be sent to what are called boarding-schools for education, and must take such as can be got for them near home.

"Those paying 3s. per quarter, and 3d. per week, are cases where it was thought right to relax the rule as to 6s. per quarter, from something peculiar in the case;—the father perhaps, although nominally a tradesman, yet not much better off than the common labourer.

"The above numbers include the infant school, 35; but the numbers in this class will increase considerably when they get into the new cottage, which is much larger than the present one.

"Of those paying 10s., 7 are girls and 23 boys; of those paying 6s., the numbers are equal,—13 of each.

"The payments, as they stand at present, will be a very considerable increase even on the amount of last year, supposing the other quarters to be like this.

From the preceding table it appears that there are at present

* The infant school, 35 in number, is included in this total.

in these schools 152 children of agricultural labourers, and 70 of farmers and tradesmen. The last-mentioned being taken, as I understand it, to include shoemakers, tailors, and the like, who, in villages, work on their own account, but who in towns would probably be journeymen.

When these children, belonging to different grades of society, stand intermingled in the classes of the schools, I have been unable to distinguish between them as to say which was the farmer's and which the labourer's child. Certainly there was nothing in a more intelligent expression of the countenance to mark the difference. The advantages of the farmer's child in respect to home culture had been made up to the labourer's by the school. Notwithstanding that the school offers precisely equal advantages to the children of farmers, tradesmen, and labourers, yet practically the first-mentioned class derive the greatest benefit from it; not because the labourers' children are less capable or less desirous of instruction than the others, but because they remain a shorter time. If, therefore, the farmers and tradesmen of King's Somborne continue to avail themselves of the advantages offered by the school as zealously as they do now, it is no more to be feared that the next generation of labourers should be more in advance of them than the present.

Thus the higher classes of the school include labourers' children in a less proportion than the school generally.

In May, 1847, the first class of boys was composed as follows:

First Class of Boys (15), arranged according to merit.

Standing in Class.	Age in Years.	Condition in life of Parent.	Standing in Class.	Age in Years.	Condition in life of Parent.
1	14	Journeyman carpenter.	9	13	Bailiff.
2	14	Gardener, in service.	10	14	Labourer.
3	15	Labourer.	11	12	Labourer.
4	12	Beer-shop keeper.	12	12	Labourer.
5	11	Farmer.	13	12	Labourer.
6	9	Relieving officer.	14	14	Village shopkeeper.
7	16	Labourer.	15	12	Labourer.
8	12	Dairyman.			

First Class of Girls (18).

Standing in Class.	Age in Years.	Condition in life of Parent.	Standing in Class.	Age in Years.	Condition in life of Parent.
1	16	Labourer.	10	15	Small farmer.
2	14	Widow of a poor farmer.	11	15	Widow of a labourer.
3	14	Widow, a nurse in service.	12	11	Labourer.
4	14	Labourer.	13	13	Labourer.
5	14	Widow of a labourer.	14	12	Labourer.
6	13	Labourer.	15	13	Village blacksmith.
7	13	Carpenter.	16	13	Labourer.
8	12	Farmer.	17	13	Labourer.
9	15	Labourer.	18	14	Labourer.

In May, 1848, the first class of boys had increased to 21, and that of girls to 22.

Attainments of the Children in the King's Somborne School.

The school is distinguished from most others in this district by the use of the Scriptures for the instruction of the children, in the subject-matter of Scripture only, and the use of secular books, exclusively, for their instruction in reading.

I have appended to this Report (Appendix A) a list of the books at present used in each class.

At my first inspection I examined all the classes minutely; 160 children were then present in the two schools, of whom I found 64 (being 2 in 5) capable of reading with tolerable ease and correctness. In other schools I have found this proportion 1 in 6.

Here, then, where so many other things are taught besides reading, the children are found in advance, in reading, of others, in the majority of which scarcely anything else is taught.

And this is always the case, and a fact which seems to point to the expediency, if not the necessity, of teaching children something else besides reading, that we may be able to teach them to read.

To emancipate them now and then from the drudgery of reading, cannot but make the task a less irksome one to them, and it is impossible that the instruction they receive in other things, awakening the intelligence and strengthening the memory, should not aid them in learning to read.

Whatever difference of opinion there may however be about the cause, there can be none, I imagine, about the fact, that in an elementary school the learning of one thing aids the learning of another; and that if various things be taught, not only is the knowledge thus acquired greater in respect to the aggregate, but in respect to each element. I know not where the limit is placed beyond which confusion is engendered of this variety.

The judicious selection of reading books is not, probably, a less important element of success in teaching to read than the intermingling of other subjects of instruction with reading.

My second inspection more than confirmed the favorable impression of the reading of the children which I had received from my first. The influence of the pupil teachers was apparent in the improved instruction of the lower classes, and I certainly never heard little children in an elementary school read so well.

It is not, however, only by the ability to read with ease and correctness that this school is in advance of others, but yet more by the correct emphasis and the just expression with which the elder children read, and particularly the girls. The books of reading lessons used in the school, which are those published for the Commissioners of National Education in Ireland, contain many beautiful passages of poetry; these they are accustomed to commit to memory, and some of them have learned the whole of them. I have no doubt that the feeling with which they read is very much due to the pleasure they have accustomed themselves, from the recital of this poetry, to take in that which appeals to the heart and the affections, and the perception of moral beauty.

All the children in the school, except five, write on slates; and all, except those of the lowest class, are accustomed to write, not only from copies and from dictation, but in some degree from their own thoughts.

Thus a child in the lowest class but one, when it can write words legibly upon a slate, is told to write the names of its brothers and sisters, of all the things in the house where it lives, of all the birds, or trees, or plants that it knows, and the like. Another stage in its instruction associates qualities

b

with things. It is told, perhaps, to write down the names of all the white or black things that it knows, of all the ugly or handsome things, or the tall or short ones, or iron or wooden ones. And then, when the child can write sentences, on the uses of things familiar to its observation—it writes of things used for the food of man or animals, used in building a cottage, or as implements of agriculture. Lastly, it is made to exhaust its knowledge of such things by being told to write down all it knows about them : all it knows, for instance, about sheep, or cows, or horses, wheat, iron, or copper, of the village of King's Somborne, or the neighbouring downs and hills, of the farms and holdings in the parish, or the parish roads, of the river Teste which runs through it, of the neighbouring town of Stockbridge, of Hampshire, of the island of Great Britain, of the earth, or of the sun, moon, and stars.

To summon together the scattered elements of its knowledge of these familiar things, to combine them in a certain order, and to express them in written language, is an exercise which may be adapted to each stage in a child's intellectual growth, and which seems well calculated at once to accustom it to think, and to give it the power of expressing its thoughts in appropriate words. Not the least advantage of commencing these exercises from the lowest classes in the school is, that they serve not only as a practice in thinking and writing, but in spelling, and that probably of the best kind : the subjects, and therefore language, of them being more familiar than those commonly found in books used for writing from dictation. I certainly never have examined little children who could spell so well ; and that good spelling and good reading, and skill in the expression of written thoughts, go together, may be taken as an illustration of the fact that to achieve excellence in any one subject of instruction in an elementary school (even the simplest and most elementary), it is necessary to unite with it others ; and that the singular slowness with which the children of our National schools learn to read (a fact to which all our Reports have borne testimony) is, in some degree, to be attributed to the unwise concentration of the labours of the school on that single object.

Written exercises are also used as a means of instruction in religious knowledge. In the lower classes, the children write out in their own words the substance of any simple portion of the Gospel narrative, or of a parable or a miracle. In the upper classes, they attempt to draw from such passages of Scripture the instruction they are intended to convey, or they develope, with a practical application, some Scripture character. Having tried them at my last examination in exercises of this kind, beginning from the lowest class but one, and taking care to give different subjects to those children who stood near one another, I can record a very favorable impression of the result.

Exercises of this kind are not uncommon in schools; they are, however, usually limited to one or two of the highest classes : here they are done by all except the last. As I know that at least as much attention is paid to Scriptural instruction in other schools as in this, I can attribute the fact I have recorded to no other cause than this, that the knowledge of the children in other things, and the higher standard of their general intelligence, contributes to their knowledge and intelligence of the Scriptures; that they write better on religious, because they are accustomed to write also on secular, subjects.

The exercises of the pupil teachers in religious knowledge have not, however, satisfied me. More attention to this subject is required in their course of instruction.

In all the classes of the school the children appear to have, according to their standing, a good knowledge of arithmetic ; they are, moreover, taught English grammar, geography, and English History. Mr. Dawes has adapted the teaching of these subjects to elementary education by a judicious selection, and by various simple methods, the particulars of which are detailed in his work.*

Among the most interesting features of the girl's school is the needlework. The elder girls are taught not only to work, but, by paper patterns, to cut out work for themselves ; and the dresses of the first class, on the day of my examination, were many of them thus cut out, and all made by themselves. There seems to be no reason why the economical cutting out of work should not thus enter, as a part, into the ordinary instruction in needlework in our schools. The cost of paper for patterns would be little. The fitting of different articles

* Suggestive Hints.

of clothing to the children of the school would supply an inexhaustible variety of subjects for patterns; and for such an object the school might well afford a good many failures. The exercises of the girls in *arithmetic* might even be associated with this useful object. It is, for instance, a good question in the Rule of Three, knowing what the length of the sleeve of a dress for a person of a given height is, to determine what that for a similar dress for a person of another height should be; or, knowing how many yards of cloth would be required to make the dress in the first case, to determine how many would make it in the other. There can be no reason why the girls should not know that this last proportion is as the square of the height in the one case to the square of the height in the other; that, for instance, the cloth in a dress for a person 4 feet high, is to that in a similar dress for a person 5 feet, as 16 to 25.

When a girl has cut out for herself the dress she has made, she has associated her labour, in a natural relation, with the exercise of her judgment; she has taken one step towards her emancipation from a state of pupilage, and gratified an instinct which associates the growing independence of her actions with her progress towards womanhood.

Algebra is taught to 21 boys of the first class, including the two pupil teachers, and geometry to 11 of these. I examined into their knowledge of these subjects with much care, orally and on paper. Their written exercises are now before me. Nine of them have solved correctly a proposition in the first book of Euclid, beyond which book none have yet advanced. From my oral examination I am convinced that they have been well taught the propositions they profess to know, and that they understand them. I have rarely, indeed, heard boys answer so well in Euclid as some of them did.

Knowing that a good deal of skill in Algebra may be attained in an elementary school, I have been disappointed with the exercises of these boys in that subject. Only two or three of them have worked a simple equation correctly. The great interest of Mr. Dawes's experiment in mathematical teaching appears to lie in his having established the possibility of teaching Euclid with success in an elementary school; and of giving to farmers, and tradesmen, and labourers in such a school the advantage of that incomparable discipline of the mind which results from the habit of geometrical reasoning, even if it be limited to a few propositions in the first book of Euclid. Mensuration is taught as an application of the principles of geometry. Having examined the boys as to their knowledge of some of its fundamental principles, I can bear testimony to the fact that they are "not taught these things in a parrot-like way, but led to understand them as a matter of reasoning."

I have found algebra and geometry introduced in only one other National school,* and the teaching of it was there attended with the like success, contributing greatly to the interest the children seemed to take in the school, and to its reputation in the district.

That feature in the teaching of the King's Somborne school which constitutes probably its greatest excellence, and to which Mr. Dawes attributes chiefly its influence with the agricultural population around him, is the union of instruction in a few simple principles of natural science, applicable to things familiar to the children's daily observation, with everything else usually taught in a National school. He thus speaks on this interesting subject.

"After the school had been opened rather more than two years, I began giving to the teachers, and the more advanced of the school children, short explanations of a philosophic kind, and in a common-sense sort of way, of the things almost daily passing before their eyes, but of the nature of which they had not the slightest conception; such as some of the peculiar properties of metals, glass, and other substances in common use; that the air had weight, and how this pressure of the atmosphere helped them to pump up water; enabled them to amuse themselves with squirts and pop-guns; to suck up water, as they called it, through a straw; why the kettle-top jumped up when the water was boiling on the fire; why, when they wanted to know whether it boiled or not, they seized the poker, and placing one end on the lid and the other to their ear, in order to know whether it actually boiled; why a glass sometimes breaks when hot water is poured into it, explaining the reason of the unequal expansion of the two surfaces: these and similar things I found so excessively amusing to them, and at the same time so instructive, that I have scarcely missed a week explaining some principle of this nature, and in questioning them on what had been done before.

"In subjects of this kind, and to children, mere verbal explanations, as every one will perceive, are of no use whatever; but when practically illustrated before their eyes by experiment, they become not only one of

* In the Midland District.

b §

the most pleasing sources of instruction, but absolutely one of the most useful.

"For instance, a teacher may talk to them about a thermometer, and find, in the end, they just know as much about it as they did when he began; but if he shows them one, and then grasps it in his hand, telling them to look at the fluid as it rises, or plunge it into hot or cold water, and let them see the effect, they then begin to open their eyes in a wonderful manner, light breaks in upon them, and information thus given leaves an impression which in after-life they turn to a source of instruction, by the reasoning powers of their own minds.

"The teachers here, who at first knew but little of these matters, are now well qualified to give instruction in them; to teach the mechanical principles of the tools they use,—the spade, the axe, the plough; and to explain such things as the common pump, barometer, pair of bellows; metals varying in volume, according to the quantity of heat which is in them, or, as it is termed, expanding by heat and contracting by cold; why one substance feels colder to the hand than another; the way in which metals are separated from their ores; how water is converted into steam, and again condensed; how their clothes are dried, and why they feel cold in setting in wet clothes; why one body floats in water and another sinks; how much in volume, and how much in weight, a floating body displaces of the fluid in which it floats; why, on going into the school on a cold morning, they sometimes see a quantity of water on the glass, and why it is on the inside and not on the outside; why, when their ink is dried up, does it leave a substance behind which does not go away; the substances water holds in solution; water of the springs taking up some of the soil through which it has fallen; chalk, &c.; equal volumes of water varying in weight according to its density."

To the discussion of subjects of this class Mr. Dawes brings a rare sagacity, and that quality which in education is above all others to be desired,—great practical common sense.*

The children, when they disperse, carry home with them their books, for the evening's lesson, in satchels. The sight was to me, as an Inspector, a new and a very gratifying one. My thoughts followed them to the cottage fire-side; and I was not surprised when Mr. Dawes repeated to me the following words of the mother of one of the children whom he had recently visited: "You cannot think, sir, how pleasantly we spend our evenings now, compared with what we used to do; the girls reading and getting their lessons while I am sewing,

* Mr. Dawes's work, entitled "Suggestive Hints, &c.," published by Groombridge and Sons, of Paternoster Row, London, ought to be in the hands of every elementary teacher. It will not supply the scientific information he needs for conducting a school as that at King's Somborne is conducted, but it will direct him how to apply it.

and their father working with them ; and he so disappointed,
sir, if the evening task is above him, so that he cannot help
in it."

I have no doubt that the singing of the children is among
the most pleasurable recollections of those persons who have
visited the King's Somborne school. Occasionally the singing
classes are assembled in the evening in the class-room, and
the singing through of the pieces of music they have learned
makes a village concert, to which some of the friends of the
school are admitted. I was present on one of these evenings,
and I have thought that I could not better describe the
character of their musical attainments than by appending to
my Report (Appendix B) the programme then placed in my
hands. Singing is no task to these children ; music has
found its way to their hearts ; a result which I have never
met with in an elementary school, except where, as here, a
large portion of the children are allowed to sing by ear, and
where all have thus begun. Several of the pieces were
certainly executed with remarkable firmness and precision,
and all not less to the satisfaction of the farmers and village
tradesmen (who, together with Mr. and Mrs. Dawes and
myself, formed the audience) than to mine.

For this valuable element of the course of instruction the
school is indebted to the zealous and skilful assistance of the
relieving officer of the district.

Remarks on the King's Somborne School.

The popularity of this school is altogether unprecedented.
Everywhere else the inspector is accustomed to be told of the
indifference of the poor to the education of their children.
Here he finds them manifesting an earnest desire to obtain
for them the benefits of it. Agricultural labourers send their
children from other parishes, from three to four miles daily,
to the school,* and one seventh of the resident population of
the parish daily assembles in it.

Wherever he goes, the inspector's ear is familiar with the
complaint that funds for the maintenance of the school are
deficient ; that the fees are wrung with difficulty from the
hands of the parents, who are too poor to pay them ; that the

* There are at the present time 26 children who attend the school
under these circumstances.

landlords and farmers are unwilling to contribute to the school, and that competent teachers cannot therefore be provided, or sufficient in number. Here, in a district where the rate of wages is at least as low as in others, and where, if the people be not as poor, it must be due to the operation of moral causes, he finds a self-supporting school, having more than the usual staff of teachers,* adequately paid.

At other schools one third of the children are generally absent, and if the fee be insisted upon, the inability of the parents to pay it is generally assigned as a principal reason of this irregularity in the attendance.† Here the payment of the school fee is strictly enforced, and the average daily attendance is more than eight ninths of the children on the books.‡

In other schools nothing so discourages the inspector as the inadequate supply of school-books, the injudicious selection of them, and their miserable condition ; for all this, the poverty of the school is given him as the explanation : and if he is desirous to preserve the character of a discreet man, he will not venture to hint, as a possibility, that the children might be induced to buy proper school-books for themselves.

Here he finds every child in possession of as many school-books as it wants, of the best kind, well bound, and in a sound condition ; and he finds, moreover, that the child has purchased them all for itself, the school providing none.§

* Two masters and two mistresses, and (before the appointment of apprentices) paid monitors.

† In the iron districts of South Staffordshire, at a time when the wages of a large class of workmen were 50s. per week, the irregular attendance of the children was attributed to the inability (the unwillingness ?) of the parents to pay the school fee.

‡ In the month of May, 1848, when the hooping-cough was prevalent, the attendance was as follows.

	Number on the Books.	Average daily Attendance.
Boys	92	85
Girls	93	80
Infants . . . ,	34	30
Total . . .	219	195

§ £29 14s. 6d. were paid by the children for school-books thus supplied to them in the year 1847, at wholesale prices.

Elsewhere the early age at which the children leave, is spoken of as fatal to the success of the school. Here, although the very goodness of the school has a tendency to produce this result, and does to a certain extent produce it, the parents persuading themselves that their children get to know enough in a good school sooner than in a bad one, there is evidence that a labourer is capable of making for his child the sacrifice of the weekly wages he might earn, if sent to work, that he may send him to the school.

There were in May, 1847, eleven girls in the first class above the age of 13, whose parents were of the condition of labourers : eight of these were above 14 years of age. There were of the like condition, five boys of above 14 years of age, and nine above 12.*

Your Lordships will appreciate the amount of that sacrifice which a labourer earning 9s. a-week makes, when he sends to school a boy who might add to the weekly income of the family from 1s. 6d. to 2s. 6d., and not, I trust, consider

* The following tables afford the means of comparing the ages of the children in the King's Somborne school with those of the children in 47 schools in the Midland Districts.

TABLE I.

King's Somborne School, (90 Boys, 82 Girls).	Number per Cent.				
	Under 7 Yrs.	7 to 9.	9 to 11.	11 to 13.	13 to 17.
Boys	15½	26¾	25⅝	21	10
Girls	13	23	29	14	19
Total	14	25	27	18	14

TABLE II.
(From Report on Midland Districts for 1846, p. 151. 8vo Edition.)

Midland Districts (2014 Boys in 27 schools, 944 Girls in 20 schools).	Number per Cent.				
	Under 7 Yrs.	7 to 9.	9 to 11.	11 to 13.	13 to 15.
Boys	22	28	32	14	4
Girls	19	27	25	18	10
Total	21	27	28	16	7

misplaced the expression of an opinion which this example has but confirmed in my mind,—that the poor will be found capable of making, to a far greater extent than they do now, the sacrifice involved in sending their children to school instead of to work, whenever this sacrifice shall be justified by the character of the education offered to them.

In other schools, only 23 per cent. of the children remain after they are 11 years of age; here 32 per cent. In other schools, 4 per cent. of the boys and 10 per cent. of the girls are above 13 years of age; here 10 per cent. of the one and 19 per cent. of the other. Here, finally, the average age $(10\frac{1}{17}$ years) of all the children in the school is nearly that of the monitors in other schools.*

There is no sacrifice made for the cause of education so great as that of the agricultural labourer, who, when he might send his son to work, sends him to the school. Nor is this a less sacrifice to make at King's Somborne than in other agricultural parishes; but, on the contrary, a greater, there being a custom of sending the children out to tend cattle in the large fields or open downs, which is in some degree peculiar to the place. Neither are the farmers more disposed to promote the education of the labourers' children there than elsewhere. They claim them at the earliest available age for what is called bird starving, pig watching, &c. There is no occupation, however slight, which does not stand, in their estimation, before the school, and they look upon their further education after they are able to go to work, as an unjust deprivation of their labour, and an unwarrantable interference with the privileges of their own children.†

* See Report on Midland Districts for 1844. The average age of 3756 boys in 46 schools of the Midland Districts was from $6\frac{3}{8}$ to 8_6 years; and of 2301 girls in 33 schools, from $7\frac{1}{8}$ to $9\frac{1}{4}$ years.

† Mr. Dawes speaks thus judiciously on this subject:

"In agricultural districts the employer does not encourage the labourer to educate his child; on the contrary, his mode of thinking and of acting is in every way against it. He has no feeling that the respectability of the labouring classes would be advanced by education; or, if he has, he immediately becomes jealous of their being brought nearer to himself, not seeing that the class to which he belongs will in the end be equally advanced. In fact, he has no notion of worth in the labourer, as a man, or as a fellow-creature, but only values him as a machine or instrument by which a certain quantity of work is to be performed; and

To complete the contrast of this school with all others known to me: whilst I have found the success or failure of other schools attributed to the personal influence of the clergymen and other respectable inhabitants over the parents, by a moral violence, compelling the children to the school, here there is obviously, on both sides, the most complete independence; the school offered on the one hand, and accepted on the other; an education provided such as the parents think likely to benefit their children, and the parents availing themselves of it for their benefit; the father consenting that out of his week's wages the school fee should be paid, and the price of the school-books; the mother yielding to the school her daughter's labour in the household, and both, that their child may enjoy a privilege of which they have themselves no experience, submitting to the privations which must be endured, when the small weekly earnings of the family are diminished by the 1*s.* 6*d.* or 2*s.* 6*d.* which that child might have earned.

That explanation which it is easiest to give of the unprecedented popularity of the King's Somborne school is, to attribute it, not to any peculiar adaptation to the wants of the people it is intended to benefit, but to extraordinary skill

does not think that, although he professes to be a Christian, it is any part of his duty, as such, to endeavour to improve the moral condition of the labourers about him, by making them more intelligent, more sober, and better conducted in every relation of life, or that, by doing so, he adds to his own respectability.

"In the eyes of too many of the employers, the labourer who spends his money at the beer-house, neglects his family, and is perfectly regardless as to how they are brought up, is considered quite as useful as the one who would struggle hard to get his children an education, and try to raise them above those low and degraded habits to which they have hitherto been accustomed. Let those who act thus, if higher motives will not influence them, weigh well the observation of a modern writer, that 'independent of moral grounds, the kindness, sympathy, and attention of an employer to his workmen is the safest and most profitable money speculation in which he can engage.'

"I have never known a single instance of a farmer encouraging the labourer to send his children for a longer period to school, however trifling the work for which he wanted them. I have known instances of a parent wishing to continue a child, but his employer preventing him by requiring his services when so young, that it would have been far more creditable to have employed an older boy."—*Hints on a Self-paying System of National Education,* p. 19.

on the part of the master, or to remarkable tact and aptitude for teaching and school-keeping on the part of the rector. Were this the case, it would be impossible for me, in recording the results of my examination, to speak of them as generally attainable, and the example of the King's Somborne school would lose half its value. I trust, therefore, that I shall be pardoned, if I record the impression that the qualifications of the master are not in advance of those of the masters of very many other schools not equally successful; and that the rector (whilst the result shows him to be a very able teacher) would, I think, lay no claim to extraordinary technical skill or unapproachable readiness, or simplicity, or aptitude in his way of dealing with children. He takes no pains to make the public exhibition of a winning manner in teaching, and is certainly the last man in the world to compromise, in his intercourse with children, the dignity of his character or of his station.

His success has, in point of fact, been accomplished by honester and better means; and holding, myself, the opinion that he has had precisely the same kind of difficulties to contend with that other clergymen have, and that any earnest and enlightened man who followed in the same path would achieve the same results, I have thought it the more expedient to record this opinion, as I have constantly heard the whole merit of the school attributed to certain gifts and graces peculiar to the rector himself. The probabilities of the case are all, in point of fact, opposed to such a supposition. Mr. Dawes is a distinguished member of the University of Cambridge, and was for many years resident in that university as fellow and tutor* of his college; and a parish school was to him an unaccustomed place, when, a few years ago, he opened that of King's Somborne.

When I hear it asserted that such an education as that given in the King's Somborne school cannot be offered to the poor of the whole country, because it is not to be expected that such a rector as Mr. Dawes can be placed in every parish, I do not dispute the premises, but I see nothing to justify the conclusion. The example of the King's Somborne school would be of little value if it did not embody a principle; and

---

* For twenty years tutor of Downing College.

there is no reason why, if that principle were duly appreciated, our training schools should not supply masters qualified to carry it out; or why, if such masters were provided, one mind such as Mr. Dawes's should not control many such schools.

It is true that the attention given to the school by a highly educated man like Mr. Dawes raises it above other schools in the estimation of the people about him; and, considering what has been the previous training of our present national schoolmasters, this is not to be wondered at; but I speak of another state of their education, and I see not why men, duly and specially educated for the office, should not create everywhere the same confidence, and accomplish the same or yet greater results.

Influence of the King's Somborne School on the Moral Condition of the Parish.

Mr. Dawes conceived the idea of working out, within the walls of his school, a moral reformation in his parish.

He found it a parish thoroughly demoralized by the operation of the old poor law. According to information I have received from the neighbouring clergy, and from other persons acquainted with it before the time of his incumbency, I have reason to believe that there was no parish in the surrounding district which stood, in respect to the character of its inhabitants, so low.

The average annual amount of the parish rate for the seven years terminating with 1835 was £1600,* on a population of 1025. The population has now increased to 1125, and the rates are reduced to £1000.

From a state which gave to it an unenviable notoriety as the opprobrium of the country round, it has emerged into a village remarkable for the orderly deportment of its inha-

---

* It had been the habit for a long series of years to employ a large number of able-bodied men, thirty or forty at a time, upon the parish roads for six or seven months in the year (nominally for the purpose of repairing the roads, but in reality to run them on until the season of the year comes when they are wanted), at wages varying with the number of children each had to support. The influence for evil which a system like this exercised on a number of families in the parish may be imagined—it was to pauperize them.

c

bitants, their regular attendance at the parish church, the neatness of their abodes, the cleanliness of their children, the punctuality with which they send them to school, and the sacrifices they make that they may do so.

Probable Causes of the Success of the King's Somborne School.

We break off a fragment from our own education, and give it to the poor man's child in charity.

We consult neither his judgment in the matter nor his independence. We have no faith in his affection for his child, or in his willingness to make sacrifices for its welfare; and thus we give him no encouragement to make them, and scarcely an opportunity.

It is the fault of all the eleemosynary good we seek to do, that we claim the right of doing it in our own way. When we spend our own money, we spend it as we like. What we give, we give to whom we like, and in the manner we like best. It is with us rather a matter of sentiment and impulse than of deliberation. We do not make this expenditure with the same forethought, and caution, and thriftiness as we do others, or with the same reference to a profitable result; and thus it is that we so often give in vain.

If our education has failed of its results, if we find the poor but little benefited by our schools, careless of sending their children to them, and ready to take them away on the least chance of profitable employment, let us remember that they have themselves had no voice in the matter; that in the education we offer to their children, the springs of opinion among them have never been considered, nor their wants consulted.

It is in this that the secret of Mr. Dawes's success appears to me to lie. He has shown his knowledge of the springs of opinion amongst the poor by consulting their independence, and adapted the education he offers to their wants, by a careful study of their condition.

The King's Somborne school was commenced in the exercise of abundant faith in the affection of a labouring man for his children; and, notwithstanding that the wages of labour in the parish of King's Somborne are very low, the school fee was fixed at double that of other neighbouring schools, under the impression that he would be willing to pay more than is usually claimed of him for what he believed to be a really good and useful education, and that the higher fee would tend to create this belief in his mind.

Who are to be considered farmers, and to pay the highest fee, and who tradesmen and labourers, Mr. Dawes claims the right himself to decide,* but all are placed within the walls of the school on terms of perfect equality; they are intermingled in their seats, and in the classes in which they are taught, and precisely the same advantages of instruction are offered to all.

Here, then, is a practical recognition of the principle which your Lordships' recent measures appear to embody, and which public opinion now recognises, that education is not a privilege to be graduated according to men's social condition, but the right of all, inasmuch as it is necessary to the growth of every man's understanding, and, into whatever state of life it may please God to call him, an essential element in his moral well-being.

To *give* to a labouring man everything needful for the support of his family would be to pauperize him. To *give* him the education of his children is, moreover, to make him undervalue it. It is for this, among other reasons, that the estimation of education among the poor has for years past been sinking.

To treat labourers always as a separate and dependent class appears the likeliest way to perpetuate their state of dependence. Ir all we do—carefully to avoid intermingling with them those persons who, having emerged from their condition, have achieved some degree of independence (the employers and the employed), is to neglect an obvious means of cultivating those feelings of neighbourly consideration and mutual respect and good-will, on which the links of society depend for their permanence, and the commonwealth for its safety.

It was to embody these views, to unite in a new relation the farmers, and tradesmen, and labourers of his parish, that

---

* A difference of opinion sometimes arises on this point, but the estimation of the school with the people carries it over every difficulty. One individual, for instance, who took his children away from the school because he was not permitted to pay the fee of a labourer, and kept them away two years, declaring that he could be as obstinate as Mr. Dawes, has recently sent them back.

Mr. Dawes conceived the idea of bringing their children together in the parish school. He had a faith in the practicability of this, and he had the moral courage to act upon it. Much, no doubt, to the astonishment of the neighbouring farmers, he announced that the National school was open to their children to receive the same education as their labourers' children were receiving, on condition of their paying for the privilege a higher rate of remuneration. On the one hand were their prejudices, and on the other, the fact that their children were offered a better education at home for £2 a-year than they could get by sending them to boarding-school, for which they must pay from £30 to £40. The fact of the better education being once established in their minds, to attack them on the side of economy was to carry the day. One third of the children are accordingly those of farmers and tradesmen, and the remaining two thirds those of labourers. Thus in the King's Somborne school the foundation is laid of that mutual respect and good-will between the employers and the employed which is said once to have existed in England, but which seems of late years to have been disappearing from among us.

There is so intimate a connexion and dependence between the education of the farmer and that of the labourer, that it is impossible to conceive the existence of a class of educated workmen fostered by a class of ignorant farmers, or a class of educated farmers in constant intercourse with a class of brutalized workmen.

If the one class is to be educated, we must educate also the other; and the only place where the education they both thus need can be given to either is the parish school. The labourer can get it nowhere else, neither can the agricultural tradesman or farmer. Farmers and country tradesmen live too far apart to enable them, as a class, to maintain good day-schools for their children, and they are deterred by motives of economy from sending them to boarding-schools. When therefore our training schools have sent out a new class of schoolmasters, it is to the parish school that both classes must look for education.

But that this may be accomplished, it must offer an education adapted to the wants of both; and in this adaptation consists the chief element in the success of the King's Som-

.borne schools. What is the nature of it Mr. Dawes has himself fully detailed in his work entitled ' Suggestive Hints on Secular Instruction.' No other person having the same claim to attention appears to have given the same deliberate consideration to the subject, and no one else has, with the like success, subjected opinions thus formed to the test of experiment.

It is sufficient to say of his system, that it deals with reasons rather than with facts, and with things rather than with words: that, intended for a class of persons who are to delve out an existence from the material objects which surround them, it assumes the properties of those objects to be legitimate subjects of interest to them, and of reflection; and, as a principle, that the Almighty, in manifesting his wisdom and goodness in all material things, has, in mercy, associated the elements of thought with labour, and the means of exercising the highest intelligence with the humblest craft.

That it is for this reason that thinking and doing are associated in a pleasurable relation, so that what we do in the exercise of our judgment for some object and with an adaptation to some end we do with pleasure, but not that which is done with no exercise of our own judgment for no object and with an adaptation to no end.

Assuming, then, that in the knowledge or science of the things with which his observation is familiar, or which are associated with his labour, is to be sought a legitimate sphere for the exercise of a labouring man's reason and reflection; and that these afford the means of exercising those faculties and of developing them to the utmost limit of his powers; it gives to "the science of common things" an important place in the system of the school, and a remarkable development; and this seems to lie at the root of its success. Mr. Dawes thus speaks on this subject:

"With respect to that part of the instruction described in the foregoing pages which is of a scientific kind, I would say, and I do so from a feeling of conviction which experience gives, that in no way can the teachers in our higher class of elementary schools give such a character of usefulness to their instruction, as by qualifying themselves to teach in these subjects, n- troducing simple and easy experiments, which illustrate the things happening before their eyes every day, and convey conviction with them the

c §

moment they are seen and explained. It is a great mistake to suppose that boys of 12 and 13 years of age cannot understand elementary knowledge of this kind, when brought before them by experiment. Seeing the way in which the bigger boys were interested in it here, and the tendency it had to raise the standard of teaching, and to give rise to a wish for information, it has proceeded further than I at first contemplated ; and the result has been that the school is provided with sufficient of a philosophic apparatus for all the common experiments of a pneumatic and hydrostatic kind, a small galvanic battery, an electric apparatus, &c. One little book used as a text-book is a volume of Chambers's Edinburgh books, ' Matter and Motion,' and this is illustrated by experiment.

"The end of all education ought to be, to prepare them for those duties and those situations in life they are called upon to fulfil, whether they be ' hewers of wood, or drawers of water ;' of those who belong to the labouring, the middle, or the upper classes in life, to make them in their respective stations good citizens and good Christians ; and I think it will be found that, according as a teacher keeps this in view, making his instruction bear upon the ordinary duties of life, or loses sight of it (I am speaking of a teacher competent to his work), he will succeed, or the contrary. I am perfectly convinced that many well-meaning efforts have not been attended with the success expected from them, entirely owing to their leaving out all instruction relating to the occupations by which they were, in after-life, to earn their bread."—*Suggestive Hints,* p. 151.

If ever we are to educate the labouring classes it must, in my opinion, be by teaching them to reason and to understand about things which are connected with their ordinary pursuits ; the things out of which each is compelled to extract a livelihood, or which lie in his daily path. With the labouring man these are things so engrossing, that whatever other process of instruction we may begin in his mind when a little boy at school, the consideration of these will infallibly take the place of it when he comes to be a man, and when his education should tell upon him.

It may be difficult to teach him principles, but not when those principles are associated with results, and those results to him useful results.

I have expressed in this Report an opinion that it would be possible to create such schools as that at King's Somborne generally in the country, and with this view, that the opportunity should be afforded to the promoters of such schools of some general direction and guidance in the management of them ; and the training colleges placed on such a footing as to yield an adequate number of masters competent to teach them. It is a further condition of success that books should be provided specially adapted to the instruction of the children in these subjects, and the masters made familiar with the use of these books.*

* This appears to me an element very much to be desired in the teaching our training schools. The masters should be made thoroughly familiar with the subject-matter of the reading lessons in some one or other of the series of books provided for that purpose ; capable of putting the subjects of these lessons before the children under their simplest forms, and of adding to them all that is necessary to their completeness and to the full intelligence of them. Many of these lessons contain admirable matter of instruction for children ; but I never have met with a master capable of doing justice to them. It is, indeed, no easy matter to do so ; considerable additional reading is required to that end, and a judicious guidance. This would be best obtained at the training school. Every reading lesson he would be called upon to give might there be studied, and the student made familiar with the best way of giving it.

C. AND J. ADLARD, PRINTERS, BARTHOLOMEW CLOSE.

SUGGESTIVE HINTS

TOWARDS

Improbed Secular Instruction,

MAKING IT BEAR UPON

PRACTICAL LIFE.

INTENDED FOR THE USE OF

SCHOOLMASTERS AND TEACHERS IN OUR ELEMENTARY SCHOOLS,
FOR THOSE ENGAGED IN THE PRIVATE INSTRUCTION OF
CHILDREN AT HOME, AND FOR OTHERS TAKING
AN INTEREST IN NATIONAL EDUCATION.

BY THE
REV. RICHARD DAWES, A.M.

DEAN OF HEREFORD.

———

"MENS SIBI CONSCIA RECTI."—*Virg. Æn.*

A GOOD INTENTION.

———

Sixth Edition,

ENLARGED AND IMPROVED.

———◆———

LONDON:
GROOMBRIDGE AND SONS.
—
1853.

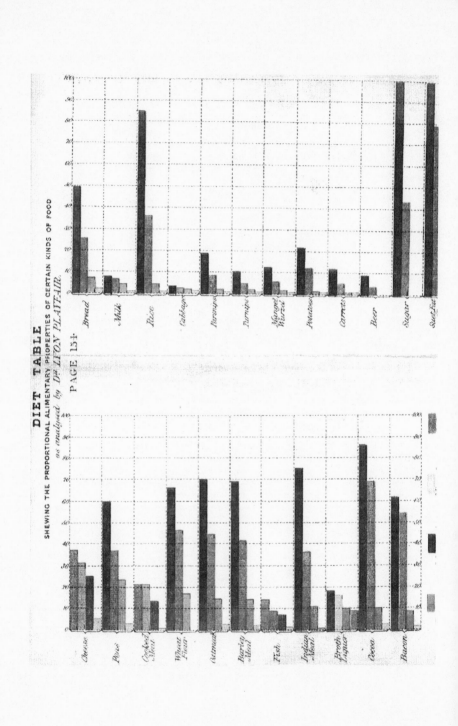

DIET TABLE

SHEWING THE PROPORTIONAL ALIMENTARY PROPERTIES OF CERTAIN KINDS OF FOOD

as analysed by Dᴿ LYON PLAYFAIR.

PAGE 151.

PREFACE.

THE reader must not expect anything like perfection in the following pages, or that the matter which they contain is arranged in the best possible order; they are intended to give an idea of what is taught in the school here, and the manner of teaching it : the Author feels that if anything of this kind had fallen in his own way when this school opened, it would have saved him much trouble; however, without apologising for their imperfections, or attempting to point out their merits (the former of which others will but too readily see), such as they are, " he casts his bread upon the waters," hoping that it may in some way or other advance the cause of education : there will, no doubt, be found in it some chaff, but not unmixed, he is willing to hope, with some wheat also, which may be worth picking out : on the whole, as the man who purchased an axe of the blacksmith, which he wished to have all over polished like the edge, to which the latter agreed on condition that he would turn the grindstone, but finding the labour of so doing greater than he expected, said, he was not quite sure that he did not prefer a speckled axe to a bright one ; so I feel myself obliged to let my axe go forth with many specks upon it ; however, such as it is, take it, reader ! profit from the bright spots, if it has any, and be lenient to the specks.

KING'S SOMBORNE; *April* 18, 1847.

In this, the SIXTH EDITION, considerable additions have
been made in the body of the work, from a wish to make
it as useful as possible, to that class of readers for which it
is intended: these additional remarks the author hopes
may not be entirely unworthy of the attention of those
interested in education, who may be desirous of availing
themselves of the experience of others in their efforts to
promote it.

DEANERY, HEREFORD; *July*, 1853.

CONTENTS.

INTRODUCTION.

ADDISON, in one of his numbers of the 'Spectator,' tells us that the common people of his day were very fond of a little Latin, and intimates that the reason of this was, because they did not understand it. Now the opinion I have formed of the people of the present day is, that they do not like a thing unless they do understand it; and although I have placed a few Latin words in the title-page of this book, this is not because I think the words will be approved of where they are not understood, nor from any wish to make the book appear more learned than it is, but simply for this reason—that the words themselves briefly express, in a portable shape for the memory, what I wish to have credit for in offering to the public a Second Edition of these "Suggestive Hints on Secular Teaching," viz. "a good intention;" and however imperfect they may be in other respects, with this impression on his mind, the reader will, I trust, overlook many defects which he might otherwise be inclined to criticise, and see something of usefulness in what is well meant, although it may not in reality be all that he had expected.

It is from no love of authorship that I am offering these remarks,—remarks, let it be observed, which have arisen entirely from experience in a parish school,—but from a wish to promote that kind of education among the middle and lower classes, which at the same time that it bears upon their industrial pursuits, leads to an improved moral condition, by instilling in early life those feelings of self-respect and self-dependence, and those principles of honesty and truth, which ought to be the guide of every one who lays claim to the character of a Christian man.

I am the more induced to do this, from seeing that the rising generation about me, and with whom I am more immediately concerned, are made happier and better by this education—that it leads to greater propriety of conduct in all the relations of life, and that those who have remained longest at school have generally turned out the best, and have given a proof, that the longer they remain the greater is the security of their becoming, in their respective stations, what the friends of education expect them to be.

The value of education of the labouring classes; or, in fact, of any other class, cannot be said to depend solely on the amount of knowledge given at school, but rather on the tendency which such knowledge has, to make them alive to the humanities of life, to fit them for their industrial occupations, to raise them in the scale of thinking beings, and make them feel what they owe to themselves and to those around them—to open out to them those sources of fireside amusement and of instruction which the art of printing has brought within the reach of all who are educated.

Now to effect this, the mere reading by rote is not sufficient; and it should be the aim of the schoolmaster, as far as he has it in his power, to give the children a knowledge of the structure of their own language—to enable them to get at the grammar of a sentence—to take it to pieces and reconstruct it ; and, unless children are left at school until this can be done, and they are enabled to get at the meaning of an ordinary book without difficulty, little use will, I fear, be made of it in after-life, and the fireside will not become, what it otherwise might be, through good books—a school through life.

A celebrated writer of the present day, has said, "The English language is a conglomerate of Latin words, bound together in a Saxon cement ; the fragments of the Latin being partly portions introduced directly from the parent quarry, with all their sharp edges, and partly pebbles of the same material, obscured and shaped by long rolling in a Norman or some other channel." Now, although this definition is somewhat geological in its language, as the author intended it to be, yet it is a very forcible one, and indicates clearly that the way to get at the knowledge of this conglomerate mass, must be by taking it to pieces, and examining the separate parts; and, when the schoolmaster can do this himself, he will be able to bring his knowledge to bear in teaching others.

How important, then that he should be able to unpack this conglomerate—to separate the cement from that which is imbedded in it to show to his more advanced classes the origin of the different words of a sentence—how words of a Saxon or a Latin origin vary in the modes of inflection—how they have been introduced—to show how some belong direct to the parent quarry ; how others, by rolling about in different channels, have had "their rough and sharp edges" rubbed off— the force and origin of the prefixes, &c.

This points out a most useful direction for the studies of the schoolmaster in this particular branch of knowledge.

With respect to this book itself, it does not profess to teach the schoolmaster the subjects he ought to have a know-

ledge of; its object is rather to point out to teachers, both
in our elementary schools and in private families, common-
sense modes of applying their knowledge, and of bringing it
to bear upon their teaching; but without particularising the
leading features of it, it is an attempt to introduce into our
elementary schools more of science, and a knowledge of scientific facts bearing upon the arts of life, and of every-day
things, than has been hitherto done.

It is a fact almost unaccountable, and certainly curious to
reflect upon, how few there are, even in any class of life,
educated or uneducated, who are acquainted with the philosophical principles of those things which they see in action
every day of their lives, and which are in so many ways administering to the wants of social life,—truths easily understood
when explained by experiment, and so important in themselves to mankind, that the names of the discoverers of them
are handed down from one generation to another for the
admiration of future ages, and as the great benefactors of
their species.

No one denies the importance of this knowledge when
applied to the arts of life, and how must the progress of
civilisation, and of the great interests of mankind have been
advanced by it, which makes it more strange that so little of
the intellect of a country should be brought to bear upon it.

This is perhaps in some measure owing to its being supposed, that a considerable knowledge of mathematics and of
arithmetic is necessary, and from a prevailing notion that
such subjects are, even when illustrated by experiment, difficult to understand; but Dr. Arnott, in the Introduction to
his Natural Philosophy, justly observes, "There are few persons in civilised society so ignorant as not to know that a
square has four equal sides, and four equal corners or angles,
or that every point in the circumference of a circle is at the
same distance from the centre. Now, so much of unity, simplicity, and harmony is there in the universe, that such simple
truths as these are what give exact cognisance of the most
important circumstances in the phenomena and states of
nature;" an acquaintance with the common rules of arithmetic, and of the measures of quantity, which fit a man for
ordinary occupations, are quite sufficient for all that is wanted
here.

Hitherto all classes seem to have taken for granted, that
the labouring part of the community had no business with
anything where the mind is concerned; but why should not
the miner, whose life may have been saved over and over again
by the safety-lamp of Sir Humphrey Davy, know something

of the principle to which he owes his safety, and of the philosophy of it—many of the accidents which occur from mere carelessness would be avoided by it; or the plumber, wh ose business it is to make a pump, be taught, however much the sense of sight may mislead him, that air and gaseous substances, which he cannot see, have weight; and that these and fluid substances press equally in all directions, and he will then understand why his mechanism succeeds, and the water rises, which, without some knowledge of this kind, must appear to him a kind of witchcraft; or why should not the labouring classes have it shewn to them during their education at school, that the burning of charcoal, or of chalk and limestone into lime, etc., gives rise to a kind of substance which they cannot see, but when breathed into the lungs is fatal to animal life, and its being heavier than common air makes the burning of charcoal in small rooms a very dangerous thing. From a want of a knowledge of this, many lives have been lost.

With a view to encourage a knowledge of the application of science to the occupations of the country in my own neighbourhood, during the autumn of last year, a course of six lectures on the Chemistry of Agriculture was given at the schoolroom by a gentleman who had made the subject his professional study, and who was well qualified to give an interest to it, not only from his knowledge, but from being a good manipulator in the experiments necessary to illustrate it.*

My first intention as to these lectures was for the instruction of the school itself, and of the schoolmasters of the neighbourhood, but finding that many of the gentlemen and also of the farmers in the neighbourhood wished to attend, I invited all to do so who were so inclined, and, with the exception of two extremely wet days, the attendance was good.

Many of the gentlemen took a considerable interest in them; and although the farmers, I have no doubt, felt they could not carry away so much as they had expected, yet the indirect effect of such lectures is good in an educational point of view—it creates a wish, and that a very natural and a very laudable one, on the part of the parents in the middle classes, that their children should have an opportunity of acquiring

* For these lectures I have to thank Mr. Edmonson, the head of the Queenwood Agricultural College, and Mr. Frankland, the chemical lecturer there, by whom they were given; both these gentlemen entered into the subject from the same motives as myself, viz., a wish to promote the education of the neighbourhood. [1847.]

a knowledge of the appliances of science to those pursuits in life in which they are so much interested.

The conclusion which I drew from the experiment, and which I think is a correct one, was, that a short course of lectures, and made as practical as possible, and repeated at intervals in different parts of a county, would be attended with great good, and in the end lead to an improvement in the education of agricultural youth, which it is most desirable to effect. It is not to be expected that those who are grown up, and whose habits are formed, should enter into it as a science ; their previous education has not fitted them for it, and their modes of thinking are against it ; nor can they stand anything like a continuous course of lectures, but they carry away facts bearing upon some particular point which they understand, talk about them afterwards, persuade themselves that such knowledge is good for their children, and in this way an influence for good on the education of the rising generation is likely to spring up.

In the schoolrooms here, these lectures were turned to good account, both as instruction to the teachers and to the older children, and the outline given filled up by experiments and explanations afterwards.

To speak even of teaching anything of science as a part of the education of village children, or of the teacher having such a knowledge of these subjects as to be able to bring it to bear upon his teaching, is, I am perfectly aware, by many looked upon as visionary, by some as useless, and by others even as mischievous. Now many of these are carried away by their prejudices against such instruction, without knowing or considering seriously what is meant by it ; but, on the subject of chemistry, for instance, when it is considered that chemical processes are involved in everything which we eat or drink ; in the preparation of every material used for our clothing ; in every change of the material world, whether animate or inanimate, with which our senses can make us acquainted, some knowledge of these processes must be looked upon both as interesting and highly important, and ought to be understood by those with whose pursuits and employments in life they are so intimately connected.

Besides, it seems to me even highly instructive that an intelligent child should be made to seize a firm hold of so much of this subject, as to enable the mind to get out of the habit of viewing all the different productions of nature as being made up of substances having nothing in common— that earth, iron, stone, air, water, animal and vegetable, as things having no single element of the same kind in their

several compositions— not having the slightest idea that all
the infinite varieties of the material world around us are only
different compounds of a few simple elements,—that the mind
should be able to correct this impression by seeing a few of
these substances taken to pieces by experiment, their simple
elements tested, and shown to be the same in each, is of itself
good, and opens out a train of thinking, which in some may
lead to most important results, by calling into use those
faculties of the mind which God has given them.

The workman who is acquainted with the facts in science
connected with his occupation, becomes less of a machine
than the one who is ignorant of them, is every way more
useful to his employer, and is himself a happier and a better
man ; for it is acknowledged, that the better educated workmen of all countries are distinguished by superior moral habits
in every respect—they are more sober and discreet, and their
enjoyments are of a more rational kind.

Of the necessity of an improvement in their social habits
among the labouring classes of this country, whether mining,
agricultural, or manufacturing, no one can doubt ; but the
Report of the Rev. H. Moseley on the State of Education in
the Midland Districts for the year 1846, addressed to the
Council on Education, which I have lately read, discloses
many features in the character of the mining population in
and about Bilston, and which of course is the same in other
mining districts, which I must confess were new to me, and
which one cannot read without great interest ; but it is an
interest of a very painful kind.

The habits of life which prevail among this population, and
their social condition, as seen in the description of the Bilston
market, and an appendix to the Report, are most instructive,
as to the effect of ignorance upon a labouring community
earning high wages—ignorance, as Mr. Moseley says, carried
out into action ; and adds, "whenever ignorance is associated
with 'high wages,' they will, I believe, become, as they are
here, a *curse;*" and the Report goes on to say, "rude as these
men are in their manners, and wholly uneducated, yet when
the opportunity has been afforded them, they have shown
themselves capable of deriving pleasure from other than
sensual gratifications and low pursuits."*

---

* The opportunity alluded to was a course of winter lectures, established for their benefit by the Rev. J. B. Owen, the incumbent, an
account of which, in a letter of Mr. Owen's in the Appendix to Mr.
Moseley's Reports, is well deserving the attention of those more
particularly who are engaged in education in populous districts.

From the Report which has lately been published on the State of Education in Wales, there is one thing which appears very remarkable, independent of the lamentable state of ignorance which seems generally to prevail, which is this : that in those districts where the people seem to have a very considerable knowledge of Scripture, the state of their morals is of the lowest and most degrading kind—in this fact the evidence of the clergy of all denominations seems to agree. Something of the same kind I have myself observed in the south of England, and it is by no means an uncommon thing to find in some, nay, I should say in many of that class, an aversion to their children being taught anything of a secular kind—as if secular instruction partook in some measure of the nature of sin ; this is no doubt a state of gross ignorance greatly to be pitied, and which will in the end be corrected by the influence of a better educated class, as this becomes diffused among them ; but the singular and almost unaccountable part of it is, that this apparent knowledge of Scripture should have so little influence on their moral conduct ; that it should never enter into their minds (or, if it does, they do not regard it) that Scripture truths are intended as rules of life ; whether the sort of familiarity which they have with Scripture phrases, and the constant habit of interweaving them into their conversation, can have led to this I do not know, but such is the fact.

Nor is this even in England confined to the labouring class ; there are many of those of the class above them, particularly of those who are uneducated, to whom the same remarks would extend. A man who gravely tells you, "I does the best I can to get an honest living," and perhaps quotes some text in Scripture to support his views, at the same time knowing that the very principle upon which he acts towards those about him makes it almost impossible for them to do so, cannot be said to make the proper application of his religious knowledge.

I observed another thing in the same Report, of a more cheering kind, that it had occurred to some of the Educational Committees to combine the education of the middle and the lower classes; and that in this way funds might be raised for proper education. One would suppose that the social state of most of the districts in Wales, the number of small farmers, tradesmen, etc., would be particularly favorable to such views, and that, if worked out as they ought to be, they could scarcely fail of success.

The present Bishop of Sodor and Man, thinking this plan well calculated for the state of society there, is endeavouring to introduce it throughout the island; and it appears from a Report lately made by Mr. Moseley to the Council on Education, that some plan of the kind had been thought of by the good Bishop Wilson, for whose memory the inhabitants retain so lively an affection, that its renewal now will be received with the greater interest. The general feeling in favour of education, as shown by "the framework," as Mr. Moseley terms it, in their laws regarding schools, and in the feelings of all classes in favour of it, dispose one to think that these matters have been much more cared for there than with us; perhaps their vicinity to Scotland, and a knowledge of its school-system, may have led to it. In their present position, and with the Minutes of Council to assist them in their poverty, they have all the elements of success.

An important feature in the school here, and one which is worthy of the attention both of school committees and of schoolmasters, is the amount of payments both for schooling and for books; this arises from the union of the children of different classes, also from many children coming from the smaller neighbouring parishes.

This amount of payment, both in a moral and in a pecuniary point of view, is important, and one in the success of which the schoolmaster is deeply interested—his improved social position almost entirely depends upon it; and if the better class of schoolmasters will reflect upon this in all its bearings, they will see how much their success in life depends upon their acquirements and their capabilities of teaching being equal to the want of the middle, as well as of the labouring classes.

What is wanted in our rural districts, most assuredly, is an improvement in the quality as well as in the quantity of instruction, and the mere extension of the Sunday-school to week-day teaching is not sufficient; but to attempt anything beyond an improved dame's school, or one fit for the younger children is, in very small parishes, on account of the expense, a thing manifestly impracticable; nor, in fact, would it be necessary with the class of schools I am advocating, numerously spread about the country, and to which the bigger children in the small parishes would resort. And in this way I am thoroughly persuaded an improved system of education may be worked out, of a very high character, almost self-paying, and which would in a few years have a firm hold on the public mind.

Nor should it be said, that in order to effect this, individuals can do little; on the contrary, they may do a great deal,— every school of an effective kind, conducted in such a way as to gain a footing for education in a neighbourhood, is of immense importance, whether it is the result of an individual effort, or not,—it is good, not only as regards the locality in which the school is, but good as an example practically worked out, and which has much more influence than a thing merely carried out on paper; and every one who reflects must see, that perfect and general plans of education must, like all other things of human contrivance, arise gradually, and cannot, in a country where opinion is so much divided as in this, be at once established.

Let the farmer and the tradesman weigh well in their minds what they will save upon each child educated at the parish school, and the kind of education he will get—let the landlord consider the interest he has in bringing a cheap education within the reach of his tenants, and how much they would rise in respectability as a class, by being better educated— and let both classes consider the mutual duties, and the moral obligations they are under to improve the condition of the labourer, both physical and moral, who is equally necessary to them both: if all would reflect in this way, and could be brought to see how much society at large would gain by this improvement in these links of the social chain, and how much the very slight fastenings which at present hold them together would be strengthened by it, the progress of education and of sanitary measures, would meet with less difficulty than it has hitherto done; and these would very soon be felt to be both a benefit and a source of increased happiness, to all classes of the community.

The rising generation of schoolmasters must not judge of the future from the past: hitherto they have been ill paid and little thought of; but very often this has arisen from their being ill qualified for the duties they had to perform : as an honest old dame said to one of the inspectors, "It is but little they pays me, but then it is but little I teaches 'em." In many cases, in such parishes as have a schoolmaster, he has been appointed, not from any fitness for the office, but because he had failed in everything else, or some labourer able to read and write, and was made schoolmaster to keep him from the parish. The schoolmaster may rest assured of this, that the better he is qualified for his situation, the more he will make society feel his worth, and instead of appointing the worst men who can be found, as the rate-payers of a parish, when they have had a voice in the matter, have been apt to do, both labourer and employer will unite and struggle to get the best schoolmaster they can—the best qualified in every respect, and one who will make the importance of his office felt, by the better education he is diffusing among them.

Although much depends on the schoolmaster in the success of a school, yet much depends also on the books which are introduced : owing to a deficiency of these, and to a want of a fitting apparatus, etc., many of the schoolmasters have no chance of success ; and I would observe here, that it is almost impossible to overrate the importance of introducing the system of the children buying their own books, the result of which is, that every fireside becomes a school.

In the selection of these, there should be no prejudices as to their being published by this or that Society : there are many which are good, published by them all ; and I have introduced here some of the Christian Knowledge Society, of the Irish National Board, and of the British and Foreign Schools. It has been found that the children in some of the lower Reading Books have them almost by heart, so that it is really necessary to introduce a more extensive range of reading, and add to their stock of knowledge.

I am aware that prejudices have hitherto existed, more particularly in my own profession, with regard to the books published by the British and Foreign Schools, and this has greatly hindered a more extensive use of them. Now, as a set of educational books in secular instruction for our elementary schools they are very good, not only good in substance as to the reading lessons, but they contain also excellent hints, which will be found most useful to the teachers. The only fault I find with them is the price, and the committee would do great service to the cause of education if they could reduce them about 25 per cent., which I have no doubt would be made up by the increased sale. Those I introduced here were Nos. 2 and 4 ; the price of the former is 9d., and it is the only book which has been sold in the school below the cost price, and which has only been done to the children of the labourer.

Arnott, in the Introduction to his Physics, speaking of a set of books of education in science, says,—" To have all the perfections of which they are susceptible, they can be looked for only from academies of science, or from an association of learned men ; and even then, they cannot be compiled by each individual taking a distinct part or parts, but by the parts being undertaken conjointly by several persons, so that he who conceives most happily for students may sketch, he who is learned may amplify, he who is correct may purge, he who is tasteful may beautify," etc. The composition of this Book of Nature (as he calls it), he adds, " might be a worthy object of rivalry between nations." What might not be done for education by a set of books adapted to our elementary schools, and got up on this principle, and how worthy such an object is of the attention of our most talented men!

Now that extreme opinions on all sides are tempered down into something of a practical plan, it is to be hoped that prejudices and jealousies will die away, and that all will unite in supporting the present plan for the advancement of education, although it may not be the best according to their own ideas, yet it certainly unites in its favour a great part of the common sense of the nation, and will, if carried out in singleness of purpose, work better in practice than those who, from mere theory, have been opposed to it, are led to expect.

With respect to the Minutes of Council on Education, so far as I am capable of judging, I have always thought them fair in principle and judicious in their detail, and characterised by a great deal of talent in the way in which they have been worked out. They offer great encouragement to the well-qualified and efficient schoolmaster, both through an increase of salary and through the assistance of the pupil-teachers in the management of his school.

Some, I know, are of opinion that the standard of acquirements of the school-teachers and of the qualifications for pupil-teachers are too high. With respect to the acquirements of pupil-teachers, I feel persuaded, if the general standard were below what is fixed upon, and what in practice the inspectors seem to require, we should soon find a numerous class of pupil-teachers totally unfit for their position, and that the cause of education would, on account of the great expense attending it, and the small proportionate results, retrograde rather than advance. No doubt a very great proportion of the present teachers are not qualified to teach what the Minutes require; but it is much better that they should be obliged to work up to a moderate standard, rather than that it should be lowered to a point which would render it totally inefficient for the advancement of good teaching.

In carrying into practice the contemplated increase of salary to masters and mistresses, the examination seems to me defective, inasmuch as it does not make sufficient inquiry into the state and efficiency of the school of which the candidate is the teacher.

A man who is just leaving a training school, or has only lately left it, and during the last year or two been practised in composition—in examinations on paper, &c., will, as the examination is conducted, do much better than many of the really good, practical teachers, and whose usefulness as teachers has been proved by the state and efficiency of their schools. In this way there is great danger of the experienced, good schoolmaster being classed far below one who may not turn out half so useful when tried in the school. I think, unless the state and condition of a school is taken into account, many useful schoolmasters, and very deserving of the increase of salary, both from their past labours and their future promise of good, will be deterred from offering themselves. I don't know how far the continuance of an increase of salary depends upon the state of a school; but it is evident there ought to be some connection between them.

I see it stated in a new periodical, the 'Educational Magazine of the Home and Colonial School Society,' "what the country really requires is schoolmasters who have *professional* skill; or, in other words, who are well acquainted with the nature of children, and the way to deal with them: (we may add schoolmistresses, also, for their patient training and happy influences are invaluable.) Faithful teachers, of steady, hard-working, pains-taking habits, with a tolerably good English education, well informed in common every-day matters, grasping what they have acquired firmly, and having it ready for use; knowing something of the art of teaching, well trained to draw out the faculties of children, to teach them the rudiments of knowledge, as well as to read with ease, and to read fluently." Now, all this is very good as far as it goes, and will, in many schools, be all that is wanted; yet there can be no doubt, the higher the acquirements of the teacher, and the more knowledge he is able to bring to bear on his teaching, the more likely he is to succeed.

Although the attainments aimed at in some of the training schools may appear of a character beyond what is wanted in the lower class of schools, yet these very men of greater attainments are by no means beyond what is wanted in our larger elementary schools, and will, if they can unite in education the children of the employer and the employed, in the end be the cheapest schoolmasters, inasmuch as I am confident they will be the means of raising up a numerous class of self-supporting schools, and make the farmers and tradesmen feel what they have hitherto never done, the real value of the village schoolmaster.

It may not be thought necessary, nor do I think that it is necessary, for the schoolmaster to teach Latin and Greek, and perhaps undue importance may have been given, or thought to have been given, to these in some of our Training Institutions, but it must be recollected that they are taught

these in order to qualify them the better for teaching other
things; and what I am holding out for is an amount of knowledge in the teacher which will make him worth having when
he is sent among us, and by his teaching make the parents
feel that education is worth paying for, and is one of the
decent wants of life.

The kind of knowledge which appears to be most useful in
our schoolmasters is sufficiently indicated in the following
pages; and I think experimental science, and a knowledge of
the science of common things, ought to form an important
part of the instruction in all our training schools.

One very serious difficulty which the Training Institutions
have had to contend with, and one really of a serious nature,
has been the small amount of knowledge possessed by the
candidates at the time of their admission; this is in general
so great, that it is a thing totally impossible to make anything of them in less than two or three years: but when
once they can draw their supplies from the best pupil-
teachers in our elementary schools, a very different state of
things will commence; they will then be supplied with young
men and young women of eighteen or nineteen, who will have
a much greater knowledge of teaching, and of the subjects in
which they are expected to teach, at the time of their admission, than many of those, who had been trained there, had
after a residence of two or three years in the institution;
and instead of three years, it will be quite unnecessary that
any of them should remain more than one   Until lately, I
was of opinion that the Training Institutions were slow in
making their usefulness felt in the country; but having had
an opportunity of judging of the kind of materials they had
to work upon (whether this may not in some measure be the
fault of those who recommend I do not know), I feel confident, if sent out at the end of one year's training, the
majority of them could not possibly be qualified for schools
even of the lowest class, and this without any blame attaching to the teaching in the institution itself.

The system of pupil-teachers, if carried out as it ought to
be, and with due vigilance on the part of the inspectors, is
admirably calculated for a future supply of efficient teachers,
and will, in a few years, entirely alter the character of elementary teaching throughout the country; on this, as well
as on every other account, the standard of acquirements
ought not to be lowered.

The reader will find at p. 40 a few short extracts from an
interesting "Educational Tour in Prussia and Holland," by an

American, Mr. Mann, Secretary to the Board of Education at Boston; they relate chiefly to the importance of the schoolmaster having a knowledge of drawing.

This, it seems, in the Prussian Schools, is almost universal; and the various ways in which a teacher will find it useful, and not only that, but in which, by means of the blackboard, it will give life to his teaching, make it a thing of great importance, and one which every schoolmaster, having the slightest taste for, ought to cultivate.*

The reception which a former edition of this little work has met with, leads me to think it has been found useful for the purposes for which it was intended; and I hope the present one, with the additions which have been made, will not be less so, and that the remarks on the effect of the kind of {education I am advocating, and its success here, may interest those who are friends to an improved social condition of the middle and labouring classes, and are anxious to bind these two adjoining links of society together by stronger fastenings than hold them at present, although they may not be actually engaged in the business of teaching; but, above all, should every friend to education feel, if he wishes to promote it, that the mass of society never can understand, or take an interest in it, from mere written theories, and can only be brought to do so step by step, and that by a slow progress, by its being brought practically home to them;— it is only in this way that the labouring classes can be made what they ought to be, and what we ought to endeavour to make them.

King's Somborne; *April*, 1848.

The occasion of a new Edition affords an opportunity of making a few additional remarks, which, it is to be hoped, may not be without interest.

That schools should be able to get the best elementary

* The same writer, who clearly does not admire the ordinary way of teaching the alphabet, gives the following anecdote taken from an American prize essay on Education:

"A Mr. Ottiwell Wood, at a late trial in Lancashire, England, giving his name to the court, the judge said, " Pray, Mr. Wood, how do you spell your name?' To which the witness replied: "O double T, I double U, E double L, double U, double O, D.' The learned judge at first laid down his pen in astonishment; and then, after making two or three unsuccessful attempts, declared he was unable to record it."

books at a cheap price, is a thing of the utmost importance; and although the plan of the Committee of Council on Education for effecting this is not, in its present state, all that one could wish it to be, yet it is to be hoped that the office will, as it gains experience, free it from those crippling conditions which make it objectionable, and which must damage the amount of good that would otherwise arise from it.

The principle of the regulations under which books are supplied, appears to be one having a downward tendency rather than an upward one; inasmuch as it is based on this —that no school belonging to the class with which the Council on Education have to do, can, by a possibility, be in a position to buy its own books at the reduced prices; and in order to be able to purchase, it is made compulsory to ask a grant in aid, limited in amount by the number of scholars: after which it is allowed to purchase to a certain extent, and applications may now be renewed for books and maps at the reduced prices, once a year, to an amount of not less than £3: a great improvement upon the first plan; the books forming a grant to be the property of the school, and lent to the children—the others allowed to be sold at the price of purchase.

Now, it surely would have been better to have made the system of buying books at the reduced prices the prominent feature of the regulation, and to have spoken of this as the pith of the matter: the grants in aid to be had recourse to in cases of such schools as are absolutely unable to purchase; making these the exceptional cases, as they ought on sound principles to have been, and not the rule, as it stands at present.

There are no doubt many schools where this grant in aid may be necessary; but there are hundreds of others rising up which, on principle, would prefer buying the books at the reduced prices, if allowed to apply at reasonable intervals; unless this making a grant absolutely necessary should suggest to them the worst of two plans—"facilis descensus Averni" —and prove to be a bait too tempting to be resisted.

The parents of the labouring class will naturally, from ignorance, prefer the lending system; and those connected with the management of schools, who have not had experience of the benefits of a contrary one, or perhaps who may not have thought much upon the subject at all, will, from an apparent saving of expense which it holds out, be led to adopt the same.

It never occurred to me as possible, that an application for books at the reduced prices on the part of any school, and without asking a grant in aid, would not be received at the Council office even with some degree of satisfaction—a sort of joy at finding a state of things sufficiently prosperous to enable it to buy books without asking for a grant, and without putting the office to any expense beyond the mere agency—so that the receiving an answer from the secretary, that the office could not dispense with the preliminary condition of asking a grant, was a matter of surprise—and it has been to me ever since a source of wonder, how so strange a principle should have found its way into practice, more particularly as an example had been set by the National Board in Ireland, which had been for some years furnishing their books to schools of a like class in this country, at low prices, and to an extent limited only by the wants of the school.

Another* thing which ought to be borne in mind, in trying to give a wholesome direction to the education of the masses of a country, is to do it upon principles as little pauperising as possible—and I feel persuaded that a child educated from borrowed books, the property of the school, and one educated from its parents buying them, and their being the property of the child, in a social sense, and for all the economic purposes of life, the two are not the same beings;—nor is the effect on the parents, or the interest they take in their children, the same in the two cases; the minds of the children

* The exclusively eleemosynary character which many attempt to give to the education of the labouring classes, is, in some respects, to be regretted. One cannot but admire the conduct of those who are at great expense in doing this entirely gratis, in their own localities; still I conceive much greater good would result by establishing moderate payments even in such cases, and any saving from this might be given to school-building when pecuniary assistance is wanted. This making them pay, many, more particularly ladies, who have schools of this kind, will not hear of: they no doubt find great gratification, and are pleased in doing so much good, but why not allow the parents to join in this feeling, by doing something towards it themselves; without this it excites but little interest in them, and altogether wants that kind of vitality which leads to the best results.

I am persuaded, with respect to my own profession, that if we relied more on improving the staple of education in our schools, and less on charity sermons, we should find better and less expensive results. The changes lately adopted in the examinations at Cambridge, and it is to be hoped Oxford may do the same, will eventually, through the clergy, have a most beneficial effect on the education of the labouring and middle classes.

are not formed in the same mould, nor are they habituated to view things, connected with the way in which they are to struggle through life, through the same medium.

No one, unless he has had experience of children in the matter of education in schools of this kind, can form an idea of the wish they have to possess books of their own, when once they have been interested in what they are learning; and if there is any one thing which more than another, from experience here, I feel entitled to recommend to managers of schools, and to those who take an interest in them, it is by all means to introduce the plan of children buying their own; a thing which, when once established and the instruction good, there is no difficulty whatever in maintaining.

The prices of these books in the Council list are so reasonable, that the great majority of schools would be able to purchase them; and there could be no greater boon to the cause of education than enabling them to do so (unrestricted by the present conditions), and to an extent limited only by their wants, and allowed also to apply for them at reasonable intervals. The dividing the list into two parts might be worthy of consideration: one of school-books used in the school, from which grants in aid, when necessary, might be made; the other, of books of a more advanced kind for pupil-teachers and masters, and to be had only at the reduced prices.

The putting in circulation a well-selected list of educational books is in itself good, inasmuch as it brings before the school-managers and school-teachers the best books of the kind, which otherwise they might not have an opportunity of knowing much about; and in this way places the education of the country in a wholesome channel, so far as books are concerned.

The restrictions with which the Council regulations are fettered, may probably in some measure arise from the booksellers and publishers being averse to this mode of supplying our elementary schools, and, of course, it is not to be expected that they can sell books at a price which is not remunerating; but if they would consider, that this is not taking away a market, which they have already had, but is opening out one in a quarter which never existed before—(the little which was wanted being supplied by the Christian Knowledge, or similar Societies)—one which, when the people are fairly in a train of being educated, so as to enable them to read when they leave school, will be of an extensive kind. If the publishers would look forward in this way, they would be anxious to supply such schools at prices which may be remunerating to the publisher, although not to the retail trade ; the latter would very soon find the benefit of this, as there is scarcely a cottage into which books, bought after leaving school, to a greater or less extent, would not find their way, when once a people are fairly educated.

The supplying our schools with educational books of the highest character, and at the lowest prices, is no doubt a great national object,—one which well merits, and will, it is to be hoped, meet with every attention from the Committee of Council ; but whether this can be best effected by the Council endeavouring to put into effective operation the talent of the country, in writing books in all those departments of knowledge which it is desirable to introduce into our schools, and be their own publishers ; or whether it can best be done through private publishers and the booksellers themselves, may be a matter of question. The prices at which the National Board in Ireland supply what are termed poor schools in this country, being a remunerating one, is encouraging to the former plan, and the increasing demand for books once well established, would enable the bookseller to do it at a small rate of profit ; but, under all circumstances, what the country may reasonably expect from the Committee of Council is,—school-books good and cheap. Whenever an important want has shown itself in this country, and one by which society would be largely benefited, it is astonishing how much private individuals have done to supply the want; and now that attention is so much turned towards education as an instrument of great public good, perhaps it may occur to some benevolent individual, blessed with the power to do it, and wishing to connect his name with the education of his country, to appropriate (as the late Earl of Bridgewater did for a high moral purpose) a sum of eight or ten thousand pounds, as prizes for the best educational books, on all useful subjects—appointing some discreet mode of carrying the object out—the copyright to rest with the Committee of Council, in order to render the books as cheap as possible. Such a sum, spent in this way, might largely benefit a whole nation, and would do more to promote the education of it, than any other conceivable application of the same amount of money.

The mode in which benevolent individuals have endeavoured to promote local education, has been by leaving property in the hands of trustees (in many cases the parish officers), and attaching some condition—such as that a certain number of children or the whole of the chidren of the poor shall be sent free; but however well endowments may have operated in Scotland (and in many instances, also, in the north of England) where, from experience of the benefit of it, a strong feeling in favour of education pervades all classes of society, and where they mix and blend harmoniously together at school, yet in this country, in the rural districts more particularly, where such endowments exist, they have become, in nine cases out of ten, a positive hindrance, rather than a benefit, to the object they were intended to promote. This indifference as to the way in which charitable endowments for education are administered, arises from an entire want of a practical knowledge, that a people can in any way be benefited by it; and it is most strange that the abuses of these charities in England should not be looked into.

In some counties in Scotland, such bequests have been so large, that the salary of the master has been very considerably increased, in almost every parochial school in the country, and this chiefly owing to the generosity of individuals who felt that their success in life was owing to an education received at the parish school, and who had a confidence that those intended to be benefited were sufficiently alive to the humanising effects of education upon their children, to see that bequests so left, would be properly administered.

With respect to apparatus of a philosophical kind, it will be found advisable to commence with absolutely necessary things, and to add to these, as the wants of the school in this way make themselves felt; otherwise, the buying expensive things at first, and afterwards, not turning them to account, might lead to disappointment.

Mr. Mosely, in his Report of last year, calls the attention of schoolmasters to a most important subject—one, not less important to their own happiness and welfare, and to that of their families, than it is to the interests of education in general—"the consideration of means for providing for support in time of sickness and of old age, and of contributing towards the maintenance of a family in case of death;" he adds, "that a mutual assurance or benefit society, formed upon a secure basis, among persons of this class, and conducted under the auspices of the Council on Education, would be an inestimable benefit."

This is a question in which the public are deeply interested, as affording the only means of protection against a master continuing to hold his situation, when, from age and infirmity, he is unfit for the duties of it; and school-managers will find some plan of this kind the only security against incompetent teachers, who have become so, from being advanced in life, and whom it would be cruel and unjust to deprive of their situations, unless they had some provision to fall back npou.

It should be the object and fundamental principle of such a plan, that every schoolmaster should be his own insurer;— to secure a provision, for instance, of from 20*l.* to 30*l.* per annum, to commence at the age of fifty or fifty-five; there would be no reason whatever, when a master is competent to his duty, that he should give up his situation when he came into possession of his annuity, but it would be in the power of the managers to prevail upon him to retire, when unfit for it, and it would also be desirable in such a plan of assurance, that the insurer should be able, in case of death before coming into the enjoyment of the annuity, to dispose, by will, of the amounts of payments made; in this way, without being very complicated, it would be something of a provision for those dependent upon him.

In a well-digested plan of this kind, all the good schoolmasters would insure; this would have the effect of retaining them in their employment, as many of them would otherwise leave it; and, in many ways, the plan seems to be so important to the cause of education, and, in fact, so necessary to its ultimate success, as to make it well deserving the consideration of those who have the power to carry it out; and the public have so great an interest in it, that the Committee of Council may reasonably be expected to give some assistance towards doing so; grounded on the principle of every man being his own insurer, no Chancellor of the Exchequer could possibly object. This ought not to interfere with any consideration, by way of reward, to those who, from great success in their vocations, and from long service, might be thought worthy of them—but it might be a part of the plan, to make some addition to an annuity, in cases of merit of a high order, in this hard-working department of the public service.*

In a letter published some years ago, as an appendix to Mr. (now Archdeacon) Allen's Report, I alluded to Lord Howick, the present Earl Grey, having suggested in the House of Commons, "voluntary examination of the schools in a district," and his having pointed out to the minister "that further encouragement might be given by occasionally conferring, on the deserving, situations in the lower ranks of the public service." Sir Robert Peel, in answer, expressed as "his only fear, that children did not remain at these schools to a

---

* The fact of its being alluded to by Mr. Mosely, in his Report, was the cause of a memorial being sent to the Committee of Council on the subject, signed by 84 schoolmasters in that part of the north which is under Mr. Watkin's inspection alone—a strong proof of the importance which the masters themselves attach to such a plan.

sufficient age to be fit for them," but otherwise seemed to receive the hint remarkably well.

It is rather singular, that the friends of education in the House of Commons, should have allowed this hint, thrown out by Lord Grey, so completely to drop, as it seems to have done ; and I fear since his lordship has been in office, and has had the power of acting upon it, that he also may have forgotten it—at least one has never seen mention made since, of this kind of encouragement in the speeches of either House of Parliament ; so that this may only have been one of those things thrown out when in opposition as having an appearance of good intention, but where there was not sufficient earnestness of purpose on the part of the speaker to carry it out, and take the responsibility of doing so when in power ; however, be this as it may, there can be no doubt that, if such encouragement be held out and if an educational test be established throughout what is termed "the lower ranks of the public service," or if carried farther, and any system be adopted of selecting from the schools in which this class of society are educated those best fitted by education or by character for such situations, many boys would be found to remain ; and not only so, but that they must remain to be well qualified for them. Many, if this principle of selection and promotion were adopted, who find their way into the very situations in question on easier terms, would remain longer at school ; and thus a wholesome channel for supplying this part of the public service being provided, it would be benefited in getting those best qualified to perform it.* There is a class in our rural districts, that just above the labourer, who would find great encouragement in this, but who from being, as it were, above daily labour, and finding nothing to do, are worse educated, and in every way worse brought up, than any other class in society ; this would hold out to some a road to useful employment ; and many of these youths, when educated in this way, might find most useful employment in our colonies ; Why should not these sources be to them what India is to the classes above them ?

But although the subject of establishing an educational test, in the kind of offices above alluded to, does not seem to attract the attention of statesmen on the ground of the principle which it involves, or of its public importance, yet it has, I am happy to say, suggested itself in one quarter, when

---

* At present such situations fall too much to the lot of the sons of those having the franchise in borough towns, by no means the class of society best fitted for them.

there is the power to act upon it, from a conviction of the good which it will do ; at the same time being a means of finding for the public service, in such departments, those best qualified for the duties of it.

About a year ago the chairman of the now Inland Revenue Board, who is in no way connected with this part of the country, and to whom I was at that time an entire stranger, offered in the kindest way to place at my disposal, for the encouragement of education here, the first situation in the Excise which he had to give, wishing it to be given to the one who, all things considered, was the best qualified for it, and it is to be hoped so good an example may find others ready to follow it.

This mode of appointment, founded on merit, has a great advantage over any other ; and it is based upon the highest and best principles, and would, if extensively acted upon, lead to a most important change, in what may be called the *morale* of the lower departments of the public service.

The minister who would endeavour to introduce an educational test in all cases of this kind, and do his utmost to carry it out would deserve well of his country ; he would, at the same time that he was indirectly promoting the best interests of society, have the satisfaction of feeling that he was filling up such situations with those most competent for the duties of them.

It is now beginning to be generally felt, that the only way to make our national and similar schools efficient, and to have them remain so, is by making them places of education, not exclusively for the labouring classes, but by having the standard of acquirement and the means of carrying it out, such as are fitted for the wants of all the industrial part of the community located in a district. This, both from experience and from the nature of the case, is now becoming evident ; and a strong evidence is given of it in the number of schools of this kind now rising up in different parts of the country, and taken up by influential individuals in a way which gives every promise of success.

The way in which we have lately seen Sir Robert Peel reorganising the school at Tamworth, and the evident interest which he takes in doing so, show clearly what his opinions are as to the mode in which the education of the country ought to be carried out, and the practical bearing which it ought to have upon the employments of after life ; and it is greatly to be wished that a man of his acknowledged talent as a statesman would not confine his interest in it to his own locality, but that he would, as a public man, give that consideration and assistance to the cause of education, which, from his position, he is well able to do ; and which, from the importance of the question, in its bearings both upon our own social relations at home and in our colonies, it so well deserves.

At a meeting in Staffordshire a few months ago, at which Lord Harrowby presided, the general feeling seemed to be of the same kind. The following is an extract from the reported speech of the chairman.

"It was pretty evident that in many parts of the country the poorer classes were placed, as regarded education, in a better position than those immediately above them ; that the labourer's children were, in fact, in the way of being better educated than those of the farmers, and that this arose from the fact that the state assisted the former, whilst the latter were entirely neglected. Those connected with farming were no doubt generally able to give their children a suitable education : but they were so divided by distance of residence and so unaccustomed to combine, that they were placed in a very disadvantageous position as compared with the inhabitants of towns. In general, the sons of farmers were sent out to school at a cost of from £25 to £30 per annum, and the expense, when there was a number of sons, was so great, that the youths were often removed before their education was completed. To remedy this evil two plans have been suggested : the first was to establish new and independent schools, and the second was to improve the common schools scattered over the country. The objection to the first of these plans was the expense, and the great uncertainty of the result ; whilst to the second was urged the unwillingness of farmers to allow their children to mix with the children of the humbler classes. He, however, did not see that the entertainment of the one scheme should preclude the consideration of the other, and that the meeting should appoint a committee to consider the subject. *Experience* had justified the establishment of schools in which all classes mixed for the purpose of education ; and the High School of Edinburgh might be pointed out as a worthy example, where the high and the low, the son of the peer and the son of the artisan, studied under the same roof, to the advantage of both. The mixture of the various orders of society in a common school, while it did not deteriorate the morals and manners of the pupils, induced the cultivation of kind and social feelings."

In fact, the whole of Scotland is an example of this. With respect to the observation of Lord Harrowby, "that the farmers are left to themselves," they in fact want no assistance ; all that is wanted on their part is the common sense to see that the only way in which they can, as a class, be properly educated, is by making our parish schools efficient for the purpose, and by their getting rid of their prejudices, and sending their children to them.

Earl Talbot, the Bishop of Lichfield, and others, expressed themselves to the same purpose ; Mr. Adderley, member for the county, added, " that he considered the plan of adopting separate schools hopeless, and thought that of improving the character of the national schools by far the most feasible He should object, however, to any plan which gave a boon to the farmers and middle classes at the expense of the labouring classes."

So far from establishing mixed schools being a boon to the farmers and middle classes at the expense of the labouring classes, I believe they will have a decidedly contrary effect, and that the establishing separate ones for sons of farmers, etc., would be in every way detrimental in the end, and bring about such a state of things in the schools exclusively for the poor, that in a very short time the character of such schools would be in no way better than it has been, and that as places of education they would entirely fail.

One resolution of the meeting, proposed by the Bishop of Lichfield, was, that it was expedient to provide from the training school or institution at Battersea,* fit and proper masters for the national schools, and that those masters should be qualified to communicate religious instruction and teach arithmetic, geography, the lower mathematics and the sciences applicable to agriculture ; and I believe they have since sent six young men to the institution there for the purpose of being educated as masters.

* This institution owes its origin, and for many years nearly its whole support, to Sir Kaye Shuttleworth and Mr. Edward Tufnell, and in 1842 it was transferred to the National Society.

The Rev. Thomas Jackson, the principal, has lately printed a statement of its views and prospective objects, to which is appended testimonials of the masters, and condition of the schools to which the Battersea masters have been sent.

These statements afford a very gratifying proof, and are strong evidence of the good which must result from establishments of this kind, conducted as Battersea is.   The education of the country must necessarily and in a great measure take its tone, and assume its character of usefulness, from the sources from which the teachers are derived; and if the opinion of one who has paid considerable attention to the educational wants of the present time, and the way in which those wants can best be supplied, were likely to be of any weight, he would strongly recommend Battersea and similar

In the present transition state of the country as to education, such meetings have a more than ordinary interest attaching to them—in fact at this moment in some measure a national one—as much depends upon what is done in the next few years, as to the direction which the education of the country will take,—a question of no small importance to the rising generation, although one, to which many of the present are perfectly indifferent.

institutions to those who have the means and the wish to aid the cause of national education. Much more good, in an educational point of view, is likely to arise from bequests and from gifts to institutions of this kind under efficient public control, than in any other way; and it is greatly to be hoped that the efficiency of good training institutions, both for schoolmasters and schoolmistresses, may not be checked for want of means.

King's Somborne;
April 7, 1849.

SUGGESTIVE HINTS,

HAVING taken a considerable interest for some years in the daily teaching of my own village school, I am, from the success which has attended it, induced to offer the following outline of what is taught, and the manner of teaching it, to the attention of teachers in our elementary schools,—as being likely to be of some assistance, at all events to the less experienced among them, and perhaps not altogether useless to those whose qualifications and training in our Normal Schools may have better fitted them for their work.

And first, it is of great importance that the teacher should be able to interest the children in what they are doing ; and this, if he takes a lively interest in it himself, he will find no difficulty in doing, even when teaching what is looked upon as the mechanical part of reading ; particularly if he know how to mix with it oral instruction of a conversational kind, and has any judgment in selecting subjects to talk to them about,—such as the domestic animals, birds, etc., and other things, with which they are brought in contact in their earliest years—the cat and dog, how they differ in their habits, manner of living, and how useful to man,—the one attaching itself to places, the other to persons ; then perhaps relating some short and amusing anecdote of the dog or other animal, for which a good teacher would be at no loss, and would always see, from the countenances of the children, whether he was interesting them or not, and would go on, or leave off, accordingly.

And again, if a cow or horse is mentioned—drawing them into a description of it—a child will perhaps say : A cow is a four-footed animal. Teacher : Yes, but so is a

B

horse; and then will point out something in which they differ. The child will then try again—a cow has got horns, but a horse has not; then the teacher will point out that some cows have no horns, and will lead them on into things, in which the cow and horse really do differ— such as the hoof; the cow having a cloven foot with two hoofs on one foot : what other animals have the same ?— difference in the way of feeding ; a cow chews the cud— ruminating : does the horse ?—what animals do ?—sheep, deer, &c. What difference in their teeth ; has a cow front teeth in the upper jaw ? a sheep ? a horse ? etc. What do you call a number of cows together ? what of sheep ?— of deer ?—of swine ?—of bees ? What are the habits of animals going many together ? mention those you know which do so. The flesh of the sheep called what ?—of the ox ? The particular noise of the sheep, cow, horse, swine, etc.? bleats, bellows. neighs, grunts. The young of a cow ? a calf ;—and its flesh? veal. The young of the horse, what ? a foal. Spell calf, calves : write them down on your slates. And in this way children may be led into a tolerably correct idea of the thing in question, and will be partly able to describe it themselves; all this they tell again at home, which has its use.

There is something extremely pleasing and interesting to children in having their attention called to the habits— difference in structure—in covering—in manner of feeding —in fact, all possible outward differences, a knowledge of which can be acquired by the eyes and by the hands (seeing and feeling) of the beasts and birds about them ; and of this a very strong proof is given, in what I have related in connection with my giving to a class of boys a lesson of the following kind, which was suggested by some obser- vations in a book on Natural History, by the Rev. L. Jenyns, on the difference of the way in which animals with which they are acquainted rise. How does the cow get up ?—hind-feet or fore-feet first? how the sheep ? how the deer, etc. ? Some will answer rightly, some wrongly; but all think and are alive to the question. Then pointing out to them ; that all these animals rise with the hind-legs first, and that they belong to the class of ruminating or cud-chewing animals—and, that if it is true that in one, two, three, four, etc., particular cases of animals which chew the cud, that they rise in this way, whether it would not be likely to be true in all cases—showing them the way of getting at a general rule, from its being true in a number of individual instances.

Then again : How does the horse, the pig, the dog, etc., rise ? hind-feet or fore-feet first ? do they ruminate ? have they front teeth in the upper jaw ? The teacher would point out how they differ from the ox, the sheep, etc.

Children living in the country are very much alive to this kind of instruction ; and I found that several of them in going home from school had observed the animals when rising, and gone out of their way to make them get up ; thus bringing to the test of experience what they had been taught, and commencing, at this early period, habits of observation on things around them ; which, in after-life, may add much to their happiness, and open out sources of enjoyment to them, to which they have hitherto been strangers.

Happening to mention that some observers of the habits of animals thought that sheep more frequently lie down on the left side than on the right, I find that many of them count a flock of sheep, as to the side they are lying on, when they see them lying down in the fold or in the field, and I have no doubt will, in time, have counted such numbers as may balance their opinions one way or the other.

Mr. Jenyns says, that he mentioned to a farmer, who had passed all his life among animals belonging to the farm, this difference in the mode of rising in the horse and in the ox—the sheep and the pig—and generally in the cud-chewing and non-cud-chewing animals, but that he (the farmer) was not aware of it ; and I recollect myself many years ago in college combination-room, a conversation arising as to whether a sheep had a double row of teeth in front, similar to the horse (and in the same way the cow), when, strange to say, although every one seemed to know that it was the case with the *horse*, yet not more than one or two were aware that the sheep had not ; and so many doubts were started about it, that two young men of the party walked a considerable distance to a field where there were some sheep, and caught one of them in order to examine it.

When able to read with tolerable ease, and when they have acquired some idea of reckoning up small numbers, which they very soon do, it will be found extremely useful occasionally to call their attention to the number of letters in a word—pointing out which are vowels, and which are consonants; for instance in the word *number*—how many letters? six. How many are vowels? two. Then how many consonants: some will reckon by looking at the book; others, and these are the sharp ones, will reason, and say; as there are six letters, and two of them vowels, the remaining four must be consonants; making it a question in arithmetic.

In this way very great interest may be excited; and when such words as *bounty, city, yearly*, occur, the teacher should point out, that at the end of words *y* is a vowel; at the beginning, a consonant; and then ask them to quote all the words they know beginning or ending with *y :* this gives them great facility in acquiring words; such questions, as, What is the first letter in such and such a word—what is the last—how many syllables in the word—what is the middle syllable—what is a syllable made up of? of letters. What is a word made up of? of a syllable or syllables. This interests much more than the ordinary way of reading without observation, and keeps up the attention.

Again, call their attention to the page of their book— say it is page ten, eleven, twelve, or thirteen—how many leaves? five, five and a half, six, six and a half; and from this they very soon will gather that when the page is denoted by an even number there is an exact number of leaves, and no odd page remaining; hence the teacher will point out to them, that all even numbers are divisible by two without a remainder, and that an odd number, when divided by two, always leaves a remainder of one. Occasionally making them reckon the leaves, in order to show that it agrees with their arithmetic, is good; in fact, there are innumerable ways in which the common sense of a teacher ought to be called forth

It will also be useful to give them correct ideas of the kind suggested by the following questions : Where does the sun rise ? point in the direction. Where is he at noon ? Where does he set ? When is he highest in the heavens ? In what direction is your shadow cast in the morning ; in what direction at noon ?—in the evening ? In what direction do you come to school ?—go home ? and as they come, of course, from very different directions, this becomes more instructive. Point to your home—towards sunset. Are the days lengthening or shortening ? Will to-morrow be longer or shorter than to-day ? In what direction is such and such a parish or striking object ? How the parish in which they live is bounded on the different sides, etc. In this way children may be made to get correct ideas as to east, west, north, and south, and the intermediate points.

The teacher should also occasionally call one of them forward, and, putting a piece of chalk into his hand, tell him to draw a line on the floor running north and south. What is the first letter of *north*, and what of *south* ? put N and S then at the proper ends ; how does he know the south from the north ? draw a line through the middle running east and west—another half way between the east and the north—the east and the south, etc. This they are all pleased in being able to do themselves, and there is scarcely a boy in the smaller classes that would not do it with great accuracy ; of course the teacher might vary it, by telling a boy to begin and make a ring (circle) on the floor as if he were going to play marbles ; then to draw a line through the centre due east and west—another north and south—and this way has an advantage ; as they improve in doing it, they will get to something like the figure of the compass.

I have observed also, that they take great interest in having their attention drawn to the particular points in which the sun rises and sets ; for instance, that on a certain day in March he rises due east and sets due west ; that every succeeding day up to the 21st of June he rises farther and farther to the north of east, and sets a little farther to the north of west, on each succeeding day, and up to this point the days go on increasing : he then returns in the same way, rising nearer to the east and setting nearer to the west on each succeeding day until the 21st of September, when he again rises due east and sets due west: then up to the 21st of December rises farther to the south of east and sets farther to the south of west, and on each succeeding day describing a smaller and smaller arch in the heavens and the days shortening.

This becomes a matter of daily observation, as a thing which they can see with their own eyes, and interests them accordingly.

Again, the teacher should point out how their shadow is longest when the sun is in the horizon—diminishes up to noon, when the sun is highest, and then increases again until sunset—what it would be if the sun were over their heads, etc.

The following verse, from one of the Lessons, will illustrate this :—

> Trudging as the ploughmen go
> (To the smoking hamlet bound);
> Giant-like the shadows grow,
> Lengthen'd o'er the level ground.

Questions like the following are also instructive.   If the sun rise at five o'clock, half-past four, three, etc., in the morning, at what time will he set ? getting them to understand what mid-day means, and that there are as many hours from sunrise to noon, as from noon to sunset—that the difference between the hour of rising and twelve o'clock will give the hour at which he sets.

As soon as children are able, the teacher should endeavour to give them correct ideas of the measures of time, of space, and of volume : ask them, for instance, What is a year ? they will answer, twelve months.   What is a month ? four weeks.   What is a week ? seven days.   What is a day ? twenty-four hours.   What is an hour ? sixty minutes : and thus driving them into a corner, they find out the answer was not the one expected, and begin to think on the subject : the teacher should then point out to them, that a year is a measure of time, as a yard is a measure of length ; that a month, a week, a day, etc., are also measures of time, but of less duration than the year ; of course they will afterwards be made to understand what duration of time the year does measure : he should then point out the great conveniences of the subdivisions of time for the purposes of civil life.

I was pleased some time ago in going into the school, to see the contrivances of some of them in making a clock-face on paper, which had been the evening task for one of the lower classes; what struck me was, the great regularity of an inner and outer circle for the face, in many instances as if made with compasses ; they had had recourse to cups or saucers or any other circular things of unequal dimensions in their cottages, but of a size which came within the compass of their paper on which they placed them, and then ran the pen round the edges ; this shows that man is a contriving animal, and I have no doubt the task afforded amusement and instruction both to parent and child.

The teacher should exercise the children on the clock-face, pointing out that the minute-hand goes round twelve times for the hour-hand once ; that the circle on the face is divided into twelve equal parts ; that while the minute-hand goes once round the whole circle, the hour-hand would only move from twelve to one, or $\frac{1}{12}$th of the whole; that when it had gone twice round, the hour-hand had arrived at two o'clock, or $\frac{2}{12}$ths ; when three times, at three o'clock, or $\frac{3}{12}$ths, and so on ; and when the minute-hand had gone twelve times round, the hour-hand would have moved over twelve of these divisions, or $\frac{12}{12}$ths : in this way they by degrees get some idea of fractions.

In the same way as to measures of length, giving them a correct idea as to the length of a yard, a foot, an inch, etc., and how many times the smaller measure is contained in the greater ; and here the teacher would do well to have a two-foot rule, and make first one and then another of the children measure the dimensions of the room—the length and breadth of the doorway, or any distance between one fixed point and another—to show them to what particular purposes in civil life these measures are used, measuring the distance between one place and another; that the yard is the measure by which they buy calico, flannel, fustian, cloth, cordage, etc., all things for the purposes of clothing:

the length only being measured, the breadth being of a standard kind.

That in speaking of the size of a room, of a garden, of a field, both length and breadth must be taken into account —of a peck, a bushel, a quart, etc., length, breadth, and depth—and the particular things measured by these should be pointed out.

Again, as to weight, the name of all the weights used, from a ton downwards, or from an ounce upwards, speaking to them of the particular things bought at the shop by weight—of those bought by volume—that fluid substances easily taking the shape of the vessel into which they are poured make the usual modes of measuring them the most convenient; that solids, instead of putting them into any particular measure, might be more easily measured by putting them into the form of some regular solid, and then taking its dimensions, etc. A friend of the author's, speaking with a large farmer in his neighbourhood on the importance of giving the agricultural labourer a better education, observed that he thought it very probable there was not one of the farmer's labourers, and he employed a great many, who knew the number of ounces in a pound, although they were in the daily habit of buying things by these weights. The farmer could not see much good in education, and thought none of his labourers so ignorant as this; but agreed to ask them the question on the Saturday night, when he paid their wages, and, to his own great astonishment, there was not one who could answer it.

When a class is able to read without spelling, the teacher should endeavour to interest them in what they are reading, by showing them specimens of anything which may be mentioned; pointing out whether it is of an animal, a vegetable, or a mineral kind—if a manufactured product how made, and the nature of the raw material—if it form any part of what they eat, or drink, or wear; how it is called into use in any of their domestic concerns; in the every-day occupations of themselves, or of their parents; connected with the mechanic trades, or with farming occupations; in short, calling their minds into exercise in every way he may have it in his power to do so.

For instance, the pen and ink with which they write? the one animal, the other vegetable matter dissolved in water ;—how the water dries away and leaves the vegetable matter behind ?—paper made from what, and how ?—when first made ?—difficulty of getting books before that, and on what written ?—printing, when invented ?—wooden types, afterwards metal types, etc., down to printing by steam : the slate they use ;—the string which fastens it round their necks ; the binding of their books, pointing out the variety of materials used, and the trades called into operation in preparing them ;—the little woodcuts which illustrate their lessons, how made, etc.

Also in the same way the manufactured articles of ordinary clothing, how made, and whether the raw material is animal or vegetable—leather, how prepared, etc. : their stockings, knit or woven ; carding, spinning, knitting.

GRAMMAR.

Grammar is taught here almost entirely through their reading lessons, and in this way, far from being the dry subject many have supposed it to be, it becomes one in which they take great interest. Any attempt by giving them dry definitions of parts of speech and rules of grammar is almost sure to fail; for one which it interests, it will disgust ten, and therefore the thing ought not to be attempted in this way. The most natural and easy manner seems to be, first,—

Pointing out the distinction between vowels, consonants, and dipththongs, from words in their lessons : when *a* or *an* is used before a noun : the difference between *a* table, and *the* table ; between a book, and the book ; a sheep, and the sheep ; a deer, and the deer : whether they would say a house or an house; a hare or an hare ; an heir, an hour ; drawing attention to exceptions as they occur.

The next and easiest thing would be the nouns, pointing out all the things which they see around them ; such as book, table, map, etc. : and thus they immediately know that the names of all visible substances are called nouns.

This being once fixed, they are soon led to the idea, that the names of things which they can imagine to exist, are nouns also ;—to distinguish the *singular* from the *plural*: that the singular means *one*, the plural more than one :— the general rule of forming the plural by adding *s* ; house, houses; map, maps; etc.; the teacher taking care to point out the exceptions as they are met with in reading, such as ox, oxen; tooth, teeth ; man, men ; loaf, loaves; church, churches; city, cities; and to observe also, where anything like a general rule can be traced out, such as that nouns ending in *ch* soft make the plural by adding *es*, as church, churches; arch, arches ; match, matches ; while in *ch* hard they follow the general rule, as monarch, monarchs, etc.; in *sh*, as dish, dishes ; fish, fishes, etc., adding *es* ; in *f*, as leaf, loaf; changing *f* into *v*, and adding *es*, leaves, loaves; nouns ending in *y* into *ies*, as city, cities; fly, flies; why such words as boy, valley, do not follow the general rule.

I would strongly recommend to all our school teachers a small book by Professor Sullivan, called " The Spelling Book Superseded," on this subject, as well as his other books, " Geography Generalized," his " Geography and History," and his " English Grammar," published by M'Glashan, Dublin, and by Messrs. Longman, in London. They are all excellent in their way, and have done good service here. The difficulty of pronouncing *s* at the end of nouns ending in *ch*, *sh*, and *x*, will show the reason for adding *es*.

The teacher would do well to exercise the children in forming the plural of any particular class of nouns as they occur; for instance, nouns ending in *f*, as leaf; spell it in the plural, leaves ; potato, potatoes ; negro, negroes ; echo, echoes ; and making them quote all the nouns ending in *f* and in *o* they could possibly recollect; the same way for others. This calls forth great emulation, and is attended with good results.

The difference of gender, also, in nouns ought to be pointed out, a thing very necessary in this county (Hampshire); everything alive or dead, male or female, coming under the denomination *he*, never by any chance changed into *him*.

They would now be able when sitting down, and without the assistance of a teacher, to pick out all the nouns in a lesson, writing them in columns in the singular and plural number; also, to write on their slates, or as exercises on paper in the evenings, things of the following kind :—

The names of the months in the year, and the number of days in each.

Of all the things in their cottages and in their gardens —of all the tools used by the carpenter, such as plane, axe, chisel, etc.,—by the blacksmith,—of all the implements used in agriculture, or in their trades and occupations.

What are the names of all the tools made of iron which we use in the village?

The names of all the trees—of the vegetable and animal products of the parish—of such vegetables as are food for man, for beast, etc.—of all articles of home consumption, etc.—of the materials of which houses are built, etc.

Describe a dog, cat, barn-door fowl :—write the names of all the singing-birds—of the birds of prey, etc. : write down six names of birds, all of which are compound words.

A year, a month, a week, day, hour, are measures of what?

A yard, a foot, an inch—of what?

A quart, a bushel, etc.—of what?

The teacher might also set each child to write down the date of its birth—to make out how many years, months, weeks, days, etc., old it was; so as to give its age in all the different measures of time.

Being now able to point out the nouns, etc., they should advance to such words as qualify them—adjectives.

The teacher, holding up an apple, for instance, will ask, Do all apples taste alike? No, sir; some are sour and some are sweet, bitter, etc. Do apples differ in any other way? Some are large and some are small—this is differing in size; some are red and some green—this is differing in colour; some soft and some hard—this is differing in the quality of hardness; some are rounder than others— differing in shape; and all these words, expressing different qualities in the noun, are adjectives. Then, perhaps, they are told to sit down and write all the words they can think of, which qualify the word apple, such as sour apple, sweet apple, large apple, etc.

Then to get at the degrees of comparison : The teacher will observe the different sizes of the children, taking two of them out and making them stand side by side. When I say that this boy is taller than the one next to him, what am I comparing ? The height of the two boys. This boy has got darker hair than the one next him—the colour of their hair : you have got cleaner hands than the boy next to you—the cleanness of my hands with the cleanness of his : such a child is the tallest in the class—is the best reader in the class. What do I compare? His or her height with the height of all the rest; his or her reading, etc. In this way they will very soon understand what is meant by degrees of comparison, and should be told how to form them : tall, taller, tallest; great, greater, greatest, etc. ; taking about half-a-dozen adjectives at a time, the children repeating them, and occasionally being set to write them on their slates. Reasoning in this way, the general rule soon strikes them, and the teacher must take care to point out the exceptions. Their very errors in following out a general rule are sometimes instructive, as well as amusing : for instance, if you give them such a word as *little*, or *good*, they will immediately begin, good, gooder, goodest, following out the general principle ; when all at once it flashes across them that the word is an exception, and the sort of knowing look they give you, as if you had tried to take them in, is most amusing.

In monosyllables, such as *hot, hotter, hottest* ; big, bigger, biggest, making them write down words which vary from the rule by doubling the final letter, and pointing out to them, that this is the case with all words of one syllable ending in a consonant, with a vowel going before it.

The teacher should now begin to point out the pronouns as they occur—what particular nouns they stand for in a sentence—what case—whether they mark possession, etc.; for instance, when *I*, or *he*, or *she* occurs, to ask them what they make in the objective cases ; what in the possessive. If *him* or *them* or *her* occurs, what is the form of the nominative; and occasionally using the pronouns in making short sentences, in order to fix a clear impression on their minds: such as, Where is my book? I saw it just now: the pen which I had in my hand: the book which he is reading; showing them in this last sentence you cannot understand what is meant by *he,* unless the noun to which it refers has been used before.

With respect to the verbs: in this school they are constantly exercised in going through all the persons and tenses, past and present, both on their slates, and occasionally by having two or three given to bring in writing, as an evening exercise: showing them they must use the present tense of the verb, or an auxiliary verb with the present participle if they speak of a thing while it is being done— the past form of the verb or the auxiliary verb and past participle, when the action is past: the teacher would write an example on the black board, such as

I work,	We work,
Thou workest,	Ye or you work,
He works,	They work:
present participle, working;	*past,* wrought.
I write, etc.,	writing; written:

particularly pointing out the auxiliary verbs when they occur with a past participle, and noting words where the past form of the verb and the past participle differ: as wrote, written; smote, smitten—calling upon the children to make short sentences to illustrate it: I wrote a letter— a letter was written; he broke a cup—a cup was broken. He should also correct such expressions as—I writ a letter; father work for farmer A.; we *works* for Mr. B.; we reads; I does, etc. It is interesting to observe how much the school is altering expressions of this kind here: the school-children of any age will all say, my father or mother works; we do, we work: or, if from habit they are led into making use of the former mode of expression, they will many of them immediately correct themselves.

This kind of teaching, young as many of them are, seems to exercise their minds, and give them a great interest in what they are learning.

In the same way their attention must be called to all the other parts of speech as they occur.

It is very important that the teacher, in exercising them in these parts of grammar, at first should select words to which they can easily attach ideas; as *nouns* for instance, the names of visible objects, such as ploughs, harrows, horses, cows, etc.; then tea, coffee, sugar, wheat, oats, things connected with their daily occupations, and the qualities of which are known to them : this soon gets them into the way of knowing what an *adjective* is. Again, for *verbs*, select such words as express some action they are in the habit of doing—to walk, to ride, to plough, to harrow; then point out the difference to them, or ask them to explain the difference, between *a* plough and *to* plough—*a* harrow and *to* harrow—*a* walk and *to* walk—*a* ride and *to* ride ; and that the noun which is in the nominative case is the doer of the action, the verb expresses the doing it, and the noun in the objective case is the thing on which the verb acts.

It will be necessary to point out the inflection of nouns, although the nominative and objective cases are generally the same, in order to show them how this ought to be attended to in the personal pronouns, etc. To notice such expressions as I saw he, I saw she, which they would invariably say here—and how they are wrong. For instance, suppose the teacher gives such a question as the following to write about : What is a spade made of, and what are its uses ? he should take care to explain why he uses the pronoun *its*, and get them into the way of using the pronouns properly by making little sentences of their own to illustrate them—how verbs are made into nouns by adding *er*, as do, doer ; walk, walker ; talk, talker ; plough, plougher, etc.—nouns into adjectives by adding *al*, as national, etc.

Compound words may be made very instructive and very amusing to them : bird-cage, pen-knife, etc. The teacher to lead them to explain what a compound word is ; if asked, they will answer perhaps, " A word made of two words ;" then show them that this is correct as far as it goes by mentioning several words made up of two, and ask what

they would call a word made up of three words : they immediately see that their definition comes short of what was
wanted ; then show them that a " word made up of two or
more words" would include every case ; this speaks to
their understanding better than if a correct definition had
been given at first.

Pen-knife—*pen* does not explain the material of which
the knife is made, but the use to which it is applied.

Oak-table—*oak*, taken as an adjective, explaining of
what the table is made ; might say oaken table : writing-
table ; made up of a noun, *table*, and a participle explaining for what the table is used.

Bring, to-morrow morning, neatly written, six compound
nouns, names of things about your houses. They will probably bring such as fire-side, bed-post, house-door, tea-pot,
sugar-basin, milk-pail. In the morning, the class to be
arranged according as they have done; the teacher to
interest them by showing how the meaning of the compound words is to be got at through the simple ones.

The word barge-river is invariably used here for canal ;
I doubt very much whether many of them know what is
meant by canal.

The importance of making the instruction turn a good
deal upon their own occupations and domestic consumption,
can scarcely be overrated ; it leads to a fire-side conversation in an evening, between parents and children, of a most
interesting kind ; and by setting the children questions of
this kind for an evening exercise the whole family is set to
work.

The reading-books used here are principally those published by the Irish National Board, numbered 1, 2, 3, 4, 5,
and those of Professor Sullivan, in connection with it : a
list of them is given at the end.

The following specimen from an easy lesson may be taken
as a mode of teaching (*Second Book of Lessons*, page 49).

" We cannot but admire the way in which little birds
build their nests and take care of their offspring. It is
easy to conceive that small things keep heat a shorter time
than those that are large. The eggs of small birds," etc.

Point out the vowels in the first line—the consonants in

the word *build*—what is *ui?* a diphthong, and build pronounced like *bild*. What is a bird? a thing. A *nest?* a thing. And therefore what parts of speech? nouns. *Birds*, does that mean one or more than one? More than one. What do you say when you mean only one? A bird, a nest. When only one, what number is that? Singular. When more than one? Plural. You say a bird, a nest; would you say *a egg?* No, sir, *an* egg; *a* before a consonant, *an* before a vowel. What are *a* and *an?* Articles, *Cannot but*, what does that mean? Must admire—be much pleased with. The teacher will point out that, if speaking in the singular number, the sentence would be : *We cannot but admire the way in which a little bird builds its nest and takes care of its offspring.* Then the class will sit down and occupy themselves in writing on their slates all the nouns in the lesson.

The pieces of poetry they learn by heart, having first made each piece the object of one or two reading lessons ; they then write down from memory, either on their slates or as an exercise on paper, about half of one of the short pieces at a time ; at first they will run all the lines together, perhaps, as in prose, or begin the lines with small letters,— write *i* for the pronoun *I*, and so on ; but in a very short time they write them out most correctly, and this exercise is a very useful one.

Again, (*Lesson Book*, No. 3, page 230.)

ON HUMAN FRAILTY.

Weak and irresolute is man,
　　The purpose of to-day,
Woven with pains into his plan,
　　To-morrow rends away.

The bow well bent, and smart the spring,
　　Vice seems already slain;
But passion rudely snaps the string,
　　And it revives again.

Weak and irresolute ; what parts of speech? Adjectives. What word do they qualify? Man. What does the prefix *ir* mean? Not. Can you quote any other words with the same prefix meaning *not?* Irregular, irreparable, etc. *Is ;* what part of speech? An auxiliary verb. In what way does it differ from *have*, as to the case which comes after it ? It always takes the nominative case both before and after it; it was I, it was he whom I saw ;—*have* follows the general rule. *Woven ;* what part of speech ? Past participle from *weave*. Are the past participle and the past tense of this verb the same ? No, sir ; wove, I wove, thou wovest, he wove, etc. What are the warp and woof in weaving ? The *warp*, the threads that run the long way of the cloth ; and the *woof*, the threads that run across : the woof is thrown by the shuttle over and above each alternate thread. Do you recollect any piece of poetry which you have learnt in which *Time* is called the *warp* of life ? Yes, sir. Quote it.

> Time is the warp of life :—Oh! tell
> The young, the fair, the gay, to weave it well.

What is meant by Time being the warp of life ? The length of life. What by weave it well? Spend it well. *With pains*, means what? With trouble. *His plan ; his*, what part of speech ? Relative pronoun, referring to man ; possessive case of *he ;* the objective, *him*. In the second verse *rudely snaps ;* what part of speech is *rudely ?* An adverb explaining the way in which the action of the verb is performed. *Slain*, what part of the verb ?

The class will then sit down, and write, in their own words, the substance of what the first two verses have conveyed to their minds, or perhaps of one verse ; afterwards get it by heart, and, as an evening exercise, bring it written from memory on paper. It is a great thing if the teacher can get them to write out in their own words at all correctly, the sense conveyed to their minds of a sentence in prose or verse.

In teaching a lesson, such as the following two verses from *Lesson Book*, No. 3.

> Thus far, on life's perplexing path,
> Thus far the Lord our steps hath led,
> Safe from the world's pursuing wrath,
> Unharm'd though floods hung o'er our head;
> Here then we pause, look back, adore,
> Like ransom'd Israel from the shore.

C

Strangers and pilgrims here below,
    As all our fathers in their day,
We to a land of promise go,
    Lord, by thine own appointed way,
Still guide, illumine, cheer our flight,
In cloud by day, in fire by night.

After explaining the first two lines, the teacher asks perhaps the grammar of a part of it, but from the words not coming in the prose order, the children find a difficulty; he should, therefore, read them thus :—The Lord hath led our steps, thus far, on the perplexing path of life; and they will at once get at the grammar of it, as well as the meaning; *safe*—what part of speech, and what word does it agree with? The verb from the same root is what? save: and the noun? safety. What does the fourth line mean? does it mean that waters are suspended over our heads? And then read to them the plain meaning of the lines in something like the following words :—

The Lord hath led our steps, thus far, on the troublesome path of life; protecting us from the pursuing wrath of the world uninjured, notwithstanding dangers have surrounded us: here, then, we stop, we review the past, we thank God for his protection from danger, as the Israelites did when they found themselves set free from the Egyptians and on the other side of the Red Sea.

We, Lord, as strangers and pilgrims in this word, go in the way in which thou hast appointed, to a land of promise, in the same way as all our fathers have done in their time; but we pray thee still to continue to guide, to enlighten, and to cheer our passage through this life, in the same way as Thou didst the Israelites in their journeyings from Egypt to the desert—in cloud by day, in fire by night.

Then referring them to the 13th chapter of Exodus—

" And the Lord went before them by day in a pillar of a cloud, to lead them the way; and by night in a pillar of fire, to give them light; to go by day and night. He took not away the pillar of the cloud by day, nor the pillar of fire by night, from before the people."

After having had the lesson explained in this way, they are then told, perhaps, to sit down and write the meaning which it conveys to their minds of one verse, and on a Monday morning to bring the first two, or any other two, verses, as an exercise written in prose.

The teacher should be in the habit of calling attention to the composition of particular words, and asking them to mention any others of a similar kind which they can call to mind; for instance—

Words with a prefix or affix, such as ungodly, unholy, inhospitable, incorrigible, irregular, occur; they should then be told to quote all the words they know with *un, in,* and *ir,* as prefixes meaning *not* when *in* is changed into *im,* as in the words improper, imperfect, etc., and why; or such words as leaflet, etc., with an affix;. ask if they know any others—streamlet, ringlet, etc. A noun ending in *ist,* as chemist; quote any others, as botanist, druggist, mechanist, copyist, etc.; or an adjective in *al, ive,* etc., such as national, local, vocal, destructive—quote others; extensive, positive, etc., and the nouns made from them.

I merely mention a few cases that occur to me at the moment of writing; but these are quite sufficient to show what is meant.

After having heard the lesson, the monitor or teacher should tell them to sit down and write on their slates a certain number (or as many as they know) of words, nouns, adjectives, etc., having any particular prefix or affix, which may have occurred in their lesson; for instance—

- Write down six adjectives ending in *al* and *ive,* six nouns ending in *ist,* in *let.*

When a word occurs which has a common root with many others, the teacher ought to ask what others we have from the same root; for instance, the word *extent* occurs as a noun; what is the word we use as a verb? extend; extending, present participle; past participle, extended: as an adjective? exten*sive*; adverb? extensively; also extension and extensiveness as nouns.

It is also useful to show them how the same word may be used as an adjective, a noun, or a verb: for instance, such a line as the following occurs:—

How calm is the summer sea's wave.

They see the word "calm" here used as an adjective; let them form a sentence, using it as a noun, a verb, etc. : there was a great calm—he calmed the sea—a calm day; and they should occasionally be asked to quote passages from their books, where the word is used in all these different ways ; to call to mind passages either in prose or in poetry containing particular usages of words. This teaches them their own language, and makes them recollect particular passages, both of poetry and prose, which they may have read. Lines descriptive of any particular country— of its physical character—character of its people—love of country, etc. ; such as Scott's—

> O Caledonia ! stern and wild,
> Meet nurse for a poetic child ;
> Land of brown heath and shaggy wood—
> Land of the mountain and the flood.

Or—

> Dear to my spirit, Scotland, thou hast been
> Since infant years, in all thy glens of green;
> * * * *
> Land of wild beauty and romantic shapes,
> Of shelter'd valleys and of stormy capes.
>
> T. GRAY.

Or the following from Cowper's "Task"—

> England, with all thy faults, I love thee still—
> My country ! and, while yet a nook is left
> Where English minds and manners may be found,
> Shall be constrain'd to love thee. Though thy clime
> Be fickle, and thy year most part deform'd
> With dripping rains, or wither'd by a frost,
> I would not yet exchange thy sullen skies
> And fields without a flower for warmer France
> With all her vines : nor for Ausonia's groves
> Of golden fruitage and her myrtle bowers.

As most of the upper children here can repeat the poetry of their Reading Books by heart, should a passage of this kind happen to be called up, they would be asked to bring it next morning written down from memory, as an evening task.

In the later printed copies of the Dublin Reading Books, I am sorry to observe they have omitted much of the poetry; as I know of nothing which has tended so much to humanize the children in this school, and improve their minds, by calling forth the gentler feelings of their nature, as the poetry of these books.

With many of the pieces by Cowper, Scott, Mrs. Hemans, and others, such as—On Cruelty to Animals—Human Frailty—The Stately Homes of England—Birds of Passage—The Graves of a Household—the more advanced children are so thoroughly acquainted, as to be able to admire their beauties and to feel the force of them : this also has given a character to their reading which nothing else could have done, and shed a softening influence over their minds which will last through life.

The following may be taken as a specimen how children may be amused into instruction if the teacher is well up to his work (page 204, *Lesson Book*, No. 3):—

> O'er the heath the heifer strays
>   Free (the furrow'd task is done);
> Now the village windows blaze,
>   Burnish'd by the setting sun.
>
> Now he hides behind a hill,
>   Sinking from a golden sky;
> Can the pencil's mimic skill
>   Copy the refulgent dye ?
>
> Trudging as the ploughmen go
>   (To the smoking hamlet bound);
> Giant-like their shadows grow,
>   Lengthen'd o'er the level ground.

In what direction do you go home from school ? West. Did you ever observe your shadow in going home? Yes, Sir. Behind you or before you? Behind me, to the east of me. Does it lengthen or shorten as the sun gets lower ? Lengthen. You who go home to the east, in what direction do you observe your shadows ? before you or behind you ? Before us. Did you ever observe them as you came to school in the morning ? In what direction are you walking when you come? Answer from one—As I go west in going home, I must be coming east when I come from home to school. Is your shadow then before or behind you ? Behind me, cast towards the west. Does it lengthen or shorten as you are going to school ? Shorten, because the sun is getting higher. Does it lengthen or shorten as you are going home? Lengthen, because the sun is getting lower. In what direction is the sun at noon? South. Point south. And your shadow cast to the north. If the sun were directly over your head, where would your shadow be? Under my feet, a point. In what countries is that the case? Twice a-year to an inhabitant between the tropics. Is this the case to an inhabitant on the tropics? Now can you explain, " Giant-like their shadows grow," etc.? Yes, Sir; as the ploughmen are going home, every step they take the sun is getting lower, and the lower the sun, the longer the shadow. Trudging means what? If it were ploughman, how must the lines be altered?

> Trudging as the plough*man goes*,
> Giant-like *his* shadow *grows*.

Now look at the last two lines of the first verse. In what direction is that window at the end of the room? West (the window is in the west end of the school-room). Does the sun shine upon it when it sets? Did you ever observe it on going home in a bright sunset, how it was lighted up, and did not that explain to you what burnished meant? Yes, Sir; it looks as if on fire.

The second verse—"Now he hides behind the hill"—would give the teacher an opportunity of calling their attention to the beauties of the setting sun on a fine summer's evening—whether behind the hill—apparently sinking into the sea—setting on a level plain—varying according to the nature of the country. From this what a very beautiful moral lesson might also be given!

Passages of this kind occurring, which may be so strikingly illustrated by things around them, a good teacher never would let slip; they give him an opportunity of making strong and lasting impressions on the mind, and add an interest to his teaching which almost commands success.

The teacher should call attention to the adverbs of time and place, in such expressions as *when* and *where*, *then* and *there*, etc.; and point out generally how adverbs qualify verbs and other parts of speech, making them form short sentences to make clear what he says; as—

He writes well—an adverb qualifying a verb.

He writes very well—the adverb *very* qualifying another adverb.

That was extremely wrong—an adverb qualifying an adjective.

The following hints of a suggestive kind may be useful when a lesson happens to be on the material of clothing, of food, etc.

The word cotton, for instance, occurs : the teacher will ask, showing them a piece in the raw state, Is cotton an animal or vegetable product? Vegetable. What part of the vegetable is it ? The lining of the seed-pod. Do you recollect any lines of poetry in your books which tell you about the cotton being the lining of the pod ? what are they ?

> Fair befall the cotton tree,
> Bravely may it grow;
> Bearing in its seeded pod
> Cotton white as snow.

A good teacher will often call upon them to quote the poetry they have learned by heart, in illustration of a lesson they may be reading.

What is meant by raw state, raw material ? The material unworked up, just as it comes from the plant. From what country do we chiefly get it ? America. Is it then called an export or import from that country ? *Ex* means from, and *im* in ; it is, therefore, an export from America, and an import into England. Into what port does it chiefly come ? Liverpool. Would you call Liverpool a manufacturing town ? No, sir ; a commercial seaport, into which the cotton is only brought, and then sent off to the manufacturing towns. Which are our principal manufacturing towns for cotton ? point them out on the map. Do you think William the Conqueror used to wear shirts made of cotton from America?—leading them to recollect that America was not known at that time : then to show them a piece of calico, to point out the different processes it undergoes, from the raw state up to the state they see it in ; how the cross threads (the woof) pass alternately over and under those running the long way, and called the warp —calico, plain and printed, bleached and unbleached—

the various articles it is made up into—how water and
steam assist in moving the machinery used in manufacturing
it—how in the transport of the material—consequent
cheapness—the numbers to which it gives employment,
etc.

Flax—showing them the plant: of course they see it is
vegetable; but in this case it is the stalk, the fibre which
runs the long way, that we use—laying a few fibres together lengthwise and twisting them into a thread, showing
the increased strength—grown at home, and in Ireland the
best—when ready, pulled up by the roots—steeped—the
quantity grown at home not sufficient for our consumption.
From what countries do we get it? the soil and climate of
New Zealand favourable to it—its uses when manufactured,
for shirting, tablecloths, smock-frocks, etc.

Hemp—take a piece of rope, untwist the threads, which
will show the material; what countries do we get it from?
—Its uses, cordage for ships, cart-ropes, etc.

Silk, animal or vegetable—on what particular leaf the
worm feeds, and the countries we get it from, and the kind
of manufactures. The uses of different dyes, animal, vegetable, and mineral.

Wool, leather—their shoes, etc.; animal products—to
explain how leather is tanned, the processes which the raw
hide undergoes before it comes into the shoemaker's hands,
and the various uses to which both wool and leather are
applied; when the woollen manufacture was first introduced
into this country, and where it is now chiefly carried on.
To show them the difference between a natural and a
manufactured product; for instance, that shoes do not
grow in gardens, like cabbages, but that the materials of
which they are made are sewn together by hand, etc.

Tea, sugar, coffee—the countries they come from, what
particular parts of the plant, and how prepared for the
market; from what other plant sugar has been extracted,
so as to be made an article of commerce;—maple-sugar
from Canada—from beet-root in France and Germany.
That, at the present moment, thousands of people are
employed in China, India, America, and every part of the
world, in preparing things for our consumption in England,
and to point out to them such as come into their cottages—

what we send out in return, and how the commerce is carried on.

In the same way the things they are in the habit of using which are home-made, cutlery, knives, scissors, etc.; pottery, soap, etc. That, in cutlery, we excel all other nations, and that wherever they go they will find English knives, axes—point out the difference between iron and steel, showing them the steel of the knife-blade welded on the iron to make the cutting edge, and asking them the names of other instruments of this kind which they know —the advantages of a people who know the use of iron, and are able to turn it into steel—how they would manage to cut down a tree, or cut their meat without iron and steel —that if it had not been for these they would have been little better than savages, picking the meat off the bones with their nails; or, in a district like this, where flints abound, using little pieces with sharp edges to scrape it off; —how they would have managed to cut down a tree—the savage making his canoe, etc.

The writer of an account of the New Zealanders in the " Library of Entertaining Knowledge," observes : " The especial distinction of the savage, and that which, more than any other thing, keeps him savage, is his ignorance of letters. This places the community almost in the same situation with a herd of the lower animals, in so far as the accumulation of knowledge, or, in other words, any kind of movement forward is concerned ; for it is only by means of the art of writing, that the knowledge acquired by the experience of one generation can be properly stored up, so that none of it shall be lost, for the use of all that are to follow. Among savages, for want of this admirable method of preservation, there is reason to believe the fund of know-ledge possessed by the community, instead of growing, generally diminishes with time. If we except the abso-lutely necessary arts of life, which are in daily use, and cannot be forgotten, the existing generation seldom seems to possess anything derived from the past. Hence the oldest man of the tribe is always looked up to as the wisest, simply because he has lived the longest; it being felt than an individual has scarcely a chance of knowing anything more than his own experience has taught him. Accordingly the New Zealanders, for example, seem to have been in quite as advanced a state when Tasman discovered the country in 1642, as they were when Cook visited it, 127 years after."

Then again, soap—made of animal fat, vegetable oils—its importance to our personal comfort and cleanliness—in washing our linen, clothes, houses,—its civilizing effect. The teacher taking occasion to remind the children always to be neat and clean in their persons and dress, and how much this adds to their respectability—that no one looks upon a child of dirty habits with the same respect as on one that is clean (showing them something like neglect when they are dirty has a good effect). To enforce cleanliness of person and dress in the children of a school is a thing of some difficulty, and requires attention. Opportunities of reminding them of the importance of truthfulness —of cleanliness—ought never to be lost.

It must be recollected, that although children of the better educated classes may be in the habit of hearing all this from their parents in conversation, yet those who attend our elementary schools have no such advantage.

The following extract from the Introduction to Arnott's " Physics," published in 1828, ought to have a place in one of our Lesson Books. I give it here, as I think it may suggest many useful hints to the village schoolmaster :

" In our cities now, and even in an ordinary dwelling-house, a man is surrounded by prodigies of mechanic art; and with his proud reason, is he to use these as careless of how they are produced, as a horse is careless of how the corn falls into his manger ? A general diffusion of knowledge is changing the condition of man, and elevating the human character in all ranks of society. Our remote forefathers were generally divided into small states or societies, having few relations of amity with surrounding tribes, and their thoughts and interests were confined very much within their own little territories and rude habits. In succeeding ages, their descendants found themselves belonging to larger communities, as when the English Heptarchy was united, but still remote kingdoms and quarters of the world were of no interest to them, and were often totally unknown. Now, however, every one sees himself a member of one vast civilized society, which covers the face of the earth ; and no part of the earth is indifferent to him. In England, a man of small fortune may cast his looks around him, and say with truth and exultation,'' I am lodged in a house that affords me conveniences and comforts which even a king could not command some centuries ago. Ships are crossing the seas in every direction to bring what is useful to me from all parts of the world. In China men are gathering the tea-leaf for me—in America they are planting cotton for me—in the West India Islands they are preparing my sugar and my coffee—in Italy they are feeding silkworms for me—in Saxony they are shearing the sheep to make me clothing—at home powerful steam-engines are spinning and weaving for me, and making cutlery for me, and pumping the mines, that minerals useful to me may be procured. I have post-coaches [now steam-carriages] running day and night on all the roads, to carry my correspondence. I have roads, and canals, and bridges, to bear my coals for my winter fire ; nay, I have protecting fleets and armies around my happy country, to secure my enjoyments and repose. Then I have editors and printers, who daily send me an account of what is going on throughout the world among all those people who serve me. And in a corner of my house I have *Books!*—the miracle of all my possessions, more wonderful than the wishing-cap of the Arabian Tales, for they transport me instantly, not only to all places, but to all times. By my books I can conjure up before me, to vivid existence, all the great and good men of antiquity, and for my individual satisfaction I can make them act over again the most renowned of their exploits. The orators declaim for me—the historians recite—the poets sing; and from the equator to the pole, or from the beginning of time until now, by my books, I can be where I please.' ''

As the exercises which the children have to write on their slates at school, and on paper in an evening at home, are, in my opinion, very instrumental in its success, I have added a few questions, in the hope that they may be useful as hints to the teachers of village schools, who have not yet attempted any thing of the kind; although the getting anything like tolerable answers may be attended with great trouble at first, and success appear to be a hopeless task, yet, in the end, it will amply repay the teacher for any pains he has to bestow upon it.   In the Somborne school, in hearing a lesson read, the teachers are in the habit of leading the children to give the substance of it in their own words, as they would relate it to their mothers at home, and in this way they are led to simple descriptions of animals, and to explain in words what is passing in their own heads.   In a short time some of them get very expert, and will ask for pet animals of their own to write about, such as they think they can describe best.

The questions are of the following kind :—
Write down the names of all the implements used in farming—in gardening, etc.
The names of all the birds you know, which of them come in spring, and go away at the end of summer.
Tell all you know about the swallow, how she builds her nest, feeds on the wing, etc.; about the cuckoo, etc.
Describe a sheep, and how it helps to clothe or feed you.
A cow the same, and its habits.
A horse, and the uses to which we turn it in the parish.
A dog—domestic fowl.
Write down the names of all the trees and shrubs you know, and mention which are evergreens.
What is the work which the farm labourer does in the different seasons of the year ?
Describe one of the four seasons, etc.
Describe a waggon and its uses—a plough—harrow—an axe—a saw, etc.
Give a description of any of the vegetable products of the parish, and their uses.
What are the uses of soap, and in what way does it increase our comforts, civilize us, etc.   What is it made of ?
Give the best account you can of all the purposes to which iron is applied in your cottages, in agriculture—in glass, lead, tin, etc.

In what ways is the power of making iron into steel useful to us ?—point out all its uses in your cottages—in any other practical things you can.

Glass, what are its peculiar properties, and in what way useful to man ?

What are the advantages which a people, knowing the uses of iron and steel, have over one which does not—point out any of them that occur to you.

Mention the materials of your own clothing, from what countries the raw materials come, and whether animal or vegetable.

What are the plants in the parish that furnish food to man ?—food for animals.

How were books made before printing was invented, and what is the material of which paper is made ?

John of Gaunt used to live where this school stands. Do you think he had tea and coffee with sugar for breakfast?— give your reasons for thinking he had or had not.

Where do we get coals from ?—describe how they are brought from the coalpit to us.

Explain what are the processes of ploughing, harrowing, and what the ground undergoes in preparing for a crop of wheat—of turnips—of barley, etc.

The different ways in which milk of the cow is presented to us for food.

The oak and the elm, their properties as timber, and how each is more particularly used ; bring a small twig of each to-morrow in full leaf, and let us point out how they differ in leaf, bark, hardness of wood, etc.

Describe wheat from its being sown until it is bread— how the grain sprouts, making one shoot downwards, which is the root, another upwards, which is white until it reaches the surface of the ground, and is then the green blade— then the straw—then the ear—when ripe, the harvest— then stacking in the farm-yard—then thrashing. What is said in Scripture of the mode of thrashing corn ?—pointing out how done, how in many southern climates—then win- nowing, and going to the mill where it is ground (what in Scripture about grinding), and is then called flour—and so bread.

GEOGRAPHY.

Having made them acquainted with the different bearings of particular objects of a local kind—of the towns and villages in the neighbourhood—how the parish is bounded, etc., and having well fixed on their minds the cardinal points—children very soon form tolerably correct ideas as to the nature of a map; and it is always better at first, if convenient, to have a map on the north wall of a school, as the four sides then correspond with the cardinal points where the observer is standing. This helps towards forming correct ideas; and as they generally become familiar with the map of England before any other, it is well to draw their attention at first to those counties on the extreme east or west—extreme north or south—showing them how they lie between particular meridians, or between particular parallels of latitude—to show them between what extremes of latitude and longitude the whole country is, of which the map is a representation; in this way they get a knowledge of the use of these fixed lines: until they do which a map is not properly understood; and it becomes therefore of consequence to show them their use, and the particular points from which we reckon—to show them that, having the latitude north or south, and the longitude east or west, the intersection of the two lines necessarily fixes the place wanted. They should then, for instance, pay attention to all the countries on the coasts, noting the river mouths, etc.; and thus by degrees fill up the whole, so as to have a correct representation of it in their minds, and know at once the bearing and position of every county on the map.

Every school should be provided with a compass, the teacher pointing out that the needle does not rest due north and south; but drawing a line parallel to it when at rest, and knowing the number of degrees which the north point of the needle is from the true north, he will very easily manage to teach them to draw a line nearly due north and south. By placing it on the floor, and having explained its directive power—that in this latitude the north point is now about 22° 30' to the west of north—then describing a

circle and drawing a diameter parallel to the needle, it will
be easy to set off an arc of about 22° towards the east of
the north end and towards the west of the end nearest the
south, and a diameter drawn through these points will be
the true meridian. The teacher of course will by degrees
call their attention to the difference of counties in physical
character — in mineral wealth — whether agricultural or
manufacturing—why the seats of our manufacturing industry should be in those counties where coal and iron are
found—how the agriculture or commerce of a country is
likely to be affected by geological character—how this bears
upon the character of its inhabitants.

A globe, however small, is extremely useful, and from
which, among other things, not to be learned from maps,
children may be made to understand how the sun comes
upon the meridian of different places at different times, or
perhaps speaking more correctly, how the meridians of different places come in succession under the sun—that the
time of a place to the east of them is before, and to the
west after the time of the place where they are—that all
the meridians pass in succession under the sun in twenty-
four hours ; and this being understood, it may at once be
explained how a degree in longitude corresponds to four
minutes in time, etc.; the arithmetic of it they must of
course be made to work out.

In the school here there are several mechanical contrivances for giving them a correct idea of the two motions of the earth, on its axis, and in its orbit, and its different positions at the different seasons of the year ; also to
illustrate what is meant by the hemisphere on which the
rays of light fall, and that only one half of a sphere can be
illuminated at the same time—this is shown by pieces of
thread, supposed to represent rays of light, fastened to a
globe of wood (the sun), and then being stretched over a
smaller globe (the earth), it is made visible to the eye what
part of the earth will be in the light, and what in the dark;
and that if made to fall upon a plane surface, the sun would
shine throughout its whole extent at the same time.

It is not sufficient merely to tell the children to look at
a map and point out any particular place upon it; this does

not make geography an exercise of the mind, which everything they learn ought to be. They ought to be made to
understand that a map is constructed on a particular plan
and scale : that if one country is larger than another it
will occupy a larger space in proportion upon the map—to
give them ocular proof of this by showing them the different
sizes of the counties on a map of England—that if two
places one hundred miles apart are one inch from each
other on the map, two places four hundred miles apart
would be four inches, and so on—to show them how to
find the distance between places, if on the same meridian,
by taking the sum or difference of latitude, and turning
the degrees into miles ; if on the same parallel of latitude,
by finding the difference of longitude, and multiplying the
length of a degree of longitude in that latitude by it—or by
applying a thread to the map, and measuring the distance
between the two places—to apply this to the degrees of
latitude, and point out why we cannot apply it to degrees
of longitude.

If a school is provided with a variety of maps, then attention should be drawn to the different scales on which
they are made, and why a map, perhaps of Europe or of
England, is much larger than one of the world ; asking
them such questions as, why is not the equator found on
the map of Europe ? Why does not a map of England
extend from the equator to the pole. Simple questions of
this kind puzzle them very much, while at the same time
they instruct them, and I have known children, after having
been learning geography for some time, look at a map of
Syria, for instance, or the Holy Land, for some minutes
for the equator or the pole, and wonder why they could not
find it. In looking at a map on the wall of the school, of
any country not reaching to the equator or poles, they are
generally made to apply a carpenter's rule to the side of
the map, and make out the scale upon which it is made ;
and then mark, below or above, as the case may be, on
the wall were the equator would be, and in like manner
to show the pole to which all the meridians ought to
converge.

The being able to make out the difference of time from

the difference of longitude, gives rise to a set of questions instructive in arithmetic, as well as in geography. The schoolmaster looking at the clock, observes, perhaps it is eleven; what is it in London (Greenwich)—what at Yarmouth in Norfolk? What is the difference in time between Yarmouth and the Land's End—what the difference in time between the extreme east and west of any country they may be looking at the map of. They will then be directed to look at the map, and work out the results themselves.

Short lessons of a conversational kind should occasionally be given, pointing out the mountain chains—their relative heights in the different parts of the world, and the directions in which they run—the course and length of the principal rivers, comparing them with our own—their directions, and the seas into which they empty themselves —the commercial advantages which one country has over another, either from its position, its rivers being navigable far inland, projecting arms from the sea running far into it —showing them the advantages of England, Scotland, Ireland, Holland, etc., in this respect—tidal rivers, such as the Thames and the Scheldt; and hence such towns as London and Antwerp; pointing out the coal and iron districts in England, and how they have in consequence become the manufacturing districts—that settlers in new countries invariably fix themselves on the banks of large rivers, or in parts of the country where branches of the sea run up far inland, instancing America, etc.; the reasons why they do this. Also such things as the quantity of water discharged by them compared, for instance, with the Thames, taking this as unity, that by the Danube is 65, the Volga 80, the Nile 250, the Amazon 1300, etc.; then the kind of reasoning which such facts suggest to the mind.

Again, explain the two motions of the earth—one of rotation on its axis—the other of progress in its orbit; what would be the effect, as regards day and night, if the rotation on its axis were stopped at any given time—for a day—for a week—for a year, etc.—how it would affect the vegetable world—the stability of bodies on the earth, etc.

What would be the effect on the seasons if the progress in its orbit were to cease for a time—for a continuance; all this would suggest a multitude of questions.

Such lessons as these, a teacher ought to be able to give, as they not only interest and exercise their minds, but are highly useful to them.

But in order that children may get an accurate knowledge of geography, it must not only be taught as a formal lesson, but as occasion may call it forth in the reading lessons. For instance, the inhabitants of America or Asia are mentioned—that will lead the teacher to ask, what country do *you* inhabit? Some will answer, Europe: yes; but what part of it? England, an island in the west. But what part of England? The south. Yes: but merely saying the *south* of England does not point out with sufficient accuracy where you live. Oh! in Hampshire. Well, but the English counties are subdivided (what is meant by subdivided? division of a division) into parishes; what parish are you in? and in this way working them down to the very spot.

Again, in their reading perhaps something occurs about France and Spain. The teacher: How are the two countries situated with respect to each other? in what part of Europe?— separated by what chain of mountains? Are the Pyrenees the highest mountains in Europe? What is their height compared with the highest mountains in England? Between what two seas do they run, and in what direction? How do you get out of the Atlantic into the Mediterranean? Passing through the Straits of Gibraltar, what country is on your right hand? what on your left? Do you pass Cadiz before you get at the strait or after? Then give them some account of the rock. Supposing a ship was sailing from Gibraltar to Constantinople, through what remarkable straits would it pass? What country is on the east and what on the west of the Dardanelles? On what sea is Constantinople?—built by whom? Are all the states of Europe Christian?—any other exception besides Turkey? What do we get from Smyrna, Constantinople, etc.? and to show how the commerce of the world is facilitated by the Mediterranean running between the Continents of Europe and Africa, and up to Asia.

Or if anything about St. Petersburgh or Stockholm occurs, make them point out the course of a ship from London to either of these places—what it would be likely to take out and bring back ? By whom was St. Petersburgh founded ? How long since Peter the Great lived ? What is the ancient capital of Russia? — then to tell them about Moscow being burnt in 1812—to point out the course of the Volga, Vistula, the Don, and into what seas they empty themselves. How is Europe separated from Asia? observe the course of the rivers in the north of Asia, and their emptying themselves into the North Sea, consequently the mouths of them frozen up during great part of the year.

The following may be taken as an example of questioning the children when teaching a lesson such as that on America (*Book of Lessons*, No. 3).

America, or the New World, is separated into two subdivisions by the Gulf of Mexico and the Caribbean Sea. Soon after it was discovered, this vast continent was seized upon by several of the nations of Europe, and each nation appears to have obtained that portion of it which was most adapted to its previous habits. The United States, the greater part of which was peopled by English settlers, while they possess the finest inland communication in the world, are admirably placed for intercourse with the West India islands, and with Europe, etc.

In what direction from Europe is America? By whom discovered, and about what time ? In the service of what nation was Columbus, and what were the names of its sovereigns ?—the teacher telling them his difficulties, and interesting them with the story.—Who was king of England at the time? (explain the word *contemporary*.) Was the passage round the Cape of Good Hope to India known then? No, sir; discovered a few years later. In the service of what nation was Vasco de Gama ?—and then point out to them how this discovery affected the line of commerce with the East—its course through the Mediterranean previously—the attempts made at discovery by

England about the same time—Newfoundland—Sebastian Cabot—the variation in the polarity of the needle.*

The lesson says "Soon after it was discovered, each nation appears to have obtained that portion of it which was most adapted to its previous habits." What does this mean?—look at the map.—What is there that would lead you to fix upon the parts taken possession of by the English?—anything in the names of places—the names of rivers—of divisions of the country—pointing out James-town, New England, and New Hampshire. Where would the early settlers be likely to fix themselves? Why upon rivers? Why particularly navigable rivers? What would guide you in your choice if you were going to an unsettled country?—the teacher to point out such things as attract an agricultural people. What is the most remarkable mountain chain in the two Americas—its direction, and how it runs into the Rocky Mountains—the rivers on one side flowing into the Pacific, and on the other into the Atlantic—those into the Pacific a short course, and probably rapid, and not navigable—those into the Atlantic, as the Amazon, of great length, lazy, sleepy, running through a flat country, and therefore likely to divide into many branches—slow, navigable—the character and employments of a people how affected by this? Do you recollect any passage in your book about a river being *lazy*? Yes, sir :

> Remote, unfriended, melancholy, slow,
> Or by the lazy Scheldt or wandering Po.

Reading at other times on this subject, the teacher would

* The teacher, placing the compass before them, should show what is meant by the directive power of the needle—what by its variation, dip, etc., "The variation was unknown until the time of Columbus, who observed on his first voyage that the needle declined from the meridian as he advanced across the Atlantic. The dip of the magnetic needle was first observed by Norman in 1576. The line of no variation passed through London in 1658, since that it has moved slowly to the westward, and is now near New York in America. The needle is also subject to a diurnal variation, which in our latitude moves slowly westward in the forenoon, and returns to its mean position about ten in the evening; it then deviates to the eastward, and again returns to its mean position about ten in the morning."

draw their attention to the Gulf of Mexico—the rivers that run into it—the course of the equatorial current, splitting into two on the coast of the Brazils; one branch going to the south, the other into the Gulf of Mexico, and called the gulf stream—most rapid between the coast of Florida and the Bahamas, striking against the coast of Newfoundland, and meeting the polar current, is again sent back across the Atlantic to the Azores, and so into itself again;—in the time of Columbus, remains of trees, also two dead bodies, were found at the Azores, washed over by this stream—how and why this encouraged him in his views.

The connection of North America with this country, when declared independent, etc., and, in like manner, how the other divisions of this large continent were, at an earlier period, connected with other European nations—Canada with France—the Brazils, etc., with Portugal—Mexico, etc., with Spain.

It is not meant that all this is to be taught to children at one lesson, but in the course of their reading the lessons on the subject of America, introduced into their school-books; this is the sort of information given by the teachers in the school here.

After a first lesson, they would be made to sit down and write on their slates the meaning conveyed to their minds by such a sentence as the one quoted above, which occurs at the beginning of their lessons: " Soon after it was discovered, each nation," etc.;—at another, to sit down before the map and make an outline of the coast bordering on the Gulf of Mexico, noting the river mouths, towns, etc., or to put down on their slates the longitude of the extreme east and west points of South America, and then to work out the difference in time.

The first class of boys are reading Sullivan's " Geography Generalized," one of the most useful books on this subject for the purposes of teaching I have ever seen.

By most of them questions of the following kind would be answered with a good deal of intelligence: what is the difference between a great and a small circle on the same sphere? What sort of circle is the parallel of latitude on which we live? What parallels of latitude are great circles?

Is the sun ever vertical to the inhabitants of Europe? In what direction is he seen, when on the meridian, by an observer north of the northern tropic? Always south. To an observer between the tropics? Explain why he would appear north or south of him at noon, according to the time of the year? To an observer in a higher southern latitude than 23½°, where would he appear at noon? Always north.

Explain how and why the rising and the setting points of the sun shift on the horizon every day during the course of a year.

What arc of a circle would measure the angle between the point of the horizon on which he rises on the 21st of June, and that on which he sets on the 21st of December?

To the question, if the sun rises at five or at seven o'clock in the morning, what time will he set? in nine schools out of ten you will get in answer, At five and seven in the evening: explaining that there are as many hours from sunrise to noon as from noon to sun-set, at once opens their eyes on the subject.

Two men walking out of the school, the one direct east, the other west, and always keeping equally distant from the equator and pole, on what line would they walk supposing the earth a sphere? Is it a straight line? How would their reckoning of time vary? Supposing each to walk a degree a day, how would their respective noons differ from the noon of the place where they started from and from each other?—at the end of one, two, three, etc., days—at the end of 360 days? When would they meet a first, second, third, etc., time? When they come to the place from which they set out, how many times will the one walking east have seen the sun rise? How many the one walking west? What is the circumference of the circle on which they walk, supposing them to start from a place in latitude 51°?

Two men starting from the same point on the same meridian, latitude 51°; point out their course, supposing one to go due north, the other due south, and always to walk on the same meridian. Will they have described a greater space when they meet than the two walking on the same parallel of latitude? How much longer? How will their reckoning of time differ? How long will it continue to be noon to both at the same time?

The sun is said never to set on the Queen's dominions—how is this? would he set on a belt of land running from pole to pole?—on a belt one degree wide on each side of the equator, and running round the earth?—$\frac{5}{6}$ths of the equator is in seas—$\frac{1}{6}$th in land—show this on the map, reckoning the exact number of degrees through which sea and land run.

Point out the advantage of knowing the figure of the earth, in answering the above.

Supposing a ship to sail from the Red Sea along the east coast of Africa, round the Cape of Good Hope, and so to Europe, would they always see the sun south of them at noon? Answer: No, sir. Point out, then, where they would begin to see him north according to the time of year—how this direction would vary in different latitudes up to the Cape of Good Hope. That to a people ignorant of the figure of the earth, and of its motions, and never having been beyond the Tropic of Capricorn, seeing the sun to the north of them at noon would appear as something supernatural.

Now, we find in a book written before the time of our Saviour, that in the time of Pharaoh Necho, king of Egypt, some Egyptians had made their way in a boat, setting out from the Red Sea, along the east coast of Africa, turned round what is now called the Cape of Good Hope, in passing which they would have, with their faces to the west, the sun on their right hand and towards the north of them, their left hand to the south, and of course their backs to the east. They then coasted along the west coast of Africa, found their way into the Straits of Gibraltar, which perhaps were known to them, and so sailed up the Mediterranean until they came to Egypt again, having thus coasted along the entire sea-coast of the continent of Africa. They took three years to do this in, and when they came back told people that they had seen wool growing on trees, *and the sun at noon, when their faces were to the west, on their right hand.* At that time there were reasons for not believing

the account; but with us who know more of the figure of
the earth than people did then, and something about cotton,
they confirm the truth of the story.

On the subject of *Physical Geography*,* which is one of
great interest, many things suggest themselves—such as
the varying altitude of the snow-line in different latitudes—
why it should be higher near the tropics than at the equator—and why the line of the same temperature should
recede further from the equator in the old continent than
in the new—the limits of the different vegetable productions, and why on high mountains, even within the tropics,
those of all climates, from the equator to the pole, may be
found, etc., showing the effect which elevation above the
level of the sea has upon climate—illustrating the explanation by instances of the vegetation of mountainous districts
in low latitudes, and of low levels in high latitudes, and
how it is that the temperature of the air decreases as the
height above the earth's surface increases—state facts in
proof of this.　If the lands in the equatorial seas were increased, an increased temperature of climate would arise—
if those of the polar regions, the temperature of the climate
would be diminished.

The following extracts from an Educational Tour in
Germany by Horace Mann, Esq., Secretary to the Board
of Education, Mass., U.S., are given for the purpose of
recommending linear drawing to school-teachers; a thing
not much practised in our schools, but of the usefulness of
which there can be no doubt.

Speaking of one of the first schools he entered, he says :
" The teachers first drew a house on the black board, and
here the value of the art of drawing—a power universally
possessed by Prussian teachers—became manifest.

" The excellence of their writing must be referred, in a
great degree, to the universal practice of learning to draw
contemporaneously with learning to write. I believe a child
will learn both to draw and to write sooner, and with more
ease, than he will learn writing alone.　I came to the conclusion that, with no other guide than a mere inspection of
the copybooks, I could tell whether drawing were taught in

* See p. 217.

the school or not—so uniformly superior was the hand-
writing in those schools where drawing was taught in connection with it.

"I never saw a teacher in a German school make use of
a ruler, or any other mechanical aid, in drawing the most
nice or complicated figures. I recollect no instances in
which he was obliged to efface a part of a line because it
was too long, or to extend it because it was too short. If
squares or triangles were to be formed, they came out
squares or triangles without any overlapping or deficiency.
Here was not only much time gained or saved, but the
pupils had constantly before their eyes these examples of
celerity and perfectness, as models for imitation. No one
can doubt how much more correctly, as well as more rapidly,
a child's mind will grow in view of such models of ease and
accuracy, than if only slow, awkward, and clumsy movement, are the patterns constantly before it."

The following passage on the subject of teaching geography, as taught in the Prussian schools, is well worthy of the
teacher's attention: Here the skill of the teacher and pupils
in drawing does admirable service. I will describe, as exactly as I am able, a lesson which I heard given to a class
a little advanced beyond the elements, remarking that,
though I heard many lessons on the same plan, none of
them were signalised by the rapidity and effect of the one
I am about to describe.

"The teacher stood by the black board with the chalk in
his hand. After casting his eye over the class, to see that
all were ready, he struck at the middle of the board: with
a rapidity of hand which my eye could hardly follow, he
made a series of those short divergent lines, or shadings,
employed by map engravers to represent a chain of mountains. He had scarcely turned an angle, or shot off a span,
when the scholars began to cry out ' Carpathian Mountains,
Hungary; Black Forest Mountains, Wurtemberg; Giants'
Mountains (Riesen-gebirge), Silesia; Central Mountains
(Mittel-gebirge), Bohemia,' etc.

"In less than a minute the ridge of that grand central
elevation, which separates the waters that flow north-west
into the German Ocean from those that flow north into the

Baltic, and south-east into the Black Sea, was presented to
view—executed almost as beautifully as an engraving. A
dozen wrinkled strokes, made in the twinkling of an eye,
represented the head waters of the great rivers which flow
in different directions from that mountainous range; while
the children, almost as eager and excited as though they
had actually seen the torrents dashing down the mountain
sides, cried out, ' Danube, Elbe, Vistula, Oder,' etc.   The
next moment I heard a succession of small strokes, or taps,
so rapid as to be almost indistinguishable, and hardly had
my eye time to discern a large number of dots made along
the margins of the rivers, when the shout of ' Linz, Vienna,
Prague, Dresden, Berlin,' etc., struck my ear.   With a few
more flourishes, the rivers flowed onwards towards their
several terminations, and, by another succession of dots,
new cities sprang up on their banks.   Within ten minutes
from the commencement of the lesson there stood upon the
black board a beautiful map of Germany, with its mountains, principal rivers, and cities, the coast of the German
Ocean, of the Baltic, and the Black seas, and all so accurately proportioned, that I think only slight errors would
have been found, had it been subjected to the test of a scale
of miles.   A part of this time was taken up in correcting a
few mistakes of the pupils, for the teacher's mind seemed
to be in his ear as well as in his hand; and, notwithstanding
the astonishing celerity of his movements, he detected erroneous answers, and turned round to correct them.   Compare the effect of such a lesson as this, both as to the
amount of the knowledge communicated, and the vividness,
and of course the permanence of the ideas obtained, with a
lesson where the scholars look out a few names of places
on a lifeless atlas, but never send their imaginations abroad
over the earth; and where the teacher sits listlessly down
before them to interrogate them from a book in which all
the questions are printed at full length, to supersede, on
his part, all necessity of knowledge."—MANN's *Educational
Tour in Germany*.

The following from an article in the " Quarterly Review,"
on Physical Geography, affords an instructive hint.

" Of the thirty-eight millions of square miles, forming in

round numbers the total area of land, nearly twenty-eight millions lie to the north of the equator; and if we divide the globe longitudinally by the meridian of Teneriffe, the land on the eastern side of this line will be seen greatly to exceed the western; another manner of division into two hemispheres, according to the maximum extent of land and water in each, affords the curious result of designating England as the centre of the former or terrene half—an antipodal point near New Zealand as the centre of the aqueous hemisphere. The exact position in England is not far from the Land's End; so that if an observer were there raised to such height as to discern at once one half of the globe, he would see the greatest possible extent of land; if similarly elevated in New Zealand, the greatest possible surface of water.

" An increase of land above the sea between the tropics raises the mean temperature, in higher latitudes depresses it; and every such vicissitude must be attended with some corresponding change in the nature and conditions of organic life."

NATURAL HISTORY.

The subject of Natural History, both of plants and animals, so far as they differ from each other in external form, in habits, etc., may be turned to very good account, and made the means of a great deal of useful instruction in our elementary schools.

" All this, it has been observed, children are capable of understanding—it consists in attending to the objects with which Nature presents us, in considering them with care, and admiring their different beauties, but without searching out their causes, which belongs to a higher department of knowledge: for children have eyes and do not want curiosity: they ask questions and love to be informed, and here we need only awaken and keep up in them the desire for learning and knowing what is natural to all mankind."

The children here are in the habit, as the spring and summer advance, of bringing to the school plants and flowers when they first come out—small twigs of the diffe-

rent trees of the parish, as the foliage begins to expand—
aquatic and other plants; all these, so far as a knowledge
of them can be had from the organs of vision, with a little
of the mind and of common sense to help it, are made
vehicles of instruction.

For instance, the names of the different parts of a flower,
from its root upwards, and the functions which each part
performs—the nature of the root, whether bulbous, fibrous,
or tap-rooted—the uniformity in number of the petals,
stamen, pistil, etc.,—running through the same class of
plants;—difference in the shape of leaves—some are
notched and some are plain—some rough, others smooth;
some oval, some round; some bright green, others dark—
the under side of the leaf differing in colour from the
upper, etc.: the different kinds of soil on which they find
the wild plants—showing that the soil on which any particular plant is generally found, is most likely one best
suited to its habits—that some plants, and pointing out
which (this they ought to know from their own observation),
are only found in shady places; while others will not grow
at all in the shade; that, when a flower or leaf withers,
it is from the juices making their escape into the atmosphere, and the plant, being separated from its roots, cannot
get a fresh supply; how aquatic plants, differing in structure from those on dry land in their air-cells, are calculated to float.

Then again, the small twigs of the different trees or
shrubs they may bring, the oak, and the elm, and the
beech—place a little twig of each side by side—how many
differences in external appearance—in the leaf, the bark,
the texture of the wood—the bark of the oak used for
tanning, and the difference in time in the leaf coming out,
and in its fall—the value of each as timber.

The acacia and the laurel—beauty of the leaves, how
uniformly the leaflets of the acacia are set on, one opposite
another,—how regularly in some plants the leaves are
placed directly opposite to one another, others, again, alter-
nating on opposite sides of the stem; point out the framework of the leaves, how the skeletons of them differ—to
observe this in decayed leaves.

Another morning they bring different twigs of the pine tribe—the larch, the Scotch fir, spruce, or silver fir—pointing out their thread-like leaves—that the larch is deciduous, the others not, etc. In this way they become acquainted with all the trees in the parish. That when a tree is cut down, the number of concentric rings on the face of a section of the stem marks the number of years' growth; that when they observe one ring smaller than another, it would denote a small growth for that year, and might have been caused by some peculiarity in the season, etc., such as a hard winter.

The great age of some trees, particularly yew.

These kind of observations should be made with the plants before their eyes, otherwise they have but little effect: the teacher would then tell them to sit down and describe a leaf, a twig, etc., of any of them; or some take one, some another, which is better, as this does away with the temptation to get hints from each other.

Again, calling their attention to some of the more striking differences in animals in their outward appearance and habits—the migrating of birds, and when they return, getting them to observe it; difference in the teeth and in the articulation of the jaw, in animals of prey and of those which ruminate, the jaw of the latter being capable of a rotatory motion, which enables them to grind, the other not, and having long tearing teeth: the air-cells in the bones of birds so beautifully adapted to the purposes of flight—the feathering of water-birds—the down on their breasts—the peculiarity of their feet, and how differing from the feet of those that roost, etc.

But more particularly will a teacher interest his school in this department by making observations of this kind and comparisons, etc., among the birds they are in the habit of seeing, such as the cuckoo, swallow, tom-tit, sky-lark, woodpecker, jay, or ducks and geese.

In this way they become observers of the external world with which they are in contact; it adds both to their happiness and to their usefulness, inasmuch as all these things have a practical bearing on social life.

These are thy glorious works, Parent of good—
Almighty! Thine this universal frame,
Thus wondrous fair: Thyself how wondrous then,
Unspeakable! who sit'st above the heavens—
To us invisible, or dimly seen
In these thy lowest works; yet these declare
Thy goodness beyond thought, and power divine.—MILTON.

In teaching ENGLISH HISTORY, the Outlines by the
Society for Promoting Christian Knowledge have been used
here, being the only book on the subject which, on account
of price, is attainable by the generality of children in a
school like this; when reading, instruction of the following
kind, in a conversational way, is given to them—on the
different people who have invaded us at different periods
of our history—Roman, Saxon, Dane, Norman—the Roman
and other remains in this neighbourhood—the Roman road
between Winton and Sarum, running through part of the
parish, and anything of this kind of a local nature—how a
people invading another, and remaining among them, is
likely to affect their language, manners, etc.—traces of
this are shown in our language; the manners and customs
of particular periods—how people were housed, and clothed,
and fed—the little intercourse there could be .between
people living even in different counties, for want of internal
communication afforded by roads, etc.—there might even
be famine in one county and abundance in the adjoining
one;—how such evils are remedied by roads, canals, etc.;
—the different inventions in science, etc., and dwelling
upon the more remarkable ones, bringing with them great
social improvements: paper—printing, the Reformation,
impulse given to it by this—nations contending for the
honour of the invention—how this enables one generation
to start from the point where another leaves off—how
rapid the progress of colonies from the mother country in
consequence; the improvements attending the introduction of turnpike-roads—post-office;—application of wind,
water, steam, etc., as the moving power in machinery.
How the introduction of the manufacture of cotton among
a people, to anything like the extent of it in this country,
must alter the mode of dress—the domestic employments

of families, doing away with spinning, carding, knitting, etc., as home occupations; comparing the employments of a family in agricultural life at the present day with what they were at different periods. Again, the time which it took at no very distant period to travel between London and the provinces, and how done;—the great men that have risen up at intervals in science, literature, etc., and in other ways; —the number and extent of our colonies, giving them such popular explanation of the nature of the constitution, one part of the legislature being hereditary, another elective, etc., as is within the comprehension of children;—the comforts and conveniences within the reach of every class in society compared with those of earlier periods; and thus, instead of making it a dry detail of the chronological order of reigns, which in itself would not be instructive, endeavouring to give an interest to it, by speaking of those things in past ages which bore upon their daily occupations, and showing how they may improve the future by reflecting on the past.

Dr. Johnson observes in the Rambler: "That not a washerwoman sits down to breakfast without tea from the East Indies, and sugar from the West."

The following is the copy of a card which used to be, and perhaps is still preserved at York, in the bar of the inn to which it refers:

"York Four Days' Coach, begins the 18th of April, 1703. All that are desirous to pass from London to York, or from York to London, or any other place on that road, let them repair to the Black Swan in Holbourne, in London; and to the Black Swan in Coney-street, York, at each of which places they may be received in a stage-coach, every Monday, Wednesday, and Friday—which performs the whole journey in four days—if God permit."

The same distance is now travelled by railroad in eight or nine hours.

ARITHMETIC.

Arithmetic should be made an exercise of the mind, and not merely an application of rules got by heart; in fact, it ought to be taught on a sort of common-sense principle, beginning with very simple things, and leading the children on, step by step. It is difficult to fix on their minds ideas of abstract numbers, and therefore, at first, the numerals 1, 2, 3, etc., should be connected with visible objects; such as books, boys, girls, etc., and thus they should be made to understand that a number, when applied to things or objects, means a collection of units of that thing or object, but that the same kind of units must run through-out; that in a class of children each child is a unit, and that, when we speak of a hundred children in a school, we speak of a hundred units, each of which is a child; but that we must have units of the same kind, or we could not class them all together; that we might say a hundred children when half are boys and half are girls, because the word child means either boy or girl, and in that sense either of them is a unit; but we could not say one hundred boys or one hundred girls when there are fifty of each sort; the unit, of boys or girls, not running through the school, but only half way : we might say a hundred head of cattle, when half were sheep and half were cows, but we could not say one hundred sheep or one hundred cows. In the same way the sportsman says a hundred head of game, meaning by that hares, rabbits, etc., but in all a hundred separate heads of animals.

It will help very much to facilitate the future steps, if the teacher can get the children to form correct ideas as to the local value of each figure, and this may be done by altering the position of the same figures, so as to make them represent different numbers; as 56, that is five tens and six units; 65 would be six tens and five units; 678 is six hundreds, seven tens, and eight units,—876, etc. : that 0 has no value in itself, but being placed on the right hand of a figure makes its value ten times as great as it was, because it shifts the first figure from the unit's to the ten's place, and so on; as 6 by placing 0 on the right hand becomes 60, and so on, and from this to infer that by placing a 0 on the right-hand side of any number, you multiply it by ten. This is to be a sort of induction or conclusion they are to arrive at, as a general rule drawn from testing it by particular instances.

In the same way he would point out that any other figure placed on the right hand of a number multiplies that number by ten, inasmuch as it advances each figure one place to the left, and at the same time increases the number by the number of digits it contains; two figures by 100, etc.; thus 95, placing 6 on the right hand, become /956, or 900+50+6; placing 65, becomes 9,565, or 9 00+500+60+5. That 5, 6, etc., are always so mar units, but the unit of value rises in a tenfold proportion every place the figure is advanced to the left.

When they know a little of numeration, the teacher should write on the black board, and make them thoroughly understand writing down numbers in the following way: 69, or 60+9; 756, or 700+50+6; 1050, or 1000+0 hundreds+50+0 units, making them say seven hundreds, five tens, six units; one thousand, no hundreds, five tens, no units: this they ought to be exercised in until they know what they are about.

In exercising them as a class by the repeated addition or subtraction of the same number, it may be made more of a mental exercise by checking them every now and then, testing what has been done; for instance, adding by sevens, and they have come up to 63; stop there, and ask the boy whose turn is next, whether they are correct as far as they have gone; perhaps he says, yes. Why? because $\dfrac{63}{7} = 9$,

or seven added nine times to itself gives 63; and the probability is they are right, and one would generally conclude so; but here the teacher will point out to them—there may be an error of seven, or any multiple of seven, and in that case the result would still be divisible by seven, and at the same time wrong: tell them to reckon the boys, and if nine, the proof is complete. Again, supposing them to have gone on adding by sevens until the sum is 77: ask, right or wrong; the boy will answer right, because $\dfrac{77}{7} = 11$;

then go on a little further, and a boy says, for instance, 99: divide, there is a remainder of one; it was right at

E

77 when the eleventh boy answered, therefore the error must be with the last three boys.

They should always be practised in asking such questions as : How many divisors has the number 12 above unity— how many 15 ? thus $12 = 2 \times 3 \times 2$, or $15 = 5 \times 3$ splitting the number into its factors : that all even numbers are divisible by 2, and that no odd number is. This seems simple, but if constantly repeated has a good effect,*

3 may be written $1+1+1$, or 3
4   „ $2+2$
5   „ $1+1+1+1+1$, or 5
6   „ $2+2+2$, or $3+3$
9   „   in separate units, or $3+3+3$;

that a class of nine children may be made to stand out as units, but they cannot be made to stand out in twos without a remainder—in sets of three but not of four.

Thus showing them that up to 20, a class containing an even number of children may be made into more sets without a remainder, than a class containing an odd number ; it is well to illustrate this practically, either by parcelling

---

* If the teacher is acquainted with a little Algebra, he would do well to apply it to a few of the common properties of numbers. Thus in this case:

Every even number may be represented by the form $(2n)$
Every odd number by . . . . . $(2n+1)$
giving to n in each of these forms its successive values, 0, 1, 2, 3.

$(2n)$ becomes 0, 2, 4, 6, etc., all the even numbers.
$(2n+1)$ „   1, 3, 5, 7, etc. all the odd numbers.

Now it is clear $\left(\dfrac{2n}{2}\right)$ giving the quotient (n) that all even numbers are divisible by 2 without a remainder,—

$\left(\dfrac{2n+1}{2}\right) = n + \dfrac{1}{2}$, therefore the odd ones are not.

Again, the square of $(2n) = 4n^2$.
the square of $(2n+1) = 4n^2+4n+1$.

Or, $\dfrac{4n^2}{4} = n^2$

$\dfrac{4n^2+4n+1}{4} = n^2+n+\dfrac{1}{4}$

Therefore the square of every even number is divisible by 4 without a remainder.
The square of an odd number is not.

out a class, or a number of small pieces of wood, thus carrying conviction both to the eye and to the mind. There is no exercise which has a better practical effect than pointing out all the factors into which numbers up to a hundred, for instance, can be broken, such as—

$$24 = 2 \times 12, \text{ or } 3 \times 8, 3 \times 2 \times 4, \text{ or } 3 \times 2 \times 2 \times 2.$$

This subject of the number of divisors without a remainder, would lead the teacher to speak of the subdivisions of a coinage, from which he would show that a coin value twenty shillings, would be much more convenient than one of twenty-one shillings, as admitting of more divisions without a remainder, and therefore of more sub-coins without fractions.

Having made them well acquainted with the first four rules, they must then be made to understand the coinage. the measures of space, time, and volume.

To get a correct idea of the comparative length of an inch, a foot, a yard, etc., and how many times the shorter measure is contained in the longer, the common carpenter's two-foot rule is of great service—show them by actual measurement on the floor what is meant by two, three, four yards, etc., as far as the dimensions of the school will permit.

The motions of the hands on the face of the clock should be pointed out—what space of time is meant by a minute, an hour, and a year—all words in use as measures of time —the same as to measures of volume. Many of the labouring class in agricultural districts, even when grown up to manhood, cannot read the clock face.

When the children understand these things, it will be found most useful to practise them in little arithmetical calculations connected with their own domestic consumption, or applying personally to themselves, such as :—

Supposing each person in a family consume $16\frac{1}{2}$lbs. of sugar in a year, consider each of you how many your own family consists of, and make out how much sugar you would use in one year.

How much would it cost your father at $5\frac{1}{2}d.$ per pound, and how much would be saved if at $4\frac{1}{2}d.$ per pound ?

This village consists of 1,120 people, how much would

the whole village consume at the same rate? How much the county, population 355,004?

Each boy adapting the first question to the number of his family, varies it without trouble to the teacher, and thus no temptation is offered to any one to rely on his neighbour. In arithmetical calculations they can easily catch a result from others; this the teacher should in every way discourage, or he will very soon find that two or three of the sharper boys in a class know something about it, the rest nothing. Tell them to rely upon themselves, and ask questions if they are at a loss.

In this way a great variety of questions connected with sugar, coffee, their clothing, such as a bill of what they buy at the village shop, groceries, etc.—a washing bill, etc., may be set; and when told to do a question or two of this kind in an evening at home, it will very often be found to have been a matter of great interest and amusement to the whole family.

In teaching them arithmetic, such simple questions as the following occasionally asked will, by degrees, lead them to form correct ideas of fractional quantities.

How many pence in a shilling? Twelve. Then what part of a shilling is a penny? One twelfth. Then make them write it $\frac{1}{12}$ on their slates.

How many twopences in a shilling—threepences, etc.?

Then what part is twopence, threepence, etc? $\frac{1}{6}$, $\frac{1}{4}$, etc.

Again, how many shillings in a pound? Then what part of a pound is one, two, three . . . . nineteen shillings?

$\frac{1}{20}$, $\frac{2}{20}$, $\frac{3}{20}$, and so on to $\frac{19}{20}$, $\frac{20}{20}$ or a whole.

In the same way with measures of space, thus leading them by gentle degrees to see that in numerical fractions what is called the denominator denotes the number of equalparts into which a whole is divided, and the numerator the number of parts taken.

When sufficiently advanced to commence the arithmetic of Fractions, the teacher will find it of great service in giving them correct ideas of the nature of a fraction, to call their attention as much as possible to visible things, so that the eye may help the mind—to the divisions on the

face of a clock—or of the degree or degrees of latitude on the side of a map, thus ||||||||||||| show-
$$\underset{50^\circ \qquad\qquad\qquad 51^\circ}{|\ |\ |\ |\ |\ |\ |\ |\ |\ |\ |\ |}$$
ing that a degree, which here represents the unit, is divided into twelve equal parts—and then reckoning and writing down

$\frac{1}{12}, \frac{2}{12}, \frac{3}{12}, \frac{4}{12}, \frac{5}{12}, \frac{6}{12}$, (or $\frac{1}{2}$), $\frac{7}{12}, \frac{8}{12}, \frac{9}{12}, \frac{10}{12}, \frac{11}{12}, \frac{12}{12}$, or units,

showing how these may be reduced to lower terms, and that the results still retain the same absolute value—that the value of a fraction depends upon the relative, and not upon the absolute value of the numerator and denominator;

as $\frac{2}{12}$ and $\frac{1}{6}, \frac{3}{12}$ and $\frac{1}{4}, \frac{4}{12}$ and $\frac{1}{3}, \frac{6}{12}$ and $\frac{1}{2}$, etc.,

have in each case the same absolute value.

In casting his eye round a well-furnished schoolroom, the teacher will see numberless ways in which he may make the nature of a fraction clear to them, as counting the number of courses of bricks in the wall—say it is fifty, as they are of uniform thickness, each will be $\frac{1}{50}$ of the whole height—placing the two-foot rule against the wall and seeing how many courses go to making one foot, two feet, etc., there will be such and such fractions—or supposing the floor laid with boards of uniform length and width, each will be such and such a fraction of the whole surface, taking care to point out that when the fractional parts are not equal among themselves they cannot put them together until they are reduced to a common denominator, and the reason of all this. In this way, and by continually calling their attention to fragments of things about them and putting these together, children get a correct idea of numerical fractions at a much earlier age than is generally imagined.

The following kind of question interests them more than very abstract fractions; the teacher should try to form questions connected with their reading.

What are the proportions of land and water on the globe? $\frac{1}{3}$ land, $\frac{2}{3}$ water. What do you mean by $\frac{2}{3}$? A whole divided into three equal parts, and two of them taken. Here the teacher would put a piece of paper into a boy's hand, and tell him to tear it into three equal parts, and show the fractions; or by dividing a figure on the black board.

What proportion of the land on the globe does America contain ? $\frac{1}{3}$. What Asia ? $\frac{1}{3}$. Africa ? $\frac{1}{5}$. Europe ? $\frac{1}{15}$. And Oceanica ? $\frac{1}{15}$. Now, putting all these fractions together, what ought they to give ? The whole land. The unit of which they are the fractional parts was what ? The land on the globe. Work this out. Africa $\frac{1}{5}$ or $\frac{3}{15}$; Europe and Oceanica, each being $\frac{1}{15}$, these with Africa will be $\frac{5}{15}$, or $\frac{1}{3}$. America and Asia together are $\frac{2}{3}$, and adding $\frac{1}{3}$ to this gives $\frac{3}{3}$, or 1 for the whole.

Having been taught this and decimal arithmetic, they should be taught to work out most of their sums decimally, and made to reason about them as much as possible, rather than to follow a common rule—for instance :

What is the interest on £500 at 5 per cent. for two years ? —5 per cent. means what ?—the interest on a hundred pounds for a year : then the interest of £1 will only be the one hundredth part of that : work it out, ·05—the interest of £2 will be twice as great; of £3 three times as great; and of £6 six times as great, etc. Having the interest for one year, the interest for any number of years will be the interest for one, multiplied by that number.*

Children sometimes get into the way of working out questions of this kind, without having any definite idea of what is meant by so much per cent., etc. ; this they should be made thoroughly to understand, as bearing upon many other questions besides those on interest, as will be seen

---

* The following algebraic formula may be useful:
Let P = the principal.
　　r = the interest of £1 for one year.
　　n = the number of years, or the time for which it is put out.
　Now if r is the interest of £1 for one year, it is clear the interest of 2, 3, 4, etc., P£ will be twice as much,
　　　　　or 2r, 3r, 4r . . . . Pr interest for one year.—
The interest for 2, 3, 4 . . . . n years will be
　　　　　2 Pr, 3 Pr, 4 Pr . . . . nPr,
　　　　　　(1) the interest = nrP,
we have the amount, being the principal added to the interest,

from the examples given; also what is meant by so much
in the shilling, so much in the pound, etc.,—that if a person

---

$M = P + nrP$. Now, in this equation there are four quantities, any
three of which being given the fourth can be found.

Ex. Interest on £250, for $2\frac{1}{2}$ years, at 5 per cent.

Here $P = 250$

$$r = \frac{5}{100} = .05.$$

$$n = 2\frac{1}{2} = 2.5.$$

$$\therefore \ I = 250 \times (.05) \times (2\cdot5) = 31\cdot25£,$$
and $M = 250 \times 31\cdot25 = 281\cdot25£$

But the above formula is much more important than the ordinary
rule, inasmuch as it accommodates itself to every possible kind of
case.

A certain sum put out to interest at 5 per cent., in four years
amounts to £250 10s.; what was the sum put out?

In this case, M, r, and n are given to find P.

Or the sum put out was £30, and in two years amounted to £33;
what was the rate per cent.?

Here M, P, and n are given to find r.

The cases where all, rate per cent., time, etc., are fractional, are
quite as easy as the rest, except in having a few more figures to
work out.

The whole expenditure of a family in a year is A pound, of
which a per cent. is spent in bread, b in tea, c in clothes, d in house
rent, e in taxes, etc., what part of the whole income is spent in each
of these articles, and give an expression for the whole?

$$\frac{a}{100} = \text{part of every £ spent in bread, and } \frac{Aa}{100} = \text{what is spent in a year.}$$

$$\frac{b}{100} = \text{the part of each £ in tea, and } \frac{Ab}{100} \text{ of the whole income.}$$

In the same way $\dfrac{Ac}{100} = $ that in taxes in the year.

Therefore $\dfrac{Aa}{100} + \dfrac{Ab}{100} + \dfrac{Ac}{100} + \text{etc.} = A.$

Or, $\dfrac{A}{100}(a + b + c + \text{etc.}) = $ the whole expenditure.

And if the annual income of a family is $P£$ per annum, $P - \dfrac{A}{100}$
$(a + b + c + \text{etc.})$ will be the state of the pocket at the end of the
year. When this express... is negative, it means they have exceeded

spends twopence in the shilling in a particular way, and lays out two, three, ten shillings, he spends 4d., 6d., 20d., etc., in that particular thing.

---

their income. When it is $= 0$, they have just spent their income; and when it is positive, they have saved money.

A mass M of three metals, of which c per cent. is copper, s per cent. silver, and g per cent. gold; how much of each?

$$\frac{Mc}{100} = \text{the copper.}$$

$$\frac{Ms}{100} = \text{the silver.}$$

$$\frac{Mg}{100} = \text{the gold.}$$

Or, $\quad M - \frac{M}{100}(c + s).$

Suppose the mass 1000lbs., of which 25 per cent. copper, 40½ per cent. silver, and the rest 34½ gold: how much of each?

Here $\qquad M = 1000, \ c = 25, \ s = 40.5, \text{ etc.}$

$$\therefore \frac{Mc}{100} = \frac{1000 \times 25}{100} = 250 \text{ lbs. of copper.}$$

$$\frac{Ms}{100} = \frac{1000 \times 40.5}{100} = 405 \text{ lbs. of silver.}$$

$$\frac{Mg}{100} = \frac{1000 \times 34.5}{100} = 345 \text{ lbs. of gold.}$$

The skilful teacher who knows a little algebra may see a very extensive application of it in this way, and the satisfaction and instruction to a boy in being able to work out easy formulæ of this kind, and adapt them to particular cases, is beyond comparison greater than being taught by rules.

This makes it highly desirable that all our schoolmasters should be able to teach so much of the rudiments of algebra as to apply it to simple calculations of this kind. The merely being able to substitute numerical values for the different letters in an algebraical formula is of service.

For instance, that

(1.) $(a + b) \ (a - b) = a^2 - b^2$: that this means that the sum of

A penny in the shilling is twenty-pence in the pound, twenty pence in one pound is one hundred times that in a hundred pounds, and would be called so much per cent'. The same in the common rule of three ; they get into the way of stating their questions mechanically ; but what the teacher should do, is, instead of saying as 1 yard : 2*s.* 6*d.* : : 50 yards to the answer ; he should say, if one yard cost 2*s.* 6*d.* two yards will cost twice as much ; three yards three times ; 50 yards 50 times as much, having recourse to the common-sense principle as much as possible.

The following questions, with those at the end of this section, may be useful to the teacher, as bearing upon the economic purposes of life, and will suggest others of a like kind :—

The population of the parish in 1831 was 1,040, at the census of 1841 it had increased 7 per cent., what is it at present ?

In the population of the parish, 20 per cent. of them ought to be at school ; in this parish, containing 1,040, only 12 per cent. are at school ; how many are at school ? and how many absent who ought to be there ?

The population of the county in 1841 was 355,004 ;— 82·8 per cent. were born in the county, 14·2 in other parts

---

two quantities multiplied by their difference is equal to the difference of their squares.

(2.) That $(a + b)^2 = a^2 + 2ab + b^2$, or that the square of the sum of two numbers is equal to the sum of their squares, increased by twice their product.

(3.) That $(a - b)^2 = a^2 - 2a + b^2 = ab^2 + b^2 - 2ab$, or that the square of the difference of the numbers is equal, or the same thing as adding the squares of each separate number together, and then diminishing this by twice their product.

In each of these cases let $a = 6$, and $b = 4$; then $(a + b)(a - b)$ would become $(6 + 4) \times (6 - 4)$, or $10 \times 2 =$ the square of 6 or 36, diminished by the square of 4 or 16, or $(6^2 - 4^2) = 20$.

(2.) $(6 + 4)^2$ or $10^2 = 6^2 + 4^2 + 2 \times 6 \times 4$.
$$\text{or } 36 + 16 + 48 = 100.$$
That is, it is the same thing if you add the two numbers together, and square the sum, or square each number separately, add them, and to this add twice their product.

(3.) $(6 - 4)^2 = 2^2$ or $4 = 6^2 + 4^2 - 2 \times 6 \times 4$.
$$\text{or } 36 + 16 - 48 = 4.$$

of England, 0·5 in Scotland, and 0·9 in Ireland; what number were born in each country ?—how many in number, and what per cent. are unaccounted for ?

Give the average of the parish, how many to the square acre; number of the houses, how many to a house, etc. These questions ought also to be the vehicle of a good deal of instruction on the part of the teacher.

A sheet containing the names of the towns in each county, arranged by counties, and giving in a tabular form the population in adjoining columns, according to the census of 1831 and of 1841, is to be had for a shilling, and offers great facility to a master for making questions of this kind ; as well as affording useful statistical information.

In teaching them superficial and solid measure the following mode is adopted :—

They are first shown, by means of the black board, what a square inch, foot, yard, etc., is, by proofs which meet the eye ; that a square of two inches on a side contains four square inches; of three inches on a side, nine square inches, and so on ; or, in other words, that a square of one inch on a side, could be so placed on a square of two inches, as to occupy different ground four times, and in doing this it would have occupied the whole square, one of three inches, nine times : thus showing clearly what is meant by a surface containing a certain number of square feet, etc.

The same illustration with an oblong, say nine inches by two, three, etc., two or three drawings or diagrams of figures so divided are painted on the walls.

Solid Measure.

The teacher takes a cube of four inches on a side, divided into four slices of one inch thick, and one of the surfaces divided into sixteen superficial inches ; to this slice of one inch thick, containing sixteen solid inches, add a second, that will make 32, and so to the fourth, making 64 ; so that they now have ocular proof so simple, that they must understand ; that the superficial inches in a square, or rectangle, is found by multiplying together the number in each side ; the contents of a regular cube by multiplying the number of linear inches on one side by the number of slices.

To apply this:

The master tells one of the boys to take the two-foot rule (a necessary thing in a village school), measure the length and breadth of the schoolroom. Yes, sir.

Length 26 feet, breadth 16 feet. What is the figure? An oblong—sides at right angles to each other. Multiply length and breadth—what is the area?

To another—Look at the boards of the floor; are they uniform in width? How are they laid? Parallel to each other. The breadth of the room you have got, and, as the boards are laid that way, you have the length of each board; measure the width of a board. Nine inches. Reckon the number of boards. What is the area of the room? Does it agree with your first measurement? If not, what is the source of error; the boards will turn out to be unequal in width.

The door—what is the shape of the opening? An oblong, with one side a good deal longer than the other. Measure the height—the width: now what number of inches of surface on the door?

The rule again. Measure the thickness. Now how many solid inches?

The door-posts. Measure the height, width; now the depth. How many solid inches of wood in one post? How many in the whole door-posts? How many solid inches in a foot? Turn it into feet.

In the same way they may apply the rule to find out the surface of a table, a sheet of paper, surface of a map, a page of a book, etc., but always making them do the actual measurement, first taking one child, then another.

Again the room—we have got the area—tell us how much water it would hold, if we could fill it as high as the walls; we have got two dimensions, what is wanting?—The height. We cannot reach up, sir.—Take your rule. Measure the thickness of a brick with the mortar.—About four inches.—Measure the first three courses.—A foot, sir. —Reckon the courses of the wall.—Thirty-six.—Then the height is what?—Twelve feet. Now find out the solid contents of the room.

Find the surface and solid contents of a brick.

In fact, the two-foot rule is to the village school what Liebig says the balance is to the chemist.

Another practical application, which works well in giving fixed ideas of linear measure, is the following :

Take a hoop, say of two feet diameter ; apply a string to the circumference; measure it.—Rather over six feet.— Another of three will be found to be nine, and by a sort of inductive process, you prove that the circumference is three times the diameter : when farther advanced, give them the exact ratio, 3·14159, which they will work from with great facility.

Boys ! make a mark on the hoop : let it rest on the floor, the mark being directly opposite the point which touches the floor ;* trundle it stopping every time when the mark rests upon the floor, and let another boy make a chalk mark where it touches ; now take your *two-foot rule* and measure between each mark.   What is it ?—Six feet, twelve feet, eighteen feet, etc.—And the hoop has been round how many times at each mark ?   One at the first, twice at the second, three times at the third, etc.—Now, you see, if you trundle your hoop over a piece of level ground, and reckon the number of times it has gone round, you can tell the length of space it has gone over.

How many miles to Winchester ?—Nine, sir.—Measure the height of your father's cart-wheel, and tell him how often it will go round in going to market.   Tell him he must not zigzag.   The teacher should point out the sources of error.   The philosophy of common life and every-day things is most attractive to children, and a book of this kind, if well done, would be a most useful one for our village schools.

This two-foot rule, and other appliances, setting to work both hands and head amuses, at the same time that it instructs, and gives a sort of certainty to their knowledge,

* The teacher who has sufficient mathematical knowledge, may exercise himself in trying to make out the nature of the curve traced out by any given point in the surface of the hoop, between two successive contacts with the floor.   A curve of very curious properties, which interested mathematicians very much about 200 years ago, and was made out by the famous Pascal when labouring under a fit of toothache, is the curve in which the pendulum keeping true time vibrates.

fixing it in a way that learning things by mere rote, never can.

In order that they may get correct ideas of what is meant by lines parallel and inclined to each other, and of a square, a circle, a triangle, etc., I have had painted on the upper part of the walls, above the maps, four series of simple figures, marked, Series A, No. 1, 2, 3, angles and triangles. Series B, No. 1, squares and parallelograms. Series C, circles, etc,, a square and a rectangular parallelogram, divided into linear inches. These figures are easily re-ferred to, extremely useful, occupying no space which is wanted for other things, and cost nothing.

Of the simple solids the school is also provided with models, and these, with the figures on the wall, may be called into use in almost numberless ways.

What is the shape of the room...of the door—of a brick —of a book—table, etc. ?—a square or parallelogram on Series B, No. 1, No. 2. Look at the beam running be-tween the walls, what are the figures of the two surfaces ? What of a section perpendicular to either surface ?—what slantwise ?

The stove in the room, what is its figure ?—A hollow cylinder.—The pipe carrying away the smoke ?—The same. —What would the figure of a section of the stove parallel to the floor be ?—of the pipe ?—A circle, No. 2, Series C. —What of a section perpendicular to the floor ? etc. The different sections of a cube—or any solids which may be about the room—but always referring to the exact figure on the wall. These figures will often supply the place of the black board.

Again, tell a boy to turn the door on its hinges as far as he can—to find out what solid it would trace out if he could turn it entirely round.—A cylinder like the stove, but much larger.—What is the section of the solid part of the stove ?—A ring inclosed between two concentric circles. —Concentric, what ?—If the door were a right-angled triangle, what figure would it generate by going quite round on the hinges ?—A cone, like a sugarloaf.—What if a semicircle, the line between the hinges the diameter ?— A globe : and so on. Then again, the outer edge of the door and a line parallel to it, at 2, 3, etc. inches apart, would trace out a solid ring. What would the door trace out, if, instead of revolving round its hinges, it revolved round one of its ends; and to illustrate this still further, fasten two pieces of string of unequal lengths to the top of a stick, which place perpendicular to the floor, then let two boys taking hold one at each end, walk round the stick, they will clearly see, that the finger of the short-stringed boy describes the inner surface, and of the long-stringed the outer surface—that every point in a circle is equally distant from the centre—explain what is meant by circles being in different planes—what by concentric circles—and then the teacher will ask them, if the strings were 2, 3, 4 feet, etc. long, what the circumference would be; at first some of them would say six feet, nine feet, etc., not seeing that their piece of string was the radius and not the diameter; difference to be pointed out, and that the circumferences of circles are in proportion to their diameters.

Here they may be shown that the area of a circle is the circumference $\times \dfrac{\text{radius}}{2}$ or the circumference $\times \dfrac{\text{diameter}}{4}$, and since 3·14159 is the circumference of a circle whose diameter is unity, $3·14159 \times \frac{1}{4} = ·78539$ is the area, and that the areas of circles are to each other as the squares of their diameters; this expression they can work with practically afterwards, in measuring timber, etc.

The contents of a cylinder :

The teacher should not be content with merely showing them how to find the contents of a cylinder, or any other regular figure, but should point out to them, in this case, for instance, anything in the room of a cylindrical form, such as the stove if round, the pipe which carries off the smoke, etc. ; and taking the diameter of a section, and from this finding the area of it, and multiplying into the height or length would give the solid contents : that for an iron roller, or any other roller hollow in the middle, they must take the diameter of the outer and inner surface, get the area of these sections, and subtracting them from each other, would give the area of a section or ring which, multiplied into the length of the roller, would give the quantity of solid matter in it; thus calling their attention, and actually measuring vessels, etc., the shape of which they are familiar with.

This, of course, applies to other regular solids than the cylinder.

In the case of the cylinder, let $d =$ the outer diameter, d' the inner, then

$(\cdot 78539) \, d^2 =$ area of outer circle,

$(\cdot 78539) \, d'^2 =$ area of inner circle;

and $(\cdot 78539) \, (d^2 - d'^2) =$ area of section of the ring;
and if h denote the height, the solid contents will be

$(\cdot 78539) \, (d^2 - d'^2) \, h$; then to give particular values to d, d' and h, and work out the results.

Examples for Practice.

A boy at the age of 15 begins to save $7\frac{1}{2}d.$ per week, what will he have saved at the end of one, two, three, etc. years.

What will his savings amount to when he reaches the age of twenty-one? And what would it be if put into the savings' bank at the end of each year, interest three per cent.

Supposing at the age of 21 he begins to save $1s.$ per week, and at the end of each year puts it into the bank, what would he have when he is 31 years of age?

Such questions ought to have their bearings and application to every-day life explained to the children.

A goes to the village shop and lays out $10s.$ per week on an average, for necessaries for his family, every week in the year; but, for want of thought and of understanding his own interests, has got into the habit of running a bill, and having his things booked, as it is called; for this the shopkeeper is obliged to charge 10 per cent. more than for ready money. How much does A lose by this in the year? —or how much more does he pay than the ready-money customer?

Supposing the whole expenditure of a parish in rates to be £920 10s. in the year, and the whole property rated at £5276 9s. 4d., what is that in the pound?

Supposing the number of acres in the parish to be 7000, what would that be per acre?

A spends £250 10*s*. 6*d*. per annum; of this 3*s*. in the pound is paid for house rent, 9*s*. 8*d*. in food, 3*s*. 4*d*. in clothing, the rest in sundries; how much in the pound is paid in sundries; and what is his absolute expenditure in each of the above things?

Supposing him to save £80 per annum out of the above income, and his proportionate expenditure in each article as above, what would be the sum spent for each?

The whole amount of taxation in this country is upwards of 50 millions, supposing it is this sum, and that every twenty shillings paid in taxes is disposed of as follows:

	s.	*d.*
Expenses of the army and navy...................	7	2
King's judges, etc., and other departments of state..	0	10
Interest of the national debt	12	0

What is the exact sum paid to each?

What would be the expense of digging three acres, two roods, and 20 perches of ground at 4*d*. per pole? What of double trenching it for the purpose of planting, at 10*d*. per pole?

How many trees to plant an acre at such and such distances, etc.?

A pole or perch of land is 16½ feet square, the usual measure, but here they have a measure for underwood called wood measure, a pole of which is 18 feet square. How much is the wood-acre larger than the ordinary acre?

A labourer agrees to move a piece of earth 25 feet long, 15 feet wide, and 10 feet high, a certain distance at 1*s*. 6*d*. per cubic yard, what would his work come to?

A pair of horses plough ¾ of an acre in one day, the width of each furrow is one foot. How many miles will the boy walk who drives the plough?

Supposing the furrows were only nine inches or six inches broad, how far would he have to walk? Work this out, and reduce the difference into yards.

A window is five feet nine inches high, four feet six inches broad. How many square feet of glass for a house of ten windows.

How many panes, each nine inches by twelve inches, and what would the cost be at   per foot.

The following extract from " An Educational Tour in

Germany," etc. affords a very useful and practical hint to the schoolmaster:

"*In Holland I saw what I have never seen elsewhere, but that which ought to be in every school—the actual weights and measures of the country.* These were used not only as a means of conveying useful knowledge, but of mental exercise and cultivation.

"There were seven different liquid measures, graduated according to the standard measures of the kingdom. The teacher took one in his hand, held it up before the class, and displayed it in all its dimensions. Sometimes he would allow it to be passed along by the members of the class, that each one might have an opportunity to handle it, and to form an idea of its capacity. Then he would take another, and either tell the class how many measures of one kind would be equivalent to one measure of the other, or, if he thought them prepared for the question, he would obtain their judgment upon the relative capacity of the respective measures. In this way he would go through with the whole series, referring from one to another, until all had been examined, and their relative capacities understood. Then followed arithmetical questions, founded upon the facts they had learned,—such as, if one measure full of anything costs so much, what would another measure full (designating the measure) cost, or seven other measures full? The same thing was then done with the weights.

"In the public schools of Holland, too, large sheets or cards were hung upon the walls of the room, containing fac-similes of the inscription and relief—face and reverse —of all the current coins of the kingdom. The representatives of gold coins were yellow, of the silver white, and of the copper, copper colour."—Mann's "*Educational Tour*," with Preface by W. B. Hodgson, LL.D.

GEOMETRY.

A knowledge of some of the more simple parts of geometry is quite necessary for any schoolmaster who wishes to be thought competent to his work, or to stand in what may be looked upon as the first class of teachers in our elementary schools. For this purpose, it is highly desirable that they should at least know so much of the subject, as would enable them to teach the first three books of Euclid, with a few propositions out of the other books. Many of the propositions in the first three books are of easy application to the mechanic arts; particularly to the carpenter's shop, to the principles of land-measuring, etc, and an edition of these, pointing out such propositions and their application, with a few practical deductions, would be of great use in our elementary schools.

There are many of the appliances of the carpenter with his tools, and of other mechanic trades, so strictly geometrical and so easy of proof, as to be easily learned, and the workman who knows them, instead of being a machine, becomes an intelligent being, and has sources of enjoyment opened out to him, which many of them would turn to a good purpose.

Even a knowledge of the axioms of Euclid, such as "things which are equal to the same thing, are equal to one another."

"If equals be added to equals the wholes are equal."

"If equals be added to unequals, the wholes are unequal," etc., suggest modes of reasoning, which are extremely useful ; and a thorough knowledge of the kind of reasoning in the propositions of the three books, gives a man a habit and a power of drawing proper conclusions from given data, which he would scarcely be able to acquire with so little trouble, in any other way.

Children may easily be made to understand what is meant by the terms perpendicular, horizontal, right angle, and lines parallel to each other, by referring to the things in the room.

Thus the walls are perpendicular, or at right angles to the floor—the boards are horizontal and parallel to each other—the courses of bricks are parallel—the door-posts perpendicular to the floor, etc. ; the beams, rafters, etc., of the roof, all might be referred to as illustrating things of this kind.

The way in which the circle is divided ought to be under

stood; the number of degrees in a quadrant, etc.; that the three angles of a triangle are equal to two right angles; and therefore if a triangle is right-angled, or has one right angle, the remaining two must be equal to a right angle.

The proposition that if two sides of a triangle are equal, the angles opposite are equal, and the converse.

To bisect a given rectilineal angle.

The following is a very interesting and useful application of this proposition in showing how a meridian line may be laid down by it:

Tell the boys to stick in the ground, and in the direction of the plumb-line, a straight rod, to observe and mark out the direction and length of its shadow on a sunny morning before twelve o'clock, say at eleven : to observe in the afternoon when the shadow has exactly the same length; join the two extremities of the shadows, and on the line which joins them, which is the base of an isosceles triangle, describe an equilateral triangle; a line drawn from the point where the staff goes into the ground to the vertex of this triangle will be the true meridian, or by simply drawing a line from the stick to the middle of the line joining the extremities of the shadows.

Place the compass on the line, and let them observe how much the two meridians differ : that the length of the shadow, at equal intervals from noon, will be the same both in the morning and in the afternoon, etc.

To draw a perpendicular from a given point in a line, or let one fall on a line from a point without it.

The one, that either of two exterior angles is greater than the interior and opposite angle—showing from this, how the angle under which an object is seen, diminishes as you recede from, and increases as you advance towards it.

The proposition about the areas of triangles and parallelograms, as applying to the superficial measurement of rectilineal figures.

The 47th in the first book, that the square of the side opposite the right angle is equal to the sum of the squares on the other two sides. All these from the first book are particularly of practical application.

It will be found very useful for fixing on their minds any particular geometrical truth likely to be of use to them afterwards, if the teacher tests it by application to actual measurement, and not to rest satisfied with proving it merely as an abstract truth; for instance, in this school-room there is a black line, marked on two adjoining walls, about a foot from the floor; as the walls are at right angles to each other, of course these lines are also; they are divided into feet and divisions of a foot, numbered from the corner or right angle, then taking any point in each of these lines, and joining them by a string, this forms a right-angled triangle. The boys have learned that the sum of the squares of the two sides containing the right angle is equal to the square on the third side, the teacher will tell them, for instance, to draw a line between the point marked six feet on the one and eight feet on the other; square each number, add them together, and extract the square root, which they find to be 10; then they apply the foot-rule—measure the string, and find it exactly ten feet by measurement.

Again, draw the line between the point marked five feet on one and seven on the other : work it out, and they get a result 8·6 feet; the teacher would ask, is ·6 half an inch or more ?—More by a tenth.—They then measure the piece of string which reached between the extreme points, and find it perfectly correct.

The teacher would then point out that this would always be the case when the walls stand at right angles to each other. The bricklayer knows this, and, laying out his foundation walls, measures eight feet along one line, and six along the other, from the same corner; he then places a ten foot rod between the extreme points, and if it *exactly* reaches, he is satisfied his walls are square.

Through the middle of the line on the end wall a vertical line is drawn, and divided in the same way, and higher up on the wall are marked three parallel lines ‗‗‗‗‗ an inch, a foot and a yard in length; these are very convenient to refer to as a sort of standard of measure, and to show what multiple of an inch, a foot, a yard, etc., any lengths of the other lines are.

It is recorded, that in the time of Henry the First, the length of the king's arm was the standard yard : this gives an idea of the rudeness of the age.

A teacher with a little knowledge of geometry will see numberless ways in which these lines may be made useful. I feel a difficulty in entering further into this without having recourse to diagrams, which in the printing of this book I did not contemplate.

The following occur to me as simple :—Tell a boy to measure the width of the door and its height; now what length of string will it take to reach between opposite corners ? work it out : then to take a piece of string and measure,—they correspond ; the same for his book, slate, a table, etc. Measure the two sides of the room—find the line which would reach from corner to corner.

Again, let one of the boys hold the string against a fixed point in the upright wall, say four feet high, and another extend it to any point towards the middle of the floor—they see this forms a right-angled triangle ; another boy takes the rule, measures from the point where the string touches the floor to the base of the black line, taking this as one side, the height four feet as the other, they work it out, and then measure as before. This testing of theory by practice, gives them a great interest in what they are doing.

As an example of the carpenter applying a proposition in Euclid, take this :—

Not having his square at hand, he wishes to draw one chalk line at right angles to another, from a given point in it.

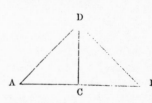

From C in the straight line AB he marks off with his compasses on each side of it, CA and CB, equal to each other, he then places his rule in the direction, CD, as nearly perpendicular as he can guess, and draws a line, CD, along it ; from the point D he stretches a string to A, and if turning it on D he finds the same length exactly to reach to B, CD is at right angles to AB.

If he wanted to fix a piece of wood CD in AB, and at right angles to it, he would of course measure in the same way ; if AD were longer than DB, he would lean it towards

A until they were equal, if shorter he would have to move it in the contrary direction.

If he take his square, and place one side on the line AC, the other will fall in a direction perpendicular to it, and he could run his chalk line along the edge.

The teacher would also point out, that when the lines are perpendicular, the angles ACD DCB are equal; that if CD lean more towards A than towards B, the angle ACD will be less than DCB, etc.

Again, another very easy application of a simple proposition in the first book, to show that if AB is a straight line,

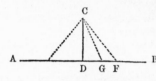

from C a point without it, the perpendicular CD is the shortest line from C to D; any other line CF, CG, etc. would be greater than CD, as being opposite to the greater angle in the same triangle, and although every successive line CF, CG, keeps lessening as it gets nearer to D, yet at D it is least, and and when it passes through that point, the length of a line from C to any point in AD goes on increasing as that points gets farther from D. It will easily be seen on what proposition in Euclid these remarks depend, and the young schoolmaster may profit by them, and apply other propositions in the same way.

Take this as a case where the eye may be made to help

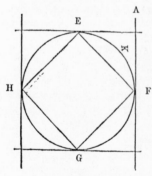

the mind; take a square thin piece of deal, say one foot on a side, and a circle of the same one foot in diameter : place the circle on the square so that it becomes inscribed on it, the figure will be this. They see clearly that the difference between the area of the square and the inscribed circle is the sum of the four irregular corners AEKF, etc., contained between the sides of a triangle and the arc in each case.

Find this difference, divide it by four; that will give any one corner AEKF: then inscribe a square in the circle: the difference between this and the first square will be the four triangles AEF, etc., and which will be found equal to the inscribed square FEHG. Dividing by four will give one of the triangles.

Let the side of the square $= a$, which will also be the diameter of the circle :

Then the area of the square will $= a^2$,

area of the circle $= (3 \cdot 14159)\dfrac{a^2}{4}$; $\left(\begin{array}{l}3 \cdot 14159 \text{ being the area} \\ \text{of a circle, radius 1.}\end{array}\right)$

$$= (\cdot 78539)\ a^2,$$

$\therefore$ the area of the four corners, FBEG, etc.,

$$= a^2\ (-\cdot 78539),$$
$$= a^2\ (\cdot 21461);$$

and area of one of them $= (\cdot 051365)\ a^2$.

Again, $\mathrm{EF}^2 = \mathrm{AE}^2 + \mathrm{AF}^2 = \dfrac{a^2}{4} + \dfrac{a^2}{4} = \dfrac{a^2}{4}$, which is the area of the inscribed square, and is one half of (a^2), the circumscribing one; and any one of the triangles AEF will $= \dfrac{a^2}{8}$.

Again the area of the triangle $\mathrm{AFG} = \dfrac{\mathrm{AE.AF}}{2} = \dfrac{a^2}{2} \times \dfrac{a^2}{2}$, and this divided by two, or $\dfrac{a^2}{8}$, as by the other method.

These are given merely because of the pieces of wood making visible what is to be done.

The following, offers a practical application of the 47th and other propositions in the first book of Euclid.

Imagine a line drawn from the eye of the spectator to the top of a tower, or of any other object standing on a plain, and at right angles to it, and another from the same point parallel to the horizon, making an angle of 45°; then the height of the tower above the level of the eye is equal to the distance at which the observer is standing from the base; adding to this the height of the eye, would give the height of the object above the surface of the ground; if, when the observer takes his station, the angle is above 45°, he must recede from the tower—if less, he must advance— bringing to bear upon this the proposition "that the exterior angle of a triangle is greater than the interior and opposite." An approximation to accuracy in observing an angle of this kind may be made by making a sort of quadrant out of a piece of deal; holding one side horizontal, and looking along a line drawn from the centre through the middle of the arc.

At all events, this is sufficient to make boys understand the theory of it, and the object of this is obvious to make them reason, that—

If one angle of a triangle is a right angle, the other two taken together must be a right angle, because the angles of a triangle are 180°, or two right angles; if one of the two is 45°, or half a right angle, the remaining one must be the same—as the angles are equal the sides are equal.

A stick 5 feet 3 inches high is placed vertically at the equator, what is the figure traced out by its shadow during the 12 hours the sun is above the horizon? What is the length of the shadow, and of a line joining the top of the stick and the extremity of the shadow, when the sun's altitude is 45° and 60°? Work out the result in the latter case to four places of decimals.

The particular propositions bearing upon this, the teacher will easily see.

In teaching them land-measuring, they should be made to understand on what principle it is that they reduce any field complicated in shape to triangles, squares, and parallelograms; why they make their offsets at right angles to the line in which they are measuring; to be able to prove the propositions in Euclid as to the areas of these figures, etc.; that a triangle is half the parallelogram on the same base and altitude, etc., and not to do everything mechanically, without ever dreaming of the principles on which these measurements and calculations are made.

Some time ago the observation was made to me, arising out of some boys having been seen to attempt carrying the

above into practice : " Well, the worst thing I have heard
of you lately is, that you are having trigonometry taught
to the boys in the Somborne School."

This odd sort of compliment has often come across me,
not knowing exactly what it could mean. I suppose those
who make such observations, do not mean that there is any
thing positively wrong in teaching *trigonometry ;* but that
it is wrong to teach it to that class of boys usually attending our parish schools. Now, one of the leading features
of the school here, and in my opinion, one of the most important, is, that it unites in education the children of the
employer with those of the employed ; and that to many
children of the former class the elements of this subject
may be most usefully taught, as applying to practical purposes connected with their after-life.

However, I have myself no objection that this or any
other *ometry,* a knowledge of which may be likely to advance
the interest and the civilization of mankind, half as much
as trigonometry does, should be taught to promising boys
in our parish schools, whose parents have been able to
keep them there to a sufficient age, and who have acquirements enabling them to learn it—these will be exceptions,
and not the rule.

But why among the words, supposed to be of suspicious
termination, attack the *ometries ?* they, of all others, are the
most harmless—dealing in weight and measure of an exact
quantitative kind ; so demonstratively true, that there is no
chance of getting wrong—no possibility of their being *anti-*
anything whatever. There may be something of wrong-
ness in some of the *ologies,* as they leave room for the
wanderings of fancy, and do not deal in measured quantity
as the *ometries* do. Here scientific men may, and perhaps
sometimes do, become bold and speculative to a degree
which may startle those of a more sober-minded temperament, and who have not paid attention to the subject on
which they treat ; still, I think we may rest satisfied that
where theories are advanced not based on truth, they will
be but short-lived, and not do much mischief in the end.

Surely these objectors do not consider themselves as
living in a railroad age—if they have ever travelled in the

heavy Falmouth mail of olden times (for the distance between that time and this is, in social improvement, as regards locomotion, not a part of a generation, but whole centuries)—or if they have ever gone between Paris and Geneva in a French diligence without stopping, let them call this to mind, and they will no longer object to trigonometry.

As an instance of the force of meaning in a word when it once gets good hold on the public mind—happening to go to a book sale in my own neighbourhood, where there was a copy of an early edition of the Encyclopedia Britannica, when it was placed on the table for sale, a man, employed by one of the booksellers in London, rather drily, perhaps cunningly, observed, — " Why, you won't find the word railroad in it." Not another word was said; but after that I observed there was not a bidder besides himself.

ELEMENTARY DRAWING.

This is a subject not mentioned in former editions of this work; but as it is most desirable it should be taught in our elementary schools, the following observations will, I trust, be useful to those for whom this book is intended :—

Hitherto drawing has been a branch of instruction mainly confined to schools for the upper classes, in which it has too often been loosely and inefficiently taught as an accomplishment merely—but there is no reason why it should not form a recognised and most useful part of the routine of instruction of every school. By the aid of the appliances and opportunities of instruction now offered by the Department of Science and Art, any teacher may make himself master of as much of the theory and practice of drawing as will enable him to impart an extent of knowledge in this direction, better digested and really greater in amount than has been hitherto, in nine cases out of ten, given in schools in which it has formed an expensive extra. Efficient examples and illustrative manuals, following each other in proper sequence, are now supplied, on well-devised terms, by the new department of the Board of Trade; and by the aid of these the study of drawing may, in almost every case, be introduced to a certain extent.

By the term *drawing*, however, we must, in the outset, clearly understand that the end of the study, as introduced into elementary schools, is not necessarily " fine art " in the production of pictorial manifestations. Drawing, strictly speaking, should be looked upon as a mechanical exercise, analogous in fact to writing, and regarded, if I may so express it, as *graphic language*—that as ideas are expressed by words or by writing, so they may be embodied by drawing.

It would be useless to enlarge on the utility of this study: every person must have experienced either the benefit, or the want, of a knowledge of drawing, at some period or other of his life. In many trades a proper grounding in this art will obviously make a man a more efficient workman, enabling him to perform various manipulations with greater certainty and quickness, and, consequently, to obtain higher wages. But even if, as in the majority of cases, its use is but to sharpen and improve the perceptive faculties generally, a great good will have resulted. In this sense it will do for the mechanical instrument of the will what logic does for the mind, teaching the hand and eye to work in unison with the judgment: and when these are thus trained to act together, the judgment itself is strengthened and a sense of power induced, giving increased certainty and command to all manual operations.

Our limits will not allow of as complete an illustration of drawing as could be wished, especially as there is a difficulty in the study in the necessity for explanatory engravings, of which the plan of this book will not admit. An abstract of the main features of the system promulgated by the Board of Trade may, however, be given, premising that it has evidently been an endeavour in framing the course to give it a thoroughly practical and unambiguous character, leaving nothing to the imagination, and providing full and complete appliances for every stage.

The Department divides the course of elementary drawing for common schools as follows :—

First stage—free hand outline-drawing from flat examples; second—rudiments of geometry as applied to drawing; third—drawing from solid models; fourth—theoretic perspective; fifth—advanced outline-drawing of ornament and the figure from flat examples and from casts in relief; sixth—shading; seventh—rudimentary instruction on the theory of colour.

The first, second, and third of these divisions may be taught in every school, and, by the help of the "Illustrative Manual" and examples, any schoolmaster may speedily qualify himself to commence the study. In the first stage, a set of twelve sheets of examples, containing a great variety of rectilinear and curved figures, is issued, accompanied by an illustrative manual, which minutely describes the method of procedure to be adopted in copying each figure. Nothing can be simpler and easier than this first step; the examples follow each other in due order, both of subject and relative difficulty, and have the great advantage, with respect to children, that each figure is a representation of some known object, thereby awakening and keeping alive the interest of the scholar, in a much more effective manner than would be the case if mere abstractions were placed before him. At the same time the objects chosen are such as are either quite flat, or at least do not obviously require the aid of perspective for their correct delineation, it being thought advisable to separate, as far as possible, the simple geometrical delineation of figures from that of solid bodies, to represent which properly would be impossible, at this early stage, the pupil as yet knowing nothing of those fundamental facts of perspective, a knowledge of which would be indispensable.

The examples are drawn on a large scale, so that they may be pinned up on a board before the entire class, and the pupils copy them first, with white chalk on a slate or black canvas, the latter being preferable, and afterwards on a smaller scale with lead pencil on paper. The first few copies chiefly consist of the right-lined letters of the alphabet, such as the letters I E H X V etc., the doubled lines of which, and the various angles, are useful exercises on parallels, vertical and horizontal lines, perpendiculars and angles. The various examples will be found, from the first, to suggest many useful geometrical definitions, of which the experienced teacher will know how to avail himself, and explain to his scholars.

The results, with pupils who have gone through this first stage, will be evident in the increased command of hand, which I have no doubt will be perceived in their simultaneously writing exercises—in a juster and more acute perception of the forms, proportions, and dimensions of all objects, whilst a certain facility in imitating natural objects will be the first evidence of, as we have before termed it, the new language acquired. At the conclusion of this stage, proper manuals and text books on *geometry*, in reference to drawing are provided; and the pupil after going through as much geometry as will at least enable him to understand the various terms and definitions, which occur in drawing and perspective, will next proceed to draw from *solid models* of simple geometrical forms. At this point of his studies, he enters upon perspective, the most obvious facts of which are, by model-drawing made familiar to him in an easy and insensible way—so that by degrees, almost as it were intuitively, he acquires such a knowledge and familiar habit of appreciating the various changes in the appearance of solid objects to the eye, that theoretic perspective, which will afterwards be an important consideration, is thereby rendered of easy comprehension. Model-drawing, hitherto frequently held up by its advocates as the sole method of judicious teaching, will be found, I believe, to occupy its proper position as an essential part of a complete system of instruction, not as hitherto, a substitute for all other modes.

The number of models used then has been very much reduced, they now consist of a few only of the most obvious and useful forms of lines and geometrical solids; such as a straight wire line, solid cube, pyramid, cylinder, sphere, wire circle, disk, cone, etc.: these with the stand and universal joint, proper for displaying them to the class, form a set of apparatus which may now be procured, at such a reasonable cost, as to be within the reach of the most humble means ;* whilst an accompanying manual, shortly to be issued by the Department, will afford the necessary assistance and information in putting them in use.

Having described the system thus far, I may here say, that to this extent drawing may certainly be taught, in ordinary schools, without the aid of a special master, for, as I have said before, there is nothing up to this point, that may not be speedily mastered by any person, who will devote some little time and attention to the subject : and it ought to be the case of every teacher in future, to master thoroughly these elements.

The succeeding stages touch more or less on the province of fine art, and will require in the teacher more decided special knowledge—to acquire which, time and study will be necessary : theoretic perspective, it is true, offers no great difficulty, it is a definite study which, by the aid of the necessary works, may soon be mastered in its broad features.

Free hand, drawing from *the round*, and shading, however, offer greater difficulties : these, to be effectually taught, will demand experience in the teacher, obtainable only by long practice. Here, however, the being in the possession of good copies and examples will be of great use, and at any rate beneficially supersede the random chance-medley copies, often far too elaborate and difficult, at which, we now so often see unfortunate children labouring with such ill-directed zeal. Besides, the examples in the advanced lists of the department of science and art being beautiful and interesting objects in themselves, will, when properly arranged and kept before the eyes of the pupils in their daily class-rooms, necessarily exert a most beneficial influence on them. Casts from beautiful antique works in sculpture, world-renowned works, for purposes of art as good as the originals in marble, cannot be made familiar

---

* Public schools may obtain complete sets of the solid models and accompanying stand from the department of science and art at half the cost price, by making proper application ; the cost being £1 13s.; the cost to ordinary schools being £3 12s. 6d.

as household objects to the young intelligence without powerfully manifesting their refining power, which is a virtual teaching.

Lastly (and very important), the subject of *colour* should be mooted in our schools, and will most appropriately form a part of all art-teaching. Children may soon be taught as much of the laws of colour, as will enable them to avoid those glaring errors which we every day see perpetrated by those who are ignorant of such elementary knowledge ; familiar demonstrations, assisted by collections of coloured papers and other aids, will soon render the subject quite familiar. A most excellent and useful little manual on this subject has been prepared for the Department by Richard Redgrave, Esq., R.A., and should be in the hands of every teacher : by the aid of this, and of the coloured diagrams issued along with it, all that is requisite may be accomplished.

From this short sketch of what is doing in the cause of elementary teaching in art by the Board of Trade, it will be seen, that the publications of that department will form the best possible texts in aid of drawing in all its branches; and the simple practical character which pervades all of them, will, I have no doubt, tend greatly to remove that feeling of uncertainty and dubiousness which has hitherto deterred numbers of intelligent teachers from introducing the study into their schools, though fully alive to its importance.

MECHANICS.

The teacher should understand the more simple properties of the mechanical powers, and if not equal to the mathematical proofs of them, he should be able to show their application in the tools they are in the habit of using, and in many other things of common life—such as the common steelyard—turning a grindstone—raising water from a well by means of a rope coiling round a cylinder, and the nature of the momentum of bodies—what is meant by the centre of gravity, etc. A skilful teacher, with models of the mechanical powers to assist him, will make this a subject of great interest. For instance, in the lever, assuming that the power multiplied by the distance from the fulcrum equals the weight multiplied by its distance, he might take a rod four feet in length and divide into feet and inches; at one end he fixes a weight, and placing the fulcrum at different distances from the weight, shows how the theory and practice agree, by actually testing each particular case, showing that the calculated weight produces an equilibrium. This is a sort of proof by testing it in particular cases, and then by a process of induction assuming it to be generally true.

Then instance their own attempts at moving a block of wood or stone by means of a lever, placing the fulcrum as near the stone as they can, in order to gain power.

Boys balancing each other on a piece of wood over a gate, and adapting the length of the arms to their own weights.

Taking a spade, and supposing it to be pressed into the ground, and pulling at the handle in a direction perpendicular to it, the teacher asks where the fulcrum is—points out it must be the surface of the ground—the arm the power—the earth pressing against the spade the weight. Show if the power (the man's arm) is exerted at an acute angle with the handle, power is lost, part of it being employed in forcing the spade deeper into the ground ; if at an obtuse angle with the handle, or an acute angle with the handle produced, power is again lost, part of it being employed in dragging the spade out of the ground ; that pressing on the handle at a right angle is to work at the greatest advantage : this they perfectly feel from their own experience ; also the necessity of having the spade of a substance specifically heavier than the handle.

The poker in stirring the fire—a pronged hammer in drawing a nail (the teacher drawing one) — the axe when they place it in a cleft of wood edgewise, and press upon the handle to make the opening larger— a pair of scales, the steelyard—drawing water from a well by means of the windlass — the pump-handle, scissors, etc.

The knife — the blow of an axe in cutting down' a tree—the coulter of the plough, etc. belonging to the wedge.

In the same way on the inclined plane when the power acts parallel to the plane, and taking for granted that the power is to the weight as the height of the plane to the length, or $P : W : : H : L$; any three of which quantities being given, the fourth may be found.

Then, for instance, knowing the height of the plane and its length, with a given power they will calculate what weight can be raised, or for a given weight what power must be applied.

It is in working formula of this kind, where a little algebra is required, and this with a knowledge of a few elementary propositions in geometry, which the boys who remain longest at school are getting here, that gives a practical usefulness to their education, which is of great value.

The teacher should point out what an immense addition to human power all these mechanical appliances are, and besides these, others of a more striking kind, such as wind, water, steam, etc.

On this subject, the following, taken from Babbage on the " Economy of Machinery," and given as an experiment related by M. Rondelet, " Sur l'Art de Bâtir," offers considerable instruction. A block of squared stone was taken for the subject of experiment :

	lbs.
1. Weight of stone	1080
2. In order to drag this stone along the floor of the quarry, roughly chiselled, it required a force equal to	758
3. The stone dragged over floor of planks required	652
4. The same stone placed on a platform of wood, and dragged over a floor of planks required	606
5. After soaping the two surfaces of wood, which slid over each other, it required	182
6. The same stone was now placed upon rollers of three inches diameter, when it required to put it in motion along the floor of the quarry	34
7. To drag it by these rollers over a wooden floor	28
8. When the stone was mounted on a wooden platform, and the same rollers placed between that and a plank floor, it required	22

From this experiment it results that the force necessary to move a stone along

	Part of its weight.
The rough chiselled floor of its quarry is nearly	$\frac{2}{3}$
Along a wooden floor	$\frac{3}{5}$
By wood upon wood....................................	$\frac{5}{9}$
If the wooden surfaces are soaped	$\frac{1}{6}$
With rollers on the floor of the quarry	$\frac{1}{32}$
On rollers on wood....................................	$\frac{1}{40}$
On rollers between wood	$\frac{1}{50}$

From a simple inspection of these figures it will appear how much human labour is diminished at each succeeding step, and how much is due to the man who thought of the grease.

Care should be taken in introductory books containing formula to work from, the proofs of which the teacher perhaps does not understand, that the expressions are correct. I am led to make this observation from the following circumstance : when I first introduced this working from formulæ in the school here, I happened to go in one day when the boys were working out practical results between the power and weight of an inclined plane ; this they were doing by taking the power to the weight, as the height of the plane to the length of the base, in the case of the power acting parallel to the plane; I was at a loss to conceive why master, boys, etc. should look so confident, even after I had pointed out to them the absurdity it led to in a particular case, instancing that if P : W : : H : length of the base,

and $P = W . \dfrac{H}{\text{length of base}}$, when the base became nothing

and the plane vertical, the power, instead of being equal to the weight, became infinite, the expression becoming $W . \dfrac{H}{0}$;

but taking it as the length of the plane, when the plane was vertical, L and H were equal, and the expression $P = W . \dfrac{H}{\text{length of plane}}$ would become $P + W . \dfrac{H}{H} - W.$

as it ought to be.

This I found arose from their having been reading a lesson on the inclined plane; and the error was, in the formula given in the note to the lesson : the confidence of the boys in the authority of the book, made it rather amusing to observe the shyness with which at first they received my explanation.

The great art in teaching children is not in talking only, but in practically illustrating what is taught; for instance, in speaking of the centre of gravity of a body, and merely saying it was that point at which, if supported, the body itself would be supported, might scarcely be intelligible to them ; but showing them that a regular figure, like one of their slates, would balance itself on a line running down the middle, the lengthway of the slate, and then again on another through the middle of that, and at right angles to it, they see, as the centre of gravity is in both lines, it must be where they cross ; and accordingly if this point be supported the body will be at rest—this they understand.

Again, balance a triangle of uniform density on a line drawn from one of its angles to the middle of the opposite side—the centre of gravity will be on that line—balance it again on a line drawn in the same way from one of the other angles—the centre of gravity of the body will be in the intersection of these two lines.

In the same way methods of finding the centre of gravity of other regular figures mechanically might be pointed out.

The teacher should also make himself acquainted with the theory of bodies falling by the force of gravity—that it acts separately and equally on every particle of matter without regard to the nature of the body—that all bodies of whatever kind, or whatever be their masses, must move through equal spaces in the same time. This, no doubt, is contrary to common experience—bodies, such as feathers, etc., and what are called light substances, not falling so rapidly as heavy masses—smoke, vapour, balloons, etc., ascending ; all this to be accounted for from the resistance of the atmosphere.

The spaces described by a falling body being as the squares of the times—that if it describes $16\frac{1}{12}$ feet in one second, in 2, 3, 4, etc. seconds it will describe 4, 9, 16, etc., multiplied into $16\frac{1}{12}$.

To show that while the spaces described in one, two, three, etc. seconds are as the numbers 1, 4, 9, 16, etc., those actually described in the second, third, fourth, etc., successive seconds are as the odd numbers 3, 5, 7, 9, etc., showing very strikingly the accelerated motion of a falling body.

To apply this also to the ascent of bodies projected directly upwards, with a given velocity.

Again, the moving force of bodies being equal to the mass multiplied into the velocity : How a small body, moving with a great velocity, may produce the same effect as a large body with a small one—as a small shot killing a bird—a large weight crushing it to death.

Interesting observations of a simple kind might be made on the strength of timber—weights suspended on beams between supports, such as the walls of a building—these coming under the principle of the lever, etc.; also such simple things as the following might be asked : Why is it easier to break a two-foot rule flatwise than edgewise ; and why joists are now always made thin and laid edgewise ?— which our forefathers did not understand. Although the reasons are sufficiently simple, very few even amongst the tolerably well educated can give a satisfactory explanation of them. The usual answer, that " it breaks more easily because it is thinner" will not do.

Wood, and all fibrous matter, is much stronger in the direction of the fibre than across it, and the strength varies as the square of the dimensions in direction of the pressure, multiplied into the dimensions transverse to it, when the length is given, or generally as the $\dfrac{\text{breadth} \times \text{depth}^2}{\text{length}}$.

It is a curious fact, but completely proved by experiment, that hollow tubes are stronger than solid ones of the same quantity of material—how beautiful this provision of Nature, as shown in the structure of the bones of animals, more particularly in those of birds and the larger quadrupeds, giving them the greatest strength, and encumbering them with the least possible weight.

As a means of testing with accuracy and of forming some definite idea of the strength of the hollow stems of plants, etc., the following simple experiment, which I witnessed, by the late Professor Cowper, of King's College, London, is very instructive :

He placed a length of one inch of wheat straw in a vertical position in a hole bored in the lower of two parallel boards, held together by a hinge of the same height, one inch, and then brought down the upper board upon it. This he loaded with a load of sixteen pounds, without any appearance of breaking, and stated that he had known a straw bear as much as 35 lbs. placed in this position, before it broke.

NATURAL PHILOSOPHY.

Nature herself seems to give a very instructive hint on this part of education, in the amusements of early childhood. We see a child as soon as it can use its hands, trying to move, or to lift anything which it can, placing it first in one position, then in another, and trying it in all the various ways which its senses admit of—in fact, making a variety of experiments with it, and this is generally looked upon as a mere amusement: but children when thus employed, are, as has been observed by Dr. Reid, " acquiring the habits of observation, and by merely indulging an undetermined curiosity, are making themselves acquainted with surrounding objects. If some new effect occurs from any of their little plays, they are eager to repeat it. When a child has for the first time thrown down a spoon from the table, and is pleased with the jingling noise upon the floor, if another or the same is again given to him, he is sure to throw it down, expecting the same noise to occur ; but if a piece of wood is given, he very soon finds out that the same effect does not take place, and is no longer anxious to repeat the experiment. So long as the noise goes on, the child has pleasure in repeating it, and if two objects are given, one of which produces a noise when thrown down in this way, and the other not, he very soon finds out the difference, and acts accordingly, and this is, in fact, the method of induction. The child is thoroughly persuaded that a jingling noise is sure to follow his throwing down the spoon, and goes on repeating it till he is tired.''

'' Such,'' observes the same philosopher, '' is the education of kind Nature, who, from the beginning to the end of our lives, makes the play of her scholars their most instructive lessons, and has implanted in our mind the curiosity and the inductive propensity by which we are enabled and disposed to learn them.''

It is an observation of the late Professor Daniel, in some of his works, '' that the principles of natural philosophy are the principles of common sense,'' and from my own experience here in introducing this kind of teaching into the school, I am confident that, with those who have been able to remain to an age to profit from it, it has given an interest in what they are learning, and a kind of practical character to it, which no other teaching could give.

I recollect many years ago, going into a school in Germany, and a German gentleman with whom I was, observed of something they were teaching, '' das ist kein practicables ding,'' that is no practicable thing—the impression made at the time has remained on my mind ever since. We look upon the Germans, as a people fond of theories, but this appeared to me a sensible remark.

The following hints are intended to show to our schoolmasters, of the class for which this book is intended, the importance of being so far instructed in subjects of this nature ; as to be able to point out in a common-sense way, some of those results in science which bear more immediately on the occupations of life ; these will be found not only interesting and instructive to the children while at school, but may be most useful to them after they have left it.

As a class, no doubt at the present day the far greater number of our schoolmasters are not qualified to give this instruction, but there are many, and that number, I hope, increasing, who are;—to such, although the following pages may not add much to their knowledge, they may perhaps suggest something in the way of imparting it, and in bringing it to bear upon their teaching. They will also point

out to others some things with which they may easily make
themselves acquainted, and a few simple experiments which
are easily tried.

Among the more striking of these things will be such as
the following : the elastic and other properties of air—the
nature of aeriform fluids—of water—how the pressure of
fluid bodies differs from that of solids—how these properties enable man to turn them to useful purposes, such as
windmills, watermills, etc.

Civilized man is able to take advantage of these properties, and avail himself of them as motive powers in the
business of life ; the savage, on the contrary, observes the
trees torn up by the winds, stones and rubbish carried down
by mountain torrents, but is unable to turn this observation
to any useful purpose.

Archbishop Whately, in his ' Introductory Lectures on
Political Economy,' observes : " Many of the commonest
arts, which are the most universal among mankind, and
which appear the simplest, and require but a very humble
degree of intelligence for their exercise, are yet such that
we must suppose various accidents to have occurred, and to
have been noted—many observations to have been made
and combined—and many experiments to have been tried
—in order to their being originally invented.

" And the difficulty must have been much greater, before
the invention and the familiar use of writing had enabled
each generation to record for the use of the next, not only
its discoveries, but its observations and incomplete experiments. It has often occurred to me that the longevity of
the antediluvians may have been a special provision to meet
this difficulty in those early ages which most needed such
help. Even now that writing is in use, a single individual,
if he live long enough to follow up a train of experiments,
has a great advantage in respect of discoveries over a succession of individuals; because he will recollect, when the
occasion arises, many of his former observations, and of the
ideas that had occurred to his mind, which, at the time, he
had not thought worth recording. But previous to the use
of writing, the advantage of being able to combine in one's
own person the experience of several centuries, must have

been of immense importance; and it was an advantage which the circumstances of the case seemed to require."

And first, of the atmosphere—a sphere of air surrounding the earth—has substance and weight, but is invisible—elastic, can be squeezed into a less space by pressure—expands again when the pressure is removed—expands by heat and contracts by cold. This may easily be made intelligible to them in the following way :

Take a tumbler and invert it—or better, take a jar used for gases, with an air-tight stopper, and placing its mouth horizontally on the surface of the water, in a pneumatic trough, or in any vessel of sufficient depth, having a shelf for support, show them, by letting them feel it, the difficulty of pressing the jar down—it offers resistance—increase the pressure, the air occupies less and less space, but the water inside the glass does not rise so high as on the outside ;—difference owing to what ?—point out. Diminish the pressure, it again expands, showing its elasticity. Of course the attention of the children must be called to the surface o f he water inside and outside the jar.

Take out the stopper, the jar sinks by its own weight, proving clearly that the resistance was offered by the air.

Again, allow the jar to fill with water, put in the stopper, and raise the jar nearly to the surface of the water in the trough—explain why the column of water is supported, and would be supported if the jar were 33 feet high at the ordinary pressure of the atmosphere—take out the stopper, the water immediately falls ;—or while the column of water remains, show how the jar may be filled with air, by carrying down successive tumblers of it until the jar is filled.

From this, the method first used of taking down barrels of air into a diving-bell is easily understood.

Why is it necessary to have a vent-peg in a barrel—or how does it happen that the teapot sometimes will not pour ? etc.

Air expands by heat. Experiment: a half-blown bladder placed before the fire, the wrinkles disappear, the air expanding it; remove it, the air again contracts.

Place the same under the receiver of an air-pump, it expands from diminished pressure.

Air has weight. A bottle exhausted of the air is lighter

than when full—difference, the weight of a volume of air equal to the contents of the bottle—this means air at the ordinary temperature and pressure of the atmosphere—100 cubic inches dry pure air weigh 31·0117 grains, being for a cubic yard $4\frac{1}{2}$ oz. Balance the bottle when full of air at one end of the scale-beam; then take it off and exhaust it by means of the air-pump, and when again suspended, the other end of the beam will preponderate; restore the equilibrium by pieces of paper, etc.

Drinking through a straw. The teacher, taking a straw and a basin of water, shows them, if the mouth or orifice of the straw is not wholly immersed, or under water, the water will not rise ; wholly covered—when they begin to draw out the air the water immediately rises, and why ?— What takes place if a hole is made in it above the surface of the water ? Water does not rise.—What if you plunge it deeper, so that the hole made in the straw is below the surface ?—It immediately rises again.—Reasons for all this, which, if they comprehend, they will at once understand the barometer, and common pump.

A model in glass of a common pump will be found a very instructive piece of apparatus, and if fitted into a small glass cylinder which can be made air-tight at pleasure by means of a screw, it becomes a much more useful and perfect instrument for teachers, as the pump will work or not according as the vessel in which the water is, is made air-tight, or not air-tight.

Again, a piece of wet leather with a string attached, called a sucker ;—press it with the foot against a stone— remove the air between the leather and the stone,—leather, say a square piece three inches on a side, ought to support 9×15 pounds, only supports, say 80lbs.—reason why ? The vacuum not complete. Then take a circular piece, three inches diameter, let them find the area, and calculate how much it ought to support. This is the principle on which a fly is able to walk along a pane of glass, or across the ceiling.

The common syringe. The pop-gun they are in the habit of making out of a piece of the elder tree—how, by pressing down the rod, the elasticity of the air forces out the pellet at the other end ; when they cease to press the rod of it down, the elasticity of the air within forces it back.

A pair of common bellows. Show them the construction —the valve, or trap-door in the bottom board, opening only inwards—the bellows fill with air when the boards are separated—valve shuts down, and the air goes out at the nozzle when they are pressed together—will not work when turned upside down, why ?—the current of air makes the fire burn better ; the reasons for all this. The teacher should have a pair .of bellows, and show what takes place at each movement of the board, and let them handle them themselves.

The barometer. The teacher shows them the instrument, how constructed, and what it is for ;—pressure of the air supports a column of mercury about 30 inches—a column of water about 33 feet—the height of the column being less in proportion as the specific gravity of the fluid is greater—not so high if carried to the top of a mountain, and why ?—temperature at which water boils varies with the height of the barometer—boils at a less heat on the top of a mountain than at the bottom. The mode of ascertaining the height of mountains by means of the barometer. —Why this method is more to be relied on in tropical climates than in high latitudes, etc.

Pascal, in France, about the year 1647, was the first to make this experiment, which he did at the summit and foot of a mountain in Auvergne, called Le Puy-de-Dôme, the result of which led him to conclude that the air had weight. He also tried it at the top of several high towers, which convinced him of the weight of the atmosphere.

To register the daily altitudes of the barometer and the thermometer, would be a very useful exercise for the pupil-teacher—and in its bearings branches out into a great many things.

The principle of the common pump might now be explained — how the atmospheric pressure which supports the mercury enables them to pump up water — having a model of a pump, or even with paper and pasteboard, showing the kind of tubes and nature of the valves, this may be clearly explained—pointing out how the valves act at each separate movement up and down of piston-rod

—the limit to which water can be raised—the experiment of Torricelli, etc.

Supposing the atmospheric pressure about 15lbs. on the square inch—how much on five square inches?—how much on five inches square?—on a square three inches on a side:—on the surface of the floor or the table?—making them have recourse to the two-foot rule; pressure on the animal body: etc., and how counteracted. A fish under water has the pressure of the air, 15lb. on a square inch, besides the pressure from its depth in the water;—a basin of water with a live fish in it, when placed under the receiver of the air-pump and exhausted, the air-bladder expands, and the fish turns on its back.

Children may easily be made to understand that the atmosphere is an aeriform fluid surrounding the globe, acted on like other bodies by the force of gravity, consisting principally of two airs or gases, varying in weight, and partly of a third, heavier than either of the others, but if placed upon each other in the order of their specific gravities, the heaviest nearest the surface of the earth, next heaviest in the middle, and the lightest at the top, that they would not remain in this order of superposition, as, for instance, the three fluids, quicksilver, water and oil, would do; but the heavy one at the bottom would rise up and travel through the pores of the other, and the lighter one would descend, this being a property peculiar to bodies of this nature, and called the diffusion of gases. That, in addition to this, there is an atmosphere of vapour of water, arising from evaporation from the surface of the earth and of water, and which is in itself lighter than dry atmospheric air; a cubic inch of water at the common atmospheric pressure forming about 1700 cubic inches of vapour; therefore a cubic inch of vapour of water is about $\frac{1}{1700}$ of the weight of a cubic inch of water—a cubic inch of common atmospheric air about $\frac{1}{800}$.

Having called their attention to the fact that a substance lighter than water will, if plunged into it, rise to the top; that of two fluids the lighter will rest upon the heavier; arranging themselves according to their specific gravities—as water upon mercury—oil upon water—cream upon milk—they will easily understand why bodies lighter than air ascend in it, as the smoke from their chimneys—tell them to watch it, particularly on a still calm day—why it stands still and does not rise higher; the principle on which a balloon ascends, a soap-bubble, etc.

Again, why there is a draught up the chimney;—the air rarefied, how this takes place;—why a current of air under the door and towards the fire—and another perhaps out of the room at the top of the door?

The kind of resistance offered by the air to a falling body—this increases with the density—that, under the receiver of an air-pump, a guinea and a feather would fall at the same time.

As a simple experiment, showing the effect of rarefaction of air, the teacher might light a piece of paper, and while burning, place it in a teacup, and invert the cup in a saucer of water—the water will immediately be driven into the cup with a gurgling noise.

Again, in the practice which cooks have of putting an inverted teacup in a fruit pie, as they think with a view to prevent the syrup running over as the pie bakes, the air in the cup becomes rarefied, and is driven into the pie-dish, through the crust, into the atmosphere—when taken out of the oven it cools, the rarefied air in the cup is condensed, but as the mouth of the cup is surrounded with the juices of the pie, air cannot get into it, but it forces the liquid up.

The teacher explains why the resistance of the air in moving along is so little felt—some of the consequences of its being disturbed, and causes of its being put in motion—a breeze, a hurricane, etc.; he would also speak of the forces of these at different velocities—the force varying as the square of the velocity. This short table might be the subject of a lesson:

Velocity of the wind in miles per hour.	Perpendicular force on one square foot in pounds.	——
5	·123	Gentle wind.
10	·492	Brisk gale.
20	1·968	Very brisk.
40	7·872	High wind.
80	31·488	Hurricane.

It will be easy to calculate the force of the wind acting on a given surface, doing so in particular cases will be instructive.

Tell them they may form an idea of the velocity of wind, by watching the shadows of clouds, or the clouds themselves, and if ever they should travel by railroad on a sunny day, to observe the shadow of the train as it passes over one field after another, and from this they may form some idea of the speed at which they are travelling.

Air as a vehicle of sound.

A bell under the receiver of an air-pump when exhausted, is not heard.

Bodies which produce the sensation of sound on the ear are in a state of vibration, as in a bell—the running a wet finger along the rim of a common drinking-glass, etc.

Here having to do with the instruction of children engaged in country occupations, I have called their attention in this, as in other subjects, to things coming under their observation, in a way something like the following:

Did you ever observe a woodman cutting down a tree at a distance; you could see the hatchet fall, and some time after that the sound of the blow came to your ear. Do you know the reason?

Teacher. Light travels so fast that the time it is in coming from the hatchet to you is so small that it cannot be reckoned; so that when you see the hatchet fall, that is the instant the blow is given; but sound, coming at a very slow pace (1,142 feet in a second), takes as many seconds to get to your ear as when multipled by 1,142, would give the number of feet between you and the man cutting down the tree.

For instance, if it were 2″, his distance would be 1142 ft. × 2, if 3″, 1142 × 3, and so on.

Did you ever see a man firing a gun at a distance, and, after seeing the flash, wonder why you did not hear the sound, or that you were kept considering how long it would be before the sound came? Do you know the reason — can you explain it? Because sound lags behind, and the flash takes up no time in coming to the eye.

Supposing you were 5″ before you heard the sound after seeing the flash, how far would you be off?—5 × 1142; 6″, how far?—6 × 1142, and so on.

When we hear the Portsmouth guns here, if you could have seen the flash, do you think you could find out the distance betwixt this and Portsmouth?

Supposing a man was standing where you could see him a mile off, and you saw the flash of his gun, how long would it be before you heard the sound? A mile in feet divided by 1142 would give the number of seconds before I could hear the sound.

Teacher. How do you think the sound gets to your ear? The air in the gunpowder suddenly expands and disturbs the air immediately about it, or the hatchet causes a vibration or tremulous motion in the wood, which sets the air in motion all round about; and this makes a sort of circular wave, beginning from a point which gradually enlarges, one circle of the air of the atmosphere striking against another, until it reaches the ear, unless it meets with some hinderance in the way; just as when you throw a stone into a smooth pond, a wave, beginning from the stone spreads in every direction, until it reaches the bank. The air is as necessary to continue the sound up to your ear as the water is to make the wave come up to the bank.

Sound goes much quicker in water—nearly four times as quick as in air, and in solids from ten to twenty times quicker; so that if you splash in the water at one end of a pond, the fish would hear you much sooner than a boy standing at the opposite side would do.

Now, in order that you may understand how well solids convey sounds, the next time you see a solid log of deal, or timber not very knotty and broken in the grain, at the carpenter's shop, set one of the boys to scratch at one end of it, and the rest of you go and listen at the other. Try the same on a block of stone, marble, etc.

But perhaps this will amuse you more: when you see the kettle on the fire, and you cannot tell whether it boils or not, place one end of the poker on the lid, the other to your ear, and it will tell you. If you strike with a hammer on a solid wall at one end, and some of you go and fix your ears against the other, you will most likely hear the sound of the blow twice—the first going along the wall you may call the wall-wave (coming more quickly), the second, a little after, through the air, coming with the air-wave we have talked of before. Try if you can hear two reports of the same knock by tapping with a hammer at the end of a log of wood—one along the wood, the other along the air.

You have heard of the wild natives of America—when they think their enemies are near, they lie down on the ground, and, by applying their ears to it, they can judge of the distance, and hear sooner than through the air.

Did you ever hear what is called an echo?

Supposing you were to clap your hands violently together, that creates a wave in the air which carries the sound along with it; now, if this wave happens to meet with a wall or a rock, or any obstacle in its way, it is checked and beat back, and so brings the sound with it a second time to your ear; and again, after passing you, if it met with the same sort of obstacle on the other side, it would be sent back again, and so strike your ear in passing and repassing, losing a little every time until it entirely died away. This would be called an echo; people living in a flat country have not so many opportunities of observing it as those who inhabit a craggy and mountainous one.

Water—a fluid at the common temperature of the atmosphere. Have you ever seen it solid? In winter—in frost—it is then ice.—How high does the thermometer stand when water begins to freeze? 32°.—Look at the thermometer in the room, how high is it? 52°.—How many degrees above the freezing point?—Does it increase in volume when it becomes ice? Water from the temperature of about 39°, expands as it grows colder, and at 32°, when it becomes ice, expands so as to crack water-bottles, water-pipes; a piece of ice floats in water, part of it being above the surface; if it were of equal weight with the same volume of water, it would just sink so as to have no part above.—You should never let water stand in leaden pipes, or in vessels likely to be broken by its freezing in severe frosts. This expansion of water in becoming ice, how serviceable to the farmer, in some soils, in pulverizing and making them fit for vegetation — good for gardens, etc.

"That water contracts in reducing the temperature to about 40°, and below that again expands, is easily shown, by taking two equal thermometers, the one filled with water and the other with spirit; placing them in melting ice, the spirit one will gradually fall to the freezing point, but the other will fall to about 40°, and then begin to rise. By Act of Parliament the temperature at which the specific gravity of spirits is determined by the excise, and at which the standard weights and measures are adjusted, is 62° of Fahrenheit."—DANIEL's *Chemical Philosophy.*

Quicksilver, unlike water in this respect. contracts and becomes denser in becoming solid. It has been ascertained, by leaving it exposed to the cold in high latitudes, where it has assumed a solid form, and observing the temperature at which it begins to thaw, that the freezing point is about 40° below zero of Fahrenheit.

Attention may be called to the way in which the roads are raised up in winter by the freezing of the moisture within them—how after a thaw a loaded cart or waggon sinks in, causing deep ruts—how rocks and stone, which have absorbed much moisture, split after frost—parts of buildings peel off, etc.

Can water be made into a vapour — something you cannot see? By heat it becomes steam, thermometer 212° at the average pressure of the atmosphere; one inch of water makes about a cubic foot, 1728 inches, if further heated it exerts a greater pressure in trying to escape, pressing on the surface of the vessel in which it is. This is the property which makes it so serviceable to us in grinding our corn, moving the machinery for spinning and weaving, of steam-boats, etc., and as a motive power on our railroads, carrying us forty or fifty miles in an hour. If cooled below 212° it immediately falls back, shrinks up into one inch, and becomes visible water again, giving out a great deal of heat;—instance steam raising the kettle-lid.

Why does the teakettle, just before boiling, very often

force out a quantity of water from the spout? Because the air, driven from the water by heat, and the steam which is forming from the water, rise to the top, and the lid happening to be air-tight, it cannot escape, and being lighter than water it cannot descend, so the vapour or steam under the lid increases and expands, aud, pressing upon the surface of the water, forces it out at the pipe.— Did you ever see on a frosty day, when you were going with a team, what you call the breath of the horses, or your own breath? Yes, Sir.

Teacher. The warm air from the horses' mouths, or from your own mouth, containing vapour which you cannot see when the air has a certain degree of warmth in it, as soon as it comes in contact with the colder air gets cooled, and the steam or vapour becomes water (is what they call condensed), or perhaps watery vapour, which you can see, instead of a vapour which you could not see.

Did you ever see sugar or salt melted in water? No, Sir; but we have seen sugar in tea.—Then the teacher takes a small phial containing water, and puts in a certain quantity of salt, when entirely melted they see the fluid perfectly clear; increase the quantity beyond what the water will take up, this remains undissolved. If the temperature of the water were increased, it would take up more; in the same way the air will take up a greater quantity of vapour the warmer it is, and coming from the mouth warm, it holds more vapour than it is able to do, when it comes in contact with the cold air, and throws some of it down, so that you can see it; thus water on the inside of the window in frosty weather—dew on the outer surface of a bottle of cold water in hot weather, etc. —the quantity of watery vapour in the air in hot climates greater than in cold, hence torrents of rain when it is suddenly cooled, etc.

About London, latitude 51° 30', the average fall of rain in the year is about 23 inches; while in Rome, latitude 41° 54', it is 38 inches; at Calcutta, latitude 22° 34', it is 81 inches; and in climates like the West Indies upwards of 100 inches; but though the quantity of rain falling in hot countries is greater than in the temperate ones, the number of wet days is greater in the latter than in the former; there is more moisture in the air in our climate in summer than in winter; but from the greater temperature it is held up, and is not so sensible to us. By inches of rain is meant the depth at which it would stand on every square inch of surface on which it falls, supposing none to be absorbed by the soil or to evaporate.

Two fluids in the same vessel, one lighter than the other, which would get to the bottom ? The heavier one.—Give instances. Milk and cream, water and oil, quicksilver and water, water and air.

The teacher, holding up a glass : What is this glass full of ? Atmospheric air.—If I pour in water, what does that do ? Drives out the air, because it is the heavier fluid ?— If I pour quicksilver into a glass of water, what would take place ? The quicksilver would drive out the water for the same reason.—If water upon mercury, or oil upon water ? The water or oil, being the lighter fluids, would rest on the top, and the same thing would take place if carbonic acid or any gas heavier than air were poured in. —Another instance : fill a small phial with water, leaving room for a bubble of air, and then cork it ; holding it in a horizontal position the bubble rests in the middle, elevate one end, the bubble rises to the top ; show how this may be used as a spirit-level.

Look at that cubical vessel on the table, divided into two equal parts by a division in the middle. Suppose one division full of mercury, the other of water, and the partition suddenly withdrawn, what happens ? The mercury immediately covers the bottom of both parts, and the water rises to the top.

Take a bottle of water from a cool spring or from the pump ; place it in the sun or in a room—for instance, as you see it sometimes in a bedroom. You will observe air-bubbles form themselves on the surface of the glass—at the bottom and the sides—this is air contained in the water. As it takes the temperature of the room these air-bubbles form themselves, expand as they rise, come suddenly to the top, the water being of equal temperature throughout. Why does the bubble expand as it rises ?

The pressure upon its surface varies as the depth, and therefore the nearer the surface the less the pressure.

How is it, then, if you place water in an open saucepan on the fire to heat, we see at first bubbles form themselves at the bottom, like pieces of glass, rise up a little way, and then lost before coming to the surface?

The air in that part of the water in contact with the bottom of the saucepan, immediately it begins to feel additional warmth, forms a bubble, rises up a little way, and although the pressure is diminished, it becomes again compressed, in consequence of coming in contact with cooler water as it rises. This it is, I believe, which causes what is called the hissing of the kettle.

If you were to boil a quart of water until it has all, as you call it, boiled away, what has become of it?—All turned into steam.—If water with salt or chalk in it?— The water would go into vapour, and the chalk or salt be left behind, at the bottom of the kettle.

Did you ever see a white crust at the bottom of your tea-kettle? Yes, Sir; but we don't know what it is.— Don't you know we live upon what is called a chalk soil here, and the rain that falls makes its way through the chalk and comes out underneath it, having taken up some of the chalk in its way through. If our hills had been of iron ore, lead, or salt, the water would have taken up some of these substances in passing through them, as it always takes up some of the earth through which it filters—as it is a fluid in which many things are soluble; thus, we get water with chalk in it—when you boil it, the pure water goes off in vapour, and leaves the chalk behind, which falls to the bottom of the kettle: besides this, although hot water will hold up or melt more sugar or salt than cold, yet it will not hold more chalk, on the contrary less, as the heating drives off a particular gas or air (called carbonic acid gas), which has a great liking for the chalk, and holds it up in the water, so that what falls to the bottom partly belongs to the water which is driven off, and partly to that which is left in the kettle. These are two reasons, therefore, why your kettle has a white mass of chalk at the bottom.

Taking off the lid of a kettle when the water is boiling, turning it up, what do you observe? Drops of water. These are formed by the steam coming against the lid, cooling it down so that it becomes water—the lid being in contact with the atmosphere conducts off the heat from the steam—this is distilled water or pure water, containing no lime, salt, etc.

Two fluids mixed together, which become vapours at different temperatures, may be easily separated—thus a mixture of spirit and water; heat the mixture up to the temperature at which spirit becomes vapour, it goes off and may be collected, the water remaining behind.

That the boiling point of water or any other fluid varies with the atmospheric pressure—how this may be applied to find the altitude of mountains—that water at the top of Mont Blanc, for instance, boils at a temperature of about 187°—that a difference of 1° in the boiling-point corresponds to about 530 feet of ascent, and this difference in boiling will denote a fall of about 0·589 inch of barometric pressure—that, under the receiver of an air-pump, water may be made to boil at a very much lower temperature than in the air. This and other things of a similar kind I find, from experience, may be made most instructive and useful to them, and more particularly if a school is provided with a philosophical apparatus with which the experiments can be shown. A table of the temperatures at which different fluids boil and freeze should be suspended on the wall.

Heat water to boiling in a Florence flask, cork it well when boiling, and turn the flask upside-down; having removed it from the lamp it now ceases to boil; sprinkle water on the surface of the bottle, the steam within is condensed, and it again begins to boil; when it again ceases to boil, from the elasticity of the steam within, repeat the sprinkling, and it commences boiling again; thus the application of cold makes the water boil.

Archdeacon Wollaston invented an apparatus of such delicacy for ascertaining this, that the difference of the height of a common table from the ground would produce a difference in the boiling-point, which was clearly shown by the instrument.

The different ways in which water and metals are heated —hot current ascending, the cold water descending, and metals from particle to particle; point out also the difference in the process, in attempting to heat water by placing the fire above and not under the vessel containing it. The conducting power of fluids is very small, and it has been found that water may be made to boil in the upper part of a tube, without imparting much heat to the water below it, and that it may be brought to the boiling-point within one fourth of an inch of ice without its immediately melting; and that ice is melted eighty times slower when it is fixed at the bottom of a cylindrical vessel with water above it, than when it floats upon the surface of warm water.

Salt is got from sea water by exposing it to the air in large pans; the water goes off in vapour and leaves the salt behind; the greater the surface exposed to the air the more rapidly the water goes off. Shallow pans better than deep, and why : Do you not observe the water lessen very much in summer in your sheep-ponds, even when you do not take cattle to drink at them ? It is taken up by the air ;. in the same way a good brisk wind rapidly dries the hay, corn, and clothes after washing; and if you want anything that has been washed to dry fast, you unfold it as much as you can in order to expose all its surface to the air. For the same reason you spread out the grass and leave the corn in the field, in order that the fluid matter contained in them may be taken off.

Salt also is found as a mineral in Cheshire, Poland, etc,; and salt-springs are very often found in the coal-mines in some districts, particularly in Durham and Newcastle, where a great part of the salt used by the miners for their own domestic purposes is supplied by the salt springs in the mines.

The following is an easy instructive experiment : Take a small quantity of rock-salt and also of saltpetre, the crystals of which differ very much, dissolve them together in water, they form a clear limpid fluid. Pour this solution of the two into a small dish and let it evaporate; crystals of pure salt and saltpetre will be the result, the beautiful long crystals of saltpetre being totally devoid of salt. This shows clearly that the atoms of salt have an attraction for and seek for their own atoms—the same of the saltpetre, and that if there is any attraction of the one for the other, it is less than that among themselves.

Dew. When it is once understood that the air of the atmosphere holds up a considerable quantity of vapour, and that the greater its temperature the greater is the quantity which it holds, it will be easily understood that, when any portion of air comes in contact with a body colder than itself, that it will throw down some of its moisture.

During the daytime, the earth, plants, etc., absorb heat from the sun ; when he goes down they radiate or give off part of the heat they have absorbed, and consequently cool ;—this cools the air in contact with them, and when cooled below the point which enables it to hold up all the vapour which it had taken up during the day, it lets it fall again—this is called the dew-point. Now, some plants and some leaves, and earths give off heat faster than others— on such a more copious dew will be deposited. On the contrary, gravelled walks, stone, etc. give off heat less rapidly, and on them little or no dew falls.

This all know from experience, or at least may easily ascertain it : — then to call their attention to the beautiful drops of dew formed on the leaves—the service they are to the plants—the beautiful provision of the Almighty in causing the dew to fall more copiously on the vegetable world, which wants it, than on the mineral—attraction of cohesion keeping the globules together, etc. Why they disappear in the morning, again becoming vapour.

Little or no dew on cloudy nights : why ? An umbrella overhead in an evening prevents the falling of dew on the person—on the clothes—the philosophy of this—the clouds are an umbrella, and the reason why no dew falls on a cloudy night applies to the umbrella—held over the head.

Any schoolmaster taking an interest in this subject, will see some very simple but curious and instructive experiments in Griffiths' " Chemistry of the Four Seasons." They consist in taking equal portions of dry wool of a given weight, and placing them in the evening — one on gravel, another on glass, another on grass, but sheltered by

a slight covering a little elevated above it, and then at sunrise taking them up and weighing them; of course the
increased weight, which will in all these positions vary very
much, is the weight of water deposited in the shape of dew.
These and a variety of phenomena connected with this
subject, easy of explanation—such as the mists—the fogs
rising in damp, marshy places—following the course of a
river, and many appearances of a like kind, which those
living in the country are in the habit of witnessing, may be
studied with great interest: but, as it is merely my object
to throw out what I conceive to be useful hints, I will not
pursue it further.

The force with which the absorption of moisture by
porous bodies causes them to expand, is much greater than
those who have never thought on the subject have an idea of.

As an instance of this, and of turning it to practical purpose, Sir John Herschel, in his " Discourse on the Study of
Natural Philosophy," gives the following very interesting
one, as a process which is had recourse to in some parts of
France where millstones are made: " When a mass of
stone sufficiently large is found it is cut into a cylinder
several feet high, and the question then arises how to sub-
divide this into horizontal pieces, so as to make as many
millstones. For this purpose horizontal indentations or
grooves are chiselled out quite round the cylinder, at distances corresponding to the thickness intended to be given
to the millstone, into which, wedges of dried wood are
driven. These are then wetted or exposed to the *night
dew*, and next morning the different pieces are found
separated from each other by the expansion of the wood
arising from its absorption of moisture."

This is a very curious instance of a simple natural power
doing what would require great trouble and expense to
effect; either by chiselling through, or by any machinery
of sawing, sometimes used for dividing blocks of stone.
The same author also mentions another instance where a
knowledge of the laws of nature, although acting here in a
different way, is called into action. In this case the heat
first expanding, and then the application of the water
causing a sudden contraction. In the granite quarries

near Seringapatam the most enormous blocks are separated from the solid rock by the following neat and simple process. The workmen having found a portion of the rock sufficiently extensive, and situated near the edge of the part already quarried, lay bare the upper surface, and mark on it a line in the direction of the intended separation, along which, a groove is cut with a chisel, about a couple of inches in depth. Above this groove a narrow line of fire is then kindled and maintained till the rock below is thoroughly heated; immediately on which a line of men and women, each provided with a potful of cold water, suddenly sweep off the ashes, and pour the water into the heated groove, when the rock at once splits with a clean fracture. Square blocks of six feet in the side, and upwards of eighty feet in length, are sometimes detached by this method.

The following practical way of giving an insight into the principle on which bodies float in fluids lighter than themselves, and of estimating their weight by the quantity of fluid displaced, has been found very serviceable :

They* have two tin vessels, a larger and a smaller one, the large one having a small spout level with the top, so that, when filled with water and running over, it may discharge itself into the small vessel placed by the side of it; the small one of known dimensions, say nine inches square at the bottom and six inches high, with a graduated line on one of the sides, so that it may be immediately seen to what height the water rises when flowing into it, and of course knowing the area of the base, and multiplying this into the height at which the water stands, will give its volume.

Then they are provided with a number of cubes of wood, the woods of the parish, oak, elm, ash, etc., four inches on a side—together with other pieces of any irregular shapes, for the purpose of experiment.

Having filled the larger vessel with water up to the spout, and placed the smaller one under it, the teacher takes a cube of oak, for instance, floats it on the water, which immediately begins to flow into the smaller vessel, and when it has ceased to do so, the height at which it

* This is speaking of the boys in King's Somborne school.

stands is observed. They then calculate the number of cubic inches of water displaced.

This they know is equal to the number of cubic inches of oak under water—(the teacher should show them the proof of this)—that it is equal in weight to the piece of oak. *Proof*—then knowing that the weight of a cubic foot of water, temperature about 62°, is 1,000 ozs., and why it is necessary to specify the temperature—they calculate, for instance, the weight of a cubic inch, by dividing 1,000 by 1,728, the number of inches in a foot.

Then multiplying the weight of one inch by the number of inches, this gives the weight of water displaced, and the weight of the wood.

They then take the piece of wood, tie a string round it, weigh it by a spring-balance, and find this exactly agrees with the figures they have worked out; and it is this weighing which gives such a character of certainty to what they have been doing, which makes them take pleasure in the work. Weighing before floating it is better.

Again, knowing the measurement of the piece of wood, supposing it to be one of known dimensions, subtracting the number of solid inches under water from the whole, gives them that part of the body above the surface, and which is floating in air.

The same would be done with pieces of ash, elm, fir, etc. Also in winter, pieces of ice afford a teacher who understands the subject an opportunity of giving a useful lesson, —pointing out how water becomes solid at a particular temperature—that although water freezes at this particular point, yet pieces of ice may have a temperature far below this—that a piece of ice, temperature 20°, as measured by Fahrenheit, would be of more service for cooling butter, water, etc., than one at 32°, and so on.

The teacher might ask such a question,—What is the atmospheric pressure on the surface of the water in the vessel? making them calculate it, and showing how it varies with the barometer.

It is by repeating these questions over and over again, in a practical way, that they tell on the minds of children.

Again, take a small square, or oblong, or a box of any

shape—a piece of wood hollowed out like a boat—a tin, such as tarts and bread are usually baked in: floating these, and loading them with weights until the water reaches the edge—they then see clearly that the quantity of water displaced is equal to the measure, in volume, of the vessel and the material of which it is made : and that a boat will just float, when the weight of the cargo and the weight of the boat taken together are equal to this displaced volume of the fluid in which it floats, and that any weight beyond this will sink it.

Calculating the weight of this volume of water displaced, and subtracting from it the weight of the boat, gives the extreme weight which the boat would carry without sinking.

Applying this to boats made of iron, or any other heavy metal, it is evident, that so long as the weight of the boat is less than a weight of fluid on which it is floating, the volume of which is equal to the whole size of the boat and material included, it will carry some cargo—that the limit to the thickness of the iron, so that the whole may float, is that which would make the weight of the boat equal to the weight of fluid of its own volume—that the thinner the material (due regard to safety being had), as in all cases the less the weight of the boat itself, of a given size, the greater cargo it would carry—that a boat which would sink in one fluid, would float merrily in another which was heavier, etc. ; for instance, a load which would sink in fresh, would float in salt water, and be buoyant in mercury. The teacher would naturally point out that the same boat would carry a heavier cargo on salt water than on fresh. What would it be on oil, milk, mercury, etc.?

The number of things which the principles connected with floating bodies may be called upon to illustrate is very great.

It may be well also to point out that a floating body is stable, when a line joining the centre of gravity of the body and that of displaced fluid is vertical.

Having made them understand what is meant by the term specific gravity, and that by taking the weight of a certain volume of water as a standard, we calculate the weight of other bodies, it will be well to have a table of the specific gravities of substances in common use, metals, woods, etc., suspended on a card in the schoolroom; and to show them by experiment how these results are arrived at. It is quite a mistake to think that boys about twelve or thirteen years of age cannot be made to understand them, and not only that—they will take a great interest in them.

A short list is added, merely for the purpose of working an example or two from it. Taking water as 1.

Distilled water	1·	Copper	8·788	Coal	1·250
Sea water is ..	1·026	Tin	7·291	Oil	·940
Platina	22·069	Iron (cast)	7·207	Oak	·925
Gold	19·258	Iron (bar)	7·788	Ash	·845
Mercury	13·586	Zinc	7·100	Maple	.755
Standard silver	10·474	Flint glass	3·329	Elm	·60C
Lead	11·352	Marble	2·700	Fir	·550
Brass	8·396	Ivory	1·825	Cork	·240

A simple inspection of this table may be made a useful lesson, by pointing out to them the comparative weight of those substances they are continually handling, the difference among them being much greater than they are in the habit of thinking it—that those substances the specific gravity of which is less than 1 will float. In this way the comparing one thing with another makes them think. Also why distilled water is a standard—that water varies in weight with the substances it holds in solution—that its boiling-point varies with these substances.

Assuming the weight of a cubic foot of *distilled* water, and at the temperature of 63° Fahrenheit, to be 1000 ozs. (why distilled water, and why a fixed temperature?) let them show that the weight of a cubic inch $= \dfrac{1000}{1728}$, and why the divisor is 1728.

When we speak of the specific gravity of lead being 11·352 and of iron 7·788, we mean that the weight of any given volume of lead or iron will be so many times that weight of the same volume of water, and knowing the one, the other is easily calculated.

Thus a cubic foot of water weighs 1000 ozs., therefore a cubic foot of lead weighs 1000 ozs. × 11·352=11352 ozs., of iron 1000 ozs., × 7·788, or 7788 ozs., of an inch in the same way.

The specific gravity of dry oak is ·925, of fir ·550, of elm ·600, therefore any given volume of these woods would float, being lighter than the same volume of water. A cubic foot of dry oak would be 1000 ozs. × ·925, or 925 ozs.; of fir 1000 ozs. × ·550, or 550 ozs., a little more than half the weight of oak.

As applied to these substances, a good deal depends on their state of dryness, sap in them, etc.

The following questions of a practical kind may suggest others :

What is the weight of a block of marble, granite, etc., of regular figure (or any other which they can measure), base of it fifteen feet six inches by five feet two inches, and four feet high.

A given number of feet of oak, elm, ash, etc.? A given mass of metal, what would be its weight? The weight of metals is exactly known from measurement, supposing them to be pure.

In this way they will easily see what horse-power, or man-power—moving power—it will take to move given masses of these materials; and would, if called upon to put it into practice, contrive accordingly—strengthening their machinery, etc. adapting it to the work required to be done.

From this also may be shown the reason why heavy bodies appear so much lighter when moved in a fluid like water — the heavier the fluid the easier they move — as when they raise a bucketful of water from a well; its increased heaviness the moment it gets to the surface of the water—given size of the bucket how much increased in weight?—would it be heavier if raised out of the water into a vacuum, and how much ?—moving masses of stone, as granite, under water—floating beams of timber, etc. Having given the volume and the specific gravity of the fluid in which they are moving, to calculate what they lose in weight.

Suspend a cubic foot of lead by a chain from one end of a balance : what weight would balance it at the other end, or over a single pulley ? A weight equal to itself.—Now let it fall into a vessel of water : will it take the same weight to balance it as before ? Nc, Sir ; a weight less than itself, by the weight of a cubic foot of water.—What does a cubic foot of water weigh ? 1000 ozs.—Well, I don't recollect the weight of a cubic foot of lead, but what is its specific gravity ?—look at your table, 11·352 ; therefore the weight of the lead in air is 11,352, and deducting 1000 ozs., the weight of a cubic foot of water, which is the weight lost by the lead, gives 10,352, the weight necessary to balance the lead when in water.

Suppose a cubic foot of lead resting on a pile under water, what force must be exerted to pull it off, supposing no resistance from friction on the pile ? About $\frac{9}{10}$ths of its own weight.

From this to explain how, it is that the sand, stone, shingle, etc., are so easily tossed about on the sea-shore— how the human body floats, etc.

Questions : A vessel full of mercury, the bottom of which is nine inches by 4·56, and the height ten inches, what is its weight ?

Suppose a cistern, twelve feet long, five feet wide, and four feet six inches high, made of lead a quarter of an inch thick, what would be its weight ?

What is the weight of a cylinder of iron thirty inches in diameter and six feet high ? Of a block of granite in the form of a circle, four feet six inches in diameter and twenty inches thick ?

A statue of marble is placed in a vessel full of quicksilver, and causes six cubic feet to run over, what is its weight ? Would it sink ? Would a statue of cast-iron sink ?

Why is the line of the angler more likely to break after the fish is out of water than when it is in it ?

Do you see any connection between the weight of a given mass of matter and the altitude of the barometer ? and how might a dealer in any bulky commodity profit by observing that connection ?

The specific gravity of ice is to that of water as 8 to 9, and a field of ice of uniform thickness, has 10 feet above water, how many feet below it?

A cubic foot of a metal weighs 1000 lbs. when weighed in air; the weight of a cubic inch of air being about $\frac{1}{800}$th part of a cubic inch of water at a temperature of 63°, what would be the weight of the body in vacuo; also if weighed in water—and if in air of half the density,—work out the arithmetical results.

Making them reduce the fluid measures into cubic inches, feet, etc., is a good exercise.

How many cubic inches in a pint? 34·659.
>in a quart?
>in a gallon, etc.?

Then of course they easily calculate the weight of any of these measures filled with a fluid, the specific gravity of which is given.

In aeriform bodies, common atmospheric air is taken as a standard instead of water, the weight of which is about one eight-hundredth part of the former: therefore, as a cubic foot of water weighs 1000 ozs., the weight of a foot of air will be $\frac{1000}{800}$ or 1·25 oz.; ten feet will be 12·5 ozs., 100 feet 125 ozs., etc.; then having the specific gravities of other gaseous substances, some of which are heavier, some lighter, than the atmosphere, they may be made to calculate the weights of given volumes.

The principle of the thermometer should be explained—how it is made—how graduated—and how the freezing and boiling points are determined—why the tube is of a narrow bore, etc.

In the Boys' school at Somborne there is a barometer and a thermometer, which they are in the habit of observing; registering the height when they go in, and noticing the course of its rise from increased temperature; this is registered three times a day, and a thermometer kept in the open air. The height of the barometer—the taking a weekly and a monthly average—forms an exercise of their arithmetic.

Attention might be called as to how such averages of the thermometer are affected by swampy and marshy

grounds of great extent—improved drainage*—how this
is likely to affect the temperature of a district, so much so,
even as to advance the period of harvest—how the height
of the thermometer may be affected by particular aspects
—whether the line of country slopes towards the north or
south, or is a level plain, etc.

The subject of heat† is one of great interest, and one on
which the teacher may bring to bear a variety of experiments not attended with much expense, and having this
additional recommendation, that they have an intimate
relation with many of the comforts and conveniences of
life.

Heat is present everywhere and in every kind of matter:
we cannot measure its quantity, but we can measure the
quantity in one body relatively to that of another.

The general effect of heat upon matter is to expand
it, that is, an increase of heat in the same body produces an increase of volume, in some proportion to the
increased temperature.

This increase of volume for a given increase of temperature varies in different kinds of matter; air and gases
expand most, fluids next, and then solids.

Instances of each have been mentioned—as a full kettle
swelling and flowing over just before it boils—a round
piece of iron fitting exactly into a ring when cold, when
heated is too large.

Then, again, heated bodies impart heat to every thing
around them until all have acquired the same temperature;
as the heater of a box-iron for ironing linen, when put
into the fire becomes red hot like the cinder; when taken
out it is put into the box, communicates heat to it, and so
to the linen; and, when used for a certain time, becomes
of the same temperature with the things around it.

* I was told by an experienced farmer in the county of Cambridge,
that he believed the average period of harvest in that county was
earlier by *ten* days, within the memory of man, owing to improved
drainage.

† The volume on Heat in Lardner's "Cyclopædia" will be found
a very useful book for the schoolmaster, and as an introduction to
practical science for pupil teachers.— *Walker's Edition of Joyce's
Scientific Dialogues.*

We call things which we touch, hot or cold, according as they are hotter or colder than the human body, but in this the sense of touch deceives us; when we touch a body hotter than the hand, we receive heat from it—when we touch one colder than the hand, it receives heat from us; but experience tells us that all the things in a room, when measured by a thermometer, have an equal temperature, yet they do not feel equally so to the hand.

The different degrees in which bodies conduct heat have been ascertained by experiment; air and gases, when confined, are very bad conductors : metals varying in degree among each other are good ones—generally the more dense the body, the better conductor it is.

Porous bodies are bad conductors, as are any bodies which contain air confined in cells, such as the feathers of birds—the fur of animals—the bark of trees. All these how beautiful a provision for the preservation of animal and vegetable life!

Then, again, straw, reeds, etc. are bad ones; so that a thick covering of thatch is a much better covering for a cottage, so far as warmth in winter and coolness in summer are concerned, than either tile or slate.

Tile, being rather a thick and a porous substance compared with slate, is better than the latter; and every one who is in the habit of visiting the cottages of the poor will have observed that the bedrooms of those covered with slate are in the summer extremely hot, and in winter equally cold. .

Slate, again, would be better than iron.

The teacher would do well to observe the variety of fur and hair in animals, varying with the climates they inhabit; in warm climates the hairy coat of animals being short and thin, in the colder ones becoming thick and woolly. The birds of colder regions, that live in the air, have a much greater quantity of plumage than those of the warmer ones; water-fowl, such as ducks, geese, etc., have the interstices between their feathers filled up with down, more particularly on the breast. In the cold weather in winter, the birds may often be seen shaking and ruffling up their feathers in order to increase the quantity of air among them, which, being a bad conductor, helps to keep them warm.

Earth is a bad conductor, and the sharpest frosts in consequence scarcely ever get more than a few inches deep into the ground. The temperature of the earth, a very little below the surface, is the same in every climate.

In covering up a potatoe-pit for the winter, the lighter the soil, and the more of a covering of straw or leaves between it and the potatoes, the better they will be preserved. When it is said the frost gets to the potatoes, the thing really meant is, that the temperature of the air becoming lower than freezing point, the surface-covering of the potatoe-pit first gives out heat to the air, then that nearest the surface to the particles adjoining, until, last of all, the potatoes give out heat to what is resting upon them, and so the water of the potatoes gets cooled below freezing and becomes solid, and the potatoe spoiled ;—hence the necessity of covering them with bad conductors—not to make the soil over them a solid, but as light as possible.

On the same principle, a covering of snow is a great protection, in very severe frosts, to the more delicate plants ; although the temperature may be very far below the freezing point, and in some climates where the cold is great, the thermometer is even down to zero, yet the temperature of the ground, under a covering of snow, would be very little below freezing. Thus water in pipes below the surface, and in springs is never frozen. In the winter, to prevent water freezing in pipes which are above ground, they are wrapped round with straw or some bad conducting substance, etc. Ice-houses with double walls—rooms with double windows are all instances of the same kind. The application of a kettle-holder, having wood or ivory handles to teapots made of metal, etc., belong to the same principle.

The following, by way of a lesson on one of the metals, *iron*, with the experiments which follow, will convey some idea to the teacher of the mode of proceeding here, and may serve as a model for the way in which he would treat the other metals :

Iron—found in the earth as a mineral—how obtained

I

from the ore ?—is a metal a solid ?—can it be made fluid ?
Yes, sir, by great heat. Have you ever seen it fluid ?—At
the little foundry at the blacksmith's shop.—How does it
become solid again ? By cooling.—What effect has heat
upon metals ?* It expands them, makes them longer—it
would make an iron ring larger.—Have you ever seen this
property of expanding by heat turned to a useful purpose ?
Yes, sir ; the village blacksmith hooping wheels ; he makes
the hoop a little too small, heats it red hot, which makes it
larger, and it just fits the wheel—he then pours water upon
it ; it immediately contracts and makes the joints of the
wheel close up and crack, and so it fits tight—riveting
bolts, etc.—the experiment of iron bars bringing the opposite sides of a building to an upright position from leaning
outwards.

I am told, in testing the anchors in the dockyard at
Portsmouth, that the largest anchors have a strain on them
of perhaps 150 tons, and being in length about 30 feet, and
as thick as the body of a man, that immediately the strain
is taken off they will collapse as much as an inch, and that
this shrinking is visible to the eye of a looker on.

The difference between the heat of summer and winter
will cause such a variation in the length of the ordinary
seconds pendulum as to affect its time of vibration ; and in
the building of iron bridges, allowance is obliged to be
made for what is called the play of the iron, between
summer and winter heat, or the whole would come down,
and I believe in some of the large tubular structures of iron
lately erected over rivers, allowance has been made for the unequal expansion of the metal on the sunny and shady sides.

The teacher will point out the various uses to which iron
can be applied—how useful from its extending under the
hammer—welding (which most other metals do not), and
other properties. What is welding ? Heating two pieces
of iron to a very great heat (called a white heat), then
placing them together on the anvil, and beating them with
a hammer, they unite as one piece ; silver and gold will
not do this. Platina welds.

Cast-iron—melted and run into a mould for shape, for

* See p. 215.

grates, saucepans, boilers, teakettles, part of the plough, rollers, door-latches, gate-latches.

Did you ever in winter, in frosty weather, find out that it was colder to the hand to touch iron than wood? Yes, sir.—Why? Do not know, sir.—Teacher (making the children touch subtances of different conducting powers, a piece of marble, stone, wood, wool, flax, cotton, etc., pointing out to them that all have the same temperature as the room, which is below that of the hand, and ought, so far as this is concerned, to affect it equally) : Because iron is a better conductor of heat than wood or any of the others ; being very cold in frosty weather, and much colder than your hand, it carries away the heat much more rapidly than wood, and it has very little to give back in return; this rapid loss of heat causes a very unpleasant sensation; if you hold the iron long enough, it will get the same degree of warmth as the hand, and the unpleasant effect will cease; the stream of heat from the iron to the hand, and the hand to the iron, will exactly balance each other ; that is, the two substances, your hand the one, and the iron the other, will then impart equal heat to each other.

They may also be told to touch the different substances, marble, wood, stone, iron, etc., with their lips, which, as they are much more sensible to cold, will point out to them more strikingly how much the sense of touch deceives them.

Experiment. The teacher taking a polished cylindrical piece of iron, with a piece of white paper held tightly over it, holds it in the flame of a candle, and observes it does not char—the same on a piece of wood, and exposing it in the same way, it immediately turns black; the iron being so good a conductor does not allow the heat to rest with the paper, but immediately takes it away, etc.; the wood not conducting it so rapidly causes the paper to burn.

On this principle, water may be made to boil in a paper kettle, or in an egg-shell — when boiled away, both substances would immediately burn.

Experiment. Metallic rods of equal lengths and substance, one of each smeared with beeswax, and immersed in a heated fluid, the heat travels along each rod, from

particle to particle, and the one on which the wax melts
first is the best conductor, the one on which it next melts
the second best, and so on—the order in which the wax
melts being the order in which the rods conduct the
heat.

The following experiment, which is easily tried, shows
the way in which a fluid, as water, is heated by a flame
placed under it: take a glass tube, open at one end, and
about an inch or so in diameter; pour water into it, so
that there may be a column of several inches in length,
and place it over a spirit lamp. As the flame heats the
water, drop sand into it, and a double current will be
observed, one downwards along the sides of the vessel,
the other upwards through the centre of the fluid: apply
the heat to the surface on the sides of the vessel, and the
currents will be reversed. The reason of all this to be
pointed out.

Glass—a solid, can be softened by heat, so as to be
drawn out into a fine thread—allows light to pass through
it; in what way does man turn this property to his use?
Windows, lanterns, spectacles, telescopes, etc.; does not
allow the heat of the fire to pass through it—the heat
of the sun does—What other substances allow light to
pass through them? Water, horn, air, etc.

Why will a glass sometimes break by pouring hot water
in it?

Answer. Solids convey heat from particle to particle,*
and some solids do this more slowly than others; glass
conveys it very slowly, and the hot water in contact with
the inner surface causes the inside surface of the glass to
expand, but the outer one, not being so hot, will not follow
it, and so snaps, being very brittle. Thin glass will not
break so readily as thick, the distance between the two
surfaces being smaller, the heat gets through sooner, and
the inner and outer surface are almost instantaneously

* The following question is very suggestive, as an application of a
domestic kind: one joint of meat is roasted, another is baked on a
hot metallic plate heated by connection with the bars of the kitchen
fire, and a third is boiled:—in what way is the heat transmitted in
each case by which these joints are cooked?

raised to the same temperature—hence chemists use thin retorts.

On the subject of metals used for the various purposes of social life, the class of teachers for whom these pages are intended may give a great deal of useful instruction.

They might draw attention to the different ores, showing specimens of them, and mentioning the kinds of earths and other substances with which they are generally mixed—where found in our own and other countries—the per centage of metal found in an ore, in one case making it what is called a rich one, in another so small as scarcely to make it worth working—anything peculiar in the way in which metallic veins run, not being stratified, etc.—depth of mines—the number of workmen employed in the mining of any particular ore, the method and necessity of transporting it from the place where it is found for the purpose of smelting, either from the people not knowing how, or for want of coal, etc.,—great inconvenience of this in a commercial point of view, from having to transport so large a proportion of the ore which is useless (there may be other substances mixed with it which are useful).

"When a mass of matter is to be removed, a certain force must be expended ; and upon the proper economy of this force the price of transport will depend. A country must, however, have reached a high degree of civilization before it will have approached the limit of this economy. The cotton of Java is conveyed in junks to the coast of China, but from the seed not being previously separated, three quarters of the weight thus carried is not cotton. This perhaps might be justified in Java by the want of machinery to separate the seed, or by the relative cost of the operation in the two countries. But the cotton itself, as packed by the Chinese, occupies three times the bulk of an equal quantity shipped by Europeans for their own markets. Thus the freight of a given quantity of cotton, costs the Chinese nearly twelve times the price to which, by a proper attention to mechanical methods, it might be reduced" (BABBAGE on the Economy of Machinery).

Again, the mode of separating the metal from the different

ores—in some cases breaking it into small pieces and roasting it—thus driving off volatile substances, which become vapour at a comparatively low temperature—why breaking it before this process—smelting—that when a mass of any particular ore is heated to the point at which the metal fuses, it sinks down in this fluid state to the bottom of the furnace;—to point out how certain other substances are sometimes used, called fluxes, to assist in the fusion of minerals; that when a sufficient quantity has accumulated in a fluid state, and sunk down from the earthy and other matter in the ore, the furnace is tapped, and it runs off into moulds—called pigs, sows, etc., by the workmen.

Swansea, in Wales, a place where a good deal of ore is carried for this purpose—from Ireland, and also foreign ores are taken there.

One mode of separating silver from the other substances in the ore is by pouring in quicksilver, which unites with the silver, and is afterwards pressed out.

The metals themselves, pointing out those which are called precious metals, those which are most useful—the particular properties which make them so useful, such as being fusible, ductile, malleable, and the different degrees in which they are so; their melting-point, and the temperature at which they do melt, showing a very wide range (by calling their attention to these extremes, the instruction becomes more striking, and is more attended to)—their specific gravities, which may be pointed out from a table, making them handle the substances—platina and gold, how heavier than any of the others—twice, three times, etc., heavier than some—the property of welding only belonging to iron and platina—how much this increases the usefulness of the former.

It is easy to see the rougher and more every-day purposes of life for which the metals are used, but it will be also useful, more particularly in the schools in our large towns, to call their attention to the uses in the arts; why one metal oxidizing rapidly in the atmosphere or in water, and another not, would, in certain cases, make the latter preferable, as in the copper sheathing of ships, etc.

Again, a union of metals is called an alloy—when one is

quicksilver, an amalgam ; an instance of the former, bronze, consisting of copper, with a small proportion of tin, and sometimes other metals, and used for casting statues cannon, bells, etc. ; of the latter, an amalgam of tin, with which looking-glasses are covered on the back surface ; mercury very readily combines with gold, silver, lead, tin, bismuth, and zinc, but more difficultly with copper, arsenic, and antimony, and scarcely at all with platina and iron. Mercury, from the circumstance of its dissolving completely many of the less valuable metals, is very often adulterated.

Some metals have so little of affinity for each other that they have never yet been known to form an alloy, and even many whose fusing point is nearly the same will not unite ; the density of an alloy is sometimes greater than the mean density of the two metals of which it is made up, which shows that a decrease of volume has taken place, as bronze ; —others again are lighter, showing an increase of bulk.

Alloys which consist of metals that fuse at different temperatures will often be decomposed by heating them to a temperature at which one of them melts ; this is practised in extracting silver from copper. The copper containing silver in it is melted with three and a half times its weight of lead, and this alloy of three metals is exposed to a sufficient heat—the lead carries off the silver in its fusion, and leaves the copper in a spongy lump—the silver is afterwards got from the lead by another operation.

Alloys containing a volatile metal may be decomposed at a strong heat, driving off the metal which is volatile, as water is driven off at a less temperature from any salt it may contain.

The specific gravity of an alloy is a means of finding out the proportion of two metals in a given substance.

The substances used for soldering are instances of alloys; they are mixed metals for the purpose of uniting metallic bodies, but it will be necessary that the solder should melt at a lower temperature than the bodies to be soldered.

Those which are called hard solders will bear hammering, and are generally made of the same metal with the one to be soldered, mixed with some other which makes it more fusible.

Soft solder, such as tin and lead in equal parts, used by the glaziers, melts easily, and cannot be hammered; tin, lead, and bismuth, in equal parts, melt still more easily. In the operation of soldering, the surfaces should be made clean, otherwise they would not unite so well. The glaziers use resin with the solder, to prevent the metals rusting, uniting with the oxygen of the air.

A bar (whose length at 32° is taken at unity) of the following substances will, when heated to 212°, the boiling-point of water at the ordinary pressure of the atmosphere, expand: glass, $\frac{1}{1116}$ of its length; steel about $\frac{1}{307}$; iron, $\frac{1}{846}$; copper, $\frac{1}{58}$; silver, $\frac{1}{524}$; tin, $\frac{1}{462}$; lead, $\frac{1}{351}$; or a rod of iron whose length (temperature 32°) is 846 inches, will, at the heat of boiling water, expand one inch, and become 847; tin, length 462 inches, would become 463.

In consequence of this expansion of iron by heat, it is necessary to make allowance for it in building bridges, otherwise the difference between winter and summer heat might cause an expansion which would bring down the bridge.

Again, on the absorption and radiation of heat by different substances a few useful lessons may be given, and the simple and well-known experiments of Leslie, which are easily tried, may be made very instructive.

From these it is shown that smooth polished surfaces of metal reflect heat, and absorb comparatively little; that scratching or in any way roughening the surface of a metallic body increases its power of absorption, and blackening it with anything increases it still more.*

Experiment. Take, for instance, three circular pieces of metal, as tin, nine inches in diameter, and raised on a stand of a few inches high—one smooth, another scratched and roughened, the third blackened—the back of each being smeared with tallow, or some substance which melts at a low temperature; then placing a red-hot ball of iron at equal distances from any two of them, it will be found that the tallow on the blackened one will very soon melt, that

---

* See List of Apparatus at the end of the volume.

on the roughened surface next, while the smooth surface would remain nearly at the temperature of the room; of course this experiment might be tried with different substances, and metals scratched and blackened in different degrees.

Another of Leslie's experiments. Take a cubical vessel, made of tin, one surface blackened, a second scratched, the third more roughened, and the last smooth; fill it with boiling water, and place the differential thermometer near it, and turning each side in succession towards it, it will be found that the quantity of heat radiated, or thrown off from the different surfaces, will be in the order mentioned above. Professor Leslie covered the surface of the vessel with thin plates or layers of different substances of different colours, and noted the number of degrees which the thermometer rose, and thus ascertained the radiating power of each particular covering.

Lamp-black	100°	Clean lead	19°
Writing-paper	98	Iron, polished	15
Tarnished lead	45	Tinplate	12

He then, instead of blackening or otherwise meddling with the faces of the tin vessel, made it perfectly smooth, and covered the bulb of the thermometer with the different substances, and found by the way in which it was affected, that they absorbed heat much in the same way as they had before radiated it when on the tin vessel.

His experiment of heat reflected from parabolic reflectors is a very curious one, and they are well worth the expense of purchasing, in order to try the experiment, from the instruction it gives. A pair of these reflectors is a useful apparatus in a school.

Although heat is emitted from every point in the surface of a hot body in all directions, it is not emitted in all-directions with the same intensity. The intensity of the heating ray is as the sine of the angle which it makes with the surface, and therefore those rays have the greatest heating power which are emitted at an angle of 90°.

As an instance of roughened bodies absorbing heat and

then radiating it again, and of polished surfaces reflecting it—take the case of a blackened rough fender and polished fire-irons—the latter are generally nearer the fire than the fender, touch them and they will be found much the coolest; the fender having absorbed the heat, the irons reflected it.

The different degrees in which bodies absorb heat depends also on colour.

Dr. Franklin observed that when he laid pieces of differently coloured cloth upon snow, it melted more rapidly under the dark colours than the light. And black and red inks, for example, when exposed to the sun, become heated in different degrees from their absorbing the light which falls upon them, and consequently the heat in different degrees; while pure water seems to transmit all the rays equally, and is not sensibly heated by the passing light of the sun.

The teacher should also note the difference between the radiation of heat from the sun and that from any other bodies—that from the sun passing through air and glass, water, etc., the other not, or if so, in a very slight degree.

The following experiment, attended with no expense, affords a good practical hint—two old tea-pots will serve, one of white metal, the other of black earthenware.

Fill them with boiling water, or with hot water from the same kettle—after standing a given time, place a thermometer in them, and it will be found that it will stand much higher in the metal one than in the other; showing that for the purposes of making tea the metal one is the better, not radiating the heat so rapidly; but if placed before the fire the black one will absorb heat better than the other. A black earthen teapot loses heat by radiation, in the proportion of 100; while one of silver or other polished metal loses only as 12.

Thus hot water running in a blackened pipe or rough one, will give out its heat more rapidly than in a polished smooth one.

A solid, when changed into a fluid state, absorbs heat—some solids soften in melting, as wax, tallow, butter, and then become fluid; others, as ice, change at once.

In changing from a fluid to a state of vapour, heat also

is absorbed; on the contrary, bodies in passing from vapour to fluid, and from fluid to solid, give out heat.

Water in freezing gives out heat, while in the melting of snow and ice heat is absorbed; hence the chilling cold felt in a thaw, after there has been a great fall of snow; also the gradual melting, in consequence of the latent heat in changing from snow into water.

Fluids become vapour also at different temperatures, their boiling-points depending upon the pressure of the atmosphere, which varies with the altitude above the level of the sea, as well as from other causes; they may also be heated beyond their boiling-point in the atmosphere, by subjecting them to artificial pressure.

The following questions will suggest a few important things, on which the teacher who wishes to understand this subject may inform himself.

Why, as water in boiling becomes vapour, and as it were boils away, does its temperature not rise above 212°? When all converted into steam at 212°, what would take place if immediately condensed? What has become of all the heat required to convert the water into vapour, and how would it show itself when the steam is condensed?

If the steam were heated above 212°, how is its expansive force increased? Simply as the temperature, or in a higher ratio?

The disruption of vegetable substances produced by the passage of the electric fluid through a tree is caused by the intensity of the momentary heat converting the fluid of the wood into steam.

At what temperature does water vaporize?

What do you mean by saying that a liquid boils?

Describe the relation between the boiling power of a liquid and the pressure of the atmosphere above it—specify the effect on this boiling-point.

1. By artificially attenuating ⎫ this atmosphere.
2. By artificially condensing ⎭

What is high-pressure steam?

Why, when a mass of ice is dissolved from the heat of a room, or in a vessel on the fire, does the temperature of the water not rise, so long as any ice remains undissolved

—(test this by placing a thermometer in melting ice), and why does it rise as soon as it is all melted ?

Water being kept perfectly still, may be cooled many degrees below the freezing-point, but if shaken, ice would immediately be formed. The extent to which it freezes at once when shaken depends upon this, whether the quantity of heat given out on freezing is sufficient to raise the temperature of the rest higher than 32°. If, for instance, the mass is cooled to 10° below the freezing-point, then only $\frac{1}{14}$th is immediately frozen, and in becoming solid it has given out sufficient heat to raise the temperature of the rest up to the point of freezing.

The circumstance of water, when cooled below 39° of Fahrenheit, expanding when further reduced in temperature, should be noticed—this is shown from ice being lighter than water—from the bursting of water-pipes when frozen.

How beautiful the design of Providence in this arrangement, that when the surface water is near the freezing-point, being lighter than that which is underneath, it cannot sink. If it had followed the general law, rivers would begin to freeze from the bottom, and become a solid mass of ice—fish and all the other inhabitants of the water would be destroyed : ice is also a bad conductor.

Why can the human body bear to be brought in contact with air at a much higher temperature than with a fluid— with a fluid than with a solid, such as hot iron ?

A fluid boils, when its temperature is raised to such a point that the elasticity of its vapour is sufficient to overcome the pressure which is acting upon it : whether from the cohesiveness of the substance itself, the pressure of the atmosphere, or any other artificial pressure.

This explains the principle of a vessel called Papin's Digester, made to extract all the nutritive matter from bones. It is a cylindrical vessel, capable of resisting great pressure ; closed by a stopcock, which will resist a pressure of many atmospheres. Of course, in this, water may be heated far above the ordinary boiling-point, and from its greater heat, most animal substances are made to dissolve.

The boiling-point is not changed by bodies mechanically mixed in a fluid—as sand in water; but it is by all those chemically united with it. All soluble salts retard the boiling point of water, and substances such as starch, mechanically mixed with it, retard its cooling.*

The processes in the arts and manufactures carried on by distillation and evaporation should be noticed. The continual evaporation going on at all temperatures from every part of the surface of the globe—land and water, animal and vegetable—increasing the transparency of the atmosphere, sometimes when most charged with vapour it is most transparent—at others forming clouds, descending in rain to supply our rivers and springs, and to sustain the whole animal and vegetable world.

Formation of vapour absorbs heat, and therefore produces cold—instance a wet towel applied to the temples in case of headache—sometimes wrapped round a bottle containing any thing which requires to be cooled—damping the mats in a doorway—a damp bed a very dangerous thing, for want of exercise to generate heat in the body, so as to counteract the cold in drying, etc. That evaporation produced cold had been known in warm climates from an early period, but this had escaped notice in the more temperate ones, until after the invention of the thermometer, when it was soon perceived that on the bulb being wetted, the mercury immediately fell in the stem.

The following may be taken as a way of applying this knowledge to the teaching of children :

Sugar from the sugar cane. The juices are pressed out by passing the cane between heavy rollers; this contains, besides sugar, a great deal of water—the water is driven off by boiling—will go away slowly by evaporation.

A current of air over anything that is wet takes the moisture up in vapour, as it passes over the surface; this changing the wet upon anything into vapour is called evapo-

* The reader will see some interesting tables on the freezing and boiling points of liquids, etc., on the melting-points of solids, such as fat, metals, etc., at the end of the volume on Heat in Lardner's " Cyclopædia; " as also on their expansions at different temperatures. See pp. 214—216.

ration, and produces cold; dip your finger in water, when
there is so little wind that you do not know from what
quarter it comes, and you will find the finger colder on one
side than the other; this is the side on which the wind
blows, and it is colder because there is a greater evaporation on that side of the finger than the other. The sailor
knows this, and when he is becalmed at sea, and does not
know from what quarter the wind blows, he wets his finger
in his mouth, and holds it up to the air, the cold side is the
wind side.

After a shower of rain on your clothes, and whilst they
are drying on your back, do you not feel much colder than
you did before?—this is the cold arising from the wet on
your clothes becoming vapour—and for this reason you
should not sit in your wet clothes after you get home.

Why does your ink get thick by standing in the ink-
stand? This, after what you have heard, you can answer
yourselves.

In cold weather you will sometimes observe a quantity of
water collected at the bottom of the panes of glass in a
room—you recollect warm air holds up more vapour than
cold—the warm air in the room coming in contact with the
glass, which is cold from being in contact with the cold air
of the atmosphere, is immediately made cooler; this causes
the vapour in it to condense on the surface of the glass—
become water—it then runs down, and collects in large
drops on the wood. What becomes of it? Point out how
it is perhaps first absorbed by the wood—is changed again
into vapour—again mixes with the atmosphere—reappears
in rain—fertilizes the fields, etc.

With the aid of a sectional model of the steam-engine,
and knowing something of the elastic power of vapour—
that its force of elasticity increases in a much higher ratio
than that of its temperature—that when reduced below a
certain temperature it is immediately condensed — the
teacher would be able to explain many of the more important parts of the machine, showing how steam may be
adapted to the purposes of man as a moving power.

He would explain how the steam enters alternately
below and above the piston rod, and is carried off—by its

elasticity giving an up and down motion to the large beam which sets the machinery in motion — pointing out the parallel motion at the end of the beam, causing the piston rod always to move in the same vertical plane—the up and down motion of the beam causing two dead points, one at its highest, the other at the lowest point of its motion—how the contrivance of a fly-wheel, by its momentum when once set in motion, carries the machinery over the dead points, etc.

Then again—the importance of having a great quantity of fire surface in the boiler, in order to generate steam rapidly—the saving of fuel by this—the different kinds of boilers in order to effect it—the nature of safety-valves—that a safety-valve is, in fact, a weak part of the boiler made to give way when the elastic force of the vapour, from increased temperature, becomes so great as to endanger its bursting—the valve opens (or ought to do), at a pressure much below that which would burst the material of which the boiler is made—gauges for measuring the pressure on every square inch of surface at which the engine is working —nature of an atmospheric safety-valve opening inwards, and why wanted, etc. ; that if the steam inside the boiler is suddenly condensed, the boiler would have a tendency to collapse, and an atmospheric valve would guard against this.

Again, when the water in the boiler is very low, the fire-surface of the boiler above the water would become heated in a very high degree ; danger from this, in an engine not stationary, as in a steam-boat, of the water, from the rolling motion of the boat, being thrown over the heated surface, and all converted into steam, and an explosion taking place —not perhaps immediately, but after the heated surface was cooled down to a certain temperature.

The boiler of the locomotive steam-engine is of a tubular kind, in order to expose as much surface as possible to the fire ; and in this engine, as there can be no fly-wheel to get over the dead points, there are in each machine two engines at work, the dead points of which are at right angles to each other, so that they never occur together.

The following from Herschel's " Discourse on the Study

of Natural Philosophy," will give the reader some idea of these hidden powers of nature when called into action, and show him how much they are perhaps beyond anything he may have been in the habit of imagining them.

" It is well known to modern engineers that there is virtue in a bushel of coals, properly consumed, to raise seventy millions of pounds weight a foot high. This is actually the average effect of an engine at this moment working in Cornwall. Let us pause a moment and consider what this is equivalent to in matters of practice.

" The ascent of Mont Blanc from the valley of Chamouni is considered, and with justice, as the most toilsome feat that a strong man can execute in two days. The combustion of two pounds of coal would place him on the summit.

" The Menai Bridge consists of a mass of iron, not less than four millions of pounds in weight, suspended at a medium height of about 120 feet above the sea. The consumption of seven bushels of coals would suffice to raise it to the place where it hangs."

It will, perhaps, be difficult to understand the following description of what may be called the mechanical effects of a jet of steam without having recourse to diagrams; but they are curious, and as the same thing may in some measure be tried by a current of air blown or sent rapidly through a hollow tube, this may suggest simple things of an interesting kind.

A jet of steam issuing outwards in any direction, but suppose vertically from an orifice, will ascend into the air, with greater or less force, according to its temperature and elasticity, and will by its momentum displace the air which it meets with in its upward course. The jet will be rendered visible by the steam being condensed, and the effect of this jet upon the flame of any burning substance—or any light substances brought near to the axis of it—by its attracting them (a current of air setting in on all sides towards the axis of the jet), is striking and worthy of attention.

Take a piece of tow, dipped in spirits of wine and placed at the end of a rod, set it on fire, and approach the flame near the axis of the steam jet; when held a little above the orifice from which the steam proceeds, the flame will be attracted in a slanting direction, and the angle which the flame makes with the axis of the jet increases as the distance from the orifice increases, up to a certain point, when it becomes a right angle; elevated above this it again assumes the position it had below this point, until it is elevated beyond the influence of the jet, when it of course assumes a vertical position.

This is better shown by taking a circular piece of iron, with a handle attached, and wrapped round with tow : moisten it with spirits of wine and kindle it, then place the circle of flame across the axis of the jet—up to a certain point above the orifice, the flame will assume a conical appearance; here it will set itself at right angles to the jet, and appear a flat disc of flame—above this point the flame will again become a conical surface, until being farther elevated, it gets beyond the influence of the jet, and assumes an undisturbed position.

Light bodies when placed in the jet, or heavy bodies within certain limits, when placed in it, will be supported, or a flat surface of any kind held in the hand at a certain distance from the orifice will be forced upwards; but brought close to it or in contact with the surface in which is the orifice of the jet, it will be held down with considerable force.

It is from these properties of a jet of steam, that it has been proposed to ventilate coal and other mines, by creating a strong current of air up one shaft, to be supplied by a down current from another, which could be regulated at pleasure, and in such a way as to produce even a gentle breeze or a perfect hurricane in the mine.

The same principle may be shown by taking a hollow tube of glass, or of tin, having two arms at right angles to each other for the convenience of blowing through; otherwise, a straight tube would do as well, and one end terminating in a perforated pasteboard, or tin disc, of a few inches diameter, through the centre of which the tubular opening runs, then blowing violently through it, and placing another piece of pasteboard, or tin, over the opening from which the air proceeds, it will be found to adhere, and to be violently attracted—if the apparatus be

K

turned downwards, so that the current instead of ascending is blown towards the ground, the under surface will be lifted up.

If water is poured into a bent glass tube, open at both ends, and a current of air is blown violently across one end, the water in it will be found to rise.

On the subject of light there are many simple things easy of explanation, connected with experiments of so simple a kind, that the teacher may with advantage turn them to account in his teaching.

That some bodies, such as the sun—the stars—flame of all kinds—bodies heated to a red heat, are self-luminous, possessing in themselves the power of throwing off light; others again, not being themselves the source of light, reflect that which they receive from self-luminous bodies. The flame of a candle is seen by the light which proceeds directly from it; the things in the room are seen by the light thrown upon them from the candle, and reflected back to the eye.

Why does the light passing through a window light the whole room, and not appear a mere column of light, the base of which is equal to the size and figure of the window, and why any light on each side of this column ? Or, rather why is it not a set of separate columns, as many in number as the panes of glass, and having circular, or square bases, etc., according as the panes may be circles, squares, diamonds, etc., with dark spaces of the thickness of the bars of the window between each column of light; so that a person walking from one side of the room to another would pass through alternate sections of light and darkness—th same, also, vertically, from the bottom to the top, caused by the cross bars : each column of light, supposing the floor to be horizontal, and the window at right angles to it, would be inclined to the plane of the room, at an angle equal to the angle of incidence on the glass.

In bringing candles into a room during twilight, whether would there be more or less light in the room by closing the window shutters ?

Light is sent off from luminous bodies in every direction, and proceeds in straight lines.

through a small hole into a dark room—if there is dust or smoke in the room its progress will be distinctly observed proceeding in a straight line—if it is received on a dark surface, at the opposite side of the room in which it enters, most of the light is absorbed, and the room scarcely lighted at all by it—if on a white surface, such as a sheet of paper, much more light is reflected on the objects around.

Also beams of light from the sun, passing through the opening in a cloud, darting in straight lines to the ground —the outline of a shadow, being always that of the object seen from the luminous point shows the same.

Hold a flat object between the candle and the wall, the image is of the exact form of the outline of the object—the image of a globe—of a flat circle of the same diameter, held parallel to the wall, and to the flame of the candle—of a cylinder, with its end towards the centre of light, is the same, and these different bodies would not be distinguished from each other by their shadows.

The shadow of a flat circle, when held slantingly, would differ, etc. How? what would it be when the circle is held with its plane perpendicular to the surface on which the shadow is cast? The darkness of a shadow will not be in proportion to the real darkness, but in proportion to the quantity of light on the surrounding objects; try the shadow of a hand on the wall, as made by one candle, and then place another so that the shadows from the two candles coincide; it will be seen that this appears much darker than the former one, and why? Vary the position of the candles so that part of one shadow rests on the other—the comparative darkness will be very visible.

When the body from which light comes is less than that which causes the shadow, the shadow will be greater than the body—the shadow of a hand on the wall (luminous body, flame of a candle), of a small paper figure of a man, may be made of any size greater than itself, by varying the distance of the candle and object from the wall.

When the body from which light comes is greater than the body causing the shadow, the latter will always be less than the object; this is the case with the shadows of all the planets and of the earth, because less than the sun—the nearer to the body causing the shadow, the greater the shadowed surface.

When light falls upon any body whatever, part of it is reflected, part of it absorbed, and either lost in it, or proceeds through it; when on a brightly polished surface, most of it is reflected, and the remainder lost,—when on glass or water, very little is reflected, and the greater part transmitted through it.

"The quantity of light which is reflected by a substance of any kind, depends not only on the nature of the substance, but also on the obliquity of its incidence; and it sometimes happens that a surface which reflects a smaller portion of direct light than another, reflects a greater portion when the light falls very obliquely on its surface. It has been found that the surface of water reflected only one fifty-fifth part of the light falling perpendicularly upon it—that of glass one fortieth, and that of quicksilver more than two thirds : but when the obliquity was as great as possible, the water reflected nearly three fourths of the incident light, and the glass about two thirds only."—Young's *Lectures.*

A given quantity of light or heat, such as that from a candle or from the sun, will be less intense the greater the space it is spread over—the intensity of both diminishes as the square of the distance increases; a person standing near a fire (the heat given out remaining constant), if he remove to twice the distance, will only receive $\frac{1}{4}$ of the warmth, at three times only $\frac{1}{9}$, at four times $\frac{1}{16}$; the same of light.

Light falling on polished metals, or any polished surface, is reflected at an angle made between the reflected ray, and a perpendicular to the reflecting surface, which is equal to the angle which the incident ray makes with the same perpendicular.

A glass mirror reflects the light without the heat absorbing the latter; while a metallic mirror reflects both light and heat, so that it is not quickly warmed, unless its surface is blackened.

When a ray of light falls perpendicularly, it is sent back in the same line.

The image of an object, placed before a plane mirror, appears to be at an equal distance from the glass with the object, but on the opposite of it.   Place a boy or hold an object in such a position that the rays fall obliquely on the mirror; a person, in order to see it, must stand in a direction making the same angle with the other side.

Place two looking-glasses parallel to each other, and a lighted candle between them, and observe an infinite number of images, each in succession dimmer than the one before it, and why.   Explain also the distances from each other and from the glass.

Light passes through some substances, as glass, water, ice, rock-crystal, etc., but, on entering, is bent at the surface ; and in going out, if it passes through, is again bent at the other surface.

A ray of light entering from air into water is bent downwards—in passing from water into air, it is bent from the perpendicular to the surface of the water ; so that a body in the water, as a fish, or the bottom of the river appears elevated, and the fish higher, or the water less deep than it really is—people not knowing this, mistake the depth of water ; if looking perpendicularly downwards, the object appears in its true place.

Exp.   Put a shilling into an empty basin, place it on a table, and recede until the eye entirely loses sight of the shilling, or in fact of any particular point in the bottom of the basin, keep the head in that position, and let some one pour water into the basin, and the shilling will gradually appear—parts of the bottom surface of the basin will come in sight which before were not visible.   If spirits of wine were used for this experiment, the shilling will appear more raised, and if oil still more ; but in none of these cases will it be thrown aside to the right or to the left of its true place, however the eye be situated.

The ray having once entered one of these transparent substances, passes on in a straight line, and, when coming out on the other side, its direction is parallel to that in which it first entered.   The different refractive powers of transparent liquids vary, but so constant is it in the same substance, that the purity of oils can be tested as a matter of commerce by their refractive powers, and that this mode of examination is had recourse to, in order to test whether an oil has been adulterated or not.

A ray of light from the sun, when it enters the atmosphere, which increases in density the nearer the earth, moves in a curve which is concave towards the earth, this causes the sun to appear to us in the horizon before he is actually above it.

Light proceeding from the sun, as well as heat, the more of the atmosphere they have to pass before they reach us, the less intense they will be—much of both being lost in the passage. The stratum of air, also, in the horizon is so much more dense than that in the vertical, that the sun's light is diminished 1000 times in passing through it, which enables us to look at him when setting without being dazzled. The loss of light and of heat by the absorbing power of the atmosphere increases with the obliquity of incidence. There is no known substance which is perfectly pervious to light : all transparent substances absorb in different degrees the light falling upon them. The clearest crystal, the purest air or water, stop some of the rays of light on its passage through them, and of course the thicker the medium the greater the quantity of light absorbed; on this account objects cannot be seen at the bottom of very deep water, and there are more stars visible to the naked eye from the tops of mountains than from the valleys: the quantity of light incident on any transparent substance is always greater than the sum of the reflected and refracted rays. Bodies which reflect all the rays appear white, those which absorb them all seem black ; but most substances, after decomposing the light which falls upon them, reflect some colours and absorb the rest, and appear of that colour the rays of which they reflect, for they all receive their colour from their power of stopping or absorbing some of the colours of white light and transmitting others.

From the quantity of watery vapour in the atmosphere varying, objects at the same distance at one time appear more distinct and larger than at another.

The experiment of letting light from the sun fall on a triangular prism of glass, will interest—seeing the separation into the different prismatic colours—let them observe the order in which they follow—the image being white, excepting when the rays proceed from the prism at a particular angle; cover first one side of it with paper and then another, which shows to them on which side it enters and which it goes out at—otherwise they will not understand. This separation of colours by refraction is perhaps the most striking thing which can be brought before them belonging to this class of experiments.

Tell them when they see a rainbow to observe the order of the colours—the order in the secondary bow. Calling their attention to things of this kind even in this simple way is of great service.

Many of them have seen a heated coal, or the red-hot end of a stick whirled rapidly round, or moved quickly in a straight line ;—show them that the fiery end cannot be in every point of the circle or of the line at the same time ; and that it must be moved with such rapidity, that the impression of it on the eye while at any particular point must rest until it comes there again ; the stick in one case appearing a circle, in the other a line of fire.

The impression of light lasts on the retina about one sixth of a second, therefore it must whirl round six times in a second, or come from any one point in the line to the same again in one sixth of a second, as the least velocity which would produce this effect.

Of the same kind a meteor, called a falling star, which is a luminous point in rapid motion—the motion of a rocket, etc.

The following is a very instructive experiment : Take a circular disc of white pasteboard, or perhaps better, paste white paper on a circular piece of board, and having divided the surface into sections of proper proportions, and painted on them the prismatic colours — when made to revolve rapidly it will appear white—if whirled round in a dark room, and with the same rapidity which before produced white, when lighted by an electric spark, all the colours are as distinctly visible as if the wheel were at rest ; in this case the wheel has moved through no visible angle, while the light lasted, and may be taken to have been at rest ;

if lighted by a flash from gunpowder, they will be less distinct, but here the duration of light is longer.

"It has generally been supposed, since the time of Newton, that when the rays of light are separated as completely as possible by means of refraction, they exhibit seven varieties of colour, related to each other with respect to the extent that they occupy in ratios nearly analogous to those of the ascending scale of the minor mode in music. The observations were, however, imperfect, and the analogy wholly imaginary. Dr. Wollaston has determined the division of the coloured image or spectrum in a much more accurate manner than had been done before; by looking through a prism, at a narrow line of light, he produces a more effectual separation of the colours than can be obtained by the common method of throwing the sun's image on a wall. The spectrum proved in this manner consists of four colours only, red green, blue, and violet, which occupy spaces in the proportion of 16, 23, 36, and 25, respectively, making together 100 for the whole length; the red being nearly one sixth, the green and violet each about one fourth, and the blue more than one third of the length."— YOUNG'S *Lectures.*

Transparent substances, as glass, may be made into such forms that the light falling on them, after passing through, may be brought to a point at particular distances.

The eye is of this nature, and it collects the light which falls upon it from objects around, and brings them to a point on what is called the retina—when they are exactly brought to a point there the sight is good;—when the surface of the eye is too round, the image is not in its proper place, and as people get older, in the generality of cases, the eye becomes too flat;—to assist them in both casss, lenses (when used in this way called spectacles) are had recourse to, and by the assistance of these, the image is formed at the proper point;—when the eye is too flat, the image is behind the retina, when too round, between the retina and the eye; but in neither case can people see well.

Short-sighted people have the eye too convex, long-sighted too flat; this latter defect comes with age, or increases as people get older, which is the reason why they cannot read without spectacles.

This does not increase the quantity of light, as light is lost in passing through the spectacles.

The effort which every one whose sight is beginning to fail feels himself making in order to read, or see anything which is indistinct, is to bring the lens of the eye into such a form, that the image may be formed in its proper place.

Then a teacher would ask them if they had never observed the effect of going out from a lighted room on a dark night, how little they could see at first, and the sort of muscular action going on in the eye, so as to adjust it to collect more light;—the contrary, going from dark to great light, as in opening the shutters of a bedroom window on a bright morning, causing a sort of involuntary effort of the eye to contract, and exclude part of the light—reflection of light from snow causing pain, etc.

Owls, etc., and animals which see well at night having the power of dilating the pupil of the eye, so as to take in more light.

To have a perfect sight, the lens of the eye must be so shaped that the image is formed exactly on the retina.

Sir John Herschel, in his "Discourse on the Study of Natural Philosophy," mentions, among others not less striking, the following instance of theory and pure mathematical analysis leading to results such as no ordinary practical reasoning would be able to get at, being contrary, as it were, to one's every-day experience.

"An eminent living geometer had proved by calculations founded on strict optical principles, that in the *centre of the shadow* of a small circular plate of metal, exposed in a dark room to a beam of light emanating from a *very small brilliant point*, there ought to be no darkness—in fact, *no shadow*, at that place; but on the contrary, a degree of illumination precisely as bright as if the metal plate were away. Strange and even impossible as this conclusion may seem, it has been put to the trial and found perfectly correct.

"Cases like this," he justly adds, "are the triumph of theories."—HERSCHEL's *Discourse on Nat. Phil.*

ASTRONOMY.

There are a few facts connected with Astronomy, and, when properly explained, not very difficult to comprehend, which ought to form a part of the instruction given in our schools.

The apparent motion of the heavenly bodies—that this is caused in part by a real motion of the spectator, which he himself is not aware of—that the movements we see of the sun, and among the stars, are not all real ones, but owing to our point of view changing every moment

That all these bodies appearing to be in a blue concave sphere, in which we see them on a fine night, and at nearly equal distances from us, are not really so—that some are millions and millions of miles farther from us than others —some are fixed and do not change their position with respect to each other, and are called fixed stars—others, again, are moving in circular orbits round the sun, in the same manner as the earth does, of which a certain number are known—their distances from the sun—the time of revolving in their orbits accurately calculated; that is, the time from one of these bodies leaving any one point in its orbit until it comes to the same point again—these are called planets —some of them, again having statellites or moons revolving round them, in the same way as the moon round our earth.

Again, that some of them are self-luminous bodies, like the sun, as the fixed stars—others like our moon, are not in themselves luminous, but appear to be so by reflecting the light thrown upon them by the sun—this explains the various phases of the moon, new moon, full moon—otherwise, if she were a luminous body, she would always appear the same, etc.

These and similar things which they may be taught are no doubt quite opposed to their preconceived notions, so far as they may have notions at all, or have ever thought on the subject; but I can say, from my own experience, that when explained in a simple way they excite a very lively interest, and are not only highly instructive as to the facts themselves, but may be made a means of imparting to the youthful mind strong feelings of a religious character.

> I saw the glorious sun arise
> In morning's early gray,
> I saw him light the eastern skies,
> And melt the shades away.
>
> Who made the sun to shine so bright
> The heavens to adorn?
> Who turn'd the darkness into light,
> And gave us back the morn?
>
> 'Twas God who made the sun so bright
> The heavens to adorn;
> 'Twas God who made the darkness light,
> And gave us back the morn.

Sung in the school by the children.

Having become acquainted with the different lines on the surface of a terrestrial globe,* they should be made to understand the two motions of the earth, one in its orbit causing the variation of the seasons, the other of rotation, causing day and night, and that this motion on its axis from west to east causes an apparent motion of the sun and stars from east to west.

Turning the globe from west to east (having first elevated the pole to the latitude of the place), it is easily understood that a point on the surface near the pole describes a very small circle, and that every point which is more distant describes a larger one, till we reach the equator, any point on which describes a great circle, and that from the equator to the south pole these circles go on decreasing.

Hence the teacher would call attention to the tendency which a body would have to fly off from the surface of the earth, caused by this rotation—that the more rapid the motion, the greater this tendency—that the motion being greatest at the equator and decreasing towards the poles, this tendency to fly off, would be greater there than at any other point; and would in all cases diminish the weight of

---

* "This earth of ours is a huge mass, self-poised, supported upon nothing, hung upon nothing—enveloped by the air which we breathe, and surrounded by the space of the heavens.

"How many thoughts does the mind embrace in this idea!"

MOSELEY'S *Astro-Theology.*

bodies, and that this was found by experience to be the case ; a body at the equator loses from this $\frac{1}{289}$ of its weight.

This tendency to fly off is always at right angles to a perpendicular to the axis of rotation, and at the equator is at right angles to the direction of gravity.

The centrifugal force at any point on the earth's surface acts at right angles to a perpendicular let fall from that point on the axis of rotation, and varies in magnitude as that perpendicular which is the cosine of the latitude ; at the equator this force is at right angles to the direction of gravity, and is a maximum, the latitude being 0, and the cosine equal to radius ; at the pole it is nothing, the latitude being 90°, and cosine of 90° is 0.

Why is a bird in its flight not left behind by this rotation of the earth on its axis ? or, why does not the lark soaring in the sky find the field moved from under her when she descends ?

He might then instance the dirt or wet flying from a cart or carriage-wheel in rapid motion over dirty roads— the water from a wet mop when twirled round—from a grindstone when the blacksmith is grinding tools ;—then to show how easy it is, from knowing the properties of a circle, to calculate the absolute space moved through by any point on the surface of the earth in twenty-four hours, or in any given time ; that any point must revolve from west to east, and will in a complete revolution describe the parallel of latitude in which it is ; giving them the length of a degree of longitude in that latitude, they would work out the arithmetic of it, and for one, two, three, etc. hours, as the case may be ; ask—what points on the earth's surface describe the greatest space, and what the least, in twenty-four hours ?

The difference between the polar and equatorial diameter. Again, pointing out that every section of a sphere must be a circle, and that knowing the circumference they can find the diameter—or the line which would reach from any one point to the one differing in longitude 180° from it—also the area of the section or slice of the earth which the plane of a parallel of latitude makes.

The following questions may interest a teacher who has a tolerable knowledge of the subject, and suggest others.

(1) The length of a degree of longitude in our latitude is 37·76 geographical miles : compare the velocity of a point on the earth's surface here arising from the motion of rotation, with the velocity of a point on the equator.

(2) If the earth's diameter were only one half what it is, what proportion would the mass, the surface, and the different land divisions of this new globe bear to those of the present one, and what would be the size of each in square miles.

The teacher should work this question out numerically to its final results; it only requires a knowledge of the properties of a circle and of a globe, that the circumferences of circles vary as their diameters, the areas as the squares; and that the solid contents of spheres vary as the cubes of their diameters.

Archimedes more than two thousand years ago discovered that the superficies of a sphere is equal to the convex surface of the circumscribing cylinder, or to the area of four of its great circles ; and that the solidity of the sphere is to that of its circumscribing cylinder as 2 to 3. He was so pleased with this discovery, that he ordered a sphere inscribed in a cylinder to be placed on his tomb, and the numbers which express the ratio of these solids.

As a means of giving correct ideas of the apparent motions of the heavenly bodies, a celestial globe will be necessary. This, to an unpractised eye, seems a mass of confusion, but by confining the attention at first to a few particular stars, particularly those near the pole, and by degrees extending it to others, it will be found very simple.

It is essential to make them understand how the elevation of the pole, or the apparent place of the pole-star, varies—that at the equator the poles are in the horizon, and at the poles directly over head.

Having elevated the pole according to the latitude, and otherwise regulated it for any particular day and hour in the year, they may conceive the equinoctial and ecliptic as the corresponding lines of the terrestrial globe swollen out to the blue vault of the sky—the teacher would point out, for instance, the constellation of the Great Bear, and how to find the pole-star from it; others, as Capella in Auriga, etc., which never get below the horizon—that the stars near the pole-star appear to move in circles round it from east to west—that this is in consequence of their own motion with the surface of the globe from west to east— that the farther a star is from the pole star, the greater the circle it describes, until you get to those which rise due east—that such a star would describe a greater circle than one rising either to the north or south of east, and that stars rising further to the south will appear to describe smaller and smaller arcs in the heavens, until you get to those which only just make their appearance on the horizon —such as a star of the first magnitude (Fomalthaut) in Piscis Australis—those further south not rising to us at all, but describing circles round the south pole, in the same way as the stars in the Great Bear and others do round the north.

Then by degrees to call the attention to others, such as a star (Vega) of the first magnitude in Lyra—Acturus, Regulus, Antares in the Scorpion, etc., marking those in and near the ecliptic—point out also the direction of the Milky Way, and the particular stars near it on each side, east or west of it.

Then turning the globe from west to east, show the rising, etc., or particular parts of the heavens where the more remarkable stars are to be found, at hours when they may themselves observe them—where they will be at eight, nine o'clock, etc., near the horizon in the east—or that they must turn their faces to the south, the west, etc., to see them; as also their apparent distance from the pole-star; and they will have the greatest pleasure in hunting them out and watching their motions.

When a right conception of the apparent motion of a few of the more important stars is formed, that of the rest scattered among them becomes an easy matter of reasoning which is soon filled up, always bearing in mind their appa-

rent distances from the pole-star—watching those which
never set, in their highest and lowest points, beginning in
the east; conceive how the observers must turn in order to
see them in the different parts of the circle they appear to
describe, until they come to the same point again.

That if they can observe one of those stars to change its
position with respect to any star which they know to be
fixed—if they find its angular distance from a fixed point
increase or decrease—that this is called a planet—that the
planets move in orbits inclined to the plane of the ecliptic,
but that their path is never far from that of the sun—some
nearer the sun—some farther from it than the earth—the
difference this must cause in the quantity of heat and light
falling upon them—that in one it would melt iron and lead
—that they would not be known as solids, water only as
an elastic vapour—while in another, perhaps, quicksilver,
water, etc,, would be solid substances, capable of being
quarried out in blocks like Aberdeen granite—gases would
become solid, etc.

Then to point out their respective distances from the
sun — their periods of revolution in their orbits — their
satellites, etc.—the exactness with which astronomers are
able to make all these calculations—changes of the moon
and her different phases.

That if the plane of the orbit in which the moon moves
were extended, it does not lie in the plane of the ecliptic,
but inclined to it, at an angle of about 5°; that at new
moon, the sun, moon, and earth are in a straight line, and
that side of the moon which receives light from the sun is
turned entirely from us, so that none of her reflected light
can reach the earth—that by her motion in her orbit she
separates herself, moving to the east, about 13° daily from
the sun—that a day or two after the change we see a small
crescent of light, concave towards the east; this goes on
increasing daily with her angular distance from the sun,
until she appears in the part of the heavens directly opposite to him, when it is full moon—the whole enlightened
surface of the moon being turned towards the earth. She
now goes on decreasing, rising later on successive evenings,
the waning side being convex towards the west.

Call attention also to the points of the horizon on which she rises — when due south — the arc described in the heavens—her varying distance from particular stars—and why the difference in time between successive risings of what is called the Harvest Moon, is less than at any other time of the year. That the orbit in which the earth moves is not a circle, but an oval or ellipse with the sun in one of the foci—show how an ellipse may be described— that the sun is nearer the earth in winter than in summer —how the point°of the horizon on which he rises varies, being farthest to the south in winter, and to the north of east in summer—how his altitude when on the meridian varies, being much greater in summer than in winter; the effect of this, so far as heat is concerned—that the length of time between sunrise and sunset varies, as you leave the equator, all the way up to the pole—the duration of twilight short at the equator, longer at other places as the latitude increases, and why? The sun not getting so high in the heavens in winter as in summer, the rays fall in a more slanting direction on the earth's surface, and on this account at this season, as well as from his not being so long above the horizon, less warmth is communicated to the earth than in summer. On fields with an aspect to the north, the rays will fall still more slantingly than on those turned to the south or on a horizontal plain, and in such situations less warmth will be given to the soil or to any substances upon it; hence vegetation in the spring is not so forward in a northern as in a southern aspect—the hoar frost in autumn remains up till noon, or even the whole day, in aspects turned to the north, but vanishes early in those to the south—the same of snow remaining on the north side of hills—other reasons also, such as cold winds from the north. What must be the inclination towards the north on any given day, that the rays may fall parallel to the surface? What the inclination to the north beyond which the surface would be entirely in the shade? What the aspect to the south, that the rays of the sun may fall perpendicularly to the surface on any given day?

Light travels from the sun to the earth in $8\frac{1}{4}$ minutes, at the rate of 192,500 miles in a second of time.

It moves through a space equal to the circumference of the earth in ⅛th part of a second—a space which would take the quickest bird three weeks to fly over.

Again, point out the difference between sidereal and solar time—day—year : how a solar day is not always of the same length—clocks regulated by mean solar time, etc. : how the period of time we call a year does not consist of an exact number of days, as 365 ; and hence the difficulty in regulating the calendar.

That the sidereal day, or the time between any meridian leaving a particular star, and coming to it again, is always the same ; the star not having moved in the interval—that this is not the case with the sun—that in the interval between any two successive passages of the same meridian under him, he has moved on towards the east, and this daily motion being unequal, causes the length of a solar day to vary.   A clock tells mean time, and is therefore sometimes before, and sometimes behind solar time.

That the time of the earth's making a complete revolution in its orbit is 365 days 5 hours and 48 minutes; so that if leap-year is made to occur every four years, this would be too often, and require correction.

" Hipparchus, the most celebrated astronomer of antiquity, and who lived about a century and a half before Christ, first paid great attention to the rising and setting of the stars; he discovered that the period of 365 days 6 hours, which had been considered as the true length of the solar year, was too great by about 5 minutes, and observed that the four parts, into which the year is divided by the solstices and equinoxes, are by no means equal, the sun occupying 94½ days in passing from the vernal equinox to the summer solstice, and only 92½ from the same solstice to the autumnal equinox, and that therefore the sun remained 187 days in that part of the ecliptic which lies north of the equator, and only 178 in the other part."

Laplace concludes that the mean heat of the earth cannot be altered by 1° of Reaumur since the time of Hipparchus, inasmuch as the dimensions of the globe would be thereby changed in a small amount, its angular velocity increased or

L   .

diminished, and a sensible difference be made in the length of the day—and this is found not to be the case.

On the subject of Eclipses. There is no phenomenon connected with the appearances and motions of the heavenly bodies which creates so much astonishment among those who have never thought on the subject, as an eclipse of the sun or moon ; and that the time of its having happened, or of its happening for the future, can be so exactly computed, is a subject of no less wonder.

It is familiar to every one, that an opaque body of sufficient size may be so placed between a luminous body and the eye of an observer, as to stop all the light proceeding from it, and in this case the luminous body becomes invisible.

Now an eclipse happens in consequence of one of the opaque bodies, the earth and the moon, being so placed as to prevent the light falling upon the other.

The moon coming between the sun and earth causes an eclipse of the sun, and this happens at new moon, when she is between the earth and sun, and hinders the rays of light from falling upon the earth.

The earth coming between the sun and moon causes an eclipse of the moon, and happens at the same instant of absolute time to all observers—longitude calculated from this.

The shadow of the earth or moon is conical, having the area of a great circle for its base. The length of the earth's shadow is 216·511 semi-diameters of the earth.

What is meant by the transit of a planet over the sun's disc ? How is it that the transit of Mercury, on the 9th of November, 1848, could not be seen to its termination by an observer in Paris, but would by one in Ireland ?

Facts of this kind, when understood, many of which they will be able afterwards to verify by their own observation, will to many, I have no doubt, be a source of rational enjoyment in their homes, and make them feel that they belong to a class of beings of an intellectual kind ; instead of being unmoved or stupefied by the grandeur of the

appearances about them, they will turn their thoughts to
that God who made them, and call to mind the lessons
they have learned at school in their childhood.

Child of the earth ! O lift your glance
To yon bright firmament's expanse !
The glories of its realm explore,
And gaze, and wonder, and adore !

Doth it not speak to every sense
The marvels of Omnipotence !
Seest thou not there the Almighty name,
Inscribed in characters of flame?

Count o'er those lamps of quenchless light,
That sparkle through the shades of night;
Behold them!—can a mortal boast
To number that celestial host?

Mark well each little star, whose rays
In distant splendour meet thy gaze;
Each is a world, by Him sustain'd,
Who from eternity hath reign'd.

Each, kindled not for earth alone,
Hath circling planets of its own,
And beings, whose existence springs
From Him, the all-powerful King of kings.

Haply, those glorious beings know
No stain of guilt, nor tear of woe;
But raising still the adoring voice,
For ever in their God rejoice.

What then art *thou*, O child of clay !
Amid creation's grandeur, say ?
E'en as an insect on the breeze,
E'en as a dew-drop lost in seas !

Yet fear not thou—the sovereign hand,
Which spreads the ocean and the land,
And hung the rolling spheres in air,
Hath, e'en for thee, a Father's care.

Be thou at peace ! the all-seeing eye,
Pervading earth, and air, and sky,
The searching glance which none may flee,
Is still, in mercy, turn'd on thee.

MRS. HEMANS.

CHEMISTRY.

The subject of Chemistry is one which may be made both interesting and useful, perhaps more so than almost any other of a secular kind, in the class of schools for which these pages are written, whether in towns or in the rural districts.

About two years ago, the subject of chemical agriculture was introduced in this school, with Professor Johnston's Catechism as a text-book, and sufficient apparatus for the experiments required to illustrate it. What has been done, and the way in which it has been received, is a sufficient proof that instruction in this might form an important feature at the larger class of schools in our rural districts, where the teachers are qualified to give it, or where those interested in the school have an inclination to introduce it ; this would attract the attention of the farmer as regards his own children, not that I think that is wanted ; when the education in our parish schools is in other respects good, they will, in the end, avail themselves of it. The difficulty is in finding qualified teachers, but let them once be properly remunerated, and society made to feel and estimate at its proper value the real worth of a sound practical education, preparing them for the duties of this life as well as for a future existence, this difficulty will cease, and qualified teachers will soon be found : nor is it too much to expect from the most advanced nation in the world, as to its political and social constitution, science, and wealth, that it should grant a liberal allowance to the education of its youth : were it to do so, the gain, even in a pecuniary point of view, would in the end be great, independent of those moral considerations which ought never to be lost sight of.

The first object of the farmer is to produce food for man and beast in the cheapest way he can—to get the most productive crops, at the least possible expense ; and although experience is not to be despised, yet, assisted by science, much more may be done than without it—this it is difficult to persuade the farmers ; some knowledge of

manures, they think, may be of service, but beyond the
"Muck Manual," in the way of book-learning, very few
of them are inclined to go—still they are on the march,
and when they see their way, through experiments successfully tried, prejudices will give way ; there is something
of wisdom in not abandoning a tolerably good plan, unless
you have confidence in the one which is recommended
being better, and the road to confidence is practical
proof.

One of the first questions naturally would be—of what
are all these plants composed ?—On inquiry, they are all
found to consist of two classes of substances, varying with
different plants, one of which is volatile, called organic, the
other, which remains after combustion, in the form of ashes,
and called inorganic—these again are analysed into their
separate elements, and it is thus seen what the plant is
made up of.

Now, it is evident that if the seed, after it is sown and
germinates, as well as grasses, during their growth, cannot
find such substances as they are composed of, the crop
must necessarily be an unproductive one, and that in proportion to the deficiency of the substances required. The
next question is—

Where are they to find all the things which enter into
their composition ?—which of them can be supplied by the
industry of the farmer ?—and which of them must he trust
to atmospheric influences to supply ?

To this, science gives an answer—the farmer judges from
experience—the agricultural chemist would analyse the
soil, and find out its separate elements—he knows the
elements of the crop he wants to grow, and knowing which
of these are to be found in the soil, and for which he must
trust to the atmosphere, he would use that kind of manure
which would supply the rest—and that such substances as
any particular crop is known to take away, must be supplied
in the shape of manure, otherwise the land will be worn
out.

A knowledge of the particular substances which a crop
of any kind, as wheat, barley, etc., takes out of the ground,
and of what is wanted by the crop which is intended to

follow, would point out a good rotation of cropping; and, in addition to this, knowing the composition of the soil, would lead to a proper economy in not casting useless substances upon the land as manure—such substances as did not contain the particular things wanted.

This does not apply merely to grain crops, but to all others; and although long experience may have taught the farmer a right course as to the ordinary crops; yet, take the case of a new plant, a grass, or other plant which is recommended, he is then at a loss as to the soil he ought to try it in; he therefore goes by guess—if he hits upon a favourable soil he pronounces in its favour; if not, it is condemned; and it will only be after a long time, and after many successful or unsuccessful trials and much expense, that it is found out what soil will suit this plant and what will not. Now, here science might help to a speedier and less expensive mode of trying it — burning the plant, examining the ashes, and analysing the soil in which it is intended to to be tried, would show whether they suit each other or not.

Thus, science, with caution, may at once point out a right course, when it would take years of experience to find it out.

Then again, with respect to manures, although a substance thrown on the ground may contain the ingredient wanted, it may not contain it in such a form that the plant can avail itself of it. Here, again, science steps in, and teaches that the nourishment which plants take up by the roots must necessarily be in a fluid form—that they cannot assimilate to themselves any substance in a solid state; although it may be the very thing they like best, and therefore it will be necessary to use such manures as are soluble in water—by the rains which fall, or which, from exposure to the atmosphere, become so—that after decomposition every animal and vegetable substance returns in one shape or other—the organic parts through the atmosphere in a gaseous form—the inorganic as solid substances thrown upon the ground, for the future nourishment of plants, and through them, of animals.

Also, with respect to the food of animals, chemistry

points out what particular food is best fitted for a required purpose; the proximate principles of fleshy matter, such as form the muscles, fat, etc., are formed in the plants; the stomachs of animals dissolve the compound substances into their proximate principles, they circulate through the blood, and are thus assimilated to the differents parts of the body.

For instance, the farmer wishes the calf, the lamb, or colt, to become a well-grown animal, to have muscle, bone, and sinew; the cow to give milk which will yield a great deal of butter and cheese, excepting in large towns, where they want quantity and not quality; the ox he wants to feed on such substances as will leave the most of fat on his bones.

In all these cases, from knowing the composition of the different vegetable substances, such as turnips, swedes, mangel-wurzel, different kinds of hay, etc., there is something of a guide as to what plants would be best suited for any particular purpose.

The farmer knows that one grass field is better than another for young stock, for milk, for fattening, etc., which is nothing more than that the grasses in one field are of that kind which have more in them of those substances of which bone, or muscle, etc., is made—in another more of the substance of milk—and in the third of fatty matter; here experience has taught that which science would confirm, if the agricultural chemist were to analyse the grasses which most abound in such pastures.

Calling attention, also, to the influence of light—heat—moisture, etc., in the atmosphere—wet and cold seasons, etc., on vegetation—that a great deal of rain has a tendency on many soils to produce more straw in our cereal crops than dry weather, etc.; in fact, calling the thinking faculties of man more into action in the business of agriculture; and not making it in the same degree that mechanical routine sort of thing which of all other occupations carried on in this country it has hitherto been; and thought to require less of intellect than anything else. Of all occupations it is that which is most natural to man, and that without which we cannot exist.

When a knowledge has been obtained of the simple elements of which vegetable matter is composed, and of the substances, starch, gluten, oil or fat, and inorganic matter, which a healthy animal ought to derive from its food, it will be found useful and instructive to call attention to the ascertained quantities of each of these in given weights of particular kinds of grain — or other substances of a nutritive kind, such as the following:—

According to Johnston, in his " Chemical Catechism," " 100 lbs. of wheaten flour contain about 50 lbs. of starch, 10 lbs. of gluten, and 2 or 3 lbs. of oil.

" In 100 lbs. of oats there are about 60 lbs. of starch, 16 lbs. of gluten, and 6 lbs. of oil.

" In 100 lbs. of potatoes, about 75 lbs. of water, and from 15 to 20 lbs. of starch ; and in 100 lbs. of turnips there are about 88 lbs. of water.

"And of animal substances, 100 lbs. of butter contain from 10 to 12 lbs. of water, about 1 lb. of curd ; the rest is fat.

" 100 lbs. of cheese contain from 30 to 45 lbs. of water; skim-milk cheese from 6 to 10 lbs. per cent. of butter ; full-milk cheese from 20 to 30 lbs. per cent. of butter, and about as much pure curd."

Tables, also, similar to the following, connected with the chemistry of food and of nutrition, and which is taken from Brandt, may be made a means of suggesting most useful observations. This shows the change which takes place in the proximate elements of barley, in the process of malting:

	Composition of Barley.		Composition of Malt.
Starch	598	......	431
Gluten	57	......	12
Albumen	4	......	0
Diastasse	0	......	2
Sugar	46	......	154
Gum	44	......	150
Oil	4	......	4
Salts	5	......	5
Husk	136	......	136
Water	106	......	106
	1000		1000

The most remarkable change being of a large quantity of starch into the substances sugar and gum.

The following, shewing the functions of animals and vegetables, suggests many useful hints :—

AN ANIMAL IS AN	A VEGETABLE IS AN
Apparatus of combustion	Apparatus of reduction
Is locomotive	Is fixed
Burns carbon	Reduces carbon
„ hydrogen	„ hydrogen
„ ammonia	„ ammonia
Exhales carbonic acid	Fixes carbonic acid
„ water	„ water
„ ammonia	„ ammonia
„ nitrogen	„ nitrogen
Consumes nitrogenous matter	Produces nitrogenous matter
„ fatty matter	„ fatty matter
„ starch, sugar	„ starch, sugar
„ gum, alcohol, etc.	„ gum, alcohol, etc.
„ oxygen	„ oxygen
Produces heat	Absorbs heat
„ electricity	„ electricity
Restores to the air and earth its elements	Takes from the earth and air its elements
Changes organised into mineral matter.	Changes mineral into organised matter.

An exact knowledge of the nutritive properties of vegetable substances—food for man and beast—and the exact proportions, both quantitative and qualitative, in each, is of great importance to an agricultural people, as having a tendency to induce them to cultivate the most nutritive kind ; and one can scarcely conceive a people having such knowledge, and bringing their mind to bear upon it—cultivating, for instance, the potato — as food for man —considering also its perishable nature, to the extent which the Irish have done, in preference to crops of a cereal kind.

That great permanent benefit will be conferred upon the farming classes by the introduction of such instruction into our schools there can be no doubt, not only in an increase of produce arising out of improved modes of culture as regards the soil, but, in addition to this, it will lead to an improved culture of the mind in the rising generation of agricultural youth, and make them, as a body, a much more intelligent class of men than they are at present.

The following table, which is an analysis by Dr. Lyon Playfair of different kinds of food, and the coloured diagram in the frontispiece constructed from it, offer most useful hints not only on the properties of food, but on illustra-- tive modes of instruction; and, also, show how a mixed diet may be both more nutritive and healthy than one which is confined either to animal or to vegetable substances only.

The coloured table will give at a glance an idea of what

Substances used in Dietary.	Nitrogenous Ingredients.	Substances free from Nitrogenous Ingredients.	Mineral Matter.	Carbon.
Bread	·07	·49	·02	·25
Cooked meat	·22	·14	·00	·22
Carrots	·01	·12	·01	·05
Turnips	·02	·10	·01	·05
Potatoes	·01	·22	·01	·12
Oatmeal...........	·14	·70	·03	·44
Barley meal........	·14	·69	·02	·41
Peas.................	·23	·60	·03	·36
Rice................	·05	·85	·01	·36
Wheat flour	·17	·66	·00	·46
Sugar	·00	1·00	·00	·43
Suet, fat, or butter..	·00	1·00	·00	·79
Milk	·05	·08	·01	·07
Bacon	·08	·62	·00	·54
Parsnips...........	·02	·18	·01	·09
Cabbage....	·02	·04	·02	·03
Fish	·14	·07	·01	·09
Indian meal........	·11	·75	·01	·36
Mangold wurzel ..	·02	·12	·01	·06
Cheese.............	·31	·25	·05	·37
Cocoa	·10	·86	·03	·69
Beer	·00	·09	·00	·04
Broth liquor........	·10	·18	·16	·09

is meant ; and the more exact proportions will be learned by the decimal points in the table.

This table and the diagram may also suggest more exact and instructive methods of teaching other useful lessons, which a teacher might wish to bring before his school. It is, I believe, the intention of Dr. Lyon Playfair, secretary to the Board for the encouragement of Science, under the Board of Trade, to have the table in the frontispiece, with other similar ones on a larger scale, prepared for the use of schools, to be supplied to them at one half the cost price.

The village schoolmaster who attempts anything of this kind should, in addition to a general knowledge of the particular substances which constitute the ordinary crops, be able to manipulate in a few of the common routine things in general chemistry—in making the ordinary gases, hydrogen, oxygen, carbonic-acid gas, etc.—to show that this last is not a simple but a compound substance, and constitutes nearly one half of all the chalk, limestone, marbles etc. on the earth; shew the weight of a piece of chalk or limestone before and after being burnt into lime—the different specific gravities of the gases—that one is combustible—another is a supporter of combustion, and to such a degree that iron will burn in it—that carbonic-acid gas extinguishes flame, destroying animal life when breathed into the lungs—danger of sleeping in a close room where charcoal is burning, or near a lime-kiln, etc. To shew that all these, although the same to the eye, may in other ways be tested and made out. That ammonia consists of two gases, nitrogen and hydrogen, and how formed in the decomposition of plants and animals.

The quantity of carbonic-acid gas locked up in every cubic yard of limestone has been estimated at 16,000 cubic feet. The quantity locked up in coal, in which its basis, carbon, forms from 64 to 75 per cent., must also be enormous; if all this were set free, extinction of animal life, etc.; to suggest any mode of approximating to the weight of carbonic-acid gas locked up in a given weight of chalk—a cubit foot for instance—by weighing it before being converted into lime and weighing it afterwards—difference in weight arising from the gases driven off.

Five per cent. of this gas in the atmosphere would be

highly deleterious, and ten per cent. would be entirely destructive to animal life.

To make out by experiment that air is not a simple body, by burning a taper under a bell-jar over water, etc., or a piece of phosphorus, but is made up of oxygen and nitrogen, about $\frac{1}{5}$th in bulk being oxygen and $\frac{4}{5}$ths nitrogen; also the different compounds which this forms with oxygen, etc.

That water is not a simple substance, but composed of two elements, oxygen and hydrogen, in the proportion of 1 to 2 in volume and 8 to 1 in weight; and when analysed, that the two simple elements can be again reunited to form water.

The hot iron which the blacksmith plunges into his water-trough decomposes the water — the oxygen of the water uniting with the iron and forming an oxide of iron, which is sometimes seen as a flaky substance on the surface, the hydrogen being set free, mixed with some impurity which gives it an offensive smell : the same when the kettle boils over or water is thrown into the fire.

That salt is made up of a vapour called chlorine and a metal called sodium—that sulphur, mercury, and the metals, as far as yet known, are simple substances, and to point out the more common ones—to explain and make them understand what is meant by a salt made up of a base and an acid, etc.— the way in which acids and alkalies act upon vegetable colours —how they neutralize each other, tests for them, etc.

In order to form definite notions of the relative weight and substances of such bodies as the gases, of matters the existence of which is not evident to the sight, it will be necessary to have recourse to the balance: this, in the case of common air, may easily be done by exhausting the ordinary brass bottle, the volume of which is a quart, by means of the air-pump; in the case of the following the weights would be found—

	Weight of quart.		Weight of cubic foot.
Atmospheric air......	$21\frac{2}{3}$ gr.	....	$1\frac{1}{5}$ oz.
Hydrogen.............	$1\frac{1}{2}$	....	$\frac{1}{12}$
Oxygen	$23\frac{1}{5}$	....	$1\frac{1}{3}$
Nitrogen.............	$21\frac{1}{5}$	....	$1\frac{1}{6}$
Carbonic acid........	$32\frac{2}{3}$	....	$1\frac{9}{10}$

The simple fact of showing how these invisible substances can be handled—those which are heavier than common air, poured from one vessel to another, like water—can be pumped out, and even, by a dexterous manipulator, ladled out by the hands, proving that the transfer is really made by testing in the ordinary way, is of itself most instructive.

The teacher might easily show this in the case of carbonic-acid gas, by taking a quantity of bruised chalk or limestone, powdered marble, or bruised oyster shells—place them in the bottom of an open vessel (a rather tall glass one would be best), then pour sulphuric acid diluted with water upon them, when this gas would be copiously given off—would rest at the lower part of the vessel, rising as the quantity increased—then letting a lighted taper be gradually lowered, the point to which the gas had risen would soon be seen by the taper becoming dim, and when sunk a little further it would entirely go out.

To know that the gas given off from the substances above named is actually carbonic acid, it would not be sufficient merely to know that it is heavier than common air; but it must also be shown that it will not support combustion—will make lime water turbid—and is an acid, by turning vegetable blues red.

It is also instructive to collect this gas by displacement —making it in a vessel into which a bent tube will fit, giving it a direction into any vessel into which the gas can descend, and thus displace the air of the atmosphere. It will be found very instructive to perform this experiment in the following way : balance a glass jar at one end of a scale-beam, and then allow the carbonic acid to displace the air of the atmosphere: the end of the beam on which the jar is suspended will very soon begin to descend, thus showing the pouring in a heavier air than the one which previously occupied it—a thing not evident to the sight, but made so in this way : restore the equilibrium by means of pieces of paper—test the height to which the carbonic-acid gas has risen, by dipping in a lighted taper.

Also, show that it is a compound substance formed by the chemical union of carbon, a solid, with oxygen—that one atom of carbon unites with two of oxygen, the chemical equivalents of which are 6 and 16, forming a compound substance, of which 22 is the equivalent—the resulting gas not being an increase in volume over the oxygen with which the carbon united, but an increase of specific gravity, by the interpenetration of the substances.

For instance, if the exact quantity of carbon were burnt in a jar containing the exact quantity of oxygen with which the carbon would unite, the result would be carbonic acid, equal in volume to the volume of oxygen, but of course specifically heavier, and having all the properties of the former, the solid carbon thus united having become invisible.

This carbon may be thrown down again, and would show itself in a volume of smoke—the black and restored carbon.

The mode of weighing a gas lighter than the air of the atmosphere, would be by inverting the jar, having the open mouth downwards, and placed at the end of the balance as before—in the case of hydrogen, for instance, allowing it to ascend into the inverted jar, it will soon be shewn by the other end of the balance descending—it may be shewn to be hydrogen by ladling it out and bringing a lighted taper into contact with it.

The following experiment, which is easily made, would show the change which atmospheric air undergoes by being passed through the lungs.

Take a jar with an air-tight stopper, and such as is used for pneumatic purposes—if open at the lower end it must be placed over water—take out the stopper and place the mouth over the opening—inhale and exhale the air several times by breathing with the mouth over the opening, and taking care that no air from the atmosphere gets in ; put in the stopper, and then test the air—it will be found to have all the properties of carbonic acid—will put out a light, make lime water turbid, etc.

It is found that lungs of an ordinary capacity will take in about 160 cubic inches of air, and the greatest about 295. A man of five feet one inch takes in about 160, and eight additional cubic inches for every inch in height is found to be a very near approximation to what really takes place in life.

The same may be done by breathing through a bent tube

into an inverted jar; the upper end of which is closed; this, after having passed through the lungs and breathed out, will ascend, being heated and mixed with watery vapour, and on raising a lighted taper towards the top of the vessel, or depressing the vessel upon the taper, it will be extinguished.

The reason why this gas breathed out by animals ascends, the gas itself at the temperature of the atmosphere being heavier than common air, is, that it comes from the animal heated, and is mixed with watery vapour.

As a curious result of the chemical inquiries of the present age, it has been ascertained that the quantity of carbonic acid breathed out by a healthy man in 24 hours is about $13\frac{3}{4}$ oz., of which about 7 oz. is solid carbon; about 63 oz. by a cow, and about 70 oz. by a horse; and that an approximate calculation founded on this would give about 500 tons, breathed out by the population of London; and that the quantity of carbon breathed out by the whole animal race would be sufficient to supply all the vegetable world on the surface of the globe.

It has been ascertained by a Swedish philosopher experimenting on a healthy man about thirty-five years of age, confined in a small chamber into which air entered by a hole on one side, and examining it after it passed through at the other, that the carbon ejected per hour was 105 grs. fasting; 190 grs. after breakfast; 130 when hungry; 165 two hours after dinner; 160 after tea; and 100 sleeping; making about 7 oz. daily.

The mode of making common coal gas—the process which is going on in the burning of the gas, or of a candle —how the water which is formed during the combustion— the carbonic acid, etc.—is returned through the atmosphere again to assume the form of vegetable life, etc.—that a given weight of wood, for instance, or of any other combustible body, when consumed, if all the parts were collected, would weigh more even than the wood, and why?— that when they burn wood on their own fires, elm will leave more ashes than beech—beech than oak—oak than willow, etc., and that consequently these trees during their growth carry away different quantities of inorganic matter from the soil—that leaves make more ash than straw—straw than grain.

These are things not difficult to understand—but they ought to be taught by experiment, and all that is required may, by a person at all well acquainted with the subject, be done at very little expense. There are numberless ways of showing the principle of many of these things, not only in the arts, etc., which would apply more particularly to towns, but in the common every-day things of life, whether in town or country, and calling attention to them when an experiment is performed, is of more service in an educational point of view than those without experience are at all aware of.

Many examples might be brought forward where even the remarks of ordinary workmen have led to discoveries of a most important kind; but the two following, from Sir John Herschel's " Discourse on Natural Philosophy," are particularly striking : " A soap manufacturer remarks that the residuum of his ley, when exhausted of the alkali for which he employs it, produces a corrosion of his copper boiler, for which he cannot account. He puts it into the hands of a chemist for analysis, and the result is, the discovery of one of the most singular and important chemical elements, iodine. Curiosity is excited : the origin of the new substance is traced to the sea-plants, from whose ashes the principal ingredient of soap is obtained, and ultimately to the sea-water itself. It is thence hunted through nature, discovered in salt mines, springs, etc., and pursued into all bodies which have a marine origin : among the rest, sponge. A medical practitioner then calls to mind a reputed remedy for the cure of one of the most grievous and unsightly disorders to which the human species is subject—the goître —which infests the inhabitants of mountainous districts, and which is said to have been originally cured by the ashes of burnt sponge. Led by this indication, he tries the effect of iodine on that complaint ; and the result establishes the extraordinary fact that this singular substance, taken as a medicine, acts with the utmost promptitude and energy on goître (of course, like all medicines, with occasional failures), as a specific against that odious deformity."

Another instance affording a safeguard of human life, and a remedy for a more serious evil : "In needle manufactories, the workmen who point needles are constantly exposed to excessively minute particles of steel which fly from the grindstones, as the finest dust in the air, and are inhaled with their breath; this in time produced a constitutional irritation dependent on the tonic properties of the steel, which was sure to end in pulmonary consumption: insomuch, that persons employed in this kind of work, used scarcely ever to attain the age of forty years. In vain was it attempted to purify the air, before its entry into the lungs, by gauzes or linen guards; the dust was too fine and penetrating to be obstructed by such coarse expedients, until some ingenious person bethought himself of the motions and arrangements of a few steel-filings on a sheet of paper held over a magnet. Masks of magnetized steel are now constructed, and adapted to the faces of the workmen. By these the air is not merely strained, but searched in its passage through them, and each obnoxious atom arrested in its progress."

Also Davy's safety-lamp, lightning conductors, etc., are all instances of the application of science to the most valuable purposes of social life.

So indifferent, from habit, do the miners become, in the midst of danger, that to those unaccustomed to this class of life, their conduct appears almost unaccountable. The following was told me, by a scientific friend, as having occurred when visiting a *mine* of a very dangerous character :—

"The workman carrying the light, when he came to a particular part of the mine, stopped, and coolly said, ' Now Sir, if I were to elevate the light a few inches higher, we should be blown to atoms.' " Meaning the light would then come into contact with the carburetted hydrogen which, from its comparative lightness, was floating in the upper part of the diggings.

This dangerous gas, issuing from fissures in small quantities, and sometimes from beds below those the men are working, by means of boring is employed as a gas-jet to light the veins above. Sometimes it is carried to the surface of the ground, and a continual fire kept up by it at the surface.

Of the great usefulness of being acquainted, through experiment, with facts in science which are of a practical kind, a knowledge of which, from experience, I am convinced is attainable in our best elementary schools, the following is a striking instance. The philosophy of it is very interesting, and from its being an important practical lesson, I give it here : it shows also, that the very means we take to protect both life and property may, through ignorance, increase the danger we wish to avoid; and is an instance, where a knowledge of science prevented what might otherwise have been attended with most serious results. Being in London, I went with a friend to the Royal Institution, to hear a lecture which had been announced on the manufacture of glass, and on the application of various metallic substances in colouring it, etc. ; on arriving there, we found there was no lecture, some danger of fire having arisen from the furnaces erected for the occasion. On the subsequent Friday, Professor Faraday gave a very interesting account of this accident. The heat of the furnaces and fire resting on the bricks of the fire-place in the lecture-room, had so heated the bricks, as to char the ends of some joists on which the floor rested, and the ends of which ran up nearly to the fire-place, and were in contact with the bricks; this caused a smell of fire, water was thrown on the fire in the fire-place to extinguish it, and while this was being done, a workman went into the room below, and broke the ceiling at a distance from the fire-place, and spying every now and then a flame issuing out, thought nothing could stop it. This being pointed out to Professor Faraday, he immediately saw the water thrown for the purpose of putting out the fire, falling on the heated bricks, was decomposed, and the hydrogen, by the pressure of the steam above, was forced downwards, and coming in contact with the charred beams, took fire, the beam ends being sufficiently hot to ignite it, so that the very means taken to extinguish it were adding to the danger. He then directed the water to be thrown on the heated substances near the fire, and these being cooled down below the point which would cause the gas to ignite, there was of course no further danger in throwing water on the fire.

The facts of a scientific kind connected with this are by no means difficult to understand, and are such as an experienced workman, who had seen experiments on the composition and decomposition of water—how the compound substance could be separated into two others, by coming in contact with a heated surface, like the bricks, and that one of them, hydrogen, was very inflammable, and would ignite at a low temperature—that the oxygen would assist the combustion—would easily understand: the lesson taught him would be that, in a case of this kind, instead of continuing to throw water on the fire and on the bricks, he would immediately direct it to be poured on the heated materials around, and then pour water again on the fire; when, even if gas were evolved, there would be nothing near it of a sufficiently high temperature to ignite it.

Facts in science such as these have a direct practical bearing; and when it is seen how much of property in towns, nay, of life itself, may depend upon a knowledge of them among what are called our more experienced workmen, their importance will be understood.

A knowledge of elementary chemistry, and of what has been termed the philosophy of common things, is becoming every day more and more necessary in the schoolmaster, and greater facilities of acquiring it are placed within his reach.

The Training Colleges make it a part of their course of instruction. The managers of schools are now seeing its importance; and influential individuals who take an interest in promoting a good practical education for the industrial classes, are proposing to institute prizes in their own counties and districts for those schoolmasters who shew the greatest knowledge of such subjects, and its application to the comforts of life—*with regard to food and its cookery—ventilation of cottages, and sanatory condition of them—a knowledge of mechanics and labourer's work*, etc.: such prizes to be adjudged after examination in writing, and *vivâ voce*, by competent persons, in the required subjects: and, I would add, as shewn in their application of it, in the state of their schools.

The Committee of Council on Education will aid in providing the necessary apparatus for instruction in elementary physical science, in schools where the teachers are competent to use it; and the Board of Trade* Department for the encouragement of Practical Science and Art, of which Dr. Lyon Playfair is secretary for the former, is instituted for the purpose of promoting it, both in schools and other local institutions.

The demand for apparatus connected with this department of teaching is likely to be very great compared with what it has been; and those employed in its productio are turning their attention to simplify and cheapen it. I am told if such instruction be made common in schools, that a very great reduction in price will be the consequence.

Philosophical instruments are not essentially more expensive than tools for tradesmen, or utensils for domestic use. They are dear because the demand is small; but if made in large quantities they will, according to the common results and experience in other matters of trade, be made more cheaply.

I have received, with reference to the class of prizes already alluded to, a synopsis of what is called a knowledge of common things. It is inserted here with the permission of the promoters, and is a good outline of the

---

* The Treasury Minute establishing this department of the Board of Trade, says:—" My Lords concur in the views expressed by the Lords of Committee of Trade, that every means should be used to render these institutions as much self-supporting as possible, and that in the plans adopted, that object should always be borne in mind. My Lords adopt this view, not only because they feel it incumbent upon them to confine the public expenditure to the lowest limit, but also because they entertain a belief that the utility of such institutions is great in proportion as they are self-supporting." This remark applies equally to all our schools; and school managers would do well to aim at this in all possible cases, as a result which their efforts ought to lead to, and in the end attain.

practical turn which the schoolmaster ought to give to the knowledge he possesses on this subject. It may also, in some measure, direct him in bringing to bear what he knows on his every-day teaching.

A KNOWLEDGE OF COMMON THINGS.

I.—Sources of Domestic Health and Comfort.

A—*With regard to food.*—The value of different kinds of food, both vegetable and animal—the kinds best adapted for keeping up the strength of the body, and those fitted for preserving animal heat *—the mixing of different kinds of food so as to give really nutritious food cheaply—the best kinds of food for hard muscular exertion—the diet of young people and of the sick—the value of various kinds of foreign food, such as Indian corn (maize), rice, arrow-root, sago, etc., and the mode of using them separately or of blending them with home products so as to render them nourishing and palatable—the advantage of variety in food, and the best mode of cultivating a cottage-garden so as to secure a regular succession of crops of vegetables for domestic use without exhausting the soil—the effects of excess in drink and grossness in living.

B—*With regard to cookery.*—The best modes of making common things cheap and palatable—the different modes of boiling beef if soup be required, or if it be wanted as boiled beef—the relative advantages of boiling, roasting, stewing, and baking—the best forms of fire-places, stoves, ovens, boilers, etc.; for domestic use—the baking of bread, etc.

C—*With regard to the healthy state of a house.*—The cheapest and most effectual mode of draining, warming, and ventilating the houses of the poor—the importance of avoiding all collections of refuse and decaying matter. The connection of the common diseases of the poor, such as rheumatism, fevers, inflammations, and contagious mala-

* See Frontispiece.

dies, with the dampness, bad ventilation, want of personal
or domestic cleanliness, and the retention of decaying
matter in or about their dwellings, and the best means of
avoiding these causes of disease.

D—*With regard to personal health.*—The importance of
personal cleanliness and the most convenient and cheap
expedients for procuring it—the precautions to be taken
in peculiar sedentary and in-door manufacturing employments for the preservation of health—the clothing appropriate to different forms of labour to the seasons, etc.—the
importance of vaccination—the urgency of attending to
premonitory symptoms of cholera and other contagious
maladies. The permanent injury to health by the use of
sleeping mixtures to secure quietness in children.

E—*With regard to domestic comfort.*—The uses of domestic order, neatness, convenience, and comfort; and
with this view, a knowledge of the expedients which may
be resorted to for washing, drying, etc., so as to occasion
the least discomfort—the economy of soap—the means
of softening hard water, so as to adapt it for washing, and
to save soap—the household arrangements at night required by decency, health, or good feeling—the economy
and proper distribution of the wages of the working man,
whereby his family may enjoy the fair share of his earnings,
and the education of the children may be provided for—
saving-banks—sick-clubs, etc.

II.—Knowledge of Mechanic and Labourer's Work.

A—*Tools for hand use.*—The various forms of those in
general use—such as the various planes, chisels, hatchets or
adzes, hammers, files, picks, spades, mallets, saws, pincers
or tongs, shears, drills, punches.

B—*The cutting edges of tools.*—Such as the various plane-
irons, chisels, saws, gouges, shears—the guide-principle
in tools and its value—modes of compensating for its
absence.

C—*With regard to matters of household arrangement.*—
Viz.—the common pump—the common clock—the gas
meter—the gas-pendant—the gas-cock—the gas-burner—
the bell—its cranks and wires—the common lock and latch

—the forms of hinges and castors—the common scales—both those for standing on a table and those for being suspended—the common bellows.

III.—EXPLANATION OF NATURAL PHENOMENA.

A—*Stones and Rocks.*—What they are made of—the manner in which they have been formed—the metals, etc. found in them—petrified plants, shells, and bones—the arrangement of rocks, or the places in which different kinds are found.

B—*Animals and Plants.*—The kinds of animals—those with bones and limbs—those with hard skins and limbs—those with shells—those with soft bodies—animals invisible to the naked eye—animals that live upon animal food—animals that live upon vegetable food—plants with flowers—plants without flowers—the parts of flowers—the kinds of trees—plants and animals used for food by man.

C—*The Weather.*—The four seasons—trade winds—changing winds—revolving storms and whirlwinds—land and sea breezes—rain—hail—snow—ice—mists and clouds—dew and hoar frost.

D—*Natural Geography.*—The ocean—ocean currents—tides and their variation in different parts of the world—rivers—lakes—volcanoes—earthquakes—glaciers and icebergs—wasting powers of the sea—rivers and glaciers on the land.

E—*The Stars.*—The sun and its planets—the year—leap-year and months—the changes of the moon—comets—meteors—fixed stars.

GEOLOGY.

There are many interesting facts in Geology, particularly such as apply to the locality in which a school is situated, or which have reference to agriculture, to which attention might be called.

Boys may be easily made to understand what is meant by stratified and unstratified rocks ; that the order of superposition of the different strata is found to be the same in every country, and in every part of the globe ; and there are a few leading features which might be mentioned, without going into detail, as to the fossils that distinguish one set of beds or one formation from another—such as where a stratum is found to abound in fossils of a marine character—animals that must have lived in the sea—that these denote a submarine formation ;—that one abounding with those of a fresh-water character denotes a fresh-water formation ;—and, having formed an idea of the order in which the different strata rest one upon another, to notice the strata which prevail in their own neighbourhood—for instance in this part of Hampshire—the chalk—that this is divided into two, the upper and the lower—the one containing flints, the other without flints—the soil resting on the upper part not so good for arable purposes as for pasturage—that on the lower chalk partaking of the character of a good soil, and being of a marly nature, is better for the purposes of agriculture.

These nodules of flint when broken, will many of them appear inside of a spongy or porous texture, and the chalk being a submarine formation, they are supposed to have been formed by a deposit of the siliceous matter in sea-water around the sponge, the substance of which gradually going away has been replaced by this flinty deposit.

That the unstratified rocks form hills, mountain chains, etc., often one mass of the same material, as granite—that the stratified rocks rest upon the other, but that the hills of granite have been upheaved through these primary rocks, as is shown, by laying bare the strata, where they rest on the mountain sides.

That the mineral ingredients of a soil partake very much of the character of the rocks in the neighbourhood, and of those on which they are superposed ; if, in digging through the surface-bed of soil, we come at chalk as the prevailing substratum, the soil itself, when analysed, would be found to contain a great deal of this substance—if a limestone, it would be of a calcareous nature, etc.

Of the nature of this degradation and crumbling away, it would be easy to refer to instances in almost any neighbourhood—such as chalk cliffs, limestone rocks, deep pits, etc.—how the atmosphere is the chief agent in this—by

the action of heat and cold—of frost and thaw, etc.
Thus the depth, etc., of soil will depend much on the rock
being easily decomposed, or of a soft nature.

Then, again, the practical purposes to which a knowledge
of this superposition of the different strata may be turned.
If they come in the order 1, 2, 3, 4, etc., and you live upon
No. 2, it is of no use attempting to find No. 1 below it, or
No. 2 below No. 3—to point out the use of this knowledge
in boring for water—in looking for beds of coal—and in all
mining purposes—the needless and immense expenditure of
money which a want of this knowledge has sometimes
led to.

The alluvial deposits at the mouths of rivers, in cases
where the sea has receded, will be found containing a soil
which has been transported from great distances, as the
annual overflowings of the Nile, the Ganges, etc. These
gradually deposit an accumulation of soil over large extents
of country; and although this soil may differ from the
character of the rocks in the neighbourhood, yet the fact,
when inquired into, admits of easy explanation by the
geologist.

From what has been said on the absorption and radiation
of heat in some of the preceding pages, it will easily be
seen that the degree of warmth which a soil will acquire
from the sun's heat will depend very much upon its nature,
and this will again very materially affect the vegetation.
Professor Johnston says, that when the temperature of the
air in the shade is no higher than 60° or 70°, a dry soil
may become so warm as to raise the thermometer to 90° or
100°. The temperature in wet soils rises more slowly,
and never attains the same height as in dry by 10° or 15°.
Hence, wet soils are called cold, evaporation causing it.
This to be corrected by draining. " Dry sands and clays,
and blackish garden mould become warmed to nearly an
equal degree under the same sun; brownish-red soils are
heated somewhat more, and dark-coloured heat the most
of all."

The farmer, hitherto, never seems to have thought much
about the analysis of soils; but it is one deserving of great

attention, and can only be done by those who are well
skilled in this department of chemistry, and can pay great
attention to it.

A geological map of England, on a tolerably large scale,
pointing out the extent of country over which any particular formation extends—whether chalk, red sandstone, etc.;
also the coal fields—districts where the iron and other ores
are found—slate, tin, lead, copper—and this coloured for
the purpose, with references at the side, is a most useful
piece of school-apparatus;—it not only gives a teacher an
opportunity of pointing out where those minerals are to be
found—how they affect the agriculture of a district—the
character of its population and their employments—attracting an agricultural or a manufacturing class—but the children get a great deal of information by examining the map
themselves.   I have very often found a boy answering
questions on this subject, of which I had no notion that he
had any idea, and have found that he had got at the knowledge himself, from the inspection of a geological map on
the walls of the room.

There are many things of an ordinary STATISTICAL kind,
connected with our social economy, our manufactures, etc.,
which might be made subjects of useful lessons to the boys
in a school; such as the population of the different parts
of the United Kingdom at periods when a census has been
taken—the decennial increase, the average annual increase,
and this whether greater in the manufacturing or agricultural districts—the average number to a house, in 1831,
in Great Britain 5·62, in 1841, 5·44, so that, at the latter
period, there would seem to have been an increase of houses
in a greater ratio than the increase of population.

The average consumption of each person in some of the
common articles of life would also be interesting, as affording ideas of a definite kind as to the average consumption
of a family in a village, a town, a county, etc.

This was for the united kingdom :—

```
                        lbs.
Of sugar in 1840..........15·28 for each person.
     „      1841..........17·65   „       „
                      lbs. oz.
Of coffee in 1831..........1  5·4   „        „
     „       1841..........1  7·55  „        „
Of tea in    1831..........1  3·93  „        „
     „       1841..........1  5·96  „        „
```

Soap, in 1831, 6·23lbs. each, and in 1841, 9·2lbs. each, showing that the nation is progressing in the use of soap in a greater ratio than in an increase of population, and that, if there is not an increased consumption of it in the arts, we are progressing in cleanliness.

Then, again, the consumption of coal as fuel, and the extent of our coal-fields, how this enables us to turn large tracts of land to arable purposes, which in this climate, must otherwise have grown wood;—that every combustible substance may be considered a store of light and heat treasured up for the use of man—coal, for smelting purposes—for making gas to light our towns—this mode of lighting introduced at no very distant period, and better for the purpose than oil.

In England the coal-field is about $\frac{1}{20}$th of the whole surface, in Belgium $\frac{1}{30}$th, in France $\frac{1}{200}$th.

Different kinds of coal differ in their heating powers.

Table showing the relative heating powers of certain combustible materials.

```
Best turf.................... 1
Beech-wood................ 0·862
Danish coal................ 1·275 to 1·524
Swedish coal ............. 1·611
Faroe coal ................ 1·672
English Newcastle ........ 2·256
Scotch .. ................. 2·387
```

Economy of a Coal-Field.—JOHNSTON.

The great improvement of late years in the habits of the upper and middle classes in this country, more particularly as to drunkenness—but not a corresponding improvement in the lower and working classes in this respect—this much to be regretted.

On manufacturing subjects. The number employed in each particular class of manufacture—the potteries—cotton, silk manufactures, etc.—cutlery, and working in metals, etc.—where all these are carried on—the increased value given to the raw material when worked up—this partly in proportion to the time and skill required.

There is on this subject some very instructive information, in a tabular form, in Babbage on the " Economy of Machinery," but the calculations are made for the year 1825, and therefore would not exactly apply at present. The following are a few of them :—

Lead of the value of £1, when manufactured into—
Sheets or Pipes, of moderate dimensions.......... £1·25
Ordinary printing characters...................... 4·90
The smallest type................................. 28·30
Copper, worth £1, became, when manufactured
into copper sheeting........... .... 1·26
Household utensils .... 4·77
Woven into metallic cloth, each square inch of
which contains 10,000 meshes............... 52·23
Bar iron, worth £1, when manufactured into—
Agricultural implements, became .... 3·57
Barrels, musket   „   .... 9·10
Blades, razor, cast steel   „   .... 53·57
Blades, of table-knives   „   .... 35·70
Door-latches and bolts, from...................4·85 to 8·50
Files, common, became........................... 2·55
Horseshoes   „   .... 2·55
Saws, for wood   „   .... 14·28
Needles, of various sizes, from............... 17·33 to 70·85
etc. etc.

The above are given simply for the purpose of suggesting inquiry as to the value of labour compared with that of the material, in manufactured products;—other instances of a domestic kind would occur—such as the value of the raw material wool, of different qualities, compared with the price of a pair of stockings—a yard of flannel—of a coat of the kind ordinarily worn—of a hat, etc.

The increased value given to the skins of animals, when

manufactured into shoes, gloves, harness, saddlery, or any other thing made of leather, etc.

Increase of value in flax when manufactured into linen, tablecloths, made into sheets, etc.—pointing out the advantages to a country in being able to manufacture its raw products, whether of a mineral or a vegetable kind, over one which is obliged to export them in a raw state for the purpose of being worked up:—also to what causes it is owing that particular manufactures are located in particular districts—as that of cotton in Lancashire—woollen at Leeds—cutlery at Sheffield, etc.

Too much attention cannot be given to all these things of an industrial character, from which they can form a definite idea of the comparative money value which society pays for the various branches of industry, of skilled and unskilled labour, etc.

Of the extent to which internal communication and rapid modes of conveyance may increase the power and affect the productive industry of a country, the following passage taken from Babbage may give the reader some idea:—

" On the Manchester railroad, for example, above half a million of persons travel annually; and supposing each person to save only one hour in the time of transit between Manchester and Liverpool, a saving of five hundred thousand hours, or of fifty thousand working days, of ten hours each, is effected. Now this is equivalent to an addition to the actual power of one hundred and sixty-seven men, without increasing the quantit ofy food consumed; and it should also be remarked, that the time of the class of men thus supplied is far more valuable than that of mere labourers."

The above was written when the Manchester railroad was the only one established; the present state of things adds greatly to the interest of the observation.

A teacher ought to have a general knowledge of the ordinary things of life, so as to give a character of usefulness to his teaching, which will interest those who are taught, and also interest the parents who send them.

Short CONVERSATIONAL LECTURES, about fifteen or twenty minutes long, will be found a very effective means of instruction. Subjects like the following would naturally suggest themselves :

Truth and falsehood—industry and idleness—sobriety and drunkenness—honesty and the reverse, etc.

In natural history ; habits of birds—of animals, their instincts, etc. ; or on subjects connected with the occupations of the district—agricultural employments—mining, manufacturing, etc. ; on any particular application of substances with which they are acquainted, etc. And when a master is qualified, he might take such as the following :

The atmosphere—as a vehicle of heat and moisture—as a vehicle of sound : rain and clouds, etc., mist and fogs, etc., dew, etc.

To give an idea of what is meant by conversational lessons, the following may be taken as illustrations :

A loaf of bread.—The teacher would go on to explain, that the different substances of which it is composed are —the flour of wheat, water, barm, salt ; that these again are not simple, but each made up of many elementary substances into which they can be separated.

Flour contains gluten, starch, etc., which form the nutritive part of it as food.

Water can be decomposed into its elements, oxygen and hydrogen—two gases, which can be again reunited to form water.

Salt, of a gas, not colourless like the other gases, but yellow, which cannot be breathed, and a metal, sodium.

Barm, a froth which rises to the top of beer during fermentation. That if the smallest crumb of bread be taken, so small as to be only just visible, it will contain something of all these different elements ; that if they divide this again into a thousand pieces, so as not to be visible even to the naked eye, each of these would contain something of all the different elements of the loaf.

Again, when the loaf is cut we see a number of cells of various sizes—how came these there ? The barm causes a vinous fermentation to take place in the dough, by which an air, heavier than common air, and called carbonic acid gas, is formed; this, as the dough warms, expands, tries to escape, but the dough, by its tenacity, retains it, and in this way these cells are formed.

Then, again, the number of people it has given employment to before it became bread: from the ploughboy up to the farmer—from sowing up to threshing—from the farmer who takes it to market—the corn dealer—the miller—the baker.

How beautiful this provision of the Almighty for man's happiness, in making necessary that employment of mind and body which is required for his sustenance, and without which he could not live! what an interest this gives to life! " If a man will not work, neither shall he eat," does more for man's happiness than the thoughtless are aware of; and the labourer who has to earn his bread by the sweat of his brow is, in many instances, a much more happy man than he who, from want of employment, whatever his condition in life may be, spends his time in listless indolence or in frivolous amusement.

The cottage fire.—The fire once lighted : this heat sets free the hydrogen and other gases in the wood and coal; the hydrogen, as it is disengaged, takes fire, is supplied with oxygen from the atmosphere, heats the carbon of the fuel to such a heat that it readily unites with the oxygen of the fuel and of the atmosphere, and forms carbonic acid. This carbonaceous matter in the flame, heated to a red heat, is the principal cause of its giving out so much light. The flame of hydrogen unites with the oxygen, and produces water—the carbonic acid which is formed, being rarefied, ascends through the chimney into the atmosphere, and then mixes with it—is taken up by the leaves of trees and of plants, or descends with the rains, and is again taken up by the roots—the oxygen of it is again given out by the plants to the atmosphere to support animal life—the carbon retained in its solid state, and assimilated to themselves by the trees, adding to their solid state, and again comes back when the trees are cut down to supply us with timber, fuel, etc.

The heat of the fire not being sufficient to cause all the carbon of the fuel to combine with oxygen, the combustion is, as it were, incomplete—the uncombined carbon rises in the shape of smoke, and is partly deposited on the sides of the chimney, and is collected for manuring our lands, and again used up for vegetable life ; that part of it which ascends into the atmosphere is washed down by the rain, and so feeds the plants again.

How beautiful to watch the ascent of the smoke on a calm summer's evening — sometimes ascending merrily, denoting fine weather, at another descending the moment it has escaped from the chimney : ascending because the specific gravity of the air is greater than that of the smoke ; standing still, and in a sort of stable equilibrium on a calm evenng, when the stratum of air in which it is floating is of the same specific gravity as itself ; and descending when the specific gravity of the air is less than that of the smoke !

Here we see, in this apparent destruction of vegetable matter, that nothing is lost ; the gaseous part which went up the chimney, and which forms a very great proportion of the whole, returns again to nourish vegetable and animal life ; the ashes which remain, and contain the inorganic part of the fuel, are spread upon the ground to be dissolved through the agency of water and of the atmosphere, and so carried into the roots for the nourishment and support of fresh vegetable matter.   Not the slightest particle is lost, and if all the products of the combustion were collected— the water, carbonic acid, smoke, ashes—and weighed, their weight would be found greater than that of the fuel, having been increased by the oxygen taken from the atmosphere during the combustion.

The *flame of a candle* might be the subject of two or three conversational lectures of this kind—showing the way in which the tallow or wax, when reduced into a fluid state by heat, ascended by capillary attraction up the wick, a length of which between the candle and the flame will be seen to be moistened with it ; a higher degree of temperature changes this out of a fluid into a gaseous state, consisting of the different elements of the substance of the candle, one of which, hydrogen, ignites, the oxygen of the atmosphere supporting the flame, and the carbon, another element, ascending in the flame and being heated, increases the quantity of light. The products of this combustion, water and carbonic acid, may be collected by placing a funnel-shaped glass tube, with the larger end over the flame of the candle, and the smaller one bent and communicating with a glass cylinder kept cool, in passing into which the watery vapour arising from the flame would be deposited, and the carbonic acid passing on might be collected by an apparatus properly arranged at the other end of the cylinder, and then tested.

It has been found that the water produced by the burning of a candle is nearly equal in weight to that of a candle consumed; the collected products would be greater than this weight, but it will at once be seen that the oxygen of the atmosphere consumed explains this :—the gas collected when properly tested will be shown to be carbonic acid.

That the vapour arising from the burning of a candle or a jet of hydrogen contains a great deal of water is easily shown, by holding a cold glass in such a direction that the ascending vapour may pass into it—the glass immediately becomes dim and wet—the same may be shown by holding a cold glass over a burning piece of cotton—of paper—or a splinter of wood.

Reason why the glass should be cold.

Again, that metals, such as lead, iron, etc., in a minute state of division, are much more inflammable than tallow, oil, fat, etc., or even than gunpowder, taking fire at the temperature of the atmosphere — sodium and potassium igniting the moment they come in contact with water or with ice—and if spirits of wine in a saucer or similar vessel be set on fire, iron filings thrown on the flame will burn and fall into the saucer, when they can be examined and will be found oxydised, but grains of gunpowder thrown into the flame in the same way will not ignite.

Tallow, oil, and fat require to be heated up to a certain point, when they readily burn, but must wait to be arti-ficially heated before they do so—how beautiful this pro-vision in order that they may be turned to the purposes of mankind — lighting their dwellings — enabling them to

N

read—to work ;—how important all this to civilized life !—
and while we consider all these things " do not let us forget
Him who made them."

In giving a short conversational lecture on birds, for
instance, the teacher might speak of the way in which they
build their nests—whether in trees or on the ground—the
greater degree of skill shown by some in doing this, than
by others—but that all birds of the same kind build in the
same way—that a bird builds its nest by instinct—man
builds a house from reason, improves and profits from what
others have done in that way before him—but that birds
build now as they always have done, etc.

The striking difference of the state of their young, when
hatched and leaving the egg—the chickens of the barn-
door fowl, and of others of that class, will run about, and
seek their own food, the moment they leave the egg—want
but little assistance from the parent birds, that of the
mother alone for a short time being quite sufficient, and
the care of the male bird is not wanted in assisting to
bring up a brood of chickens—the same with the duck—
young ducks take to the water, and look out for themselves immediately.

Others again, such as birds of prey, the eagle, the hawk
—all our small birds—the young of these, after leaving the
shell, are in a helpless state for some weeks, and depend
entirely for support upon the parent birds, and require the
assistance of both, in order to find a sufficient supply of
food : these are always found in pairs, and want the assistance of both the parent birds to bring them up.

Then the structure of the bones—being hollow tubes,
and full of air-cells—caused by little, strengthening, bony
processes, which go from one side of the hollow tube to
the other—(this would be seen by splitting the bones of
fowls)—the outside bony substance of the tube being
thickest at the extremities, where strength is wanted—all
this required for the purposes of flight; but in the bones of
animals moving on the ground, these hollow parts of the
bone are filled with marrow—fewest air-cells in the bones
of those birds whose habits do not require long flight, etc.
The mechanical structure of the wing—the pinion-bone

moving in order to stretch out the feathers in the same plane with the one to which it is attached—if it admitted of an up-and-down motion out of that plane, the wing would be much less strong, and a much greater muscular power required to produce the same effect in flight, etc.

Again, on fish for instance—some breathing by means of gills, so as to get at the oxygen contained in the air of the water, all water containing air, it being necessary to the life of fish. Air contained in water being richer in oxygen by about 25 per cent. than the air of the atmosphere—this is important to fishes—although cold-blooded animals do not require by any means the same amount of oxygen in a given time as hot-blooded ones of the same size—perhaps not more than $\frac{1}{30}$th.

Some fish, such as the whale, etc., breathe by means of lungs, and take in air, for which purpose they are obliged to come up to the surface of the water.

All air-breathing fishes have a broad flat tail—a horizontal tail, giving them a mechanical advantage in rising to the surface—fishes breathing through the gills have the tail vertical, perpendicular to the water in which they float —thus to propel them forward and direct their motion— some fish, gelatinous masses, breathe at all points of their surface.'

One reason why some fish live longer than others out of water, seems to arise from their having a different kind of gill, one which retains a quantity of water, and so long as they can get oxygen from this water in the gills they continue to live.

Any one wishing to give short conversational lectures of this kind, if unaccustomed to do so, will find it of assistance to read from a book any striking passage which may occur, or which he may happen to meet with in his own reading, embracing facts easy of illustration, or describing the manners and customs of other nations; such, for instance, as the following :

" Certain insects can run about on the surface of the water. They have brushy feet, which occupy a considerable surface, and if their steps be viewed with a magnifying glass, the surface of the water is seen depressed all around, resembling the footsteps of a man walking on feather-beds. This is owing to a repulsion between the brush and the water. A common fly cannot walk in this manner on water. Its feet are wetted, because they attract the water instead of repelling it. A steel needle, slightly greased, will lie on the surface of water, make an impression as a great bar would make on a feather-bed, and its weight is less than that of the displaced water. A dewdrop lies on the leaves of plants, without touching them mathematically, as is plain from the extreme brilliancy of the reflection at the posterior surface ; nay, it may sometimes be observed, that the drops of rain lie on the surface of water, and roll about on it, like balls on a table. Yet all these substances can be wetted ; that is, water can be applied to them at such distances that they attract it."

How easy to make interesting remarks on a passage like this, and how delighted children are to have the philosophy of such things as flies walking on water, or needles floating on it, explained to them—or of any facts which come frequently under their own observation.

I have been very much pleased with the interest I have found the children would take in having any graphic passage read to them, descriptive of the modes of life, occupations, etc., of other nations or people, and have occasionally read passages of that kind myself, and am in the habit of pointing out such to the school-teachers to read. I will instance the following: while reading " Hoche-laga," a description of Canadian life, the following passages occurred to me as giving a lively picture of what it is their object to describe, and one quite coming home to the minds and capacities of children. I took the book into the school, and read them, and the interest with which they were listened to, with a few observations I made myself, would have convinced any one of the usefulness of this sugges-tion. On an occasion like this, the teacher would, as an economy of time, unite all the intelligent part of his school.

" For about three weeks after Christmas, immense num-bers of little fish, about four inches in length, called ' tommy-cods,' come up the St. Lawrence and St. Charles : for the purpose of catching these, long narrow holes are cut in the ice, with comfortable wooden houses, well warmed by stoves, erected over them. Many merry parties are formed, to spend the evening fishing in these places; benches are arranged on either side of the hole, with planks to keep the feet off the ice ; a dozen or so of ladies and gentlemen occupy these seats, each with a short line, hook, and bait, lowered through the aperture below into the dark river. The poor little tommy-cods, attracted by the light and air, assemble in myriads underneath, pounce eagerly on the bait, announce their presence by a very faint tug, and are transferred immediately to the fashionable assembly above. Two or three Canadian boys attend, to convey them from the hook to the basket, and to arrange invitations for more of them, by putting on bait. As the fishing proceeds, sandwiches and hot negus are handed about, and songs and chat assist to pass the time away. Presently plates of the dainty little fish, fried as soon as caught, are passed round, as a re··"d of the piscatorial labours. The young people of the pa. cy vary the amusement, by walking about in the bright moonlight, sliding over the patches of glassy ice, and visiting other friends in neighbouring cabins ; for while the tommy-cod season lasts there is quite a village of these little fishing-houses on the river St. Charles.

" Although the temperature is usually kept very high within doors, by stove-heat, people never seem to suffer by sudden transition to the extreme cold of the open air. I have often seen young ladies, when the thermometer was below zero, leave a hot room, where they had been dancing, and walk quietly home, with very little additional clothing ; the great dryness of the air preserves them from danger. In the very low temperatures, a razor may be exposed all night to the air without contracting a stain of rust. Colds are much less frequent in winter than summer."

" The winter markets at Quebec are very curious : everything is frozen. Large pigs, with the peculiarly bare appearance which that animal presents when singed, stand in their natural position on their rigid limbs, or upright in corners, killed, perhaps, months before. Frozen masses of beef, sheep, deer, fowls, cod, haddock, and eels, long and stiff, like walking-sticks, abound on the stalls. The farmers have a great advantage in this country, in being able to fatten their stock during the abundance of summer, and by killing them at the first cold weather, keeping them frozen; to be disposed of at their pleasure during the winter. Milk is kept in the same manner, and sold by the pound, looking like lumps of white ice."

The above passages will suggest many interesting observations on the habits of the people, climate, etc. ; that, although ice is ice, yet it varies in its temperature, and that a mass of ice (milk) at a low temperature (zero, for instance,) would do more for cooling purposes, than the same mass at a temperature near the melting point. Canadian ice is better than English ice, and why ?

Then, again, these frozen animals, etc., how is it that the animal body, while alive, is not cooled down to the temperature of the atmosphere, and of the objects around it ?—what is it which maintains this internal heat that resists the cold ?—a degree of cold in some climates far below the zero of Fahrenheit, and preserves an internal temperature in warm-blooded animals, varying but little on either side of 96°—remaining also about the same in the hottest climates—refusing to be cooled down by surrounding objects below that internal heat which is necessary for this class of animal life, or to be heated by those above it ; but the moment life is extinct, yielding itself up to the influences of either—in the one case becoming a solid frozen mass, and while in that state not decomposing—and, in the other, rapidly dissolving into its simple elements.

And again : Is every kind of animal life equally affected by heat ?—are those termed cold-blooded animals affected in the same way as the warm-blooded by the surrounding media ! No : these submit themselves within certain limits to the influence of the surrounding objects, and the internal heat of their bodies varies between 35° and 85°—when cooled down to the former point many of them become torpid—and revive again with increased warmth, but all refuse to be cooled below this, the principle of animal life supporting the heat of the body at this temperature—how curious this is, when, for months together, no new fuel is added to support this heat. In hot climates, if they submitted to a heat greater than about 85°, they would many of them, dissolve and become extinct—these preservative conditions are indeed beautiful.

What myriads of organisms necessary for the chain of existences in the world would be destroyed if either of these principles were violated!

"TEMPERATURE OF THE BODIES OF VARIOUS ANIMALS.

	Fahr.
Adult man	99·5
Child	102
Ox, sheep, elephant, hare, rabbit, dog	99—100
Narwhal, (lowest temperature of any mammal	96
Ape and bat (highest temperature of any mammal	104
BIRDS	104·5
Gull (lowest temperature)	100
Great titmouse (highest temperature)	111

Cold-blooded animals have a temperature three or four degrees above the medium in which they exist.

All animals, strictly speaking, are warm-blooded; but in those only which possess lungs is the temperature of the body quite independent of the surrounding medium."

The SINGING of the children here has been a good deal remarked upon, as being better than is usually found in schools of this kind, particularly in the country. I have myself witnessed, with great pleasure, the good moral effect, and at the same time cheerful feeling, which this gives rise to among them. They are taught by one of the parishioners, who, although busily engaged in other things, finds time to instruct the children of his neighbours; and has that pleasure in doing good to others which every well-regulated mind ought to feel. During the winter they meet every Wednesday evening at the class-room, which is well lighted and warmed, where I occasionally attend myself, and always with feelings of satisfaction, in seeing sixty or seventy children (which is the number of the singing class) spending the evening in so rational a manner. In addition to Psalmody, they sing in parts many of the moral pieces in Hullah's books as well as others, not forgetting Rule Britannia, and God Save the Queen, and have as loyal hearts as any in her Majesty's dominions.

SCHOOLMASTERS.

Having spoken of the kind of knowledge which I conceive is the most useful to be introduced into our schools, and the mode of teaching it, I will add a few observations bearing upon the duties of the schoolmaster, and the course of education, which I trust may not be altogether without interest.

At present I fear these duties are not sufficiently understood, and that society at large does not attach the importance to them which it ought to do ; but as the people become better educated they will, it is to be hoped, attach greater value to the services of the schoolmaster. In the meantime he must expect to meet with difficulties, and to find hindrances where he might have looked for support, and altogether to find the road not so smooth as he had calculated upon.

So long as there are those who prefer darkness to light —an ignorant peasantry to an enlightened one—who look upon the labourer as a machine which sleep winds up at night, to be set again in motion in the morning, and again run down on doing its daily work—who think he has sufficient knowledge of the world if he knows the order of succession in which the days of the week come—and that although God has given to the labourer a mind, it was not intended he should exercise it, it was only the body which was made for his use—so long will there be hindrances in the way of education, and it will have to struggle against opinions, and against difficulties arising out of them, which may for a time impede its progress, but must in the end give way.

But it is not learning alone which will make an efficient schoolmaster and overcome these difficulties ; there are many other requisites of a personal nature, which, if he does not naturally possess, he must endeavour to acquire. He must not only teach by precept but by example ; anything he can say will have comparatively little effect, if he is an example of the direct contrary in his own conduct.

With respect to punishment, the less of severity the better—he should endeavour to win over the children by kindness and good temper, reasoning with them in a cheerful way, and always endeavouring to discriminate, as far as possible, between idleness and want of ability. When two children are set to do the same thing, such as getting by heart a piece of poetry for instance—it may be a very unequal task—he should not be angry with a child which has done its best : this is an error I have often seen in schoolmasters.

On this point, there is an anecdote in Stanley's interesting " Life of the late Dr. Arnold," which ought to be registered in the mind of every schoolmaster in England. At Laleham (the place where he lived), he had once got out of patience and spoken sharply to a pupil, who was a plodding boy, and had taken great pains ; when the pupil looked up in his face, and said, " Why do you speak angrily, sir ? indeed, I am doing the best I can." Years afterwards he used to tell this story to his children, and said, " I never felt so much ashamed in my life ; that look and that speech I have never forgotten." This requires no comment, it speaks both to the feelings and to the understanding. Mr. Stanley adds, that he used to say, " If there be one thing on earth which is truly admirable, it is to see God's wisdom blessing an inferiority of natural powers, where they have been honestly, truly, and zealously cultivated."

In teaching children habits of cleanliness, the schoolmaster will have great difficulty if he does not set an example in his own person ; he should not go into the school unshaved, as I see many do : this has a dirty and a slovenly appearance.

He should endeavour to make them open and straightforward in their conduct, and on all occasions to speak the truth—to get rid of all those feelings of low cunning which are too prevalent among the labouring classes—to be an example himself of open, manly, and straight-forward conduct. He must not attempt to despise others for conduct which he himself is guilty of.

He should set añ example of industry, thriftiness, and good management in his own household; by this he will gain the good opinion of those around him, and very much increase his power of doing good.

In his religious teaching he should impress upon them, and show it in his own conduct, that Scripture truths are not intended as mere idle words, always in their mouths and little thought of, but are intended to be acted upon.

The following passage from a paper of Addison's in the Spectator conveys an instructive lesson, and requires no comment:

"It is of unspeakable advantage to possess our minds with an habitual good intention, and to aim all our thoughts, words, and actions at some laudable end, whether it be the glory of our Maker, the good of mankind, or the benefit of our own souls.

"A person who is possessed with such an habitual good intention, enters upon no single circumstance of life without considering it as well pleasing to the great Author of his being, conformable to the dictates of reason, suitable to human nature in general, or to that particular station in which Providence has placed him. He lives in a perpetual sense of the Divine presence, regards himself as acting, in the whole course of his existence, under the observation and inspection of that Being, who is privy to all his motions and all his thoughts, who knows his 'down-sitting and his up-rising, who is about his path and about his bed, and spieth out all his ways.' In a word, he remembers that the eye of his Judge is always upon him, and in every action he reflects that he is doing what is commanded or allowed by him who will hereafter either reward or punish it. This was the character of those holy men of old who in that beautiful phrase of Scripture are said to have 'walked with God.'"

Some of these observations may appear trite and commonplace, and I will not go on adding to them. The schoolmaster ought to see and feel that life is made of little things—that man is a " bundle of habits," and that it is therefore of importance he should acquire good habits in youth, and that although each single thing may not of itself appear of importance, it is only by attending to each separately that good as a whole, and in the aggregate, can be produced—that it is only by impressing upon the minds of children over and over again, by example and by precept, the importance of these little things and these little duties (in addition to other instruction which he has to give), that he can work out a good result, and discharge those duties to society which are expected from him.

CONCLUDING REMARKS.

In having put forward these views on the subject of secular instruction in our schools, I hope it will not be supposed that I am either indifferent, or would give less attention than ought to be given, to those Scriptural truths which are the foundation of all sound teaching, and without which an education of a merely secular kind may be a very delusive guide.

In the middle and educated classes, a religious foundation may generally be laid at home, but with the labouring and uneducated classes, this can hardly be said to be the case. My own experience tells me that the more they have of secular knowledge—the more they know of their own language, the grammar of it, etc., so as to get at the construction of a sentence, the better they will understand, and the greater interest they will take in those fundamental truths of Christianity which it is essential for them to know, and without which they cannot even be called Christians— truths which they ought to know and believe for their souls' health ; the more also they will feel that the precepts of the Gospel are intended for their guidance through life— to be acted upon, and not merely to be talked about—to guide their thoughts and words and actions—and that, if they do not take them as their guide, and, by God's help, endeavour to act up to them—whether they belong to the church or dissent from it—they are merely nominal Christians, and might as well be called by any other name. That if religion does not make them better in all the relations of life, as parents doing their duty to their children and all around them — as children*˙ obedient to their parents, grateful to them in after-life, truthful and honest in all they do—so far as they are concerned, it has failed in its intention, and that they are not doing what they profess they ought to do. That practical good conduct is the best proof which they can give that they believe what they profess—that the same substance of Christianity is contained in that beautiful passage from St. Paul, which cannot be too often or too deeply impressed upon their minds, "The grace of God that bringeth salvation hath appeared unto all men, teaching us that, denying ungodliness and worldly lusts, we should live soberly, righteously, and godly in this present world; looking for that blessed hope and the glorious appearing of the great God, and our Saviour Jesus Christ, who gave himself for us that he might redeem us from all iniquity, might rescue us from the power and dominion of sin, and purify unto himself a peculiar people, *zealous of good works ;"* and that they ought to endeavour to acquire the virtues, the temper, and disposition of a real Christian.

It has been asserted, "that man acts more from habit than from reflection," and of the truth of this no one can doubt—but how important then that, in the education of youth, the training of the mind should be such as to influence for good the habits which are then formed, and on

---

　　* And canst thou, mother! for a moment think
　　　　That we, thy children, when old age shall shed
　　　　Its blanching honours on thy drooping head,
　　Could from our best of duties ever shrink?
　　Sooner the sun from his high sphere should sink,
　　　　Than we, ungrateful, leave thee in that day
　　　　To pine in solitude thy life away,
　　Or shun thee, tottering on the grave's cold brink.
　　Banish the thought ! where'er our steps may roam,
　　　　O'er smiling plains, or wastes without a tree,
　　　　Still will fond Memory point our hearts to thee,
　　And paint the pleasures of thy peaceful home;
　　　　While Duty bids us all thy griefs assuage,
　　　　And smooth the pillow of thy sinking age.　H.K.WHITE.

which the character of the man so much depends; not only should he be made to feel that, in a worldly point of view, his success and his respectability in after-life depend upon the habits of industry, of manly virtue, and of honest, straightforward conduct, the groundwork of which is laid at this period of life—but that all his actions and all his feelings should partake of the spirit and of the devotional feeling which sees, as one of our sweetest poets has beautifully expressed it—

> " There lives and works
> A soul in all things, and that soul is God.
> Happy who walks with him! whom what he finds
> Of flavour, or of scent, in fruit or flower;
> Or what he views of beautiful or grand
> In nature, from the broad majestic oak
> To the green blade that twinkles in the sun,
> Prompts with remembrance of a present God."

Not that children should be made to feel that there is anything gloomy in religion, or in those feelings which spring from viewing the works of nature in a devotional spirit; on the contrary, I should wish to have them taught to look on the cheerful side of things, and to find lessons of happiness in the works of nature which are around them—

> Behold! and look away your low despair—
> See the light tenants of the barren air:
> To them nor stores nor granaries belong;
> Nought but the woodland and the pleasing song.
> Yet, your kind heavenly Father bends his eye
> On the least wing that flits along the sky.
> To Him they sing when spring renews the plain,
> To Him they cry in winter's pinching reign;
> Nor is their music nor their plaint in vain—
> He hears the gay and the distressful call,
> And with unsparing bounty fills them all.

> Observe the rising lily's snowy grace,
> Observe the various vegetable race;
> They neither toil nor spin, but careless grow;
> Yet see how warm they blush, how bright they glow.
> What regal vestments can with them compare—
> What king so shining, or what queen so fair?
> If ceaseless thus the fowls of heaven He feeds;
> If o'er the fields such lucid robes He spreads;
> Will He not care for you, ye faithless, say?
> Is he unwise?—or are you less than they?　THOMSON

Paley, in his "Natural Theology," after having inquired into the works of nature, comes to the conclusion that "the world, after all, is a happy one;" and, in the sense in which he intended it, this view is perfectly right, and it ought to be the duty of every teacher to train up the young to see and contemplate the goodness of the Almighty in the designs of creation—to see in everything "that happiness is the rule, and misery the exception"— to contemplate with pleasure "the air, the earth, the water teeming with delighted existence;" he goes on to say, "In a spring morn or a summer evening, on whichever side I turn my eyes, myriads of happy beings crowd upon my view; the insect youth are on the wing: swarms of newborn flies are trying their pinions in the air; their sportive motions testify their joy, and the exultation which they feel in their lately discovered faculties. A bee amongst the flowers in spring is one of the most cheerful objects that can be looked upon; its life appears to be all enjoyment— so busy and so pleased; yet it is only a specimen of insect life, with which, by reason of the animal being half domesticated, we happen to be better acquainted than we are with others. The whole winged insect tribe, it is probable, are equally intent upon their proper employments, and under every variety of constitution gratified by the offices which the Author of Nature has assigned to them. But the atmosphere is not the only scene of enjoyment; walking by the sea-side in a calm evening, upon a sandy shore, and with an ebbing tide, I have frequently remarked the appearance of a dull cloud, or rather very thick mist, hanging over the edge of the water, to the height, perhaps, of half a yard, and of the breadth of two or three yards, stretching along the coast as far as the eye could reach, and always retiring with the water: when this cloud came to be examined, it proved to be nothing else than so much space filled with young shrimps, in the act of bounding into the air from the shallow margin of the water or from the wet sand. If any motion of a mute animal could express delight it was this; if they had meant to make signs of their happiness, they could not have done it more intelligibly. Suppose, then, what I have no doubt of, each individual of this number to be in a state of positive enjoyment, what a sum, collectively, of gratification and of pleasure have we here before our view.

" The young of all animals appear to me to receive pleasure simply from the exercise of their limbs and bodily faculties. A child is delighted with speaking without having anything to say, and with walking without knowing where to go; and, prior to both these, I am disposed to believe that the waking hours of infancy are agreeably taken up with the exercise of vision, or perhaps, more properly speaking, with learning to see."

How desirable, nay, how enviable is that frame of mind which can reason thus, and find sources of happiness in watching the habits of the animal and vegetable world around them ; that can see only happiness in an action, which appears at first sight to have no meaning, the leaping of a cloud of shrimps from the water; and where an un-inquiring mind, or one of a gloomy temperament, would merely say, This is to avoid the danger of falling into the jaws of some fish-monster which is below the surface!

> These are thy wondrous works, first Source of good!
> Now more admired in being understood.

Who can listen to the carol of the lark as he soars in the air, and seems so happy, without feelings of delight and without reflections rising in his mind which tend to make him both a better and a happier man ? Who can witness the familiar habits of the robin, and see how contentedly he will perch himself on a neighbouring bush close to your side, and pour forth his song, without having his own feelings tempered down into harmony with nature ?— How can man in the midst of all this, which points out the intention of an all-wise Creator, think that he of all God's creatures is the only one intended to be unhappy !

No!—let him learn to admire the beauties of nature—let him learn to occupy his hours of leisure in trying to understand them—to find

> Tongues in trees—books in the running brooks—
> Sermons in stones—*and good in everything.*

Nature never did betray
The heart that loved her; 'tis her privilege,
Through all the years of this our life, to lead
From joy to joy: for she can so inform
The mind that is within us, so impress
With quietness and beauty, and so feed
With lofty thoughts, that neither evil tongues,
Rash judgments, nor the sneers of selfish man,
Nor greetings where no kindness is, nor all
The dreary intercourse of daily life
Shall e'er prevail, that all which we behold
Is full of blessings.   Therefore let the morn
Shine on thee in thy solitary walk;
And let the misty mountain winds be free
To blow against thee; and, in after-years,
When these wild ecstasies shall be matured
Into a sober pleasure, *when thy mind*
Shall be a mansion for all lovely forms,
Thy memory be a dwelling-place
For all sweet sounds and harmonies; oh! then
If solitude, or fear, or pain, or grief,
Should be thy portion, with what healing thoughts
Of tender joy wilt thou remember me,
And these my exhortations!   WORDSWORTH.

Nature, enchanting Nature, in whose form
And lineaments divine I trace a hand
That errs not, and find raptures still renew'd,
Is free to all men—universal prize!
Strange that so fair a creature should yet want
Admirers, and be destined to divide
With meaner objects e'en the few she finds.   COWPER.

How important the bearing and influence which such
trains of thought, inculcated in youth, might have in every
class of life it would be wise to consider; how little they
have hitherto had, is humiliating to think.   A dry remark,
many years ago, in a college lecture-room, occurs to me as
full of meaning, although at the time intended for sarcasm.
Asking an undergraduate a question on the refraction of
light, with which he was not acquainted, and who answered,
"he did not know much about refraction," the lecturer
dryly added, "nor about reflection either, I am afraid."
I hope this will not be lost upon the schoolmaster; not
that I wish him to make his remarks in the same spirit.
That the sphere of enjoyment of the labouring and
middle classes might be enlarged by education there can

be no doubt; and it was observed by a celebrated moralist, more than a century ago, that " man in all situations in life should endeavour to make the sphere of his innocent pleasures as wide as possible, that he may retire into them with safety, and find in them such a satisfaction as a wise man would not blush to take; for although the world may not be so happy as that we should be always merry, neither is it so miserable as that we should be always melancholy."

With respect to that part of the instruction in the foregoing pages which is of a scientific kind, I would say (and I do so from a feeling of conviction which experience gives), that in no way can the teachers in our higher class of elementary schools give such a character of usefulness to their instruction, as by qualifying themselves to teach in these subjects; introducing simple and easy experiments, which illustrate the things happening before their eyes every day, and convey conviction with them the moment they are seen and explained. It is a great mistake to suppose that boys of twelve and thirteen years of age cannot understand elementary knowledge of this kind, when brought before them by experiment;—seeing the way in which the bigger boys were interested in it here, and the tendency it had to raise the standard of teaching, and to give rise to a wish for information, it has proceeded further than I at first contemplated—the result has been, that the school is provided with sufficient of a philosophic apparatus * for all the common experiments of a pneumatic and hydrostatic kind, a small galvanic battery, an electric apparatus, etc. One little book, used as a text-book, is a volume of Chambers's Edinburgh books, " Matter and Motion," and this is illustrated by experiment.

The end of all education ought to be, to prepare the rising generation for those duties and those situations in life they are called upon to fulfil—whether they be " hewers of wood or drawers of water," of those who belong to the labouring, the middle, or the upper classes in life, to make them in their respective stations good citizens and good Christians; and I think it will be found that, according as a teacher keeps this in view, making his instruction bear

* See end of volume.

o

upon the ordinary duties of life, or loses sight of it (I am speaking of a teacher competent to his work), he will succeed, or the contrary. I am perfectly convinced that many well-meaning efforts have not been attended with the success expected from them, entirely owing to their leaving out all instruction relating to the occupations by which they were, in after-life, to earn their bread.

Although these hints are addressed to the schoolmaster, I am not without hope that they may be of some use to many in my own profession, and to others who take an interest in advancing the happiness and respectability of the uneducated classes in this country.

The schoolmaster, especially in the present state of things, is not able to do all that is wanted. He is very often insufficiently educated himself—his social position is not what it ought to be—the poor are inclined to resist his authority over their children—to send impertinent messages through them, etc., so that, at first, he wants strengthening in these respects. Then, again, the more wealthy do not place him in that scale of society that he ought, from his usefulness, to be placed in.

In saying this, I am not seeking for him a better position than the interests of society require that he should have, and which, in the end, his own usefulness will work out for him;—there is no doubt that the schoolmaster who conducts himself well—who can succeed in raising the standard of education in his school, and in making it what it ought to be, and what it hitherto has not been, a benefit to all classes around him—will establish claims upon all, the labourer, the tradesman, and the farmer, and upon all in his locality, which will cause him to be estimated in a very different way, and place him in a very different position from that which he has hitherto held. At present, ignorance, and jealousy arising from it, produce in many of the uneducated a sort of dislike to all the instruments of education—a sort of jealous feeling, the result of which is to endeavour to bring all those leaving school to a level with themselves—to make them mere masses of clay, animated, it is true, but in every other respect a mere " bundle " of ignorance.

Notwithstanding all the difficulties with which education is beset, but which must prove less and less every year, I hope many of those who persevere in this useful work may live to see the labouring classes of this country much more enlightened than they are at present—much more respectable in their conduct—honest, manly, and straight-forward in everything they have to do—not looking upon insolence as independence, which ignorance does, but feeling that it is a duty which they owe to themselves 'to be respectful to their superiors, civil and obliging, neighbourly and kind to all about them, and that, when they fail in these things, they are wanting in their duty both to God and man.

It is painful to observe how the uneducated classes, the labourer and those above him, will sometimes, from pure ignorance of what is due to themselves, go out of their way to insult others, from a feeling that this is, as they call it, showing their independence. When I see this, I am always sorry that it does not occur to them, that in doing so they are only lowering themselves in the scale of humanity and of civilization, and that feelings of self-re-spect ought to deter them from it; education will teach that it does not, at least ought not, to belong to civilised life.

As a means of animating those who, from their situation in life—from their education or their position, may have it in their power to assist in advancing the cause of education in their own neighbourhoods, I can only say, if they once experience the heartfelt satisfaction which arises in con-trasting the state of the educated child with that of the totally uneducated one—the intelligent countenance of the one, with the stolid, unmeaning countenance which igno-rance produces in the other—the good effect of education on their industrial habits—on their social habits—(in fact, so far as my own experience here goes, and judging from those who have left school, it makes them, generally speak-ing, a totally different race of beings),—they will not hesitate as to the course they ought to pursue.

It may not be consistent with the occupations of those engaged in a very busy and active life to pay much atten-tion to the education of those among whom they live, yet

there are many ways in which they may give encouragement to it and to the schoolmaster without much encroach-
ment upon their time. They are many of them alive to
the beauties of Nature—they can enjoy the growth and
expansion of a flower—watch each petal unfold itself, and
look with pleasure to its full opening and beauty—watch it
from its blossom to its fruit—why, not, then, take some
interest in the opening and expansion of the human mind?
What can be more gratifying to the feelings, than seeing
its gradual improvement under your influence, and that
you are rendering it capable of using those reasoning
powers with which it is endowed, and which are intended
as the source of its highest gratification?

Archbishop Whateley, in his "Introductory Lectures on
Political Economy," says :—

"The natural state of man must be reckoned, not that
in which his intellectual and moral growth are stunted, but
one in which his original endowments are, I will not say
brought to perfection, but enabled to exercise themselves,
and to expand like the flowers of a plant; and especially
in which that characteristic of our species, the tendency
towards progressive improvement, is permitted to come into
play.

"A plant could not be said to be in its natural state
which was growing in a soil or climate that precluded it
from putting forth the flowers and the fruit for which its
organisation was destined. No one who saw the pine
growing near the boundary of perpetual snow on the Alps,
stunted to the height of two or three feet, and struggling
to exist amidst rocks and glaciers, would describe that as
the natural state of a tree which, in a more genial soil and
climate a little lower down, was found capable of rising to
the height of fifty or sixty yards. In like manner, the
natural state of man must, according to all fair analogy, be
reckoned, not that in which his intellectual and moral
growth are, as it were, stunted and permanently repressed,
but one in which his original endowments are, I do not say
brought to perfection, but enabled to exercise themselves
and to expand like the flowers of a plant; and especially in
which that characteristic of our species, the tendency

towards progressive improvement, is permitted to come into play. Such seems to have been the state in which the earliest race of mankind were placed by the Creator."

That there are many among those who have paid attention to the subject of education, both of my own profession and others, who have fears of doing too much—some for one reason and some for another—there is no doubt; but if they will only look a little further into it, and see what can practically be done, and what, in those instances where most has been doing, is the good effect upon their conduct, I am well assured they will find no ground for fear.

The cry that it is teaching too much—it is teaching them astronomy, mathematics, etc., is very high-sounding, and implies much more than can be done, or even is attempted; then, again, consider the small number who remain even for this;—but the fact is, it is not teaching them astronomy, etc., but it is merely making them acquainted with facts in those subjects of a scientific kind which they are capable of understanding—which will be verified afterwards by their own experience—which open their minds, and bear upon their occupations in life—facts most useful and interesting to them, and which, even independent of their usefulness, give a greater interest to education than can be given in any other way.

It might as well, and with as much truth, be said that floating a small paper boat in a tub of water was teaching them navigation;—besides, why assume that knowledge, when communicated to the lower orders, must necessarily have a tendency to evil?—why imagine that a boy who is told how the sailor steers by the compass, and who knows a little of geography, will run away to sea and become a Paul Jones, a buccaneer, or a pirate, rather than, if he does so, that he will run in a right course—go to China, or join Mr. Brooke in Borneo, and help to civilize the world. But even in Shakspeare's time there seems to have been those who objected to much being done in this way, although I think there are few at present who would quite adopt the words which he puts into the mouth of Jack Cade, in his Henry the Sixth: "Thou hast most traitorously corrupted the youth of the realm in erecting a gramınar school ; and whereas, before, our forefathers had no other books than the score and the tally, thou hast caused printing to be used ; and thou hast built a paper-mill. It will be proved to thy face that thou hast men about thee that usually talk of a noun and a verb, and such abominable words as no Christian ears can endure to hear."

In presenting this outline of secular teaching in our elementary schools, I have done it with a view to its helping to an improved system, and towards what I think most important at the present time, the establishing schools combining the education of the labouring classes with those of the employers. This has been the aim which I had in the one here, and it is, in my opinion, one of its most important and leading features, and has, in this respect, been completely successful.

The number in the school when visited by the Rev. H. Moseley, her Majesty's Inspector, in March 1847, was 173, and their average ages throughout the school—boys, ten years and three months, girls ten years and eight months ; and although many of the labourers' children remain considerably beyond the usual ages in schools of this kind, yet, generally speaking, they leave between ten and eleven, and many even before that. It appears from the report of Mr. Moseley, in 1845, that the average age of the *monitors* in the numerous schools which he inspected is not more than eleven years.

The number of children at present (April 1848) in the school is upwards of 180, in addition to which there is a small infant school of about thirty children, kept in a cottage hard by, and managed in turn by the girls who are pupil-teachers : from this it would appear that a very large proportion of the population is at school, being upwards of a sixth of the whole, but about thirty are from neighbouring parishes.

The proceeds of the school for the year from Christmas,* 1846, to Christmas, 1847, were £152 2s. 2d., this includes books, the payments for which during the year by the children amounted to £29 14s. 6d. This is a sure test of

* See the note on next page.

the value which the parents attach to the education their children are getting.

It is now advanced in its sixth year,* and, having watched the working of it in all its bearings, from the first, with a great deal of attention, I feel that I may, with some degree of confidence offer a few observations, in addition to those I published in a pamphlet entitled *Hints towards a Self-paying System of Education*.

The reception the pamphlet met with, and the number of attempts which are being made in the same direction, and which I hope may meet with the same success, have in some measure led to this publication. I there stated, that schools for the education of the children, both of the labourer and employer, might be very extensively established in the larger parishes throughout England, by the assistance of the clergy and others interested in the education of the poor : this I still repeat, and with increased conviction of its truth. I repeat this passage from knowing that it has been misquoted and reasoned upon as if I had said *in all* parishes — a thing manifestly impossible in small ones—but these ought, and no doubt would, for the bigger children, take advantage of the neighbouring schools.

Increased experience has confirmed what I then stated, that the better the labouring classes are educated, the better they will become in all the social relations of life, and that no great improvement can be effected in the manners of the people but by the education of the rising generation.

" It is difficult, if not impossible, to change the habits of

---

* The school goes on with the same satisfactory results, both pecuniary and moral, and an increasing conviction of its usefulness to all classes: the quarterly payments and pence for the year ending with Dec. 1848, were £115 19s. 2d.; and for books for the same time, £25 9s.; for the year ending with Dec. 1849, £123 7s. 7d., and for books, £39 18s. 2d.; in addition to which, during the last year, the children have purchased tooth-brushes, hair-brushes, combs, scissors, etc., to the amount of £2 14s. 2d.

It is now in its eleventh year, continues perfectly self-paying, and, in all respects, is going on in the most satisfactory manner.

men whose characters are formed and settled.   The prejudices of ignorance that have grown up with them will
not yield to new impressions, whilst youth and innocence
may be moulded into any form you may choose to give
them."

There is one class of men in our rural districts, and no
doubt a similar class in towns, to whom schools of this
kind are the greatest possible boon, the tradesmen and
smaller farmers.   Hitherto they never have had an education for their children within their reach, but when it is
so, they show themselves willing and anxious to profit
from it.

With respect to the more wealthy farmers, and also professional men living in the country, many of them will, as
they do here, send their children to these schools, if well
conducted, when they see it is an advantage to them to do
so.   It would be folly to suppose that any prudent parent
would hesitate to send his children when a good education
is to be had at them, at a comparatively small expense,
merely because their primary object was the education of
the poor, and when he sees clearly that the interests of
both classes may be advanced by his doing so.

The gradual improvement of the labouring classes will
be such, and also of the class immediately above them,
that each will see their true interests in a better light than
they have hitherto done, and there will be no longer that
fear of coming in contact with each other in early life
which there has been, and which has been productive of
anything but good.

That the occupying farmers as a class, and I speak of
them more particularly from not having much knowledge
of the employers of labour in towns, are against the education of the labourer, there is no doubt; for they seldom
speak of it in any other terms than as " a parcel of stuff, a
parcel of nonsense ; what do they mean by attempting to
teach the children all this ;—we shall not be able to get
labourers," etc.   All this is mere prejudice, and will soon
die away.

One objection running in the minds of many of them is
this (a most ungenerous one it is true), that the children of

the labourer in schools like the one here—for I know it has been urged against this—are getting, at a cheap rate, a better education than those of the farmer. Now this would be true, supposing that the class above the labourer were to remain stationary as to education, a thing they will not do, as they will no doubt, in the end, act upon the principles of common sense, and take advantage of such schools, where they are established in their parishes or in their neighbourhood.

For what is the way in which it operates in the Somborne school? From the above averages as to age, it is evident that the children of the labourer leave between ten and eleven, many of them earlier; those who stay after that age are exceptions to the general rule.

Now surely this is not staying to an age at which any one can justly take alarm; yet I know that, even at this age, some of them are better educated than the children of many of the farmers have hitherto been; but in keeping their children at school to the age of fourteen or fifteen, the latter would secure to themselves their proper place in the social scale, and as it is in their power to do so, if they do not, they have no business to find fault. It has been said, that every class above another teaches that below it, and the establishment of good and cheap schools will not reverse this; on the contrary, strengthen it.

I feel, from my own experience, how much the classes above the labourer and mechanic are interested in a good and efficient system of education in our parish schools, and I wish to open their eyes to the importance of them, and to the good results which would arise, if all would unite in trying to establish schools with a view to meet the educational wants of the age in which we live.

The farmer, and those of the same class in our rural districts, may rest assured, that until it is brought home to them into their own parishes or neighbourhood, they never will, as a class of men, get that education it is desirable they should have; and, that by standing aloof, and feeling no interest in that of the labourer, they only augment the evil which they dread—the one is advancing in intelligence, and it is time it should—the other is standing still; and I cannot but think, that in a very few years, the employers of labour will be the class which, of all others, will take the greatest interest in those very schools of which they now think so little.

It is a remark sometimes made, that the Physical Condition of the Labouring Classes, particularly as regards the crowded state of their cottages, is such as to render attempts to educate almost fruitless, or at all events to be a very great hindrance to it.

In this there is no doubt much truth, for it will generally be found, that when families are crowded together into a small space—all ages and sexes sleeping in the same room —that they lose all sense of decency and respectability, and that education, in such cases, has great difficulties to contend with.

The remedy for this, with regard to the cottages in our rural districts, rests with the landlords rather than any one else—the farmer is indifferent to it—one sleeping-room for a family, however large, satisfies him.

The system of letting cottages in a wholesale way with farms, beyond what is necessary for farm-servants, and of letting out leasehold and lifehold cottages for the purposes of subletting, is one very much to be condemned, and which calls for the consideration of the landlords of this country. They have it in their power to do much good in this, and the mischief has arisen from want of attention on their part, and not in any feelings of indifference as to the welfare of the poor.

Ecclesiastical and collegiate bodies have much to answer for in this respect, and one can only hope they will make up for the past by better attention to it for the future.

There is also another mischief in letting cottages to a greater extent than is absolutely necessary with the farms; it introduces a sort of truck-system, and is very often a means of oppressing the labourer; the employer deducting more than a reasonable weekly rent from his wages on a Saturday night. The difficulty of getting cottages sometimes obliges the labourer to submit to this, although he may have work offered him on better terms elsewhere.

On this subject of crowded cottages, and the immorality

it leads to, I will quote the following words of Mr. Justice Coleridge, addressed to a Labourers' Friends Association in Devonshire, and which I read in the public journals some time ago. Coming from such authority and experience, they are deserving of the highest attention.

" I beg to impress upon you the importance of improving the moral and social condition of the labouring classes, with whose well-being your own interest is very closely identified. Many amongst them are wretchedly lodged. From my own experience as a judge, the painful conviction has been forced upon my mind, that very much of the crime which disgraces our country is mainly attributable to the mixture of sexes and of ages in the dwellings of the poor; a practice that debases and demoralizes the human mind, and which, unless counteracted, must effectually neutralize every effort made towards the elevation or improvement of the people."

This is a very strong opinion; but it is the opinion of one who has had the best opportunity of inquiring into crime, and he speaks of it as being forced upon him, and it is one to which every inquiring mind must come that has witnessed the low and degrading habits to which such practices lead. It is the duty of owners of property to do all they can to remedy it, as it is no less the duty of the poor to second their efforts in doing so; but such is the force of habit, that in many cases where the landlord has attempted a remedy, the cottagers themselves have taken in lodgers; or when a son or daughter marries, let them have a part of their cottage,—a proof that any great improvement in this way must be a work of time, and can only be accomplished by degrees, as the rising generation become better educated, and more alive to social comforts, and feel that such habits lead to vice and misery, and make them every way as a class less respectable, not only in their own eyes, but in the eyes of their employers.

The present generation of children of the labouring class, now leaving school, have great difficulties and temptations to contend with; they are immediately thrown with companions who have not had the same advantages in this respect as themselves—having confirmed habits of a kind

which education is intended to correct—jealous of those
who have had any education whatever, and anxious to
bring them in every way to a level with themselves—so
that they have, in fact, more than ordinary temptations to
resist.

Nor does this apply merely to their companions and
fellow-labourers working in the same occupation with
themselves, but to a very great number of others—the
jeerers and scoffers, who are continually saying, "What do
we want with this or with that? a little reading and
writing is all that the labouring man can want;" so that,
for the present, the better educated can only be looked
upon as a leaven to leaven the mass, and that from the
numerous temptations they meet with, there may, and no
doubt will be, some who fall into the low and degrading
habits of those about them; but every succeeding year
will, in this respect, bring a brighter prospect with it, and
education will in the end lead to that improvement in
society at large which its friends have reason to expect:
every one now leaving our schools at all educated as a
pioneer among these rough samples of humanity, smooth-
ing the way for a better order of things, and gradually
making it smoother with each succeeding year.

The ignorance of some in the labouring classes can
scarcely be understood by those who have not examined
into it; and I have met with instances myself, particularly
of lads just growing into manhood, whose ignorance is
greater than I could have imagined possible. The parents,
after the age of twelve or even before that, lose all control
over them; they have nothing to guide them beyond mere
animal impulse, and of course this guides them wrong—
to improve them at this age and with such habits is almost
hopeless, and in whatever light you view them, it must be
with feelings of pity and commiseration. Characters of
this kind are in such a state, and their minds are become
so completely inactive, that they work wickedness mechanically and from habit, having no idea whatever of the light
in which it appears to the respectable part of society about
them.

In extending education, and introducing it into our

schools in such a way as to reach the classes above the labourer, we might hope that more of intelligence would be brought to bear on parochial management—in those things of a civic kind, which regard our living together in small separate communities—the parts of a whole, and working together for the general good, and having to carry into effect those internal arrangements among ourselves which the law requires for the happiness of the whole— things in which society at large is deeply interested ; but notwithstanding this, they are too generally transacted in a way which loses sight of every business-principle, as well as of every principle of common sense.

In matters of this kind, it is painful to see the low standard of moral feeling which prevails in the agricultural districts, and the little regard which is paid that the public-houses, beer-houses, etc., and those places to which the labouring man resorts, should be kept within the bounds of decency, so that from the character of those who keep them, the poor man may in some measure be protected from falling into the degraded and mischievous courses, into which many of them have been led by frequenting ill-conducted places of the kind. It has been thought somewhat of a safeguard to the morals of a parish, that the keeper of a beer-house should, in order to get a license from the excise, produce a certificate signed by six inhabitant rate-payers, rated above £6 per annum, and in theory this might seem to read well, but in practice it is found to be no protection whatever, as to regulating the number of beer-houses, and proportioning them to the population, or as to the respectability of the party to be licensed ; and I can state, from my own experience, as well as from the evidence of others, that there is no character however bad, where six rate-payers in a moderate-sized parish may not be found to sign such certificate—either from what they please to term good-nature—or from a thorough indifference as to the mischief which may arise from it—or from a kind of bribery among the parties. I know instances annually occurring, where one might have supposed scarcely six men could be found in a whole county to sign such a recommendation, much less in a parish.

The mischief which this leads to, and the demoralizing effect which such practices have upon the more ignorant class of labourers, and particularly among the young men, is most deplorable, and a better state of things can only arise by the class immediately above the labourer, as well as the labourer himself, being from education brought to feel that such conduct is discreditable to themselves, and is looked upon as such by the respectable classes immediately above them, and by thus being made to see their own conduct, in somewhat the same light as others see it; in the words of the poet of Scotland—

> Oh, wad some power the giftie gie 'em
> To see themselves as others see 'em!

In general, the rule of conduct in such matters seems to be—if a man can get a living, that he is justified in doing anything which puts a penny into his pocket, no matter how much his doing so may bring into temptation and into mischief those about him. The poor labourers are many of them, in the winter, led to the beer house by the warmth which it affords, and the result is, a starving wife—ragged and uneducated children—a brutalized peasantry—and many other evils, which might at all events be materially mitigated by a different conduct on the part of their employers, and by their taking a proper interest in the moral well-being and respectability of those around them, and towards whom they are, as beings, responsible to a higher power, and from a duty both to God and man, called upon to act in a very different way from that in which the generality of them do.

The peasantry, in the south of England more particularly, have lost all feeling of self-dependance, and are by no means characterised by those feelings of manly reliance on their own exertions, for the support of themselves and those who are dependent upon them, which belong to the better educated peasantry of Scotland, and in one particular thing the contrast has struck me very forcibly—that is, with respect to those of their children, male or female, who may happen to be in any way disabled in body from following what may be called hard work : in the south of England, where this is the case, there is scarcely one parent in ten, nay, one in a hundred (at least I have found it so in my own parish, and hear of it in others), who does not, at the time his child is about sixteen, go to the clergyman of the parish for a certificate of its baptism, to lay before the board of guardians as soon after the child is sixteen as possible, in order to ask relief:—in Scotland, the feeling is, that parent and child, child and parent should mutually assist each other. In England, on neither side does this feeling exist, and in conversing with Scotch people on this subject, there is nothing in which I have found them so much astonished, as in this difference of feeling among the peasantiy of the two countries.

As an instance of the very strange notions which the poor have as regards the social relations existing between themselves and the parish, the following, although it may appear somewhat ludicrous, gives a very graphic and a very true idea. Being asked by an old man to send in his name as a claimant of a prize from the Local Agricultural Association, from his having been a number of years a member of what is called a Benefit Society, I did so, stating to him I did not think the case likely to succeed. I happened to see him soon after, and told him that he had not succeeded, and his answer to me was—"Why, sir, there's ne'er a man in the parish desarved it half so well as I did ; I have had three wives, and I married them all out of the workhouse." Now, this man was of respectable character—of average intelligence, and well conducted—and his answer was meant in all earnestness; he really thought he had done the parish a service, in relieving it of the expense, at the time of his marriage, of his respective wives.

This is but one of many cases which I could relate, evidencing the great want of better instruction on economic subjects—not only among the labourers, but among the classes above them in our rural districts, and if any one thoroughly acquainted with them would bring before the public a fair, honest, and, as far as possible, a graphic description of the real social evils of rural life, he would render great service to the cause of civilization, and would, by laying bare those vices, many of which arise from mere

ignorance, advance, at the same time, the cause of that
better education among the labouring masses of this country, which all but an unanimous feeling in the public mind
seems at the present moment to be in favour of.

That these evils have arisen to the extent to which they
now prevail, one reason among others is, I think, the
erroneous view, which many of the clergy have taken, that
to correct and expose evils of this kind is not within the
sphere of their duty—that it is of too secular a nature, and
on that account that they ought not to interfere.   In answer to this, I would ask, is it a part of the clergyman's
duty to try and make men honest, or is it not ?—to make
them tell the truth both in speaking and in acting, and not
to allow them to imagine themselves to be acting a charitable and a kind part, when in reality they are doing no
such thing ?—to see the poor crowded into cottages in
such a way as to bid defiance to any possibility of their
practising habits of decency, or of being brought up in
them ?—to see men nominally employed on the parish
roads under a plea of humanity, when, in fact, it is to run
them on in a sort of straw-yard* during the winter at a
small expense, until their services may again be wanted ?—
in short, to allow the most erroneous notions on all subjects
of a social kind to prevail without any attempt at amendment, from a fear, perhaps, of being classed among those
taking too great care of earthly things, when the doing so
might be the means of checking some of the most demoralizing influences which prevail among our labouring poor
in the agricultural districts?

I know parishes where, for a long series of years, at least
75 per cent. of the money spent on their roads has been absolutely thrown away, the value of the work actually done not
being 25 per cent. of the expenditure, the road-rate having
become a poor-rate for the able-bodied, who are employed
at a rate of wages varying with the number of their
families, the term roadman being used for, and in every way
synonymous with, the word pauper—and what is almost
unaccountable, is, the rate-payers themselves being per-

* A parish workshop—a sort of Louis Blanc-ism on a small scale
—carrying out in a parish what he wished to carry out in a nation,
and with like result.

fectly persuaded, or at least appearing to be so, that they are doing what is right, and the surveyor making oath every year before the magistrates that he has expended the parish money in such a way as the statutes relating to the highways direct. The effect of all this where it prevails, and in a greater or less degree it prevails extensively, is bad beyond description; and it is almost impossible to imagine the mischief to which it leads—in demoralizing the labourers as a class—in unduly keeping down the rate of wages and the proper remuneration of labour, and the in every way low and degraded state to which it leads.

Now if the object of religion be (what I think every one must confess it is) to make men practically good, then I think it must be allowed by all that its teachers are by no means exceeding their duty, in endeavouring to give clearer and better views in those matters nominally of a civil kind, having so intimate a relation and so direct an influence on the morals of a people, and in the healthy administration of which, almost all the links in our social chain are equally interested.

There is no subject on which both the labourer and the employer in our rural districts require more to be enlightened, than on their mutual relations with respect to the Remuneration of Labour—a thing necessary before there can be any great change in the character of the labourer in this country—before he can feel that it is a sort of moral degradation for a healthy able-bodied man to throw himself (and in the present state of things he is obliged to do so) upon the parish the moment he is out of work. Nor can the farmer think, nor does he in fact think, that the labourer is wrong in doing so. Now, in blaming the labourer for doing this, and for having so little of a spirit of independence as to throw himself unscrupulously upon the parish the moment he is sick or out of work—every one must feel that it is in reality a part of his wages, and this is implied—between both parties—the employer and the employed—the present system of wages always sup-

* During the last two years emigration and other causes have improved this state of things.

poses a third party to the contract—the parish—and never contemplates anything beyond getting on from one Saturday night to another, and in case of sickness, or work failing the parish do the rest. A system like this necessarily leads (and we all know what in times past it has led to) to an unhealthy state of society; each individual employer is willing to save himself as much as possible, in order to throw the rest on the general rate-payer—the labourer, from ignorance, has lost sight of his true interests and of what constitutes respectability and self-dependence; he is become improvident, without forethought, these being in his case not at all necessary, and is quite as contented to take part from his employer and part from the parish, as if he had the whole at once; perhaps more so, as in the one case it would imply he must take care of himself in case of sickness, want of employment, etc.; and in the other, he is taken care of by others; but at all events, the present system treats the labourer through life as a child that cannot take care of itself—as one that neither reflects upon the past, nor looks forward to the future.

The following passage from Mrs. Marcet's " Conversations on Political Economy," well expresses what ought to be the tendency of the education given to the labouring classes; she says:—

" I would endeavour to give the rising generation such an education as would render them not only moral and religious, but industrious, frugal, and provident. In proportion as the mind is informed, we are able to calculate the consequences of our actions; it is the infant and the savage who live only for the present moment; those whom instruction has taught to think, reflect upon the past and look forward to the future. Education gives rise to prudence, not only by enlarging our understanding, but by softening our feelings, by humanising the heart, and promoting amiable affections. The rude and inconsiderate peasant marries without either foreseeing or caring for the miseries he may entail on his wife and children; but he who has been taught to value the comforts and decencies of life, will not heedlessly involve himself and all that is dear to him in poverty and its long train of miseries."

It certainly appears to me to be the true theory of a healthy state of society, and certainly more consistent with honest, straightforward conduct in all parties—(for the other leads to a great deal of low cunning)—more consistent with the rights of industry—that the wages of labour should, in the case of the industrious man, be equal to all the decent wants of his class—house-rent, food, clothing, education ; and in all cases of ordinary sickness, medical attendance—that the labourer should feel that it belongs to himself and to his own character, as an honest man, to provide all these things for himself and for his family—to feel happy in providing them every comfort within his reach ; but then it is equally necessary that the employer of labour should view the matter in the same light. And although it may be difficult to arrive at this, yet it is to be hoped the tendency of education will be to point in this direction, and to enlighten both as to their true interests—that the one will respect the rights of honest industry—that the other will no less duly estimate what is owing to the employer who acts on this straightforward, manly, and honest principle (and which ought to be the commercial principle) ; which, although making the labourer earn his living by the sweat of his brow, would place him in a situation of decent comfort—happy in himself and in his family around him—happy in the blessings which this life affords him,* and equally happy in looking forward to leave it, when it shall please God to call him.

The *arithmetical constants* given below, with the tabular matter on the different subjects to which the tables relate, will, in the higher class of schools, be found of great

* "The common benefits of our nature entirely escape us; yet these are the great things. These constitute what most properly ought to be accounted blessings of Providence: what alone, if we might so speak, are worthy of its care. Nightly rest and daily bread, the ordinary use of our limbs, and senses, and understandings, are gifts which admit of no comparison with any other. Yet because almost every man we meet with possesses these, we leave them out of our enumeration. They raise no sentiment: they move no gratitude."—PALEY's *Natural Theology.*

service. Some of the walls of the class-room of the King's Somborne school are plastered, and the following matter, in a tabulated form, written upon them, in letters and figures of about an inch in size. They not only suggest observations during the progress of a lesson connected with the subject of them, but they accustom the teacher to something like arithmetical accuracy in making such observations, and enable the children to form ideas of a definite kind, and make the subjects perfectly intelligible; in fact, knowledge communicated in this way makes them close and accurate reasoners, and it is astonishing to see how much they get interested in it. These tables also suggest numberless questions in arithmetic which may be given by a teacher. In giving them here, it is merely to suggest the same things to others, and in schools, where such information is not a part of their teaching, tabular matter, connected with the ordinary weights and measures—the number of cubic inches in a solid yard, in a quart, and other measures, might supply its place on the walls of the schoolroom.

From Table I.—In comparing the rapidity of the motion of a cannon-ball with that, for instance, of the swallow, the teacher would point out the necessity of reducing them to spaces passed over in the same time, when it will be found that the cannon-ball moves at the rate of more than 1300 miles per hour, the swallow, 90; that one is a velocity so great that the eye cannot see the object moving; that there is an intermediate velocity between the two, with which, if the ball moves, it ceases to be invisible, and that it will be gradually reduced to this before its motion ceases—after striking the ground—which is called a spent ball; that the flight of the bird may be supposed to be so increased, as not to be seen in passing from one point of space to another, etc.

The outline of Table VIII, which is only partially filled up, would suggest many observations of a meteorological kind—why points of equal temperature on the surface of the earth do not follow the simple rule of distance from the equator; how affected by sea, land, mountains; accounting for the zigzag nature of isothermal lines, etc. It would also be found very useful to draw on the ceiling of the school- or class-room lines running in the direction of the four cardinal points, with a line representing the magnetic meridian in degrees, and the magnitude of the angle of variation written between them.

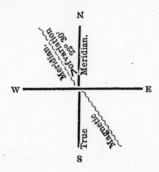

Table I.—*Numerical Constants.*

$\odot^{ce}$ of a circle, dia. 1 . . . 3·14159
Area of do. . . . . ·7854
$\odot^{ce}$ of a circle, dia. D . . . (3·14159) D
Area of do. . . . . (·7854)D²
Length of Arc 1° dia. 1 . . ·008726645
Sol. cylinder Ht D and dia. of Base D=(·7854) D³
., of sphere = ⅔ of cylinder =(·5236) D³
Surface of do. dia. D . . . (3·14159) D²
A body falls by gravity . . 16$\frac{1}{12}$ feet in 1″
" " . . . (16$\frac{1}{12}$) t^2 in t″
Length of a pendulum vibrating } = 39·1386 inches.
  seconds in lat. 51° 31′ . }
Velocity of sound . . . 1142 feet in 1″
  " of a cannon-ball . . 2000 feet in 1″
  " of light . . . 200,000 mlles in 1″
  " of rotation of point at equator 1520 feet per second.
  " of a point in lat. 51° . 830 "
  " of a musket-ball . . 1280 "
  " of a rifle . . . 1600 "
  " of a 24 lb. shot . . 2400 "
  " of quick train railroad . 88 "
  " (mean) of rivers . . 3 or 4 "
  " rapid river . . . 13 "
  " of a brisk wind . . 10 miles per hour.
  " of a high wind, about . 40 "
  " of a hurricane . . 80 "
Most rapid flight of a swallow, about 80 to 90 "

TABLE II.—*Time of Light travelling from the Sun to*

	Hrs.	Min.	Sec.
Mercury	0	3	6
Venus	0	5	57
Earth	0	8	13
Mars	0	12	20
Jupiter	0	42	29
Saturn	1	18	8
Uranus	2	37	45
Neptune	4	8	. 24
Fixed stars			

TABLE III.*·—*Specific Gravity, Distilled Water*=1·000.

METALS,
And other Inorganic Bodies.

Platinum 22·069	Zinc	....	7·100
Gold .... 19·258	Sodium	..	0·973
Mercury. 13·586	Potassium		0·865
Lead .... 11·352	Chalk	....	2·784
Silver .. 10·474	Limestone		3·179
Copper.. 8·788	Marble	..	2·742
Steel .... 7·812	Flint and		
Iron (bar) 7·788	Spar	..	2·594
Iron (cast) 7·207	Common		
Tin ...... 7·291	Glass	..	2·642

ORGANIC BODIES.

Dry Oak	·925
„ Beech	·852
„ Ash	·845
„ Elm	·600
„ Cedar	·561
„ Larch	·498
„ Poplar	·383
„ Cork	·240
„ Ivory	1·826
„ Bones of Oxen	1·656

LIQUIDS.

Sea Water	1·026
Milk	1·030
Oil of Olives	0·915
Alcohol	0·792
Ether	0·715
Nitric Acid	1·503
Sulphuric Acid	1·845
Ammonia	0·960
Weight, in ounces, of a cubic foot of water, temp. 63°	997·136
Ditto in lbs.	62·321

GASES.

Atmospheric Air	1·000
Oxygen	1·111
Nitrogen	0·972
Hydrogen	0·069
Chlorine	2·500
Ammonia	0·590
Carbonic Acid	1·527
Weight, in ounces, of a cubic foot of air	1·24642
Ditto in lbs.	·0779

* Tables of this kind, in large print, and on pasteboard, would be very useful in schools; such as those arranged by Mr. Segetmeir, and published by Messrs. Groombridge.

TABLE IV.*

Height of Barometer. Inches.	Corresponding temperature at which water boils. Fahrenheit.
26	204·91°
26·5	205·79
27	206·67
27·5	207·55
28	208·43
28·5	209·31
29	210·10
29·5	211·07
30·	212·00
30·5	212·88
31·	213·76

These inches of mercury measure also the elastic force of the vapour of water at the same temperature.

TABLE V.
Melting Points of different Substances.

	Fah.
Heat of common fire..	790°
Iron red in the dark ..	750
Beeswax	136
Lard	97
Tallow	127
Tin, 3. Lead, 2	334
Tin, 1. Lead, 4	460
Lead .	612
Zinc	680
Antimony	809
Brass	3809
Copper	4587
Silver	3937
Gold	5237
Soft Nails	21097
Iron	21637
Platinum	23177

TABLE VI.
Boiling Points of different Liquids.

	Fah.
Water	212°
Ether	96
Alcohol	176
Most Essential oils	212
Water saturated with common salt	225
Oil of Turpentine	316
Sulphuric Acid	590
Linseed Oil	600
Mercury	660
Nitric Acid	248
Phosphorus	554
Sulphur	570

TABLE VII.—*Freezing Points of Liquids.*

	Fah.		Fah.
Water freezes	32°	Mercury	— 39°
Milk	30	Vinegar	+ 28
Olive Oil	36	Oil of Turpentine	+ 16
Salt Water, 1 part salt, 4 parts water	7	Sulphuric Acid	+ 46
		Human Blood	+ 25
Brine, 1 part salt, 3 water	4	Brandy	— 7

* Tables IV, V, VI. VII, from Lardner's Cyclopædia, volume on Heat.

TABLE VIII.

Linear Dilatation.

Of Solids by Heat.

Dimensions at 212° of a bar whose length at 32° is 1·00.*

		Vulgar Fractions.
Glass Tube..............	1·000828000	.... $\frac{1}{1116}$
Platina	1·00088420	,............... $\frac{1}{1131}$
Cast Iron	1·0011110	.... —
Steel	1·00118980	.... —
Iron Wire.................	1·00144010	.... —
Iron (Dulong)	1·00118203	.... $\frac{1}{846}$
Gold	1·00146606	.... $\frac{1}{682}$
Copper	1·00172244	...........: $\frac{1}{581}$
Silver.............:...	1·00190974	.... $\frac{1}{524}$
Tin	1.00217298	.... $\frac{1}{462}$
Lead	1·00284836	.... $\frac{1}{351}$
Zinc.....................	1·00294200	.... —

Of Liquids by Heat.

From 32° to 212°.

		Vulgar Fractions.
Mercury	0·01800	.... $\frac{1}{55}$
Alcohol (Dalton)........	0·11600	.... $\frac{1}{9}$
Water..................	0 04444	.... $\frac{1}{23}$
Water, saturated with } common salt }	0·05000	.... $\frac{1}{20}$
Fixed Oils	0·08000	.... $\frac{1}{125}$
Oil of Turpentine........	0·07000	.... $\frac{1}{41}$
Sulphuric Acid	0·06000	.... $\frac{1}{17}$
Nitric Acid	0·11000	.... $\frac{1}{9}$
Whale Oil	0·08548	.... —

---

* From Ure's Dictionary of Chemistry.

TABLE IX.

PLACES.	Latitude.	Longitude.	Elevation in feet above Sea Level.	Snow Line. Between (Feet.)	Variation of the Needle.	Inches of Rain in the Year.	Year.	Winter.	Spring.	Summer.	Autumn.	Coldest Month.	Hottest Month.
London	51° 30′ N.	0°	218·5	5 & 6000	22°30′W.	23	55·4	41·45	53·37	70·47	56·07	38·75 Jan.	72·05 July
Edinburgh..	55° 57′	7°58′ W.	288·71	6 & 10,000			51·35	40·1	49·1	64·4	52·02	38·5 Jan.	65·75 July
Paris........	48° 50′	2°26′ E.	193·3	10,000			56·3	39·42	55·17	72·72	57·02	36·05	74·52
Madrid	40° 25′	8°28′ W.	2175·19	6 & 10,000			63·95	44·6	63·95	84·65	62·82	28·6	68·57
Vienna	48° 13′	16° 29′ E.	518·81	5000		16	54·7	32·45	55·62	77·67	55·62	9·00 Jan.	70·25 July
Petersburgh.	59° 56′	30° 25′		6 & 10,000			39·85	13·10	35·82	68·00	43·00	11·00 Jan.	47·5 Aug.
St. Bernard..	45° 50′	7° 11′	8606·00				34·25	14·45	27·5	45·72	32·9		
Cape of Good Hope	33° 35′ S.	18° 34′		10 & 14,000			74·97	65·3	73·85	84·65	75·65	64·17 Aug.	86·9 Jan.
Calcutta ...	22° 35′ N.	88° 26′		17,000		81	96·12	76·77	95·22	96·12	90·72	73·4 Jan.	99·27 May
Quito	0° 14′ S.	83°31′ W.	9560·34	16,000			67·10	66·65	67·32	67·1	71·37	65·3 July	68·67 Mar.
Rome	41° 54′ N.	12° 34′ E.	173·88			38	66·65	50·2	63·60	82·50	69·00	47·75 Jan.	86·00 July
North Cape.	71° 10′	25° 56′					34·25	21·75	29·00	46·50	32·00	20·75 Jan.	50·2 July
Jakutyk on the Lena	62° 1′	129° 13′	383·857	1 & 5000			10·18	*55·52	13·33	70·7	17·15	*41·0 Feb.	77·75 July

* On the —ve side of zero.

A figure like the following, in the Somborne School, on the wall at the east end of the class room, showing the meridian altitude of the sun on the shortest and longest days, and at the equinoxes, may be made the means of giving children a good idea of his varying meridian altitude at different times of the year — varying influence arising from this on the vegetable and animal kingdom, etc.

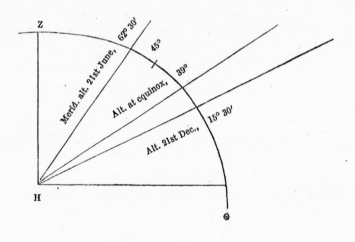

A List of some of the Philosophical and other Apparatus used in the King's Somborne School.

A geological map of England.

A pair of globes.

A compass, a spirit level, a measuring chain, and models of the simple geometrical solids.

A set of mechanical powers, lever, wheel, and angle, etc., apparatus for illustrating centrifugal force, etc.

A pair of common bellows.

Glass model of a common pump.

Glass model of a diving-bell.

Air-pump and receivers, etc., with other apparatus for various experiments.

Brass bottle-balance for weighing air, gases, etc.

Apparatus for finding specific gravity of bodies.

Apparatus for showing elasticity of steam.

A sectional model of a steam-engine.

Apparatus on heat, etc.—barometer, thermometer, pyrometer.

Apparatus for showing the different conducting powers of metals.

Leslie's parabolic reflectors.

Three plane circular discs of white metal, on stands, one smooth, one scratched, one blackened for experiments on the absorption and radiation of heat.

A vessel in the shape of a cube, with faces of different kinds for ditto.

Leslie's differential thermometer.

A magic lantern, with astronomical and other slides.

Glass prisms, lenses, etc., of different kinds.

A small chemical apparatus.

Pneumatic trough, bell-jar, etc., with stop-cock, etc., for collecting and decanting gases, retorts, etc.

Spirit-lamp, argand-lamp, oxy-hydrogen blowpipe, Davy lamp.

A voltaic battery — apparatus for showing Oersted's experiment — the principle of the electric telegraph — magnets, etc.

A small electric cylindrical machine, glass, and sealing-wax, rods, and pith-balls, stools, with glass legs, Leyden jars, discharging rods, electrometers, etc.

A number of small things, which it would be tedious to make a list of, but which have grown up here by degrees, would suggest themselves to a teacher as he proceeds.

The list given is for the purpose of suggesting to others, things which have been found by experience highly useful; but the instruction is *not* in the instruments themselves, but in the use which is made of them.

A teacher having a knowledge of these subjects may

give a great deal of useful instruction illustrative of every-day life, by means of simple apparatus of no very expensive kind. This should be added to as the wants of the school require, for fear of incurring expense by the purchase of things which the teachers might not be able to turn to good account.

The Committee of Council on Education, I have under-stood, now give assistance in the purchase of apparatus of this kind, in schools in connection with them, where it is likely to be turned to good account; and, where such is wanted, managers of schools might profit by looking at the list of apparatus which the inspectors recommend.

THE END.

Wertheimer and Co., Printers, Finsbury Circus.

Published by Request.

SCHOOLS

AND

OTHER SIMILAR INSTITUTIONS,

FOR

THE INDUSTRIAL CLASSES.

REMARKS

ON

THE IMPORTANCE OF GIVING THEM, AS FAR AS POSSIBLE, A SELF-SUPPORTING CHARACTER, AND THE MEANS OF DOING SO.

A Paper Read before the Society of Arts, April 27th, 1853.

BY

THE REV. R. DAWES, M.A.,

DEAN OF HEREFORD.

LONDON:
GROOMBRIDGE AND SONS,
PATERNOSTER ROW.
M.DCCC.LIII.

REMARKS ON THE IMPORTANCE OF GIVING, AS FAR AS POSSIBLE, A SELF-SUPPORTING CHARACTER TO SCHOOLS FOR THE INDUSTRIAL CLASSES, AND THE MEANS OF DOING SO.

A Paper Read before the Society of Arts, April 27th, 1853, and Published by Request.

GENTLEMEN, — In compliance with a request which has been made to me, I appear before you this evening for the purpose of addressing to you a few remarks on the subject of popular education. The results of my own experience and reflections on this subject have, of late, been so frequently submitted to the public, that I must begin by assuring those who are at all conversant with the progress and position of the question, that I have no new principles to advance; the substance, at all events, the drift of the remarks I shall make, will be found in that I have already published. I should therefore have insisted on its being more profitable for you to listen to some other experienced person in matters of education, had not the request been urged upon me in such a manner that I could hardly consider myself at liberty to refuse.

I have no intention of taking any general or comprehensive view of the subject: on an occasion like the present, remarks of such a kind would be ill-timed, and to so practical an audience would appear unprofitable. I will strictly limit myself to those particular points which have been announced as the subject for the evening, and upon which I can bring my own experience to bear, and also that of other practical men engaged in the work of education, whose testimony in support of the principles I am advocating, is, I think, worthy of your attention.

I shall lay before you my own conclusions as to how far the principle of self-support is applicable to national education: I shall have to tell you in what sense I myself understand this principle, — how I conceive it may be brought to bear, what due I attach to it; in a word, what it is, and what it is good at.

I have been frequently quoted as having demonstrated the success of this principle. This, however, is a remark which needs some explanation.

1

2   Schools for the Industrial Classes

The success of the schools established at King's Somborne, in Hampshire, demonstrated in the most satisfactory manner, the adequacy of the principles to effect the objects I myself had in view (what were my objects, and how I succeeded in accomplishing them, I will presently explain to you). But I do not consider that their success did prove the adequacy of the principle of self-support for certain other objects with which it was never connected in my own mind, and which must be provided for (excepting in the most favoured localities) by other means.

The expenses of a school are divisible into two distinctly marked parts. First there are those expenses which are incurred antecedently to the schools being set to work: I mean the expenses incurred in purchasing the site, in building the school and the teachers' houses, in providing suitable school-fittings and apparatus, and in educating and training the teachers. These expenses also are, to speak generally, incurred once for all.

The other kind of expenses are incurred annually: they are permanent expenses — they represent the cost of keeping the school at work, as the former represented the cost of starting it; they consist of the salaries of teachers, of the cost of books and other needful apparatus as the school progresses, of the outgoing for repairs, and a few other items of this kind.

Now it was to these latter permanent annual expenses (which I beg to observe have always been the most difficult to meet), that I endeavoured to apply the principle of self-support; and to this extent the King's Somborne schools, as you will see from the statistics I shall quote, have been, and continue to be, thoroughly successful.

In the case of Somborne, the first class of expenses to which I alluded, were met by liberal assistance from the Committee of Council on Education, from the National Society, the Diocesan Board at Winchester, and by subscriptions from myself and others connected with the property of the parish.

From the first I determined to spare no expense in anything connected with the well-working of the schools, having an entire confidence in the principle, that this would, in the end, be the best economy. These views were justified by the result; and although a considerable sum, as regards this first class of expenses, fell upon myself; this, thrown over a few years, made the school much less expensive to me, as clergyman of the parish, than the ordinary village school.

These are, however, expenses which ought not to be left to private individuals; but every parish or school district ought to be enabled to charge themselves legally with it.

The property of the parish of King's Somborne was rated at about £6000 per annum. Taking this first necessary outlay at £900, and supposing there had been the power and disposition on the part of the ratepayers to charge themselves with it — throwing it over a period of thirty years, as is done in the case of building workhouses — how very light a burden it would have been, considering the advantages resulting from it! And although I should at that time, even if there had been the power, have despaired of getting the ratepayers to agree to it, yet, with the light which has broken in upon them through the school itself during the last ten years, this question assumes a very different aspect.

You see, then, my object was a limited one; and in speaking of the King's Somborne school as a self-supporting one, the word "self-support" is intended to apply to the working of the school after it was once fairly established.

But my success in attaining it has been spoken of as if it had demonstrated the possibility of self-support in the widest sense in which the word would be made to include all the preliminary expenses: and upon this has been founded an argument, that the aid of the State, in educational matters was unnecessary, and, if unnecessary, of course mischievous. Now, as my schools did not prove this — and in fact, under the circumstances, could not be intended to do so — and as my opinions are strongly at variance with any conclusion which would reject the aid of the State, I thought it necessary to direct your attention as soon as possible to this distinction.

But as the whole value of my experiment depends upon the extent to which such schools can be raised up in other localities, I will now proceed to give you some account of it.

The parish contained, by the census of 1841, a population of 1,125, of whom about 800 lived in the village, the rest scattered over an area of about 8,000 acres. The farms were large, many of them having been formed of what formerly composed of two, three, or four occupations, making the case proportionably less favourable to the success of the plan I had in view. The parish is a purely agricultural one, and in a purely agricultural district; and at that time, and for a long period of years, the Poor-rates had been extremely heavy, giving it a bad notoriety in that respect over the neighbouring parishes.

There was, therefore, nothing in the circumstances of the neighbourhood, or parish, nor in the history or character of the people, to predispose them towards making greater sacrifices for their children, for the purposes of securing some serviceable degree of education, or of enabling them to do it, than would be found elsewhere.

My aim, from the first, was to unite in the same school the children of the labouring classes and those of their employers, being persuaded that the only means by which the children of the latter in our rural districts were likely to get an education equal to their wants, was by bringing it home to them at a cheap rate; and that if this were done, then they would, in the end, gladly avail themselves of it, notwithstanding any prejudice against the mixture of the classes, which I knew to prevail. This union of classes also was necessary to give the plan any chance of success; and the result has proved, in a most convincing manner, that where the instruction is good, and such as to meet the requirements of the parish and neighbourhood, that all difficulties may be overcome.

The schools, built on plans from the Committee of Council, were opened in October, 1842. The rates of payment were, for the children of labourers, 2*d.* and 1*d.* per week; 6*s.* a quarter for the children of the employers of labour, and for those known to be able to pay it, living with the parish; and 10*s.* for a similar class living in other parishes.

(These payments, now that parents know the value of the school, might even be increased).

The annual amount of school payments for the first eight years from its opening, is as follows:—

PAYMENTS, INCLUDING BOOKS, ETC.   BOOKS.

		£	s.	d.		£	s.	d.
1st Year, from Mich., 1842, to Mich., 1843..		56	17	3	Of this	7	5	5
2nd do.	” 1844..	68	11	7	”	8	0	5
3rd do.	” 1845..	84	6	1	”	11	5	3
4th do.	” 1846..	93	5	5	”	15	8	0
5th do.	” 1847..	145	6	6	”	24	18	1
6th do.	” 1848..	146	3	7	”	30	2	1
7th do.	” 1849..	164	16	7	”	39	2	7
8th do.	” 1850..	174	4	9	”	41	1	8

A supply of necessary books and maps, etc., were always kept on hand at the school for them to purchase from.

These figures are a most satisfactory proof of the success of the schools, both as to numbers and the classes of life from which the children came. The greatest increase in any one year is £52 1s. 1d., between Christmas, 1846, and Christmas, 1847; and this is owing to the improved process of teaching given to the schools, by the introduction of pupil-teachers, and other advantages arising from the Minutes of the Committee of Council on Education, issued in that year; and also to the impulse in favour of the schools both in the parish and district, arising from the practical conviction which had now been brought home to the parents, that their children were getting a really good and serviceable education. You will never prove this to them as a matter of theory; it can only be brought home to them by experiment.

The amount paid for books and other school necessaries, it will be observed, increased year by year, and at the end of the eighth year it is five times the amount paid in the first; in fact, so soon as the children became thoroughly interested in what they were learning, all difficulties were at an end, and the parents cheerfully and readily did all that could be expected of them.

It was the introduction of the reading-books of the Irish Board of Education, at the cheap rate at which they are to be had, which led to the purchase of books to this large amount in these schools.

For the first two or three years, the books purchased were almost entirely the ordinary reading-books: this led to a taste for the introduction of others, and of cheap maps, both into the schools and into their homes; and for every £10 spent in the purchase of cheap school-books, it has led at least to £20 being spent on other books, thus opening out a market where none existed before; so that I very much doubt whether, even on trading principles, the London publishers are altogether right in the views they have taken up as regards the books published by the Irish Board.

The amount of payments in some measure denotes the numbers attending the schools; but it will not be uninteresting to add a few more particulars on this head.

The schools opened at first with 38 children, which, at the end of the year, increased to 106; and I perfectly recollect that, during this first year, more than 30 children were taken away or sent away by myself, because they would not conform to the rules: these, almost without exception, were glad to be allowed to return.

At the end of the   2nd year.. 110 (no great increase)
     „   „   3rd year.. 144
     „   „   4th year.. 158
And at Midsummer, 1850, they had gradually increased to 219.

Of these, 31 were paying 10s. per quarter, and came from other parishes, many from a considerable distance; and there were as many as twenty lodging in different respectable cottages in the village, some from Monday morning to Friday night, going home for Saturday and Sunday; 24 paying 6s. per quarter, sons of tradesmen and employers of labour in the village, 164 paying 2d. and 1d. per week.

At Christmas, 1850, my connection with these schools terminated; and my successor in the living, not entertaining the same views as myself, I was apprehensive they might suffer from this circumstance. He, however, agreed not to interfere with them; and the letter which I am about to read to you will show his change of opinion on becoming really acquainted with the education given, and the manner in which the schools were conducted.

Of the master and mistress I had the highest opinion, both as to their abilities as teachers, and as to their zeal and industry, and in both my expectations have been fully realised. I visited the schools in March last, and was very much pleased with their general appearance. The amount of annual payments up to the present time shows, that the children, in numbers and position, are much what they were when I left the parish.

The master and mistress are both certificated teachers by the Committee of Council, and receive augmentation of salaries on that account.

The following is the letter I alluded to, from my successor at King's Somborne:—

King's Somborne, April 6, 1853

MY DEAR SIR, — According to promise, I send you a statement of the present condition and prospects of the King's Somborne Schools, together with my impression, derived from the experience of upwards of two years now since I succeeded you in the parish, as to the practical working of the system of education which you had established, and for eight years so successfully carried out. You are aware that I came here with some slight degree of *prejudice* against that system, and of apprehension as to the principles on which it was founded; being not quite satisfied that I could conscientiously support it, though readily engaging not to interfere with it. You are also aware that a very short time convinced me of the needlessness of all doubt and hesitation, and happily and completely converted me to a sense of its excellence.

It has afforded me much pleasure to be assured by you, that, in the visit which you lately paid us, you found the schools, in which you yet retain so warm an interest, in a satisfactory condition; and I have every reason to hope and believe that they will continue to maintain their high character and efficiency, and be a great means of extending the system adopted in them, and found to work with so much success, gradually and generally throughout the country. Indeed in this latter respect, they have already exercised much influence, through the many pupils that have gone forth to other schools, especially during the last two or three years; and I am constantly receiving applications from various and distant parts of the country for a boy or girl of sufficient age and attainments to introduce the benefits of our system. This assistance has been always granted to the full extent of our means of supply, which, indeed, in one or two later cases, as you are aware, have not been adequate to the demand. Of those who have been sent out from the King's Somborne Schools, in whatever capacity, the accounts received have invariably been most favourable; our numbers are still maintained, and we have, at present, some very promising children of both sexes, who will, I feel confident, do credit to themselves, and to the institution in which they are receiving their education.

So much for the state and prospects of our schools. With regard to the general character of the system of instruction and management pursued therein, every year is testing its merits, and demonstrating its value; and I feel sure that the more extensively it is known, and the better it is understood, the more it will be appreciated. In reference to one peculiar feature in this system — its "self-paying" principle — that has been, I believe, for many years completely successful; at all events, I can state that, after paying every expense connected with the schools, a balance has remained in hand at the end of each year that I have been in the parish, and had the management of them. Before I came here, I had often heard of attempts having been made to establish schools on the self-supporting principle, and to introduce it into those already in existence; but almost invariably with the same unsatisfactory issue — partial success, if not total failure; though

I believe, within the last year or two, some nearer approach to a successful result has been effected in a few instances. That the scheme is quite practicable, our own schools here, which owe their origin and their reputation to yourself, are a proof, where it is carried out to its fullest extent, and with the happiest effect. Other schools may, and no doubt in the course of time will, attain the same measure of success; but it must be by raising the present standard of education, by making the instruction offered of such a kind, so far in advance both in quality and practical usefulness, of the usual routine which has so long prevailed in our national schools, as to induce parents not only of the lower, but of the middle classes — not alone the employed, but the employers — to avail themselves of its advantages for their children. That this would be the effect I have no hesitation in expressing my conviction, from my own experience, since I have been resident in this parish. I have found, also, that the rule by which the children are required to purchase every book, etc., which they use (a rule absolutely essential towards making a school self-supporting), is still working well, and appears to afford no ground of objection or complaint, nor to have acted as a means of *exclusion* in any instance that I have heard of: so far from it, I quite believe that the labouring poor generally, in the parish, justly and warmly appreciate the efforts which have been made in favour of education for their families; and that many parents, even of the poorest, do, and many more, if necessary, would readily and cheerfully consent to make some sacrifice of their already too scanty means, to secure for their children the benefits which our schools hold out to them.

I would add a remark upon one other point only in reference to our system, upon which I have reason to believe some misunderstanding exists amongst persons who have not had an opportunity of making themselves acquainted with its nature and character, either by personal observation or from the reports of the Government Inspectors. I allude to the opinion prevailing in some quarters, that the course of instruction pursued in these schools does not include religious teaching; that it is restricted solely to subjects of "useful knowledge," to the acquisition of physical and general science — in a word, to what is commonly called a "secular education." Those who entertain this erroneous supposition have only to remember that Her Majesty's Inspectors require, at their annual visits, a sufficient degree of Scriptural information from the children generally; and that from the upper classes in all Church of England Schools some acquaintance with her doctrines and formularies is in addition expected; and, I believe, that on no occasion have they had reason to complain of any deficiency here in this respect. I have also continued to follow the excellent plan adopted by yourself, of receiving the senior children at my own house on the Sunday evenings; and I do not hesitate to say, that all who have visited our schools, and taken the trouble to ascertain for themselves, will testify that it is possible to combine a high degree of general useful knowledge with the principles of a sound religious education.

I am, my dear Sir,
Very sincerely yours,
CHARLES NICOLL.

The first comment, then, that I will make is, that in a few years the aim I had in view had been completely reached. The schools, in the sense in which I had intended them to be so, had become self-supporting. No person out of or in the parish was called upon for subscriptions or donations; nothing of the kind was needed; and I had such confidence in this principle of self-support being a sound one, that I have never even thought of asking for subscriptions for this purpose.

I had thus established the fact. The thing could be done; it had been done: and now I must tell you how it had been done.

I proposed, as my object, the establishment of such schools as would be instrumental in raising the moral tone and the intellectual character of my parishioners — schools which would not only supply profitable training for the young, but which would also be capable of interesting the parents. I calculated upon succeeding in this latter point through the medium of their parental feelings. I knew that, for these purposes, the old eleemosynary or charity school, however carefully attended to, would be utterly powerless; indeed, considering the materials upon which I had to work, that in some important points it would be worse than powerless — that it would be positively mischievous; that its effect would be, making the labouring classes feel that they were regarded as standing in a separate and degraded position, and as having no power or inclination to do anything for themselves or for their children, to confirm and strengthen the pauper spirit which I was desirous of rooting out, by creating feelings of manly independence.

The task I set myself was, to make the schools so good, that the parents might see that there was no question about the fact that their children were the better for attending them, and that the knowledge they were acquiring was in their (the parents') estimation interesting and valuable.

If the schools were of this character, I considered I should be making a strong appeal to the affections, and to the sense of responsibility of the parents, and that in this way a feeling would rise up in favor of the schools, and in favor of education, both among parents and among children, very different from that which could possibly arise from the ordinary village schools.

You have already heard how, as the school improved and became known, both in the parish and at a distance, the attendance of the children, both of employers and employed, became one of its distinguishing features.

With respect to the instruction given in the schools over and above the ordinary routine, I aimed (as you may have seen) at teaching what would be profitable and interesting to persons in the position of life which the children were likely to occupy. I aimed at their being taught what may be called the philosophy of common things — of every day life. As the wants of the school increased, no expence was spared in getting the needful apparatus for teaching this. They were shewn how much there is that is interesting, and which it is advantageous for them to know, in connexion with the natural objects with which they were familiar; they had explained to them, and were made acquainted with, the principles of a variety of natural phenomena; as well as the principles and construction of various instruments of a useful kind. Such interest did some of the boys take in elementary chemistry, that they formed a voluntary class of ten or twelve of the biggest boys, who met on a Saturday with the master; they subscribed among themselves for the current expenses of it: in this, the school had great advantage in being near Queenwood College. Two of the most promising boys went there two days a week to work in the laboratory — one for a year; and the master, by occasional visits, was greatly benefited, and enabled to give great effect to this useful branch of instruction in the school.

Instruction of this kind contributed largely to keep alive an interest in the whole of the school-work; it seemed to awaken powers of thought, hitherto dormant, which enabled them to bring to the ordinary routine of school instruction, a desire to understand and a disposition to reflect upon, and as far as possible to apply, what was taught. A practical turn was given to everything; the uses and fruits of the knowledge they were acquiring were never lost sight of.

It was a common observation, made by almost every stranger who visited the schools, that the children had not the appearance of being those of the labouring classes; this arose entirely from the cleanliness of the school, and that look of intelligence which nothing but education can give.

I trust you will not imagine there is anything egotistical in what I have been saying, because, when you invite me to address you on the subject of education, I can only suppose that you are desirous of hearing the history and results of my own educational experiments. Whatever little value my conclusions upon this subject may possess, must arise from their being the result of those experiments. I have now, however, given a brief history of them, and except as a basis for a few remarks, I shall have no further occasion to refer to them.

The great conclusion of all is, that what was done in the poor agricultural district of King's Somborne and its neighbourhood, by these schools, may be done in other places by using the same means. Small parishes of few inhabitants do not supply materials enough for such schools; to attempt it in them would be absurd; but my own experience tells me, that the best way of promoting education under existing circumstances, is — not by writing and speaking of such things and such schools as matters of theory, but by multi-plying and establishing them, and patiently working them out as model schools whenever circumstances are favorable to them.

I attach great importance to the mere attempt to invest schools for popular education with a self-supporting character — the impor-tance of their becoming such, and of thoroughly establishing the principle in the minds of the labouring, and, in fact, of all classes, that parents ought to be the instruments through which their children are to be educated, is, in a social point of view, impossible to overrate.

We ought not to accustom people to ask and receive every kind of assistance from others, and to owe nothing to themselves; but we ought to teach them, that when a good school is brought within their reach, they must exert themselves to support it.

I do not say that the attempt will always be attended with complete success; I must guard myself against misapprehension on this point. There are at present too many retarding causes; the low standard of instruction, which many are still of opinion is sufficient for the labouring classes; the want of a proper appreciation of education on the part of the parents themselves, totally uneducated as they are; the prejudices of the employers of labour against the mixture of classes; the inexperience of managers of schools, who become timid and afraid of the difficulties which arise; and last, not least, I may mention, the very feelings and opinions of many of the clergy themselves (particularly in our rural districts), are against it, from not having had a practical opportunity of seeing the great good that may be effected by a higher standard of education for the labouring classes than the one they have adopted.

But although we cannot, in all cases, hope for complete success in attempting to establish schools on the self-paying principle, yet it is to be hoped that those who have the direction of the education of the country, may not lose sight of it. At present, we must content ourselves with making it our aim in as many localities as possible, hoping that, at no distant period, public opinion, enlightened by what is now going on, may lead eventually to a system of national education founded on this basis. We have now the means within our reach of so conducting our schools, that they may lead to this result; the facilities for doing so are much greater than they were ten years ago; the well-qualified teachers from the training institutions; the encouragement and assistance which is given in various ways, by the Committee of Council on Education; the increasing feeling on the part of the people themselves; all these tend to make the establishment of schools on a self-supporting principle much more easy than it hitherto has been, and on that account more likely to be taken up by those interested in the subject.

In making these remarks, I have been speaking in a general way on the subjects taught in our schools; but I would not lose sight for a moment of the highest part of education — the moral and religious training of the children; and it is my firm conviction, the result of my own experience, that the effect of religious teaching is greatly increased when brought to bear upon the minds that have been trained to thought and reflection, and have been interested by the contemplation of the attributes of the Deity, as they are displayed in the objects and phenomena of surrounding nature.

The schools at King's Somborne very soon attracted attention in the neighbourhood, and were much visited by those interested in education. This led to great improvement of the schools in that district: a general wish to improve them on something of a similar plan was excited; better reading books were introduced; a more extended circulation was given to the reading books published by the Irish Board of Education. This, from the cheap price at which they were to be had, and the goodness of them as school books, led to the system of the children buying the books, to which I attach so much importance, and which has proved a most important element in the success of those school plans I was endeavouring to carry out.

In the year 1844, and following year, the schools were inspected by the Rev. John Allen, Her Majesty's Inspector, now Archdeacon of Salop, who gave us great encouragement in all that was being done.

In the years 1846 and 1847, they were inspected by the Rev. H. Moseley, who gave a more complete examination of them than had ever been done before; and this full and able report of them in the Minutes of Council for 1846-47, made the schools more extensively known. This year the new plans of the Committee of Council were established, and I immediately availed myself of all the advantages which they offered, and the good effects of this were soon seen, and were visible in the marked increase of payments on the part of the children which took place in that year.

Mr. Moseley, in his report speaking of the causes of the success of these schools, says — "In the education we offer to the poor, the springs of opinion among them have never been considered, nor their wants consulted.

"It is in this that the secret of Mr. Dawes's success appears to lie; he has shewn his knowledge of the springs of opinion amongst the poor by consulting their independence, and adapting the education he offers to their wants, by a careful study of their condition.

"The King's Somborne School was commenced in the exercise of abundant faith in the affection of a labouring man for his children; and, notwithstanding that the wages of labour in the parish are very low, the school-fee was fixed at double that of other neighbouring schools, under the impression that he would be willing to pay more than is usually claimed of him, for what he believed to be a really good and useful education, and that the higher fee would tend to create this belief in his mind.

"*Who* are to be considered farmers, and pay the highest fee, and who tradesmen and labourers, Mr Dawes claims the right himself to decide; but all are placed within the walls of the school on terms of perfect equality; they are intermingled in their seats, and in the classes in which they are taught, and precisely the same advantages of instruction are offered to all."

In the year 1850, the Rev. H. Brookfield was Her Majesty's Inspector who visited these schools; and in his Report, published in the Minutes of Council for that year, I was glad to see that he had corrected an opinion that had in some measure got abroad — that the boys' school was too much devoted to science, to the neglect of other things. He says:—

"As to the character of their studies and employments, all appeared to me of the most homely, useful, practical sort, just such as would qualify them for the discharge of their probable tasks in life with comfort to themselves, and advantage to their employers, and in a sense of duty to their Maker.

"They read with that fluent ease, and pleasing modulation and intelligent emphasis, which would make their reading an agreeable resource, not only to themselves, but to listeners by the cottage fireside. Their writing and arithmetic were proportionately good, and plain and industrial occupations had their proper measure of regard. There is no reason why every parish in the kingdom should not present a similar nucleus of moral improvement and cultivated intelligence. Nothing about has struck me so much as its perfect freedom from the romantic and impracticable. Good common sense, directed by a genial, a humane, and a Christian spirit, seems to be its presiding influence; and I have other reasons than those connected with an official inspection, for believing that it has been the happy nursery of many honest, industrious, intelligent, Christian men and women."

To these visits of the Inspectors the school at King's Somborne owes much; and I shall ever recollect them (associated as they were with a mutual wish on the part of Inspectors and inspected that good should arise from them) as affording opportunities of an interchange of ideas on a subject in which both the Inspector and myself felt the greatest interest, and from which we all seemed mutually to profit.

I will now mention a few out of the many cases which have been brought under my notice, instances in which have been adopted similar plans to those I am recommending.

First. — The school at Abbot's Ann, in the county of Hampshire, which is entirely directed by my friend, the Rev. Samuel Best, rector of the parish.

Up to the year 1846, Mr. Best informs me, this school, although he had paid great attention to it, and had required but very small payments, had yet been totally ineffective. In that year a favourable opportunity occurred for making a change; it was taken advantage of, and the whole system altered.

A master was procured from Battersea, the school payments were made real payments; and although, in the case of children already in school, it was not considered fair to increase them, in the case of all new scholars the payments were raised gradually, but regulated according to the class in life of the scholars. This system is now in operation, and while a higher tone has been given to the school, there has been no difficulty experienced in carrying out the rate of payments.

The annual receipts, supposing the payments in all cases to be according to the new rule (which I have an entire confidence they will be shortly with our present numbers), would be quite equal to the expenses of the school.

The children pay for their books and slates, and as the details of the payments may be interesting and throw light on the questions at issue, viz., whether the different classes can be brought together, and whether thereby schools may be made self-supporting, I subjoin the following statement of the school as at present constituted:—

17   children paying 1s. per week or 12s. per quarter.
4   paying 9s. per quarter; 17 paying 6s. ;
6   paying 4s. ; and 69 at 2d. per week.
29   come from other parishes in the neighbourhood.
11   walking seven miles a day out and home.
9   walking five ; 9 walking three ; 7 come and take lodgings in the village, paying 5s. per week, which includes board, lodging, and washing ; 3 of them are from a neighbouring parish, 1 from Surrey, 1 from Somerset, 1 from Kent, and 1 from the other side of the county of Hants.

I say nothing of the education given, as I consider that the foregoing remarks pre-suppose a good one, inasmuch as people will only pay for that which is worth its price.

Mr. Best then speaks of the influence of King's Somborne in this, and adds, that, in illustration of the preceding remarks, and in order to enforce their application, it may be desirable to state, that the parish to which they refer is agricultural, the rate of wages 8s. per week, and the population at the last census 580. He has followed the practice of the King's Somborne school in having lectures of a scientific character given at the school-room, which is well fitted with apparatus, and the school is creating a feeling in favour of education in and about his own parish which promises the best results.

He lately sent me rules of an association of a local character, for the promotion of lectures on scientific and literary subjects in village schools, which seemed to me well worthy of attention.

There are many schools in Hampshire more or less adopting the same principles:— Stockbridge; some of the schools in Winchester; at Wellow, where there is a pupil-teacher from Somborne; at Beechwood in the New Forest, from which I have the following:—

	£	s.	d.
Payments for the year 1849	46	17	6
For books ditto	6	10	0
1850 Children's payments and books	54	0	11
1851 Do. do. do.	57	14	11

Of which £7 19s. 7d. was for books; and in 1852 a small decrease.

At Downham Market in Norfolk, and Woodhill in Hertfordshire, and at Much Marcle in Herefordshire, are schools, in each of which there is a pupil-teacher from King's Somborne.

At Mildenhall, Suffolk, in a school of Sir Henry Bunbury's, the same principles are very successfully carried out; and in this school there are two boys apprenticed pupil-teachers from King's Somborne.

There is a very good school at Sudbury, in Suffolk, in the parish of which the Rev. Mr. Badham is vicar. In a small publication of his, written soon after the schools were established, he says, "An earnest hope was entertained that, in addition to the working classes, a large number of tradesmen in the town and neighbourhood would be anxious to afford their children the benefit of such a system of instruction as the schools would afford, bearing in mind the remark of the late Sir Robert Peel on the establishment of schools in connection with the Committee of Council at Tamworth, that if the farmers and tradesmen did not avail themselves of them, they would inevitably be left behind by the working classes.

"Could the children of the tradesmen and the middle classes, instead of being partially, be generally secured to the schools, which we believe, from the experience of the past year, will ultimately be the case, a moral result of no ordinary kind would take place, and the schools, by becoming self-supporting, as in the gratifying instance of King's Somborne in Hampshire, would need no further aid." And Mr. Badham, in a letter to me, dated the 18th of March last, says, "The children pay weekly, in advance 1s., 6d., 2d., according to the condition in life. Our receipts for the weekly payments for the two last years were—

"For 1851, £ 93 7s. 7d.   For 1852, £ 117 0s. 11d.   an increase of £ 23 3s. 4d. on the preceding year.

"We have no difficulty about what each child should pay, and I am rarely referred to on the subject.

"Some weeks ago, a girl who had paid two pence per week for two years, brought 6d. as the sum which her parents wished to pay in future. They had undergone no change in outward circumstances, and had not been solicited to pay more." He then adds, in this letter, "Speaking of model schools — a visit to a good school does more for the establishment of similar ones than a great deal of argument."

I have some interesting particulars from the Rev. Mr. Stephenson of the schools in his parish, Shirley, nearly Birmingham (population 1,100, engaged in agriculture). He says:—

"The introduction of a higher class of children into the school has produced a very marked change in the rest. Personal cleanliness is more attended to; ragged and dirty clothes are rarely or ever seen; orderly and respectful behaviour is the rule and not the exception. I also see that a kindly feeling is arising between the children, which, while it will not interfere with the proper gradation of rank, will be of great service in uniting in one common bond, those who will be hereafter engaged in one common interest, in the different relations of master and servant.

"There are now about 30 children of farmers and petty tradesmen in attendance at the schools, many of whom travel a daily distance of six or seven miles from the neighbouring parishes, and some of whom formerly went to boarding-schools whose charges varied from 30 guineas and upwards a year. The children that come from these latter schools I have generally found very deficient in the practical application of what they had been taught, and particularly ignorant of religious truths.

"The children are required to purchase the whole of their secular books," and he adds, "from Midsummer 1850 to Midsummer 1851, they purchased—

    485 books   ⎫
    320 copy books   ⎬   £ 14
    18 quires of paper   ⎪
    144 slates   ⎭
From 1851 to Midsummer 1852.

$$\left.\begin{array}{l}\text{292 books}\\\text{262 copy books}\\\text{12 quires of paper}\\\text{126 slates}\end{array}\right\}\quad \text{£ 12 5}s.\ 7d.$$

"Under the old regime the stipends paid to teachers were £45; they are now £158.

"To some, these details may appear dry and uninteresting; but they are facts of great importance, and from which much may be learnt.

"From Acton School, Cheshire, I am informed, the children of the farmers and the labourers have been together in the class and in the playground, with no feelings of jealousy or evil result of any kind; the farmers' sons continue at school to a greater age and attain a higher degree of proficiency than is usual with the sons of the labourer, though of these many will remain to a greater age than is usual, from the value which the parents of all classes soon learn to attach to education which is really good and useful."

Christ-Church School, Stone, Staffordshire,
April 13th, 1853

REV. SIR,— Seven years ago I entered upon my present charge, and found 50 children in attendance, very low in attainments, and the school still lower in public estimation.

After two years of hard labour, the numbers began to increase; a decided improvement was perceptible; a more respectable class of children began to attend our school.

It was then thought advisable, by my late respected clergyman and myself, to raise the payments; when the accompanying Circular, dated 1851, was issued, and a class was formed, each child paying 6d. per week. Nearly all the first class of boys at once paid the advance: no compulsion was used; but care was taken that no one was admitted for the future unless he paid the 6d. It is now become a well-known and fixed rule.

We have now a class of 30 boys on the books at 6d., and 25 or 26 of these are nearly always present; indeed, they attend much better than those who pay only 2d. We did not at that time attempt the class at 4d., as suggested by Her Majesty's Inspector in his letter; but on the appointment of the Rev. J. Ford, our present worthy minister, a second Circular was issued, raising the payment in the second class to 4d. per week, which class now consists of 27 boys.

I find the higher rates of payment are as readily paid as the lower rates used to be; while the amount of pence collected is widely different. The first year I commenced, the pence amounted to £20; last year £50. The average number of boys for last year was 124.

I am of opinion that the payments of our national schools are too low to be valued as they ought to be. If the master adapt his instruction so that it may be useful in the particular locality in which his school is situated, and the clergyman and himself go hand in hand in the great work, they will rarely fail of raising the condition of the school.

Any information which I can furnish I shall be happy to afford, if required.

I remain, Reverend Sir,

Your obedient servant,

WILLIAM DUROSE

The Very Rev. the Dean of Hereford.

The St. Thomas's Schools, Charterhouse, are a striking instance of this self-supporting character being given to schools in one of the poorest districts in London; they owe their origin and success to the energies of the Rev. W. Rogers, from whose printed account of them I make the following extract:—

"A chief feature in these schools is, the steady increase of the children's payments. When they were first opened, I found great difficulty in getting the parents to pay even 2*d.* per week for their children's schooling, and the payments amounted to about £80 per annum in the boys' school and £50 in the girls'. But gradually the people began to appreciate the benefits of the school, and in consequence of the great improvements we were enabled to introduce through the advantages offered by the Minutes of Council, 1847, we raised our school fees from 2*d.* to 3*d.*, 4*d.*, and 6*d.* per week, according to the classes.

But the most remarkable fact is, that the number of scholars has not fallen off in consequence of raising the payments; on the contrary, it has increased to such a degree, that, two years ago, I was compelled to hire a room to accommodate the overflowing numbers. And an important fact has been elicited by the establishment of this school, viz., that providing the children make progress in their learning, the parents evidently prefer paying for their schooling to sending them free of expense. In consequence of an arrangement I had made, any child residing in the district, upon application, was admitted in the free list. At first the applications were numerous, but gradually diminished, and have now almost entirely ceased.

Total numbers — between 700 and 800.

Mr. Rogers, in a letter dated the 23rd inst. says —

	£	s.	d.
The payment for 1851 was	291	15	2
Ditto for 1852 was	280	14	8

The reason for the decrease is, that during 1852, they were obliged to disband a school of 150 children for the new school-building. They are now paying at the rate of £350 per annum. This is one of the poorest districts in London.

About a year ago, the Committee of the Blue Coat School in Hereford, of which I am a member, and where the education is gratis, being paid chiefly by subscription, agreed that the children should buy the reading books, and that we should introduce those of the Irish Board; they left it to me to carry it out. There are 130 boys in the school and 80 girls, and at the end of one month there was scarcely a boy or girl who had not done so, and books to the amount of more than £12 had been bought by the children themselves. There was a case of two brothers at first not buying them, and I was anxious to look into this, as I saw clearly it was not poverty which made them refuse. I called on the father, and found he was a man of some property, perfectly able to pay for the education of his own children, and ought not to have had them in a charity school. Since that, the committee have proposed that the children should pay for all their copy-books and slates, etc., and I have no doubt, were we to establish a system of reasonable payments of school-fees throughout the schools, that few, if any, would leave; the instruction is good, the people understand and appreciate it, and would be willing to pay. By doing so, we should be doing a great good to the town of Hereford, rather than continuing the schools on the charity principle.

In this school the managers took a pupil-teacher in his last year by permission of Committee of Council, from King's Somborne, who was of great service to it, and at Christmas last he was elected to the Winchester Training School as a Queen's scholar.

There are in all places some exceptional cases which must be paid for by others — must be met either as matters of charity or from the local rates, but I will not enter upon this at present.

In the year 1849, the late lamented Sir Robert Peel remodelled a Charity School, founded by his father at Tamworth, for the clothing and educating fifty boys. He appointed a certificated master, and placed it in connexion with the Committee of Council, and admitted middle-class boys as day scholars, who were to pay 10*s.* per quarter, in advance, and purchase all books. The master, Mr. Vaughan, informs me in a letter of the present month:—

"The mixed system has worked really well. Very few parents have objected to their sons being classed with poor boys and none have expressed a wish that the fee were lower. The effect of the mixture of the two classes has been — upon the higher, to stimulate them to a greater exertion in their work, by seeing many poor boys before them in their studies; while the lower class have had their natural roughness of manner somewhat softened by contact with boys of a superior grade, who, from a better home-training, are generally more tractable and gentle in behaviour.

"By the admission of the middle-class boys, the fee required, and the advanced course of study (very similar to that you adopted in your school at King's Somborne), the *status* of the school has been greatly raised in the estimation of the most respectable inhabitants of the town and its vicinity, while the poor desire more than formerly to get their sons admitted to the foundation. My own position, too, is far superior to that which I could hope to take, were this school one for *foundationaries* only."

This school has the advantage of pupil-teachers.

The master speaks of his position being far superior to what he would have had, if the school had been for the charity boys only. There is no doubt of this; and every good schoolmaster in England is interested in giving this self-paying character to his schools. It makes their position among those with whom they live a totally different one, and gives them the proper importance due to their situation, which on the semi-charity plan they never can attain.

The letter I am now about to quote from is from the Rev. Thos. Walpole, rector of Alverstoke, Gosport, who has paid great attention to the subject before us; and although he says his school has not yet succeeded in bringing the middle-class children to it in such numbers as he expected, yet I look upon his opinion as of great value.

Alverstoke Rectory, April 20, 1853.

Partly I think from pride and partly from prejudice, the quarterly scholars have not come in any number into our school. We made a scale of payments, 2*d.* a week for poor; 4*s.* and 6*s.* a quarter for mechanics and tradesmen. We called the parents together and proposed the scheme, and all assented, and some took advantage of the education offered to them. Still there are a great many who prefer *bad* schools in Gosport for the dignity of a sort of middle class, and for the independence of all discipline and control.

I am still of opinion that our schools may be made more self-paying than they are; and in proportion as education is valued by the poor themselves, will they be willing to make those sacrifices which parents of the higher and middle classes are so ready to make for their children's education...... We have very little difficulty in making the children pay (at a reduced price) for their books, and by having a school library attached to the school, the boys acquire a taste for procuring books, which has its good results in the purchase of school-books, as well as those of a more amusing kind.

We discourage entirely the system of a *free school* — a charity school in the 19th century acceptance of the word is a wretched thing; it brings education into disrepute and pauperises. The prevailing system of 1*d.* per week schooling, in National Schools, is a great hindrance to any movement in the right direction, because labourers and their wives are frightened at the notion of 2*d.* as a large weekly sum, when in fact the labourer with his 9*s.* only per week (and I put the lowest possible sum) could as well pay 2*d.* as 1*d.*, as the children are given as pocket money more than the other 1*d.* to buy trash with. If I established a new school even in an agricultural poor parish, I should be very much inclined to charge 4*d.* per week, to say I *disapprove* of charity schools altogether, but that I should be ready to give a ticket for *half the payment* to the very poorest. We have adopted a half-ticket payment* with some success here.

*This half-payment ticket is a good idea: on the reverse of the card used in the Alverstoke School is printed —
"This ticket will free the child named on the other side of half the school payment.
"The ticket will be forfeited if the child is absent without leave.
"At the end of the quarter, if the attendance has been regular, this ticket will be signed by the schoolmaster and the rector, and may then be renewed for the following quarter."

I might go on quoting cases of a similar kind, but to do so would be tedious. I will only add one more; the School of Elementary Drawing, in connexion with the Board of Practical Art, which has been opened at Hereford, and which promises well in a self-paying direction.

The Committee of Management have been at a first cost of about £70, in fitting up a room for the purpose, and in providing the necessary models and examples for a commencement, which they get from the Board at Marlborough House at half-price.

The conditions made by the Board of Trade in sending a master are, that he should receive all the fees paid by the schools where he attended to give instruction, and, at least, one-half of those paid by the classes attending the Central School, the Board guaranteeing him a minimum salary, should the fees fall short of this. It was expected that the school would, at the end of the year, become self-supporting; and if not, the master would be withdrawn.

The master is entirely under the control of the Committee of Management, and the fees fixed by them.

There are four schools in which he attends to give instruction, three of them schools for the labouring classes, each of which pays £5 per annum; one of the Cathedral School, for the children of the upper classes, paying £10.

There is a morning class, meeting twice a week, for two hours each time, paying 2s. each per week, or 8s. per month, in which there are forty-eight pupils.

An evening class, meeting also twice a week, chiefly artisans and mechanics, paying 6d. per week, or 2s. per month, in which there are fifty-one pupils.

The school is only now in its third month, but for the two first months the sum secured was £47 6s.; and if continued during forty-four weeks of the year at the same rate, would give the master a salary of more than double the minimum fixed by the Board. The instruction is very popular with all classes, and there seems no doubt of its success.

I cannot imagine anything more interesting, or more instructive, than a visit to this school when the artisan and tradesman's class is at work. Being a witness to the interest they take in it would remove any doubts that might exist, as to the usefulness of such means of instruction for this class of the population.

Had the Board of Trade made an offer of £200 a year for the maintenance of this school (which is about the sum it will cost), on condition that instruction should be offered to all gratis, I believe it would have been a complete failure; and although, from the short time it has been at work, one cannot speak of it as a positive success, it clearly meets the wants of the town in this particular kind of instruction, from the great interest all classes take in it.

The population of the town is under 13,000, the trades entirely those connected with agriculture. It would seem, then, that if a School for Elementary Drawing succeed in Hereford (and there is every prospect that it will), we may fairly infer that a similar one would do so in all towns of an equal amount of population, when properly managed.

On the subject of school payments, and on the importance of making them in all classes of life, as far as possible, a part, as it has been termed, of the family expenditure, I will now quote a letter which I have had from the Rev. S. Norris, one of Her Majesty's Inspectors of Schools for the counties of Cheshire, Stafford, and Shropshire, which deserves to be read at length. It is dated Walsall, March 4, 1853:—

Walsall, March 4th, 1853.

DEAR SIR,— So entirely do I agree with you about the importance of raising rather lowering the payments made by parents for the education of their children in our elementary schools, and so urgently needful does it appear to me to set public opinion right on this subject at the present time, that I am quite glad that you have asked for my evidence; indeed, I take every opportunity of putting it forward.

In my Report for 1851, I have devoted several pages to the subject, endeavouring to show that a higher rate of fee is essential.

1st. In order to secure the co-operation of the parents.

2nd. In order to relieve our schools from the pecuniary difficulties under which they at present labour.

On the first head, my text, as it were, is what Dr. Chalmers said thirty years ago, that if we wish to secure the parents' interest in the education of their children, we must make it part of the family expenditure.

Nearly four years' experience as an inspector of schools convinces me of the truth of this.

If a parent pays for his child's education, he takes care that he gets his money's worth out of the school. If the boy is truant he scolds him. "My boy, I can't afford to be paying 6*d.* a week for your

schooling, if you throw away two-pennyworth of it in this way."
He feels that *he* is educating his son; and this is as it should be,
and as God meant it to be. If the school is a charity school, he
feels that the *parish* is doing it for him; he is pauperised, and
soon learns the lesson, that our charity schools have long been
teaching him that *he* (the parent) is not responsible for the
education of his child, and that he confers a sort of obligation on
his clergyman or patron in sending his child to school.[1]

To say that a parent has a right to expect the free education of
his child from the state, I believe to be neither more nor less than
communism, little better than the doctrine that he has a *right* to
food at the hands of the state.

But I am not only convinced that this is true in principle, but
also that it is practically felt by the parents. They *prefer* a school
that asks a higher fee. To show this, I collected some statistics
relating to the attendance and fees at private schools in my district
which I have given in pages 725–729 of my Report for 1851.

I am glad to say, that in my district the fees have been raised
within the last few years in nearly all my better class of schools
and with the best effect.

About 20 rural schools have adopted the King's Somborne plan.

About 40 town schools have raised the fee in the first class to 4*d.*
or 6*d.*

I have shown in the Report referred to how generally, and
almost universally, the plea, "We can't afford it," has been mis-
understood. Many a poor gentleman gladly pays one-fourth of his
income for the education of his son for several years. A poor man
is asked for one-sixteenth part, and it is considered a hardship!

But while I would urge our elementary schools to raise their fees
on these grounds, we must carefully avoid the elimination of the
very poor.

There will be some helpless cases in every parish where the fee
really cannot be paid.

What is to be done with these?

I would answer, they are to be met either (1st) by strictly private
charity, as exceptional cases, not compromising the *rule* of the
school, or (2nd) by the *Home Secretary*.

---

[1] The common answer when a clergyman expostulates about the absence of
a child is — "Well, sir, I'll try and oblige you next week." I have often
heard this myself; and if you offend them they "spite" you by keeping the
child at home.

The state should relieve our National Schools of all the pauper (out-door or in-door) children, and also of the quasi-criminal class of children.

I believe that greater injury could hardly be inflicted on any better sort of schools than would result from abolishing the school fee.

> Believe me, Dear Sir,
>> Yours faithfully,
>>> J. P. NORRIS

Mr. Norris, in this letter, refers to his Report inserted in the Minutes of Council for 1851, in which there is much important matter, which I have read with great interest, as bearing on the question before us.

To the question he often asked — "What prospect is there of this school becoming, in a greater or less degree, self-supporting?" he had, in four cases out of five, the following answer:— "If we could only teach the parents to value the education offered them, it might become so, or nearly so, tomorrow. Of course the way to make them do so is by making it good.

"That parents ought to feel responsible for their children's education is felt by all. That the State, or any other party, should take it out of their hands and do it for them is clearly a second best expedient; an argument that something is wrong, a concession to condition (real or supposed) which we must all deplore. Earnest men have ever felt this."

He then gives the statistics of numbers and payments of children to private adventure schools in certain towns in his district, and says — "The aggregate population from which my statistics are drawn may be put down at 225,000. Out of this population, it appears that 9,400 of the same class as that which attends our national Schools are attending adventure schools, and paying in fees to them a weekly sum of £235; or out of a population of 225,000, more than four per cent. are attending adventure schools, and paying an average fee of 6*d.* per week."

If this proposition be supposed to hold good for the entire population of Great Britain, it would appear that the operative and poorer classes of this country are paying more than a million a year towards the support of adventure schools; and I can state that, with regard to the town of Hereford, in which I have made similar enquiries, it most certainly is borne out by the facts which have come before me. Of the quality of the education given in these adventure schools, I have a very low opinion indeed, and no one can for a moment suppose that parents would continue to send their children to such schools, if those of an efficient character were brought within their reach. The fact mentioned by Lord John Russell, in the House of Commons, that the amount of pence at present paid by the children in schools for the labouring classes was very nearly £500,000, was an encouraging one; and this sum, with the million I have quoted above, shews the value, in a financial point of view, of the self-supporting element, among the resources we possess for defraying the cost of National Education. The following extract from Mr. Norris's Report is very instructive:—

> Mr. Norris observed, that the better the schools became, the more they approximated to a self-supporting character.
>
> In asking the parents, what sort of education they would like for their sons — the farm-labourer would like his boy to plough a straight furrow — the potter asks for drawing schools — the shop-keeper for book-keeping; — in short, they all want that kind of instruction which will pay best in their several callings. And are they unreasonable in this? Are we quite sure that we should continue to give eight or ten years to the study of Latin or Greek, if it were not the recognised avenue to the learned professions. And so it is with the parents among the operative classes; those to whom they look as the future employers of their children want good workmen, and therefore the father values no education for his son, which does not, as he thinks, tend to make him a good workman.

Mr Norris does not consider that the working-classes are unable to pay a reasonable fee; on the contrary, he says —

> It is a common notion, that the bulk of them are not only unwilling, but unable to pay such attendance fee as would requite the services of a good teacher.
>
> Excepting pauper parents whose case requires a separate consideration, I believe this to be untrue. I believe that most parents are able to pay for their children, and that the prevalence of the opinion of their being unable, is owing to a misconception of their real meaning when they say they cannot afford it, and to ignorance of the large sums actually paid by the poor to private adventure schools.
>
> When they say they cannot afford it, they mean they cannot afford to lose the time of their children when able to work.— *Rev. J. Norris Report Minutes of Committee of Council, 1851.*

A friend of mine, the Rev. Barham Zincke, who has written several interesting works on education, has sent me some calculations on this head.

The amount, for the figures are very large, may perhaps produce some little momentary astonishment; yet I am by no means sure, that it is not a tolerable approximation to the real sum which might be paid for education so carried out. He omits all consideration of Ireland, on account of the differences of the social and educational circumstances of that part of the kingdom; and his calculations are confined to Great Britain.

Taking the population of this island at 21,000,000, and the number of children who ought to be at schools of which we are speaking, at one-fifth, or 20 per cent. of the whole, he finds that, in this division of the United Kingdom, our schools ought to be attended by 4,200,000 scholars. Omitting the 200,000, and supposing that these 4,000,000, which include, of course, the children of the class above the day-labourer, as, for instance, the whole of the artizan class and small tradesmen, are capable of paying, one with another, 4*d.* a week for their schooling, during forty-seven weeks of the year; this gives him an aggregate of £3,133,333 a year.

He then verifies this by the case of King's Somborne, taking the number of children at 220, and the amount of payment for schooling and books at £165 per annum, the result of the proportion between the number of scholars and the amount of payment, when applied to the 4,000,000 of children of Great Britain, brings out a sum of about £3,000,000; very nearly the sum he had arrived at, by supposing an average school-fee of 4*d.* per week for the whole number.

Speaking hypothetically, then, if 20 per cent., which Mr. Zincke supposes is the due proportion which ought to be in the schools, that is the sum which the principle of calling upon parents to pay for the education of their children is capable of yielding. Now let us compare this sum with that spent in tobacco, or spirits, etc.:—

According to the late Mr. Porter, the following "shews the extent to which the people of England, Scotland, and Ireland voluntarily tax themselves for the enjoyment of only three articles, not one of which is absolutely necessary."

British and Colonial Spirits	£20,810,208
Brandy	3,281,250
Total of Spirits	£24,091,458
Beers of all kinds, exclusive of that brewed in private families	25,383,165
Tobacco and Snuff	7,583,607
Total	£57,063,230
Annual average consumption of Snuff alone, 5,537,344 lbs., at 6s. 8d. per lb., is of the value of	£ 1,845,781

The consumption of these articles is chiefly by the working and industrial classes, and is it not clear, that in this class of expenses with improved habits (such as I should hope education would bring), there is room for raising the average school-fee to the amount for which I have been contending. Facts like these are of great importance, and ought to be brought before the labouring classes much more frequently than they are, and might with great propriety be dwelt upon by those who have influence among them.

What a reflection on the habits of a nation! So large a sum paid for spirits, tobacco, and snuff, and so small a one for the education of their children, those who are the consumers of them!

There is more morality in arithmetic than the world gives it credit for, and if you reflect on these figures for a moment you will agree with me in thinking so. If the people would consume one-third less of tobacco and snuff, it would pay for the education of their children. The late Mr. Porter, in his Paper on the self-imposed taxation of the working-classes, says—

"There is one consideration arising out of this subject, which is of a painful, character, and which, if it were hopeless of cure, would be most disheartening to all who desire that the moral progress of the people should advance with their physical progress; it is, that among the working-classes so very large a proportion of the earnings of the male head of the family is devoted by him to his personal and sensual gratifications. It has been computed, that among those whose earnings are from 10s. to 15s. weekly, at least one-half is spent by the man, upon objects in which the other members of the family have no share. Among artisans earning from 20s. to 30s. weekly, it is said that at least one-third of the amount is in many cases thus selfishly devoted. That this state of things need not be, and that if the people generally were better instructed as regards their social duties, it would not be, may safely be inferred from the fact, that it is rarely or ever found to exist in those numerous cases wherein earnings, not greater than those of the artisan class, are all that are gained by the head of the family, when employed upon matters where education is necessary." He then says, how monstrous such conduct would be thought in the educated classes, and instances the clerk of 80l. a year, a small fraction over 30s. per week — that it would be considered quite exceptional if a fourth part of his earnings were spent upon objects in which the wife and children would have no share. "The peer, the merchant, the clerk, the artisan, and the labourer are all of the same nature, born with the same propensities, and subject to the like influences. It is true, they are placed in very different circumstances, the chief difference being that of early training — one, happily, which is quite possible to remedy, and that by means which may in many ways add to the sum of the nation's prosperity and respectability." *Papers by Mr. Porter, read before the British Association in 1850.*

The proportion of one-fifth at school may be too high; but, taking it at one-seventh in such schools, this would give, in Great Britain, three millions of scholars, and, at 4d. per week for forty-eight weeks, the produce of the pence would be £2,400,000. When we consider that a sum more than three times as great is annually spent in tobacco and snuff, in the United Kingdom, leaving out all that is consumed in spirits, and that the consumption of these is chiefly by the classes for whom such schools are wanted, can it be thought unreasonable that this sum should be paid by them for the education of their children? I think not. How much of an improved morality is concerned in this?

Now I would ask the advocates of free public schools to consider these figures. Do they suppose they will ever persuade the State to pay these £3,000,000 a year (to say nothing about all the heavy preliminary expenses of establishing and building schools, for the purpose of maintaining schools, and, I might add, according to my own views, with the effect of deteriorating education in the end, and of obliterating, in no small degree, the feelings of parental responsibility?

It is stated in the "Queen's Letter," recently issued on behalf of the National Society, that the total number of Church schools known to exist up to Christmas, 1851, is 23,000, with the number of 1,564,401 scholars. This is for England and Wales, the population of which is 18,000,000; but from the way in which these returns are made, and from the state of education which I know must prevail in the greater part of them, I can form.no favourable opinion of the education which the children receive, taken as a whole.

There remains all those who go to no school at all — those who go to schools not connected with the Church — and all those who attend what are called adventure-schools — being the children of small tradesmen, farmers, &c., who would attend the better class of schools, which are in these calculations supposed to exist. This, with the number stated above in Church schools, would not amount to less than three or four millions in Great Britain.

The census of 1851 gives the population of Great Britain at 20,193,552, and taking the per centage of those under fifteen at decimal ·365, more than one-third of the whole (which was stated to be the case in the census of 1841), and by the same, more than one-fourth of the whole, decimal ·252 per cent. under ten, we have the following:—

Children under 15 years of age   7,589,644 ⎫   in Great
Ditto   under 10   ”   5,239,975 ⎭   Britain.

So that, making allowance for the numbers in the classes of life which would not attend such schools, and for those who, from age, were unable to do so, 3,000,000 would be a near approximation to the numbers attending the schools I speak of. However, the accuracy of these calculations does not affect the argument; the less the cost of the whole education, the less the privation of the parents as to the article before alluded to.

Sir James Shuttleworth, in his valuable book on Public Education recently published, states that, in 1847, there were in all about 20,000 schools, of which 17,015 were daily schools belonging to the National Society, and about 3000 to all other religious denominations; that of those belonging to the National Society, 5,404 are in buildings not erected for the purpose, and that 3,407 are in Dames' cottages. Independent of the large sums required to place these schools on a permanent footing, as to building, etc., or erect others for them in better localities, it would require more than a million and a half of money for the annual expenditure of this 17,015 schools to make them effective to give instruction to 1,531,350 scholars; a sum in proportion for the other 3,000 schools. Doubling all these figures would be a very near approximation to what is wanted for the whole people; but we never can expect this amount, or any sum adequate to such wants, until the people take it up for themselves, on the principle, that those who are benefited by education are to pay for it — mixed schools and reasonable payments being the sole exceptional cases to be met by charity or by a local supplemental rate.

Of the state of efficiency of free schools at that time, an opinion may be formed from this — that, according to the official return up to 1847, of the 17,015 church schools, in 1,100, or in nearly two thirds of them, the incomes of the master or mistress were not sufficient to qualify them for an augmentation of salary by the Committee of Council on Education — a minimum of salary being very properly fixed by the Committee of Council, below which they will not grant an augmentation.

About 6,000 have a sufficient income.

At the end of 1851, there were only 1,173 certificated teachers, and taking the proportion of former years, this would give 782 for church schools and 391 for schools of all other denominations. At that time, then, there were 5218 church schools, in which the income was sufficient to admit the master or mistress to a certificate of competency, but in which the teacher had not attempted to obtain, or had failed to obtain, such certificate.

For this, and for other reasons already mentioned, it is quite evident, that those who form an opinion of the state of education throughout the country, from the number of schools and of children attending them, will form a very erroneous one, and that such statistics may, and do mislead those who never enquire further into the matter.

To shew the number that have obtained certificates since that time, and the progress since the system of Queen's scholars and of pupil-teachers who had terminated their apprenticeship, had come into operation, I have ascertained the number of certificated teachers up to the present time, which includes all those examined at Christmas last. The following is a correct statement of it:—

In England and Wales

	Males	Females	Total
Church Schools	1196	658	1854
British and Foreign	103	38	141
Wesleyan	89	16	105
Roman Catholic	41	22	63
Total	1429	734	2163

Out of this total of 2163 of both sexes, 1854 are in Church Schools. Making allowance for deaths and for those who may have gone into other employments, not less than 1600 (probably more) will be engaged in schools (more than double the number in 1851).

Number of Pupil-teachers in Scotland up to the present time.

	Males	Females	Total
Established Church	210	61	271
Presbyterian Dissenters	214	64	278
Episcopal	4	2	6
Total	428	127	555

Of the 6,000 schools existing in 1847 connected with the National Society, and giving an adequate salary for it, this would still leave 4,400 without certificated teachers, not reckoning that many will have gone into new schools since established.

The total number of pupil-teachers in Great Britain on the 31st of December 1851, was — Boys, 3,657; Girls, 1,950; from which the training colleges will be supplied with candidates so that a good supply of well-qualified teachers is quite certain.

With these prospects, then, of a supply of good teachers, and of the assistance of other kinds from the Educational Board, what a different state of things would result at the end of the next quarter of a century, as to a permanent and effective system of education, if those having the direction of it, and particular the clergy, would direct their energies gradually to establish on principle a self-paying system, from that which could arise out of efforts similar to those made during the last.

Having brought forward a number of cases in support of my proposition, and quoted the opinions of experienced men, in favour of giving a self-supporting tendency to our educational efforts, I will now speak in a very brief way of the proceedings of the Committee of Council, and of their bearing on the subject which I have brought before you to-night.

The Committee does not support schools, but gives aid in creating them, and afterwards in improving them, and the tendency of its policy has been manifestly to encourage the principle of self-support, understood in the sense in which I am using it to-night. The various ways in which it gives assistance have been extremely well devised, in order to meet the difficulties with which the question has been surrounded, and to prepare the way for plans of a more extended kind, as the public mind became prepared for them.

The Committee of Council is always ready to contribute liberally, as far as its funds will allow, towards the erection of schools on the most approved plan. By aiding the training colleges in the various ways in which it does, and by examining teachers for certificates of competency and of merit, it does what it can to provide a supply of competent masters and mistresses. By inspection it endeavours to keep the schools in a state of progressive efficiency and improvement. Where augmentation of salary is given to teachers of merit, an annual examination of the schools takes place before such augmentation is paid; the same with the pupil-teachers. This part of the plan, the apprenticing of pupil-teachers, has been attended with the best results in our schools, and can only be properly estimated by those who have seen the advantages of it in a well-conducted school.

I know an opinion has been expressed that the numbers of teachers rising up in this way will be far beyond the demand. I believe not; and, at all events, it will be time enough to say this when it is found actually to be the case. That many of them, particularly the female teachers so trained, will leave their occupations after a few years and be employed in other ways, there can be no doubt; nor is this to be regretted: on the contrary, they become a means of civilizing, in their new position, those around them, and diffuse a feeling in favour of education of a most healthy kind.

To the objection, that the State ought not to be at the expense of their education, if they come to leave so soon, there is a complete answer in this: the benefit to the schools from their teaching, during their apprenticeship, is well worth the money expended upon them as pupil-teachers.

This class of expenses may, as the public become enlightened, be among those met by a local rate.

In these different ways the Committee of Council have endeavoured, and in my opinion most judiciously, and, on the whole more successfully than could have been expected, to improve the state of elementary education. Experience will point out, and apparently has done so, how improvements and extensions may be engrafted on the existing plans; and it is in this way, the only safe one, that more will be done for the education of the existing generation than in any other. Great progress has been made during the last ten years: much more apparently may be done in the next.

The kind of assistance then, given by the Committee of Council, is precisely that kind which may be made most valuable in establishing schools on self-supporting principles, and, although there are some things in the Minutes of Council apparently not altogether in unison with this principle, yet, on being further looked into, that appears to me to be the drift of them.

And here, I must notice in an especial manner, the services to education of Her Majesty's School Inspectors. I have had much intercourse with these gentlemen officially and otherwise, as much, perhaps, as any other manager of schools; and I am now glad of having a public opportunity of expressing my belief, that no class of public servants can bring to the discharge of their duties — and the duties of a school-inspector are often as difficult as they *are always important* — a greater amount of temper, discretion and intelligence, than I have seen in them, and a laborious and conscientious discharge of their duties, has rendered their opinions on all questions connected with elementary education of great value. Of the many hundreds of schools which they officially visit, there can really be very few which have not derived benefit from their suggestions and advice. Their annual reports upon the general educational condition of their respective districts, and of each particular school under inspection, give a most truthful picture both of the educational progress, and of the educational wants of the country.

On the part of some Churchmen, and I believe even still more so among some classes of Dissenters, there is a sensitiveness and a jealousy against inspection, which it is difficult to understand. The Inspectors do not interfere and direct, they merely suggest, and leave the managers of a school to adopt or refuse their suggestions. No doubt inspection is a condition where parties avail themselves of the offers of Committee of Council, but this is merely to see there is a certain amount of good teaching and of instruction in the schools; and surely this is not unreasonable where aid is granted.

Next to the Committee of Council in command of funds stand our Educational Societies, which have all directed, perhaps from necessity, their attention mainly to contributions towards building schools, and providing them with efficient trained teachers; and it is, perhaps, to a co-operation with, and to being met with pecuniary assistance from, them, and from charitable individuals, that the Committee of Council have hitherto looked, rather than expecting to be aided in any considerable way by the school payments.

The aggregate amount, however, of the aid of benevolent individuals to schools in which they take an interest must be something enormous. Now, I would urge on all such persons to give to their efforts in the cause the character and direction, which, to a certain extent, necessity has imposed upon the efforts of Government and of the Societies.

I would recommend them to aim distinctly at perfecting the machinery of the schools about which they are interested, with a view of enabling them to dispense with their assistance altogether. I know this is rather a painful thing to do, and would deprive many amiable individuals of much of the pleasure which they derive from helping others — they cannot think of making poor children buy their books or pay for their schooling — but have never allowed their minds to dwell upon the healthy tendencies of their doing so, and of the unhealthy one of giving them; but when they reflect upon it, and see, that in one way more good can be done than in the other, surely they will go in the way which reason points out, and not in the way in which they would be guided by impulse.

They may depend upon it, they will do infinitely more by making the article good than by making it cheap in the way which they mean by cheapness. This is where the benevolent intentions and exertions of so many individuals have failed. They have endeavoured, often at great cost to themselves to keep up a school at which education shall be offered gratuitously, which upon several grounds I consider objectionable, but I am happy to say, I know of many gentlemen, liberal-minded men, who had been in the habit of spending large sums annually in this way, who are now turning their attention to establishing schools on principles that may lead the labouring classes to feel an interest, and to make some efforts on their own parts for the education of their own children. One good school on self-supporting principles, or on principles which will eventually lead to this, is worth any number of gratuitous ones in a public point of view. We cannot educate a nation by charity; and we ought not to teach the people that it is possible.

The teaching in two schools, the one gratuitous, the other self-paying, may be the same; their value to the public, however, is very

different — the one places a district in the right road to help itself in
one of the most important wants of society — the other leaves
things where they were; nay, more, it teaches the people to rely on
others for what they ought to do for themselves, and even retards;
nor is the result of the two modes of education the same as regards
the children themselves.

A very common complaint of the inspectors is, the early age at
which the labourers' children are taken from school: but, manifestly
the way of remedying these evils is, to awaken the feelings of
parental responsibility; and I know of no better way of doing this,
than that of interesting parents in the visible progress their children
make while at school.

This early age at which the labourers' children are almost necessarily taken away, is a complete answer to the objection which has
been raised that, these (the labourers' children), are getting a better
education than those of the employers — the children of the latter
remain to a much greater age.

This pressure from below is sure to make the class above them,
the employers of labour, avail themselves of our parish and district
schools when they are good; and it ought to be our aim, as Dr.
Chalmers observed of the schools he established in Glasgow, "to
make education so cheap that the poorest may pay for it, and so
good that the rich will be glad to get it at a higher price for their
own children," and when this is the case, there will be no difficulty
about the mixture of classes. Begin at the base of the column, make
your foundations good and sound, and the superstructure you raise
upon it will be [solid].

I am aware it is not only the penny or the twopence per week
which represents to the parent the cost of the child's education, but
in a great many cases the two or three shillings which the child,
when at a certain age, might have earned had he been at work.
This is what managers of schools ought not to forget. The only
way in which the difficulty can be met, and then perhaps only
partially, is by making the school attractive through its efficiency. In
this way you may assure some sacrifices being made; the lowness of
the school-fee is no attraction.

Sir James Shuttleworth in his Public Education, speaking of
Scotland, says:— "The amount of the school-fees paid by the
working classes, in all but certain Highland and Island parishes, is
a rebuke to our English customs, and a commentary on the effects
of education continued through several generations, in enabling

those supported by manual labour to appreciate its advantages which no statesman should neglect.

"In Scotland, education in reading, writing and arithmetic, and the Holy Scriptures, and formularies of the church, costs a poor man from 10s. to 16s. a year for each child, and yet it is so general as to be almost universal in the Lowlands of Scotland, not included in great cities. This fact becomes more significant, when it is borne in mind that it is generally the parents *who provide the school-books and all other school materials*, which, whatever the care bestowed on them, must cost at least four shillings more every year."

I observe that her Majesty's inspectors reiterate in every variety of expression the statement that, the poverty of schools renders them inefficient.

Mr. Kennedy, in his able report upon the state of schools in Lancashire, lays it down with much emphasis:— "That as are the funds so is the school." There is no denying the truth of this. But to-night I am desirous of drawing attention to the very converse of this fact. I wish it to be understood that the inefficiency of the schools condemns them to poverty. Hundreds of schools are poor because they are inefficient.

I say this, under a strong sense of the greatness of the sacrifices which numbers of the gentry and clergy, especially the latter, have of late years been making in this cause. That the exertions of the clergy have been undoubtedly great for the purpose of providing schools for the children of the labouring classes, no one can doubt.

Still, I cannot shut my eyes to the fact, that in a multitude of cases, they would have very much lessened their difficulties if they had steadily directed their attention, not to the collection of subscriptions, as if that were the best or the only way of maintaining a school, but had rather made it their great object to see in what way the school would be enabled to dispense with subscriptions altogether, and maintain itself. I know that it is a very ungracious office to have to tell those who have (as they thought), done their best and achieved much, how they might have done better; but being convinced of the truth and importance of my views, I cannot but think it right to speak plainly on this point. The difficulty is not with the people, but in getting a really practical education, such as comes home to their wants, placed within their reach and carried out in such a way as to give the experiment a fair trial. The clergy have not turned their attention sufficiently to this, nor have the laity perhaps; they do not feel, nor have they realised to themselves, what is necessary, and consequently do not set about it in the right way. They rely too much on the begging system, which is pauperising in its tendency and most unsatisfactory in its results.

Another error on their part is — the feeling that children ought not to go beyond the bounds of their own parishes, and, instead of availing themselves of a good school in a neighbouring parish, getting up an inefficient one in their own. I have seen the mischief of this in many cases.

There is another pecuniary source from which educational assistance ought to come, but from which it assuredly does not, to which I may allude, and that is the educational and other charities dispersed all over the country, and doing, so far as my experience goes, little or nothing but positive mischief.

The county of Hereford and town in which I live, unfortunately abounds in such charities — some for education, others for general purposes, and I have often said, what I will repeat here, that the greatest friend to the town and county (rather than things should remain as they are), would be the person that could get them all abolished.

It is with pleasure then, and some degree of hope, that we see a bill on this subject promised by government, and I trust the result may be, a mode of administration which may render them useful for the future, and not a positive curse to the places where they exist, which so many of them have hitherto been.

I do not think any mode of administering charities by local trustees, without some paid system of supervision by officers responsible to the public can be permanently effective. I speak this from experience; and were I to tell you the history of some of those with which I am acquainted (some connected with the Church, for I have no wish to screen my own profession from their share of blame on this head), I should only create feelings of surprise and astonishment, that funds which might be turned to useful purposes, could remain so long in the state in which so many of them now are, and that there should be no power to divert their application to new and more useful objects.

A charity of which I am trustee (and I am therefore speaking from my own knowledge), has an annual income of more than £3000 from funded property, left for food and clothing, and it is limited to three small parishes, the united population of which is 1250: and were I to tell you the mischief which this charity has done in demoralising those who are the recipients of it, and the details connected with its history in the last fifty years, you would be truly disgusted, and I believe there is but one opinion among the gentlemen in the neighbourhood of it as to its mischievous effects.

In the last session of Parliament an Act was passed giving the trustees greater power, allowing them, in as many ways as possible, to spend this income, but still to limit it to the three parishes; but, to administer so large a sum over so small an area, and so small a population, it is evident would be impossible without doing mischief. When I first became acquainted with it, and a year before the bill was passed, I suggested — that to give the trustees power in the new bill to grant in sums of £20 or £25 each annually to fifty teachers in as many of the best conducted schools in the county of Hereford, where the money was most wanted, these grants to be annually made, and only paid after inspection by Her Majesty's Inspector of Schools, and reported on for good, might be a very proper and useful way of getting rid of some of the money; but, to my astonishment, this met with no support, and I found the difficulties so great, and the chance of success so small, that I gave it up. I have within the last three months become one of the trustees, and at the very last meeting I attended, I could not but feel what a curse this charity was, both to the parishes which received it and to the neighbourhood around. Such, however, is the pugnacity of the English character, that although every educated and right-minded man feels it to be a nuisance, yet any attempt to extend it beyond the parish limits would meet with the most determined resistance. Some time ago I visited three adjoining parishes, in each of which I knew there was a small educational endowment, in two of them about £8 or £10 a year with a cottage used as school-house, and garden, and in the other about £20 or £25 a year.

In each of the two first into which I went, I found an aged schoolmistress not less than eighty, in one certainly more; they were surrounded by a few listless, dirty, ragged children — the school-cottage dirty and ill ventilated — a few torn books scattered about. Between me and one of the old women the following dialogue took place:—

"What are you teaching the children?" "I teaches 'em to read and the catechis." "Do you think they understand the catechism?" "Oh! I has the broken catechis and I makes 'em." "Do you teach the children to write?" "Lord, Sir, that doos 'em no good." Here our dialogue ended. I thought it quite in character with all I saw around me, and I am sorry to add that it is a type of school of which many still exist.

In the third parish, there was a schoolmaster, and a state of things very little in advance of the old dame's. The endowment and cottage is about £25 a year.

On another occasion, I visited a parish in which there were two endowments for education in different parts of it, in each a cottage used as a home and as a school-room. The master, a lame carpenter, taught in one in the winter, the other in summer; when I saw him, he was in his summer residence. After a little enquiry and conversation with the children I was perfectly acquainted with the state of things, and suggested to the master that he had better have stuck to his old trade — he seemed to think so too — but the certainty of the endowment (the two together were more than £20 a year), was no doubt his reason for preferring the school, certainly not his being able to teach.

These small charities are generally administered by the owners of property, on which the payments are charged, and are a positive hindrance to anything better being attempted.

After this I need not say I am anxious for the success of the bill promised by the Government, for the better administering to this class of charitable endowments.

I will now make a brief allusion to the educational grants of the House of Commons. This annual grant is no doubt small: but the house itself has always shown great readiness to vote money for this purpose.

We need therefore anticipate no difficulty from that quarter on the score of money, to carry out plans which have any hold on the public mind, when based on proper grounds in an economical point of view, and likely to lead to an education which will meet the wants of the age we live in.

It has often occurred to me that a very great portion of the money voted by Parliament for popular education finds its way back again to the exchequer in various ways through the post office.

Then, again, what are the effects of what has been done the last few years in education on the industrial habits and well-being of the people — has it had no share whatever in the increased prosperity of the nation — in the growing feeling of independence among the labouring classes, causing to them to rely more on their own industry and less on the industry of others. Are they not able, by being taught, to husband their own resources better, to spend more money in exciseable articles (the consumption of paper for instance), than they used to be. I believe they are, and that without attributing too much to it; *yet* surely something is owing to education in our present state of prosperity. In truth, I think we may make out a case for the Chancellor of the Exchequer which will shew to him, we are by no means confident that he does not get back again in various ways, the whole sum which is annually voted for educational purposes in the House of Commons. To quote the words of Mr. Henry Cole, in his address on art-education:— "Parliamentary grants made for this object are but the profitable investments of national capital — a loan to be repaid a hundredfold, and are laying the foundation for an increased demand, both at home and abroad, for skilled and therefore well remunerated labour."

Before I conclude, I may be permitted to quote the Great Exhibition, in support of the principles we are advocating to-night, and when I consider the audience I have the honour to address, and the place where we are, I trust it is by no means inappropriate that I should do so.

The Exhibition, which has given character to the age in which we live, and an impulse to industrial education all over the civilised world — great in its origin — great in its conception — great in its results, and worthy of the illustrious Prince to whom we owe it.

Supposing, that instead of having a full reliance on the self-supporting principle which the committee had, in constructing it upon the magnificent plan which they did; — they had confined themselves within much narrower limits, which they would have been obliged to do, in order to have admitted the public gratis — would the effect have been the same — would the result have been what it has been? Should we have learnt the same lesson from it which we have done? I believe not; and it is manifest what will now constitute one of the great events of modern history would have been perhaps by this time almost forgotten. The Exhibition, thus curtailed, would not have been what it was; certainly the same degree of enthusiasm would not have been felt in visiting it on such terms — the right plan was evidently that pursued — to make it worthy of all admiration, and then to leave it to the common sense of the world to appreciate it; and we know that no classes appreciate it more fully than those whom I have been endeavouring to shew this evening are quite able and ready to appreciate the advantages of a good and serviceable education.

The facts which I have brought before you this evening shew, that schools may be established to a very great extent of a self-supporting character, both in towns and in the larger rural parishes throughout the country; and, although this at present will most likely not be the general character of our schools, — yet, when the wants of education are properly felt by all classes (a result which is gradually coming about and to which the public mind is every day more and more inclined), a system of local rating in aid of education might be carried out, but when adopted, the schools must be open to, and the education fitted for, all classes of the rate-payers willing to send their children.

I say in *aid and supplemental* to the wants of a school, after reasonable payments have been made by those who are the recipients of education; because I think a rate-paying system making education gratuitous, would not work well in this country. In a social point of view, it would not have that elevating tendency in rearing up an industrious race depending in after-life upon themselves; which would arise out of a system, where all classes were obliged to pay in proportion to their means; and when school expenses were made a part of the family expenditure.

In a pamphlet which I published in 1850, I sketched out a plan of a rate in aid, and as the subject seems now to occupy the public mind, more than it had done of late, I will quote the following from it:—

"The power of rating should be for the purpose of making up deficiencies at the end of the year, when the amount of school payments has proved insufficient to defray the regular and necessary expenses, whether arising from teachers' salaries, pay of pupil-teachers, repairs and building of schools, apparatus, etc.

"Such a plan might work well in connection with the Committee of Council. The Committee of Management to fix the rate of school payments — the Committee of Council the salaries of masters and teachers — a minimum scale of salary to be fixed, to increase with the numbers.

"In this way, all would be interested in the success of the parish or district school; the rate-payers would have a motive of a pecuniary kind, in keeping the rates down, by sending their own children and making the payments reasonable, and if a good education was to be had, they would avail themselves of it. Permission to attend gratuitously to rest with the Committee.

"Parishes in a school district should each pay an amount proportioned to the population; and not simply by equal rating according to property throughout. When a school district consists of more than one parish, for instance a union of the parishes A, B, C, the whole sum to be raised on the rates should be divided into three parts, in proportion to the population in each; these separate parts to be raised in the respective parishes — the population at the last census always being taken as that of the parishes, so that any growing inequality would be periodically corrected.

"The Clergy would find great relief in having schools supported on this plan, from that pecuniary support which they at present give, and from that system of begging they are now obliged to have recourse to.

"The question, How the people of this country can best be educated, amidst the many conflicting opinions which prevail? is a very difficult one; but as in other business-matters of the world, so in this, experience will prove to be our best guide. The country does not seem yet to be prepared for a system of local rates in aid of education in places where it cannot be made self-supporting; but to this in the end, as being the most equitable system, it will probably come; the safest and, as it appears to me, the shortest way to a more extensive system than at present prevails, and one which would ultimately get hold of the feelings of the people, is by working well the existing system of the Committee of Council, and availing ourselves of all the advantages which it offers, and of those extensions of the system which can with advantage be engrafted upon it. What we want is, "not theorising, but schools in action."

The two new departments lately established in connexion with the Board of Trade, and now forming a part of our educational machinery — the Board of Practical Art, for the encouragement of elementary drawing and of art education, and the Board for the Encouragement of Practical Science. These offer immense advantages each in its department, which we have never yet had within our reach, and will give an impulse to those elements of a practical kind in our school-system, which have hitherto been almost entirely wanting. This practical character, I hope these boards will be a means of extending, not only to schools for the labouring classes, but to all those for middle class and industrial life throughout the country, and in fact, throughout our whole educational system.

No one, who takes an interest in this subject, can visit the Museum of Practical Geology in Jermyn Street, attend the lectures which are given there, particularly those in the evening for the workmen and artizans, and see the numbers who attend, and the evident interest which they take in all that is going on, and not be struck with the example which this Institution is holding out, and not see the extensive influence for good which it must have in leading to others of a similar kind in our larger towns.

The improved state of our schools, the introduction of elementary science into the best of them, will make such institutions more wanted than they have hitherto been, and will increase their power of usefulness, by introducing a class of students better prepared when they enter them.

Then again the encouragement given by the Board of Practical Art in the formation of Elementary Drawing Schools in our larger towns and to the introduction of drawing into the class of schools of which I am speaking this evening, is a most important step, and will lead eventually to its being made a part of elementary education — a very desirable thing; and I observe Mr. Norris, in his Report of this year, speaking of it, says, "Ill taught as it generally is in my district, I find it uniformly popular; and my experience would lead me to assign to drawing, as well as to singing, a decidedly humanizing effect on the characters of the children."

The example of the Hereford Elementary Drawing School, to which I have before alluded, and the way in which all classes seem to take it up, has thoroughly convinced me of the general usefulness of this kind of instruction. The principles upon which the Board renders assistance, giving the parties to understand that they must in the end make their efforts self-supporting, is one of which I most heartily approve.

I have lately visited some of the largest establishments in London, where industrial processes are carried on, upon a great scale; and when I see these, and realize to myself the various ways in which all that is now being brought into action of an educational kind, may be made to bear (in fact, must necessarily do so) on the great springs of industry in this country, and on human happiness in general, I cannot for a moment doubt that the good common sense of the people of England will enable them "to see straight," and that at no distant period, a good practical and sound education will be established throughout the land.

I will now bring these remarks to a close. I have given you facts connected with my own experience, and also with that of other practical men. It is for you to judge what these facts are worth, and how far they can be a guide to others in attempting to establish schools in the districts in which they are interested; but you must always bear this in mind with respect to the agricultural districts, that generally speaking, unless the children of employers and employed can be brought together in the same school little will be done, it will be impossible to support good schools for the separate classes; and whether the farmer, and the great body of the employers of agricultural labour, are to remain behind the rest of the community in the matter of education, mainly depends on our being able to establish such schools as I have been recommending.

Since my undertaking to read a paper before your Society on this subject, I have been asked the question — What business has the Society of Arts with education? This question may imply some degree of censure for your interesting yourselves as a Society in the matter, and I am not sure that it does not. I anticipate some feeling of the kind may arise; but whether the question does imply censure or not, I conceive it to be a matter of public advantage that you have done so; and I also feel that you have, in a greater degree perhaps than any other existing body, the power of giving an impulse to that element in our popular instruction, I mean its having a practical and industrial character, the want of which has for many years made it so fruitless, and gained for it so little hold on public opinion.

Certainly, a much more sensible question to have asked would have been, In what way can the Society of Arts most effectually promote the cause of education? Gentlemen, there are so many ways which must occur to yourselves, in which you can do this, and in which you are better judges than myself, that I will not venture to suggest them.

In the letter lately circulated by your Secretary, various and most important ways are suggested. The letter of also Mr. Harry Chester, which appeared some time ago, gave several useful hints on this subject, with regard to Mechanics' Institutes; but on these points, however tempting, I will not venture to enlarge. I will only express a hope that; in your efforts to promote the cause of education all over the country, you may not lose sight of those self-supporting principles, which appear to me so important in a moral point of view, for raising the character of the people; and so necessary to the foundation of any system likely to be permanent, or in the management of which different classes will take an interest.